Beyond Busing

Beyond Busing
Inside the Challenge
to Urban Segregation

Paul R. Dimond

Ann Arbor
The University of Michigan Press

Library of Congress Cataloging in Publication Data

Dimond, Paul R.
  Beyond busing.

  Bibliography: p.
    1. Discrimination in education—Law and legislation
—United States. 2. Discrimination in housing—Law and
legislation—United States. I. Title.
KF4155.D56   1985   344.73′0798   84-29782
ISBN 0-472-10062-9   347.304798

Preface

Since the first attempts in the mid-1960s to implement the Supreme Court's ruling in *Brown v. Board of Education* outlawing state-enforced segregation by actually desegregating schools, there has been controversy over "forced busing." As long as the issue touched only dual school systems in the rural South, the outcry seemed distant to the vast majority of white Americans. There seemed little reason to object to the assignment of children, who were already riding school buses, to integrated rather than segregated schools.

Yet in 1969 the Nixon administration developed a "Southern strategy" to curry favor with the opponents of desegregation. In the late 1960s and early 1970s, as the legal challenges to official segregation moved from rural to urban areas and from South to North, this Southern strategy became a national program of other Republican presidents and politicians of both parties. Neoconservative pundits also began to argue that racial separation in urban areas reflected primarily a natural and common ethnic clustering, the result of personal preference rather than the lingering effect of past discrimination. President Nixon promised to appoint "strict constructionists" to the Supreme Court who would construe the Constitution to halt desegregation by finding racial segregation the innocent result of de facto residential separation and neighborhood schools.

Nixon did appoint four justices to the high court in his first term. Yet at the beginning of the 1970s and over the opposition of the Nixon Justice Department, the Supreme Court required many Southern school districts—rural and urban—to dismantle historic dual systems. The great busing controversy soon engulfed the North and climaxed when United States district judge Stephen Roth ordered a metropolitan plan to desegregate one-race schools between Detroit and its white suburbs. The four Nixon appointees, joined by one holdover from the Warren Court, responded in 1974: they put the brakes on busing for the first time by limiting any remedy in Detroit to the borders of the central city. That opinion seemed to absolve suburban white America from any responsibility for the ghetto. Subsequent Supreme Court decisions in school and housing cases moved toward acceptance of the Nixon view. As a result, the white furor over integration abated somewhat, except in communities still ordered by lower courts to desegregate their schools.

Under the administrations of Presidents Ford and Carter loftier phrases about nondiscrimination replaced the Nixon rhetoric. But Ford pressed Congress and the courts to end busing for school desegregation altogether, and Carter's new "urban policy" simply ignored the issue of racial segregation. To varying degrees, both used federal funds only to prop up the flagging finances and services of older central cities while doing nothing to integrate the inner-city ghettos or to open the nearby whites-only enclaves.

For many Americans the memory of the urban riots of the 1960s and Martin

Luther King's assassination faded with the drying of the ink on the 1968 *Report of the National Advisory Committee on Civil Disorders* describing a "nation moving toward two societies, one black, one white—separate and unequal." In much of the national conscience, images of "reverse discrimination" and "benign neglect" displaced this earlier understanding. Nevertheless, as the 1970s drew to a close, the Supreme Court once again confronted the causes of urban segregation and the need for actual desegregation in another series of landmark cases in Dayton and Columbus, Ohio, and in Wilmington, Delaware.

As the 1980s unfold, few Americans understand why some black families, civil rights groups, and federal judges still seek to challenge the existence of virtually all-white rings around blacks-only ghettos in metropolitan areas. As President Reagan promised to get government "off the people's backs," he denounced busing for school desegregation, vetoed federal aid to assist in desegregation, championed tax exemptions for racially exclusive parochial schools, and promised the appointment of judges who will not intervene actively to overcome racial separation—whatever its causes. Yet Reagan just as emphatically proclaimed his opposition to all forms of racial discrimination. At some point, then, the issue raised by the segregation cases must finally confront the American conscience: is the basic issue "forced busing"? Or is the real issue the nature, extent, and causes of the racial chasm that separates black from white in this country?

In 1903, W. E. B. DuBois wrote that "the problem of the twentieth century is the problem of the color line." There is a "physical color line on the map, on the one side of which whites dwell and on the other Negroes." In the 1970s and 1980s the issue remains whether this same color line still divides metropolitan America. Does racial separation today result from economics, ethnicity, cultural pluralism, minority choice, or happenstance? Or has it been caused, in important part, by long-standing racial discrimination, both public and private? Does it continue because most in the country do not want to recognize racial separation as the enduring engine of caste? In this context, a primary goal of the school and housing cases of the 1970s has been to raise the issue whether a form of apartheid splits much of metropolitan America on a racial basis.

This book is an attempt to write *this* story of the segregation cases of the 1970s. My vision has been shaped by my role as a counsel and advisor to minority race plaintiffs and civil rights groups seeking to end what they saw as a racial caste system. This book is based on my understanding of the actions, statements, and decisions of the public officials, private citizens, lawyers, and judges who have been the central actors in this long-running drama. I was an active participant, as well as an eyewitness. The book is not a disinterested account nor a dispassionate discourse.

In order to add some perspective, I went back after the final Supreme Court decisions to interview the community leaders, witnesses, and lawyers who had initiated these landmark cases by pleading their cause in federal trial courts around the country. The voices of Ella Taylor Lowrey, Phyllis Blackburn Greer, John Harewood, Nate Jones, John Humphrey, Helen Jenkins Davis, Barbee Durham, and Louis Redding are authentic. They command attention from each of us as citizens sharing the same Constitution. They deserve to be heard. If we fail to listen now, we should not be surprised if their offspring conclude that we have broken the promise of *Brown*. We can do better than deny responsibility for what Hedley Donovan, former editor in chief of Time, Inc., described as ''America's most serious weakness—our failure to achieve civilized race relations.''

Acknowledgments

I am grateful to Nathaniel R. Jones who encouraged my prior legal work and my continuing research and writing of this book. My research assistants, Mike Stevenson, Jeff Burg, Richard Dean, Allen Dixon, Mary Hendriksen, and Craig Willis provided substantial assistance in researching and/or revising the manuscript. Gene Sperling inspired my writing of a concluding chapter long after I hoped the manuscript was complete. Deans Terrance Sandalow, Thomas Buergenthal, and John Roberts, respectively of the University of Michigan, American University, and Wayne State law schools were instrumental in providing a home for my work. Harold Howe, Jim Kelly, Bernard Charles, Arlene Kahn, the Ford Foundation, and the Carnegie Corporation provided the wherewithal to undertake the effort. Steve Wasby, Marlene Z. Bloom, and Alex Aleinikoff provided invaluable editorial insights. Despite all the assistance, the views expressed in this book can be blamed only on me.

Contents

I. To Speak against Segregation

Chapter 1.   Black Voices in White America: The Dayton School Case,
November, 1972   *3*

II. "Our Troubled Times Demand Such Sacrifices": The
Detroit School Case, 1970–74

Chapter 2.   The NAACP Challenge to Segregation   *21*

Chapter 3.   The Trial of Judge Roth, April to September, 1971   *41*

Chapter 4.   Metropolitan Conversion in the Lower Courts, October, 1971,
to June, 1973   *74*

Chapter 5.   The Detroit Case in the Supreme Court, June, 1973, to July,
1974   *97*

III. "Avoiding an Education": The First Round in the
Dayton School Case, July, 1972, to June, 1977

Chapter 6.   The Trial of Judge Rubin, July, 1972, to December,
1972   *121*

Chapter 7.   The Skirmishes between the Sixth Circuit and Judge Rubin,
January, 1973, to September, 1976   *147*

Chapter 8.   The Supreme Court Sounds Retreat, December, 1976, to June,
1977   *165*

IV. Standing and Waiting: The Floundering of the Legal
Challenges to Housing Segregation in the 1970s

Chapter 9.   Open Housing, Closed Court, 1970–79   *183*

Chapter 10.   Waiting for Gautreaux: The Chicago Public Housing Case,
1950–79   *205*

V.   The Lower Courts Answer the Supreme Court's Call to Retreat, 1976–78

Chapter 11.   Judge Duncan's Trial of the Columbus School Case, April, 1976, to October, 1977   *229*

Chapter 12.   The Sixth Circuit on Trial: The Columbus and Dayton School Cases on Appeal, June, 1977, to July, 1978   *258*

VI.   Reprise and Preview: The Wilmington School Case, 1971–78

Chapter 13.   Trial by Three Judges, 1971–75   *283*

Chapter 14.   The Interdistrict Remedy, 1976–78   *309*

VII.   The Supreme Court and the School Desegregation Cases, 1978–80

Chapter 15.   The Briefs and Arguments in the Supreme Court   *343*

Chapter 16.   The Decisions from the Supreme Court, 1979–80   *375*

Conclusion   *395*

Sources   *403*

Selected Bibliography   *405*

Table of Principal Cases   *409*

I
To Speak against Segregation

Chapter 1
Black Voices in White America: The Dayton School Case, November, 1972

Ella Taylor Lowrey

At the age of seventy-five Ella Taylor Lowrey rose with all her considerable wit and will to testify against the segregation of the Dayton, Ohio, public schools. The courtroom was filled with the conscience and aspiring spirit of a largely black audience. Mrs. Lowrey's step was quick, her resolve firm, and her voice clear. Many others had stood up before. She was ready now.

Like other blacks living in Dayton in 1900, Ella Taylor had grown up in a mixed neighborhood and attended public schools with white children. But no black teacher ever taught Taylor or her white classmates; the all-white school board assigned the only black teacher to an all-black class by the back door of the otherwise all-white Garfield Elementary School. Nevertheless, Ella Taylor determined to dedicate her life to teaching and attended Dayton Teachers Normal from 1915 to 1918.

In 1916 she served as a student teacher at Weaver Elementary School. One day the regular teacher was sick, and the principal secured permission from the superintendent to allow Taylor to fill in. As she testified in federal court,

> I went to work that Thursday morning. That afternoon, a little white boy sitting up near the front held his hands on his arms and looked up at me. . . . I said to the little boy, "What's the matter?" He said, "My mother says you are a nigger and I don't have to mind you."

Although the principal reprimanded the child and sent him home, this experiment in integrated education ended on an even sorrier note. As the witness told the court, opposition grew to the superintendent allowing "a Negro to teach white children in Dayton Public Schools." For the next two generations, the Dayton Board of Education responded by prohibiting black teachers from instructing white pupils. As a result, Taylor always taught in a segregated setting during her forty years of service in the Dayton public schools. "I never taught a white child in all that time," she testified. "I was always in black schools, with black children, with black teachers."

Recalling her first full-time teaching assignment, Taylor told how in 1918 the Dayton school board assigned her to a west-side school, the Garfield

Annex. It included "a two-story frame building with four rooms . . . two rooms down, two up," containing only black students and teachers, in back of the brick and whites-only Garfield Elementary School. To accommodate the increasing black pupil population, the board added a two-room, portable building to the blacks-only annex: "that made six black teachers with six black classes. There were no black teachers or students inside the brick building."

Taylor described the conditions in the temporary structure where she taught:

> This small frame [building] . . . being very fragile, was soon dilapidated, in bad condition. The walls were bad; the windows were bad and broken out, and the heating unit became bad. The [board] finally built what I would call a permanent building behind this frame house . . . [with] four rooms. Then the two-room portable was torn down. At that time, we had eight black classrooms with eight black teachers. . . . I had 62 children in the sixth grade room. . . . The white teacher in the brick building with all white children had 20. . . . There was no effort to equalize our classes.

In 1926 the board threatened Taylor with the loss of her job when a black parent refused to send his two children to the blacks-only Garfield Annex and instead tried to enroll them in an east-side school. When the board refused, Taylor remembered what happened.

> Mr. Reese didn't like [segregation] and he said he would not send his children back to the annex. [The board] would not permit his children to go into the brick building, [so] he sued the school board. Now the school board at that time, not knowing what was going to happen, hired we eight [black] teachers on a day-to-day substitute basis in September. . . . [The board] told us that they didn't know whether we would be there after the case was settled or not. If the case was settled and they had to admit black children to the white classes in the brick building, then there would be no reason for us [the black teachers]. . . . We were told that [we] would not be permitted to teach white children.

In the *Reese* case, the Ohio court reminded Dayton school authorities that since 1888 Ohio law prohibited the operation of separate black and white schools and granted the petition of the Reese children to enter the whites-only part of Garfield. But Taylor stayed in the annex, and Dayton kept its segregation policy. As she testified, [black] parents had to go and make a special request that their children be admitted to this brick building. . . . If they did not do that, they were assigned to the black teachers in the black annex and the black classes.

Shortly thereafter, there were more black children and black teachers than there was space in the frame annex, so the board assigned Taylor and her all-black class to a little cubbyhole in the brick building. Then, over the summer of 1936, the board reassigned the remaining white teachers and students from Garfield to other schools and assigned a black principal, an all-black staff, and an all-black student body to Garfield. Thus the board responded to the *Reese* decision—and the growing black population—by converting Garfield into a blacks-only school. So complete was the board's policy of segregation that, through 1948, blacks from a mixed orphanage "were put on buses and bused all the way across town to us at Garfield School. . . . They were bused all the way from North Main clear over to the west side of Dayton to come to this black school with black teachers."

In 1947 Taylor married, and after a six-year absence, Mrs. Ella Taylor Lowrey returned to teach in the Dayton public schools. This time she was assigned to another blacks-only school, Wogaman Elementary, on the west side. She taught there for twelve years until she finally retired, not having taught a white child in her forty years of service since her inadvertent breach of the color line in Dayton public schools as a student teacher in 1916.

On cross-examination by the school board's lawyer, Lowrey's lively wit and strong will seemed to dominate the courtroom. After one exchange that resulted in a collective chuckle from everyone in attendance, the trial judge assured her, "Mrs. Lowrey, one of the few pleasures of being a judge is to watch a witness confound a lawyer." But on one occasion the board's lawyer confounded Lowrey. In seeking to explain the causes of the concentration of black families and schools on the west side of the city, he focused on "the great Dayton flood of 1918," when the Great Miami River crested its banks. He asked, didn't the "movement [of blacks thereafter] start to the west [and] really continue ever since?" Lowrey responded: "Blacks could not get money to buy property anywhere but the west side. [We] had to come west." The school board attorney pressed, "Well, . . . [weren't blacks] also concerned about higher ground?" Now, that was confounding: weren't whites also concerned about higher ground? Wasn't there also higher ground on the east side of town? Lowrey responded, "Yes, higher ground, but [black families] couldn't buy where [they] had lived before [i.e., in other parts of town. Blacks] had to go west."

At 4:45 P.M. on November 15, 1972, Ella Taylor Lowrey left the witness stand with the same quick step and firm conviction with which she arrived.

She had borne witness to the racial insult that segregation had visited on her and all of her black children through the years.

Phyllis Blackburn Greer

Born in a mixed neighborhood in 1918 in Dayton to a father who worked as a custodian in a bank and a mother who worked one day a week in a school principal's home, Phyllis Blackburn and her eight brothers and sisters early experienced the meaning of segregation and racial discrimination. They could not sit at soda fountains at the dime store with white children; they could not try on any clothes at the department store; and at the theater or movie house, if they got in at all, they had to sit in the balcony or another blacks-only section at the back. When she questioned such practices, her grandmother counseled her not to "stand up so high, they can shoot you down; colored folks can only survive if they stay in their place." But her father told her, "It is time to stand up. You can be anything and go any place you want so long as you demand it and you earn it."

Blackburn's parents encouraged and supported her, especially in school, but they warned her that she would have to be twice as good as her white counterparts to succeed. When her grades qualified her for the National Honor Society, but she was rebuffed because of her race, she persevered. She would learn, she would excel, she would never accept a segregated society or second-class status for herself and her brothers and sisters.

But the legacy of white racism had a long history in Ohio. Laws had been passed in 1804 and 1807 "to regulate black and mulatto persons" by prohibiting them from settling in the state without a certificate of freedom from a court, a bond signed by two white men guaranteeing good behavior, and a pass from local authorities. Ohio denied blacks the right to vote and, until 1848, the opportunity for any public education. In that year, the state provided for "separate schools" for "colored children" from a tax on the property of "colored persons." In 1887, however, the legislature abolished "separate schools," but the customs of segregation enforced by the prior laws were not so easily abated. In the ensuing years, the color line only became more rigid in daily life.

As she grew up, Phyllis Blackburn had come to know that white supremacy notions continued to motivate racial segregation in Dayton. There were even separate shower areas at Roosevelt High School, one for whites, the other for blacks, and the swimming pool was only open to whites. Of course, such outlandish mechanisms to protect whites from contact with blacks would not be needed if all blacks could be herded into separate housing and schools on the west side.

When Phyllis Blackburn Greer prepared to take the witness stand in the

Dayton school desegregation case in the fall of 1972, she was concerned that her testimony might cost her job as head of equal opportunity enforcement for the Dayton school district. She had worked with the new white superintendent, Wayne Carle, and seventy-five community members from 1967 through 1971 to grapple with the causes and consequences of operating segregated schools. The final report of this broadly based "Committee of 75" concluded that segregation must be replaced at once by an integrated school system. Instead, in the November elections of 1971, the antibusing "Save Our Schools" candidates swept out the moderate board majority who supported the report and blocked any desegregation plan.

So Greer had to testify. As she recalled later, "I had to say some things that needed to be said. I had to pay a debt for those who suffered from racial segregation in the past. I wanted to put a little interest in the bank for those who might live in Dayton in the future."

So her story began to unfold in federal court.

Q. Mrs. Greer, could you describe for us when you first experienced what you considered to be discriminatory acts in the Dayton Public Schools?

A. I can remember in my second year at Weaver Elementary School [a "mixed" school with all white teachers, but some black students]. There was a Christmas play. . . . I . . . tried out . . . and wanted to take the part of an angel. [T]he teacher who was in charge of the play indicated that I could not be an angel in the play because there were no colored angels.

In the third grade, the white staff tried to make her a model for the bad "colored girls."

I was called to the platform, the little low platform in the front of the classroom and the rest of the class was told to look at Phyllis Blackburn's hair. It was braided and had ribbons on it and [the teacher said] she would like for them to come to school with their hair like this rather than with knots and bed lint in it. . . . Of course, as I went home that day, I had a little difficulty with the black children who had knots and bed lint.

She did not mind the "little difficulty" with her black classmates so much. But, as she later told the court, she did mind that the white teachers in these "mixed schools" never gave "black students . . . the option of being average. . . . You were either the best or you were below average and placed in 'slower classes' [that] were invariably black."

Phyllis attended the "mixed" Roosevelt High School in grades seven through nine. She described how black students "were counseled [that] to go into the college preparatory courses was useless and [we] should . . . take the general course." She continued,

> Blacks were not allowed to go into the swimming pools, blacks had separate showers. . . . [W]hen I was in an eighth grade social studies class, [another] teacher [told me] that even though I was a good student, I was not to sit in the front of the class because . . . the colored kids sat in the back.

But, as she was to do on so many other occasions in her life, she chose instead to sit right in the front.

Dunbar High, a citywide school with an all-black staff, opened in 1933 on the west side near Roosevelt High. Greer testified:

> I [transferred] to Dunbar because I felt that if there was going to be—if we were going to be separated by anything, we might as well be separated by an entire building as to be separated by practices.

The Dayton school board had named the new citywide school after one of the true poet laureates of the nation. Paul Lawrence Dunbar had grown up in Dayton and graduated from Central High in 1889 with the Wright brothers. They were eventually all buried in the same cemetery. Although Dunbar graduated with highest honors, edited the school newspaper, and wrote the class song, the local newspaper refused to give him a job as a reporter and told him that he ought to think about working as an elevator operator rather than seeking jobs reserved for whites.

Little wonder that the first principal at the Dunbar school, Dr. McFarlane ("Mr. Mac" as his students affectionately knew him), "taught us . . . that we must be better than anybody else in terms of achievement because that was the only way we could even get to be equal." As Greer testified, "Mr. Mac taught black pride, yes. Not black hate. I can say very honestly that my first experience [in the Dayton public schools] of anything good about myself came because of Mr. McFarlane." Of course as Mrs. Greer also noted, whites could not benefit from Mr. Mac's nurturing: although students living anywhere in the city could attend Dunbar High, *no* white child could make that choice because of the board's demeaning prohibition on any black teacher instructing white children.

In 1940 Greer returned to teach English in Dayton high schools. Because she was black, the board assigned her to the blacks-only Dunbar High. Greer then recounted how she watched the Dayton board convert Wogaman Elementary, another west-side school, over the summer of 1945 by the same overt methods used earlier to convert Garfield:

> When school closed in June of 1945, there was an entire white staff at Wogaman. When school opened in September, there was an entire black staff under a black principal . . . and at the same time [all] white pupils who lived in the Wogaman area were transferred by bus out of the Wogaman school.

In 1946 Greer began a two-year maternity leave. When she returned, the board had filled her English spot at Dunbar High, and school officials refused to consider her for vacancies in the white high schools for which she was qualified but for her race. The board assigned her to Willard, another blacks-only elementary school on the west side that it had converted a decade earlier in the same fashion as Garfield and Wogaman.

In 1958 Greer accepted an appointment as principal at Carlson, a new elementary school on the west side that opened with an all-black faculty and virtually all-black student body. She testified that the Veteran's Administration hospital complex was located in the school's attendance area and housed many white staff and their families, but the staff's white children went by bus to other schools, not to Carlson.

In her testimony, Greer also recounted the collective memory of the school system. She searched the faculty directories for every year and explored the recollections of other staff in order to identify the assignment of every black and white teacher—from 1921 through the day of the trial. This is what she found: In 1921 the board assigned its seven black teachers to the all-black classes at Garfield. By 1931 the number of black teachers had grown—there were ten at Garfield and one at Weaver, "an ungraded class for all-black boys." In 1933 Dunbar High opened with an all-black staff. In 1934 ten black teachers were assigned to Willard along with six white teachers. In the fall of 1935, the board transferred the white teachers and white students to other schools and assigned an all-black staff and student body to Willard. In the same way, the board converted Garfield into a blacks-only school the following summer. The changeover at Wogaman school followed in 1945. Throughout this period, the board refused to allow any black person to teach a white child. The result: four blacks-only schools on the west side and a reciprocal set of white schools elsewhere.

Beginning in 1951 the board began to breach this long-standing policy by substituting a new but equally demeaning segregation policy based on white sufferance that read:

The school administration will make every effort to introduce some white teachers in schools in negro [*sic*] areas that are now staffed by negroes [*sic*], but *it will not attempt to force white teachers, against their will into these positions*. The administration will continue to introduce negro [*sic*] teachers, gradually, into schools having mixed or white populations *when there is evidence that such communities are ready to accept [Negro] teachers*.

The board implemented this policy by transferring black teachers almost exclusively to those "mixed schools" on the west side that had increasing black pupil populations. Meanwhile, the board continued to assign virtually all-white staffs to schools with all-white student bodies in the rest of the system. The opening of new schools confirmed the policy of racial segregation through faculty assignments. Miami Chapel opened in 1953 on the west side with an all-black student body and virtually all-black staff. In 1954 Belle Haven opened with a white student body and a white staff. In 1957 Louise Troy opened on the west side with an all-black student body and a 95 percent black staff, and Meadowvale opened with a white student body and staff. In 1958 Shoup Mill opened with a white student body and staff, and so on, without exception.

On cross-examination, the school board attorney sought to explore possible alternative causes of this segregation.

Q.   Mrs. Greer, in the questions that have just been asked you concerning specific schools, the composition of the student body in those schools was a reflection of the composition of the neighborhood in which they were located?

A.   In some instances. As I pointed out, there were white youngsters in the Wogaman School District who lived in that district who did not go to school in that district, so this was not a true reflection of the composition of that district.

Q.   There were times when the Wogaman district was overcrowded, were there not?

A.   [Yes].

Q.   And I think you testified that at one of those times children from that district went to a white school, which was the school of the adjacent district, isn't that right?

A. That is correct. I would like to add, however, that during that time the black children from the overcrowded school did go to . . . [blacks-only] Willard, and that the white children went to [the white school].

The school board attorney then questioned Greer, as a mutual "lifetime resident of Dayton," concerning so-called natural barriers: rivers and creeks, railroads and industrial gulches, cemeteries and interstate highways. At every turn, witness Greer rebuffed the attorney's assumptions. She testified, for example, that black and white students regularly crossed such barriers to conform with board assignment techniques that promoted segregation, while the board honored these divides when convenient to preserve segregation. Rivers did not cause the color line in Dayton.

The school board attorney then returned to the theme that the changes in the racial composition of schools on the west side merely reflected changes in the racial composition in the neighborhoods. Greer countered by noting the board's assignment of white children out of the "neighborhood" when it converted a school, like Wogaman, to blacks-only. She added,

I would certainly like to re-emphasize that assignment of staff to go along with the neighborhood change was the kind of thing that gave the impression of the schools designed to be black, because black staff increased as black student bodies increased.

Greer concluded her testimony by telling the court about segregation that resulted from the creation of optional zones in changing neighborhoods to allow whites to escape to nearby white schools from schools thereby designated for transition to black.

As Phyllis Greer left the stand, she hoped that the federal judge had heard and would be fair, but she had her doubts. Nevertheless, she had bared her soul against segregation in Dayton, Ohio, for all who cared to listen.

John Harewood

On November 15, 1972, John Harewood took the stand.

Q. What is your present position with the Dayton Public Schools?

A. Assistant superintendent in charge of administration.

He was the person who made sure that the schools ran, while the superintendent and board established and fought over policy. Harewood reached his position the hard way. He was black. He was small and slight, almost fragile in appearance. He was born in 1909 and had grown up in racist small towns in southern Ohio. When his mother died, Harewood was in the sixth grade; he moved with his brothers and sisters to the county orphanage in Hillsboro.

As Harewood walked from his orphanage two miles past an all-white school to a dilapidated all-black school with an outhouse, he made up his mind to learn—even if his white fellow orphans had it somewhat better at their school that was closer to the orphanage and had better facilities. When he entered the "mixed" high school for all Hillsboro children and watched the other black students embarrassed and humiliated into the streets, Harewood determined to persevere. He graduated at the head of his high school class, but had to march at the back of the commencement procession with the only other black who survived to graduate.

Still there was no way to convince him that he was less than anyone's equal. He matriculated at Wilberforce, a predominantly black university near Dayton, worked in the school library, and graduated in 1932 *magna cum laude* with a straight 4.0 average in science and math and a high school teaching certificate.

He testified in federal court about his struggle to pursue his chosen profession.

A.   After you graduated from Wilberforce, did you apply for a job in the Dayton Public Schools?

A.   I did.

Q.   What happened?

A.   I was told—I first applied in 1932 and renewed my applications from 1932 to 1938—there were no openings for me as a high school teacher in the Dayton Public School system.

Q.   At that time where would openings have been available for you?

A.   Only at Dunbar High School.

Q.   In your experience as an administrator are those subjects [in which you majored], relative to other subjects, usually in short supply?

A.   Always, always an opening for math teachers and science teachers.

Deprived by the Dayton public schools of a teaching position solely because of his race, Harewood still had to make ends meet. So from 1932 through 1936 he sang professionally with his quartet, the Charioteers—for two years a mainstay on a local radio station in Cincinnati and for another two years a leading group in New York's finest night clubs. "Swing Low, Sweet Chariot" was their theme song, and the Charioteers shared center stage with the likes of Fred Waring and his Pennsylvanians. In 1936 the Charioteers' baritone returned to Dayton "to look for teaching assignments," but could only secure employment conducting adult education courses at night under federally funded programs in Greenfield and Hillsboro.

Q. Why did you continue to go out and look for a teaching assignment when you had the opportunity to travel and be in the quartet?

A. Because that was my training; that was my dedication. That's what I wanted to do, and I felt there was a place for me in some school somewhere.

Harewood was the first to apply for a vacancy that arose at Dunbar in October, 1938, following a teacher's sudden death. From 1938 through 1954 Harewood remained at Dunbar—five years in seventh grade math, five years in eighth grade math, five years in high school math and counseling.

Q. During that period of time was the Dunbar High School an all-black high school with an all black faculty?

A. All black, all the way.

Harewood also observed the mechanisms of intentional segregation at work. In 1945 he watched as the Dayton board converted the Wogaman school attended by his foster daughter into a blacks-only school. The board transferred the white principal, white staff, and remaining white students to other schools and assigned a black principal, black staff, and all-black student body when it reopened in the fall. As a counselor at Dunbar from 1949 to 1954, Harewood also visited the "mixed" elementary schools with all-white staff and observed blacks sitting in the back of the classes. He saw that these "mixed" schools assigned only black students to attend his orientation sessions to assist them in "choosing" Dunbar.

At first, Harewood refused to change his career goals in order to comply with the racial restrictions of Dayton's dual system.

Q. Were you ever invited to discuss a promotion to a principalship?

A.   Yes. In 1949 I believe I was requested to come to discuss the opening at Willard Elementary School to see if I was interested in becoming a principal there. I discussed that with the members at the central office staff.

Q.   What was the racial composition at Willard?

A.   Black.

Q.   And did you accept the job?

A.   No, I did not.

Q.   Why not?

A.   First of all, my training was in high school. I felt that I had ability to work in a high school situation. I felt that my relationship with high school students was such that I could make a contribution there. So I thanked them for their invitation and . . . I did not accept that position.

Five years later, however, Harewood could wait no longer.

A.   In 1954 I applied for the position of principal of Wogaman Elementary School.

Q.   And what was the racial composition of Wogaman school in terms of pupils and faculty?

A.   Black.

Q.   And why in 1954 would you apply for an elementary principalship?

A.   This was my fifteenth year in public school education. I felt that if I were going to advance in administration, there had been several openings in high schools, new schools established, other [white] high school positions which were available, and because of my conversation with [staff] at the central office they knew of my ability and there was no offer to even indicate to me that any of those positions were available for me. So I felt at this point that if I was going to make a move in administration, then I better reconsider the position I had previously taken, and since I had both elementary certification and high school certification I reapplied for a position as elementary principal.

That was the only alternative I had in a segregated system, as was said to me, even though I was qualified, and they said I was qualified, they would pick others with less experience with less qualifications than I and appoint them to positions. Either I accept no promotion or I take something else, and that's the reason that I went down and applied for the position at Wogaman school.

Q. And did you receive that position?

A. I did.

Q. And how long did you remain principal of the Wogaman school?

A. Thirteen years.

The board of education had to strive for each year of Harewood's tenure from 1954 through 1967 to keep Wogaman exclusively black. It maintained separate stacks of teacher applications by race and rejected the request of several white applicants to join Harewood at Wogaman. The personnel director also indicated to Harewood

how many different applications he had for black teachers for positions and how difficult it was for them to get positions. He showed me a stack of applications that were all black. There were some with master's degrees, wives of people who worked at the [Wright-Patterson] air force base and others, and we looked through those and he would comment what fine applicants they were, and the tragedy was that out of that many I needed one or two.

In practice, the school authorities still excluded otherwise qualified black teachers from white schools.

The Dayton board had intentionally created and maintained a core of blacks-only schools on the west side and placed Harewood in charge of the largest elementary school in the district. But Principal Harewood simply would not accept any second-class status for his students. He ran a school to train them in basic skills to compete in the larger society dominated by whites and preached a simple gospel: "You must compete with whites when you graduate, and they will eventually be forced to respect you for your own competence, drive, and human dignity." Under Harewood's leadership, Wogaman became a kind of magnet for the entire Dayton metropolitan area. In one year Wogaman received the largest number of tuition transfers from students outside the Dayton school district. As always, these interdistrict transfers were approved by the central administration. Wogaman received only black pupils, however; white schools got the white transfer students.

In 1966 then-superintendent Robert French approached Harewood about a promotion.

> He was chatting with me informally and saying that the pressure was on them to integrate the central office staff. He asked me would I be interested. I thanked him very politely, said no, because I didn't want to receive an appointment just because of race or take a token assignment. That was the end of the conversation.

In 1968 Harewood was offered the job of coordinator of elementary and secondary instruction and curriculum. Because he had teaching and administrative experience at both levels, had been president of the elementary principals' organization, and had excelled in every assignment, Harewood accepted.

On the witness stand, Harewood then tried to testify about his struggle within the central office to challenge segregation. For example, the predominantly black Edison Elementary School burned down during the spring term. The white central staff proposed to house the students by renting space in black churches to set up makeshift schools. Harewood convinced the superintendent to transfer the students to vacant space in white schools. Unfortunately, Harewood was not consulted on the assignment of these black students to "totally black-contained units [within these] white schools." Harewood began to explain to the trial judge that there was no reason, other than race, for the complete segregation of the black Edison school children and their black teachers intact within the otherwise all-white schools even at that late date in the school year. The judge cut off his answer in ruling that these classes were "transported into literally a black enclave" and nothing more need be said. Six years later, however, when the case would be sent back from the Supreme Court for rehearing, this same trial judge would find the intact busing of the Edison students to separate black classes in otherwise all-white schools "administratively sound," not based on "segregative intent."

Harewood was nevertheless able to complete the basic outline of his story for the record, including his rise to assistant superintendent under a new administration headed by Superintendent Carle that finally committed to ending segregation by all educationally sound means. At the time of trial in 1972, forty-nine of Dayton's sixty-nine public schools were virtually all-black or all-white. Seventy-five percent of Dayton's black pupils attended black schools with less than 1 percent of Dayton's white pupils in a system that was 42 percent black. Eighty percent of all classrooms were virtually all one race or the other. Every school that was virtually all-black in 1933, 1936, 1945,

1951, and 1971 remained black at the time of trial. Every one of the virtually all-white schools at the time of trial had originally opened and had continued as virtual whites-only schools. In response to the "Committee of 75" report in the fall of 1971 on the board's responsibility for this segregation, the lame-duck members had officially voted to abolish the existing school attendance zones and authorized Superintendent Carle to implement an effective plan for school desegregation. But the newly elected, antibusing "Save Our Schools" board rescinded this policy at its first meeting and reimposed the segregated assignments.

John Harewood's testimony in federal court symbolized his refusal to bow to such affronts to his struggle against segregation. As he left the witness stand, he stood tall. He was disappointed that a federal judge refused to hear all of the relevant facts and seemed uninterested in the lack of nonracial justification for official acts that resulted in segregated schools. But Harewood was sure that he would someday witness the elimination of the awful color line from public schooling.

Ella Taylor Lowrey, Phyllis Blackburn Greer, and John Harewood had waited a lifetime for their day in court. Their wait was not over: the Supreme Court would not render a final judgment on their case until the end of the decade. Decisions in several other cases challenging segregation would intervene in the interim, while President Nixon decried "forced integration" to a public opposed to "busing" or preoccupied with other pressing national issues. At the vortex of this storm, witnesses Lowrey, Greer, and Harewood did not, however, stand alone. Nathaniel R. Jones, the general counsel of the NAACP, guided their case and many others. They shared a common goal: to prevent the courts and the country from ignoring their plea to end what they saw as an invidious system of forced segregation in Dayton, Ohio, and elsewhere.

II
"Our Troubled Times Demand Such Sacrifices": The Detroit School Case, 1970–74

Chapter 2
The NAACP Challenge to Segregation

Nate Jones

In November of 1969 Nate Jones heeded the call of Roy Wilkins, long-time executive secretary of the NAACP, and left his private practice in Youngstown, Ohio, to become general counsel of the NAACP in New York. As he surveyed the NAACP and the civil rights movement, they appeared in shambles.

- His immediate predecessor had resigned in protest when the NAACP fired a staff member for publishing an article criticizing the U.S. Supreme Court for its failure to enforce *Brown v. Board of Education* and the other civil rights of black citizens.
- In a series of Northern school cases, the courts of appeal had rejected his predecessor's claim that the mere existence of heavily black and heavily white schools—regardless of cause—denied black children an equal educational opportunity.
- Instead, the lower courts had approved segregation resulting from neighborhood schools on the theory that any black family could freely choose a white school by moving to a whites-only neighborhood. The lower courts reached this conclusion only by refusing to permit evidence of housing discrimination. The Supreme Court refused to review these judgments.
- The NAACP Legal Defense Fund, long the primary litigating arm of the NAACP, split from the NAACP and shied away from challenging Northern school segregation in the face of the still-massive job of dismantling the Southern dual systems that, fifteen years after *Brown,* had not desegregated "with all deliberate speed."
- In the wake of the riots and the election of a president largely unsympathetic to minority interests, separatists called for "black power" over the vast and expanding urban black ghettos and challenged the NAACP's traditional but muted vision of an integrated America.

Jones was born in 1926 in Youngstown, Ohio, to parents who had moved from Big Island, Virginia, in the hope that their children could have the educational opportunities they had missed. His father's formal schooling stopped in the fourth grade of a ramshackle, one-room "colored school" when he went to work on the crops full time. In Youngstown, he provided for his family as a delivery truck helper, window washer, steel worker, and night janitor, often holding down two or more jobs to make ends meet. His mother's education ceased at the same grade level, but after her children were grown she attended night classes. In 1962 she graduated from high school at the age of sixty-three, the class valedictorian.

In Youngstown, Jones attended the state's traditionally "mixed" schools with black and white students but *no* black teachers or other professional staff. The children of both races got along, but some of the white adults would refer to a black by every name except his given one: "Sambo" still had a harsh ring to Jones's ear. The movie theaters, swimming pools, YMCA, and churches were all segregated in Youngstown. Schools and neighborhoods might be somewhat "mixed"—on white terms to be sure—but social and civil life were largely separate.

Maynard Dickerson was a lawyer, the publisher and editor of a weekly black chronicle, the *Buckeye Review,* and a state NAACP and local community leader. In 1936 Dickerson became Youngstown's first black city prosecutor. Dickerson befriended Jones at an early age and continued to inspire him for the next four decades. Jones would help Dickerson at the paper, sit in the front row of the forum meetings arranged by Dickerson at the all-black YMCA, and talk informally with many of the civil rights and educational spokesmen. He listened to NAACP officials debate the presidents of black colleges about racial reform. He weighed the arguments over self-help and the challenge to the color line. He witnessed firsthand the traditional split among black reformers and, then, proceeded to study the dispute between Booker T. Washington and W. E. B. DuBois about how blacks could best survive in a hostile white America. Washington had counseled blacks to learn vocational and job skills while accepting segregation, but DuBois argued for complete freedom for blacks by uniting to confront white racism.

Every Sunday, Jones also attended the Third Baptist Church. On the Lord's day, his home was the church: for the junior service, the sermon, the three o'clock service and, in the evening, for drama, speech, recitations, and singing at the Baptist Young People's Union. From his first days, Jones was a youthful organizer who talked, prodded, and questioned. He pondered how he should react to the nation's color line, and he decided that segregation and racial discrimination must be challenged—frontally and successfully—in his lifetime.

At age twelve, Jones joined the local NAACP Youth Council and participated in attacks on segregation in public theaters, amusement parks, restaurants, and soda fountains. It did not hurt his cause that he took his complaints about racial discrimination to Dickerson, who could make the justice system work.

When Jones graduated from high school, he joined the war effort and the Army Air Corps. Stationed at Wright-Patterson Air Force Base on the outskirts of Dayton, he lived in the separate black dorms and trained with his segregated black unit under the control of white officers. On leave, he visited the city but could not escape segregation: movies, restaurants, and even the public schools were designated for whites or blacks only or had segregated seating. Compared to Youngstown, Dayton "had a most pronounced color line," he recalled later. Transferred to Shepherd Field in Wichita Falls, Texas, he found that the Air Corps relegated blacks to the most menial jobs. At each step Jones dashed off letters to Dickerson and to Thurgood Marshall, the general counsel of the NAACP, to complain of the segregated conditions and the unjust courts-martial of some of his black brothers.

With the war's end, Jones enrolled in Youngstown College on the G.I. bill. His small but regular earnings from running the *Buckeye Review* for Dickerson enabled him to continue his education and training. When blacks had difficulty getting equal treatment in the school cafeteria, Jones went directly to the college president to correct the indignity. When the student activity books given to black students omitted many school social functions reserved for whites, he confronted the school's business manager, who responded, "That's college policy." So Jones again went to the president, spoke of the recent world war for democracy and freedom, and threatened a federal complaint; soon thereafter the college changed its policy and issued a full activity book to all students. When the school sent black students in physical education activities across town to the colored YMCA rather than the nearby whites-only YMCA, Jones again led the successful challenge to open the school's recreational facilities and programs.

When the city of Youngstown continued to operate segregated swimming pools, seven reserved for whites and one for blacks, he issued a challenge in the pages of the *Buckeye Review* and then led a group of Youngstown College students and community representatives to integrate the white pools. A white mob attacked them as the police looked on and warned Jones about "stirring up trouble." He then went to the city attorney and swore out a complaint against his white attackers and the defaulting police officers. When a restaurant refused to serve him on grounds of social custom, he successfully sued the owner for damages under a newly enacted Ohio law prohibiting discrimination in public accommodations.

Jones also did extra work in school. The day the Supreme Court rendered its 1948 decision in *Shelley v. Kramer* invalidating state court enforcement of racially restrictive covenants, he commandeered his political science class to discuss the case. His teacher, who also served on the law faculty of Youngstown College, told his colleagues that, with such skill and initiative, Jones would "end up a high-fee lawyer."

After graduating from college, Jones matriculated at Youngstown College Law School. He continued to run the *Buckeye Review* to make ends meet and to voice his concerns. But he contracted tuberculosis that nearly killed him and was only cured when his illness was diagnosed sixty days later. After nine months in the hospital, he returned to law school and cut back his involvement at the *Buckeye Review* to writing editorials. Dickerson then asked Jones to become an inspector for the Industrial Commission—Ohio's panel set up to hear workmen's compensation claims—a panel on which Dickerson served as vice-chairman. In his last year at law school, Jones also was named chairman of the Youngstown Fair Employment Practices Commission, a position he maintained for the next four years.

On vacation in California, Jones met a favorite niece of Shirley Graham and W. E. B. DuBois. They married in 1958, and a daughter was born in August, 1959. The mother never recovered, and she died in October. Jones had just hung out his shingle to practice law. Although his mother cared for the baby at home during the day, Jones kept a crib in his office and a blanket in his car for the many nights he kept the child while working at the law and in community affairs.

For two years, like many young attorneys, Jones struggled to earn his living handling domestic relations and criminal defense cases. In 1961 Merle McCurdy, the United States attorney for northern Ohio, convinced Jones to become one of his assistants. For the next six years, Jones prosecuted federal criminal cases with the cooperation of the U.S. Justice Department, the Federal Bureau of Investigation, the Secret Service, Treasury Department agents, postal inspectors, and local law enforcement authorities. He remained active in the local NAACP and founded the Youngstown Leadership Conference, which met for breakfast every Friday morning to discuss and to formulate community policy concerning fair employment, the administration of justice, and school segregation. But even as an assistant U.S. attorney, Jones could not escape America's color line. On the morning of his first oral argument before the United States Court of Appeals for the Sixth Circuit, he awoke in his Cincinnati hotel room to the news of the murder in Mississippi of Medgar Evers, one of the nation's prominent black civil rights leaders. When Jones went to the lobby for a haircut, the barbershop was closed—but only to blacks.

In the summer of 1967, Jones told McCurdy that he had decided to return to private practice in Youngstown. But McCurdy made a counteroffer: join the staff of the National Advisory Committee on Civil Disorders to study the root causes of the racial riots. As deputy general counsel, Jones organized and participated in fact-finding trips and meetings, scheduled witnesses and issued subpoenas, examined the law and the facts, and participated in commission discussions and the writing of its report. In the major urban areas he saw that public officials were not responsive to black needs and grievances, and there was growing black frustration with the lack of any effective means to challenge the pervasive system of segregation. He saw and felt, in the words of the commission's final report, that "our nation is moving toward two societies, one black, one white—separate and unequal."

Eighteen months after Jones returned to private practice in Youngstown, the call came from Roy Wilkins to serve as NAACP general counsel. When Jones arrived at the NAACP's New York offices, the media asked him why he had left private practice to join an organization that was perceived by many as over-the-hill if not irrelevant. Jones responded:

> The NAACP is uniquely equipped to make the American system work for all of its people. I intend to make the system of justice in this country redress the legitimate and longstanding grievances of its black citizens.

Jones also had to deal with the realities of his new position: limited financial resources, a staff that was in disarray, a caseload that had not been supervised for more than a year during the search for a new general counsel, the need to advise the NAACP on all legal matters and to arbitrate disputes among the local branches, and a growing black urban population that seemed increasingly willing to acquiesce in one-race clustering rather than to challenge the color line of pervasive segregation. Jones nevertheless determined that anything short of a sustained legal attack on the institutional barrier of segregation could only provide short-term and cosmetic reform. He knew, as had his predecessors Thurgood Marshall, Robert Carter, and Charles Houston, that school and housing segregation had to be a focal point of his legal challenge: schools because they forced so much segregation on so many people, and housing because it was another of the primary engines that perpetuated the color line.

But pending cases and new crises occupied his time from the first day on the job. The last of the so-called equal educational opportunity cases started by the former general counsel was about to go to trial in Benton Harbor, Michigan. Meanwhile, merchants in Claiborne County, Mississippi, were suing the NAACP in state court for millions of dollars in damages under a local antiboycott statute aimed at snuffing out black economic protest against public and private discrimination in local jobs and services. In California authorities charged forty black students in a three-thousand-count indictment for occupying the president's office at Fresno State University. In Goose Bay, Labrador, the Army court-martialed a black soldier on trumped-up charges. In Oyster Bay, Long Island, Grumman Aircraft claimed it could not employ many blacks because none lived near its plant. Jones had to respond to each crisis, and he did.

Jones personally represented the black soldier and won an acquittal. The base commander was transferred, and an investigation of charges of widespread racial discrimination in the Army's Goose Bay operation begun. He secured the services of the Jackson office of the Lawyer's Committee for Civil Rights Under Law to defend the NAACP and the black boycotters against the Mississippi merchants' suit. He personally defended the black Fresno State students and secured acquittals or minor misdemeanor convictions—and readmission to the campus—for most of the demonstrators. In Oyster Bay, he authorized a suit to challenge large-lot zoning that contributed to the dearth of housing open to blacks, which in turn made it difficult for blacks to gain access to the burgeoning job opportunities in distant and virtually all-white suburban enclaves.

In the Benton Harbor school case, Jones enlisted the services of Louis Lucas. After serving as an assistant U.S. attorney in New Orleans and in the civil rights division of the U.S. Justice Department challenging state-mandated Jim Crow laws throughout Tennessee, Mississippi, and Louisiana, Lucas had joined with black lawyers to form the first integrated law firm in Memphis, Tennessee. Jones's call to Lucas went out only three weeks before the Benton Harbor trial, and the cause seemed hopeless. The theory upon which the case was based—of educational disparities resulting from de facto or unintentional segregation—seemed implausible, and the Sixth Circuit had already denied that claim as a basis for finding illegal segregation in *Deal v. Cincinnati Board of Education*. The court's ruling, written by Chief Judge Paul Weick, also held that neighborhood schools gave parents "free choice" by allowing them to choose the neighborhood in which they lived, but refused to allow plaintiffs to introduce evidence of housing discrimination to rebut that rationale for school segregation. With Jones's approval, Lucas nevertheless tried to construct the theory and proof of de jure or purposeful segregation in order to get around the *Deal* ruling.

The Challenge in Michigan

In the aftermath of the riots that shook Detroit and other major cities, some Michigan blacks and white liberals turned away from the goal of integration. Whether from despair, frustration, or a new vision, the code of black power and the cry for community control became popular. In nearby Pontiac, a black federal district judge, Damon Keith, however, ordered desegregation of the schools by skirting the Sixth Circuit's *Deal* ruling after finding a pattern of deliberate actions by local school authorities to segregate students.

Meanwhile, the Michigan Legislature passed a law requiring decentralization of the Detroit school system. The bill's avowed purpose was to secure black control over Detroit's 133 virtually all-black public schools, while ceding white control of the 69 virtually all-white schools. If there was to be segregation, black pragmatists argued, black city parents should exercise the same control over their schools as white suburban parents exercised over theirs. In the process, the state steadfastly rejected consideration of an areawide decentralization alternative proposed by Detroit school board president Abraham Zwerdling to redistrict across school district lines in order to integrate Detroit and its all-white suburbs. Although the new law left most details of the redistricting and decentralization to the Detroit school board, it made one thing clear: it ratified the city's limits as the school district boundary, thereby preserving the city as a predominantly black district and protecting the whites-only status of most suburban districts.

On April 7, 1970, however, Zwerdling maneuvered the school board, by a four-to-two biracial vote, to pass a compromise plan over the opposition of white conservatives. In doing so, the board drew regional boundaries maximizing the limited potential for desegregation within the city and redrawing attendance boundaries for twelve of the twenty-two regular high schools across the color line of residential segregation.

The April 7 plan would reassign only 10,000 of the system's 290,000 pupils over three years to promote some desegregation. For the first time in the history of the system, however, a few white children would be transferred from white schools to black schools. The Detroit NAACP and many other progressive and black civic groups praised the plan as a symbolic first step to school integration. White citizen groups called for the recall of the four board members who had voted for the plan and demanded that the state legislature immediately overturn the board action. Two days later the Michigan House of Representatives responded—over the unanimous opposition of the black legislators—and reversed the board's plan by mandating pupil assignments to the nearest school. Representative Vaughn expressed black sentiment about the action:

> I think this is perhaps the saddest day—April 9 will go down in history— in Michigan history. It is the day the House of Representatives, at the State Capitol, Michigan voted officially to nullify the Bill of Rights and the Constitution and violate the basic laws of the United States Supreme Court. . . . And what did the State House today say: We *must* segregate. . . . This is what Southern senators do—plot on how to circumvent a basic rule, a basic rule that would bring the schools together.

In the following weeks of intense lobbying, the white majority made clear that the perpetuation of segregation, through rescission of the April 7 plan, was inevitable. The available choice was not between integration and segregation, but between community (i.e., black) control over black schools or white control of black schools.

For state senator Coleman Young—who four years later would become Detroit's first black mayor—this choice was easy. Despite its symbolism, he also viewed the April 7 plan as no more than "a chicken-shit integration plan." As a result, he joined in pushing through the legislature a new community control compromise that was signed into law by Governor William Milliken on July 9. Act 48 rescinded the April 7 desegregation plan, mandated neighborhood pupil assignments in Detroit schools (supplemented by "open enrollment" to allow any white stragglers in transition neighborhoods to transfer out of black schools), reimposed the Detroit school district boundaries, and vested authority to draw the regional boundaries within Detroit in a three-member commission appointed by the governor. Representative Sanders was the lone dissenting voice.

> I voted no . . . because I believe it can only have the result of furthering and intensifying segregation in education, a segregation which has been contrary to the law of the land since 1954. Many of you sat smugly in Michigan while the Southern states protested the *Brown v. Topeka Board of Education* landmark decision. You thought you were so much more virtuous in this basic humanitarian tenet of considering all men as equal and realizing that separate is not, never was and never can be equal. . . . I am disappointed—I'm deeply disappointed—I'm ashamed of your action and response to racist fears. You have helped to both divide and move our society in a backward direction.

The Detroit branch of the NAACP, the national organization's largest contributor and one of its most active locals, was shocked by these events. At the urging of the Detroit branch, the NAACP national convention passed a resolution condemning the legislature's attempt to nullify the board's original step toward desegregation. The branch also requested Jones to challenge the new state statute. Jones again called on Lucas for help. Together, they surveyed the situation with the local NAACP leadership, including Executive Secretary William Penn and Education Committee chairman Jesse Goodwin. Jones concluded that the legislature's action presented as open a display of state-imposed segregation as earlier Southern attempts to nullify *Brown*.

Yet Detroit was a huge district—the fifth largest in the country—already heavily black in racial composition surrounded by virtually all-white suburbs. The school board and administration held a national reputation as racially progressive, and the April 7 plan was largely a symbolic, albeit welcome, start toward desegregation. Moreover, the legal basis for challenging Act 48 was not sure. Although change in the law might come, much was still ahead. The Supreme Court had not yet ruled that *Green v. School Board of New Kent County,* its ruling throwing out "free choice" plans that perpetuated dual school systems in sparsely populated rural areas, even applied to urban districts in the South. The Sixth Circuit had not yet enforced *Green* in rural schools in Tennessee and Kentucky, much less reconsidered its own decision in *Deal*, which made judicial review of school segregation in the North difficult. In sum, Detroit was hardly the place to begin a grand strategy to win legal support for desegregation of Northern urban schools.

But like Coleman Young, Nate Jones felt he had no choice. The actions of the legislature validating segregation could not go unchallenged. Michigan had issued an invitation to the NAACP and the local branch that Jones could not refuse. The fate of segregation in urban America and the direction of the civil rights movement hung in the balance.

Detroit school superintendent Norman Drachler also felt that the legislature's intervention was a classic act of segregation. He, too, sought the assistance of the NAACP in challenging the act and arranged a secret meeting at Jones's New York office with Detroit NAACP officials. Drachler was represented by two of his staff and the board's attorney, George Bushnell, a progressive member of the established Detroit bar. At the meeting, school board and administration representatives stressed that they would take further steps toward integration if the NAACP could obtain a judicial declaration that the legislature's action was unconstitutional. But Lucas was wary. He countered that the case against Act 48 might well depend on proof and findings of preexisting illegal school segregation; he also suggested that a broader case could and should be made against the Detroit school board to insure actual desegregation.

Immediately responding to Lucas's threat, Bushnell said, "I'll whip your ass." But Lucas was not one to be bullied. In the Benton Harbor school case he had just convinced a conservative trial judge that school segregation was harmful to black school children even if school authorities did not cause the racial separation by acts of discrimination. Even if the Detroit school case had no firm legal precedent, Lucas was no more taken aback by Bushnell than he had been by similar challenges from scores of Southern lawyers who had unsuccessfully defended segregation during his stint at the Justice Department.

After meetings with concerned parents and children, the local NAACP joined with Detroit families who wished to sue. On August 4, in a special election, the Detroit electorate recalled the board members who supported the April 7 prointegration plan. The vote was split by race: 90 percent of the surprisingly large white turnout voted for the recall, 90 percent of the blacks voted against. There was no longer a board majority favoring school integration, even if the state's rescission of the April 7 plan were thrown out in court. The private plaintiffs, the local NAACP, and Jones all agreed that the Detroit school board must therefore be included as a defendant in the suit.

Local labor leaders offered their support if Jones agreed not to challenge the racially identifiable assignment of teachers, which mirrored the racial composition of pupils in schools. Jones refused on the ground that he could not absolve faculty segregation while challenging school segregation. The Detroit NAACP did not consult Bushnell on its decision to add the Detroit authorities as defendants, even though he was a member of its board of directors. Bushnell's resignation from the NAACP only confirmed the battle lines: the state of Michigan, the Detroit board, most of the white electorate, the teachers' union, and the established legal profession in Detroit would fight the NAACP, the local branch, the plaintiffs, a few whites and a good portion of the black community, NAACP general counsel Jones, and attorney Lucas. Whatever the reasons, neither Coleman Young nor any other representative of the black community sought to enter the case to defend community control or to oppose desegregation; there would be no rearguard attack from the flanks to the NAACP's legal challenge to segregation.

Jones sized up the case this way:

> We were groping for ways to prove that what most judges and the public perceived as *de facto* or adventitious segregation was what we knew to be . . . *de jure* or official segregation and intentional discrimination, public and private. We knew that we had to find the proof and the tools of persuasion to show that racial discrimination—not free choice, economics, or happenstance—caused the current segregation in schools and housing.

As to appropriate remedies, neither Jones nor the NAACP had a clear idea at the outset. They both hoped that some form of actual desegregation that would break the back of segregated community life in urban areas might finally be ordered, but they were more concerned about finding the ways to prove to the court and to the country that a color line, every bit as wrong as Jim Crow, still divided America on a racial basis.

On August 18 Jones and Lucas filed the complaint in the United States District Court for the Eastern District of Michigan. William Caldwell, a raw-boned product of Maggie Valley, North Carolina, and Memphis State Law School, who had just passed his bar exam and joined Lucas's law firm, assisted. He was a bit awed by the prospect of suing the fifth largest school district in the nation in a court not known for its openness to challenges to school segregation, but Lucas's indomitable spirit did not allow Caldwell too much leeway for doubt.

The complaint named the governor, attorney general, state superintendent of public instruction, Michigan Board of Education, Detroit Board of Education, and the Detroit school superintendent as defendants. It challenged those aspects of Act 48 that nullified the April 7 plan, required segregated pupil assignments, and created racially identifiable regions. The complaint asked for an injunction, pending the trial, to require defendants to implement the April 7 plan, to halt all school construction, and to cease implementation of the new state law. Plaintiffs also charged the Detroit public schools had been segregated by racially discriminatory policies, customs, practices, and usages. The complaint requested that the board submit a plan for the next school year to eliminate racially identifiable schools, but there was no request for a plan that would go beyond the boundaries of the Detroit school district. Given the extreme difficulty of the case under existing law, there was little inclination among the NAACP legal staff to include a plea for city-suburban integration at the outset. For the time being, consideration of any such metropolitan remedy was left for another day.

Judge Stephen Roth

In 1969 the Supreme Court had ruled in *Alexander v. Holmes County Board of Education* that "now" was the time to dismantle dual systems. Lucas took the Court at its word. As soon as the complaint was filed, Jones, Lucas, and Caldwell marched off to a federal courtroom in Flint to ask the district judge assigned to the case by blind draw to grant a temporary restraining order until a hearing could be held. There they met the penetrating stare of Judge Stephen J. Roth.

Stephen Roth was born in 1908 in the tiny Austro-Hungarian village of Sajo Szoged where his father was caretaker on an estate. In 1911 Roth's father immigrated to the United States where he worked at the old Buick plant in Flint, Michigan. Two years later Stephen and his mother sailed across the ocean in steerage to join him. After graduating from high school, he had worked in factories for two years and then worked his way through the University of Notre Dame and University of Michigan Law School.

In 1935 Roth returned to practice law and became involved in Flint politics as a leading figure in the conservative, blue-collar wing of the state's Democratic party. He served one term as state attorney general and in 1952 became a state trial judge in the Flint area; ten years later, President Kennedy promoted him to the federal bench. Roth claimed that he grew up in a melting pot neighborhood where racial discrimination was absent or at least no more of a problem than the discrimination suffered by a Catholic immigrant. He had made it and so could blacks if they would only apply themselves. Roth earned the reputation of a hard-working but conservative jurist who demonstrated little sympathy for minority grievances.

Judge Roth listened courteously as Jones, Lucas, and Caldwell argued that Detroit was illegally segregated and that the state legislature's passage of

Act 48 rescinding the April 7 plan was no different from similar actions in Southern states seeking to nullify desegregation decisions. The judge was unmoved when Lucas argued that the April 7 plan should be implemented immediately until a hearing could be held on the merits of the claim of systemwide segregation. The judge did show interest, however, in the suggestion that, in the interest of practicality, all school construction should be halted temporarily in order not to waste money or make the desegregation job even more difficult if the plaintiffs won. Judge Roth was a pragmatic man, and there was some logic to this argument—even if it was unlikely that the plaintiffs could prove Detroit's school segregation was unconstitutional. He therefore asked for Bushnell's position; the board's attorney said the issue was moot because no such construction was in progress. Satisfied by this answer, Judge Roth denied Lucas's request for a temporary restraining order and set a date for a hearing to begin August 27.

Sensing Judge Roth's lack of sympathy and realizing the enormity of the case, Lucas advised Jones that more legal troops were needed. Lucas secured the assistance of J. Harold ("Nick") Flannery, a courtly civil rights lawyer with whom Lucas had served in the Justice Department. Flannery worked in the civil rights division from its inception and had successfully tried the government's first Northern school case—in South Holland, Illinois—before Judge Julius Hoffman. Flannery had recently resigned to become director of litigation for the Center of Law and Education, a "backup" center for the federal legal services program, housed at Harvard University. His stentorian delivery and imposing courtroom presence often were mesmerizing, and his Irish wit and charm carried him over many rough spots and legal pitfalls that might have trapped lesser advocates. Flannery also brought with him a new attorney who had just completed a clerkship for the Honorable Clifford O'Sullivan, one of the Sixth Circuit's conservative, antibusing judges. Flannery confided to Lucas, "He throws so many punches so fast, for so long that eventually he's bound to do some damage—hopefully, some to the opposition." With that introduction, I entered the fray.

At the hearing, Judge Roth listened, but with less patience. Lucas again argued for immediate implementation of the April 7 plan pending a full hearing. Judge Roth indicated his reluctance:

> I am not computerized. I am not automated, so you can't expect push-button relief here. I am not going to move hastily. . . . I am not going to move unless I am well-informed.

Realizing the case would probably be a long one, Judge Roth sharply limited the preliminary hearing. On September 3, 1970, the judge denied the plaintiffs' request for any preliminary relief.

The proofs are not convincing that there has been a course of action which can be characterized as directed toward the maintenance of a dual system of schools, either *de jure* or *de facto*. To the contrary, the evidence before the court indicates that there has been a conscious, deliberate, progressive and continuous attempt to promote and advance the integration of both pupils and faculty. . . . We believe the best interests of the children, their parents, the school administration and faculty, and the general public will best be served at this point in the proceedings if the preliminary injunction prayed for is not issued.

Judge Roth also dismissed the governor and the attorney general as defendants in the case.

With school set to open on September 8, the plaintiffs had lost the first round. Worse, with a trial on the merits of the case set to begin November 12, there was little time to prepare. Equally disturbing, Judge Roth had announced his lack of sympathy to the plaintiffs' claim that the segregation of the Detroit public schools was the equivalent of an unconstitutional dual system.

But Lucas would not allow Roth's outlook to stand in his way; he changed directions. Lucas immediately filed a notice that he would appeal Judge Roth's decision. With Caldwell, he filed emergency papers in the Sixth Circuit seeking an order to implement the April 7 plan pending a hearing. They tracked down new chief judge Harry Phillips at his home in Nashville and persuaded him to hold an immediate hearing. On September 8, the day Detroit schools opened, Judge Phillips heard oral arguments on the emergency petition.

Harry Phillips had joined former chief judge Paul Weick's *Deal* opinion in the Cincinnati school case that had established tough legal standards for evaluating plaintiffs' claims of unconstitutional school segregation in the North. But the new chief judge was beginning to put some distance between himself and Weick's attempt to insulate school segregation, North or South, from the Supreme Court's recent command to dismantle Southern dual systems at once. Judge Phillips also maintained that the best trial and appellate lawyers come from Tennessee; he seemed to enjoy seeing Lucas, one of his home state favorites, challenge city slicker lawyers from Detroit. Besides, Lucas was making some sense as well as some noise: was there really any constitutional difference between Michigan's frustration of the Detroit board's desegregation plan and the nullification measures passed by Southern legislatures after *Brown*?

Michigan assistant attorney general Eugene Krasicky defended the state's actions. But Lucas responded caustically: "I must confess to a certain feeling of *deja vu*. After hearing Mr. Krasicky, I can't tell whether I've been listening to Michigan's attorney general or Mississippi's attorney general.'' Harry Phillips chuckled. The judge expedited the appeal procedures, required full briefs, and scheduled oral argument of the appeal before a special three-judge panel of the Sixth Circuit for October 2. The speed with which Judge Phillips moved suggested that he was interested.

We all directed our energies at this new hope: the appeal brief for the Sixth Circuit, not preparation for the trial before Judge Roth, was the key. As we met on the evening of October 1 to go over the oral preparation a final time, Flannery suggested that I should handle his half of the oral argument in order to let the Sixth Circuit know the views of one of its former law clerks. Although Lucas was hardly enthusiastic, we divided the argument the next day. Lucas rose and argued in his inimitable, rambling, but loquacious Southern fashion, drawing on every analogy he could find between Act 48 and the interposition measures passed by Southern states to challenge court-ordered desegregation. I focused on the need for immediate implementation of a plan to overcome the segregation directly caused by Michigan's reversal of the April 7 plan.

On October 13 the three-judge panel ruled that the state's action amounted to an unconstitutional nullification of the steps taken by the Detroit board to protect the rights of school children guaranteed by the Fourteenth Amendment. But the court refused to overturn Judge Roth's denial of a preliminary injunction and sent the case back to the lower court for further proceedings. The Sixth Circuit had served notice on Judge Roth and the parties involved that school segregation in the North was no longer immune from judicial review and that the Detroit school case must be heard, not ignored.

The November hearing on the merits of the case before Judge Roth now loomed. There was no way to get the entire case in shape for trial by that time. Therefore, we decided on a two-part strategy: seek implementation of the April 7 plan for the beginning of the second semester; delay hearing on the entire case to give us time to prepare for the trial of the claim that segregation was systemwide. At a minimum, a limited hearing on the first request would occupy the judge's attention; at best, it could lead to undoing of the state's action. Judge Roth agreed to hear this motion on November 4 and to postpone the hearing on the merits for one month. The judge seemed impressed that there ought to be some remedy for the state's rollback of the prodesegregation plan. On November 6 he ordered the Detroit board to submit, within ten days, "a high school attendance area plan" consisting of the April 7 plan "or an updated version thereof which achieves no less pupil integration" to be implemented the first day of the second semester.

The current school board members, none of whom supported the April 7 plan, were now lame ducks. The new, thirteen-member board of education, including eight elected from the new regions than did not fit the April 7 plan, would take office in January. The backlash forces that recalled board members who supported the prointegration plan still adamantly opposed the reassignment of any white child to a black school. When the lame-duck board held a public hearing on proposed plans in response to the judge's order, six hundred angry whites protested.

In a six-hour closed meeting, the board determined to submit three alternatives: a "magnet" plan calling for the creation of several special schools at the high school and junior high levels to draw a biracial enrollment voluntarily; a part-time plan calling for specialized courses to attract a biracial enrollment for portions of the school day; and the April 7 plan.

While the board was debating, the attorneys for the plaintiffs and the defendants attempted to prepare for the trial on the claim of systemwide segregation that was to begin in less than a month. Judge Roth also allowed the Detroit Federation of Teachers to intervene as a party defendant. Far from providing support, the union offered plaintiffs new and substantial opposition. Ted Sachs, a savvy labor lawyer and no-nonsense trial attorney, represented the teachers. He would add a considerable burden to our already difficult job of proof and persuasion. In addition, Judge Roth also permitted a group of white homeowners, represented by Alex Ritchie, to intervene to defend the marked racial separation in schools and to oppose busing.

During this same period, the Harvard University faculty advisors and director of the Center for Law and Education ordered Flannery and me to withdraw from the case because of their opposition to the case. Ironically, this drew the Legal Defense Fund into the case as cocounsel with the NAACP, the first formal joint effort since the rupture in the early 1960s over how to proceed against school desegregation. It also brought the considerable legal talents of Norman Chachkin, supervisor of the Legal Defense Fund's extensive southern school litigation, into the case. In short order, with the aid of other staff of the Center for Law and Education, Flannery and I soon returned. In addition, Edward McCroom, an attorney from Cincinnati, and Robert Pressman, a former civil rights division attorney from the Harvard Center, joined the plaintiffs' roster.

On November 9 the parties submitted pretrial statements of the issues. They demonstrated both how differently the parties perceived the case *and* how much more preparation was required on all sides. In a background interview with the press on November 23, Judge Roth expressed his desire to serve as a "peacemaker," rendering his "service to the community by helping solve this problem." At the hearing on the desegregation alternatives, the board argued for the voluntary magnet plan but suggested that it should be implemented the following September rather than the second semester. We argued that three magnet schools in Detroit had failed in the past to provide any desegregation and that the new magnet plan could promote further segregation by encouraging the remaining whites in heavily black schools to flee to the proposed "magnets." We pressed for implementation of the April 7 plan to start at the second semester.

On December 3 Judge Roth approved the magnet plan to begin in the fall of 1971 *and* postponed indefinitely the hearing on the issue of segregation until "after review of [the court's] calendar." Judge Roth said the thirteen new Detroit board members had to worry about implementing the regional decentralization plan, not preparing for federal court hearings, and that the magnet plan "resolves the most urgent issue in the case." The judge rejected the April 7 plan because its "principal aim is to improve integration by the 'numbers.' . . . [I]t does not offer incentive to or provide motivation for the student himself. Instead of offering a change of diet, it offers forced-feeding." In contrast, Judge Roth touted the magnet plan: "the students, in their quest for identity and in their inherited drive for realizing their potentials, will bring about such integration [by their free choices] as no coercive method could possibly achieve." The judge also voiced his skepticism about the plaintiffs' claim that the entire school system was unconstitutionally segregated: "We cannot at this point proceed on the assumption that plaintiffs will succeed in proving their claim, in the hearing on the merits, that Detroit is a segregated school system, *de jure* or *de facto.*" As one board member remarked: "If the court wanted an integration plan with a lot of form and no substance, then this was the plan. It will cost nothing and it will do nothing."

At an unprecedented news conference in his chambers, before the glare of television lights and microphones, Judge Roth explained why he allowed the school board to undertake a "freedom of choice plan" and postponed the trial on the merits. He called the NAACP attorneys "outsiders [who] should go away and let Detroit solve its own problems," ignoring the fact that these "outsiders" represented the Detroit NAACP and its sizable membership, as well as parents and school children in the Detroit school district. Judge Roth had publicly announced his hostility to our case, and laid bare his ideology. Whatever gain the plaintiffs might have won from the Sixth Circuit's October ruling appeared lost.

But the bulldog in Lucas only saw the judge's action as a call to fight harder. As Lucas put it: "First, we *will* persuade the Sixth Circuit to reverse Judge Roth again so that he'll pay attention to us, and then we *will* prove to him that the segregation of the Detroit Public Schools results from racial discrimination." Any person objectively viewing the court of appeals record and the predilections of the trial judge might reasonably have questioned the odds of such a strategy. But, as Nate Jones saw it, the issue had been drawn: for better or worse, Detroit was the place where the NAACP would test the constitutionality of Northern school segregation and the responsiveness of the judicial system.

Trial Preparation

Joined by a small cadre of volunteer researchers and potential expert witnesses, we began to prepare for a trial whose start now appeared more uncertain than ever. Nevertheless, we began to look into the larger questions that would dominate any hearing: was school segregation in Detroit the result of choice, economics, voluntary clustering, or discrimination? What was the interplay between school and housing segregation? Had state and local officials contributed to the segregation by discriminatory acts? The staff assembled to gather evidence on these issues was unique.

First, there was a big, fun-loving architect named William Lamson, who worked in Detroit at a loose association of city planners called the Urban Collaborative. Whether decked out in a ponytail or pointing his finger or chin at a new idea, he was a formidable sight who could create magic with boldly colored demographic maps. Lamson also seemed to know every nook and cranny of Detroit and every conceivable source of data.

Second, Gordon Foster, a Quaker and a pacifist, had devoted his professional life to school administration generally and to providing technical assistance to southern school districts undergoing desegregation in particular. He had already testified in another northern school case based on his understanding of the workings of segregated school systems, and he began to prepare the case against the school officials.

Third, Karl Taeuber, a sociologist and demographer with the appearance and demeanor of a Mr. Peepers but with the soul of an evangelical abolitionist, began to bring his insights into the processes of housing and school segregation. A noted expert on the census and racial separation, he researched whether economics or ethnicity could explain the marked separation in Detroit.

Fourth, Martin Sloane, a former director of the U.S. Civil Rights Commission housing staff and former staff attorney at the U.S. Department of Housing and Urban Development, began to put together his thoughts on the federal government's involvement in creating and perpetuating housing and school segregation.

Finally, Robert Green, the dean of urban affairs at Michigan State University, psychological chronicler of the Prince Edward County, Virginia school closings, and an academic lieutenant of Martin and Coretta King's direct action movement, brought his dominating view and inspirational presence to the dry statistics on educational inequality.

In subsequent years, these five would be called derisively Lucas's "dog and pony road show" by defense attorneys in one school segregation case after another. Their continuing viability as witnesses demonstrated their credibility, integrity, and incisive understanding of school and housing segregation. In addition, Paul Smith, an educational statistician from the staff of the

Center for Law and Education, aided this quintet in the Detroit school case. He described himself as a "custodial sociologist" because in conducting any investigation he never forgot to question those who might know every detail of an organization—including the janitors.

While our preparations for trial continued, we again appealed to the Sixth Circuit to reverse Judge Roth. The three-judge panel, however, would have nothing to do with further preliminary skirmishes. In a terse opinion on February 22, 1971, the court refused to consider the claim that the April 7 plan should be implemented on an interim basis but directed Judge Roth to proceed to hear the issue of segregation "fully and forthwith." As Lucas described the decision, "The Sixth Circuit just said 'a pox on all your houses. Stop fencing and start trying this case.' " Although we might have wished for something more, the court of appeals did at least advise Judge Roth that he must listen to the "outsiders" claims and evidence, here and now. With the Sixth Circuit's ruling, Judge Roth cleared his calendar for a trial on the merits set to begin April 6, 1971.

In the six weeks between the court of appeals ruling and the start of trial, the work of plaintiffs' attorneys, experts, researchers, and support staff never seemed to cease. A rough division of labor was drawn up: Lucas and Caldwell, with Foster and Lamson, would put together the history of the Detroit public school system and document the incidents of intentional segregation by school authorities. McCroom would work on the proof of faculty segregation and discrimination in hiring and placement. Flannery, Pressman, and I, with Lamson, Taeuber, and Sloane, would document the history of community segregation and the racial discrimination on which it was based. Chachkin with Smith, and Lucas with Green, would analyze resource and educational disparities between black and white schools.

The work overlapped, and Lucas was forever driving the others to find more proof and better witnesses. School records, school administrators and teachers, census data, local public and federal housing officials and records, real estate brokers, state licensing agencies, state court decisions, title insurers, civil rights and community relations agencies and personnel, relevant doctoral and master's dissertations, planning departments, all were interviewed or evaluated.

Detroit was a big city with a complex history. Nevertheless, a picture of a community long divided along racial lines was beginning to emerge, piece by piece. In the process, however, several problems also cropped up: school boundary and racial data prior to the 1950s were not recorded or were lost; there just was not enough time to prepare the entire case of intentional segregation by the beginning of trial; and the links between the proof of intentional school segregation and the evidence of housing discrimination and educational resource disparities had not been forged.

Attorneys for the plaintiffs had to make some firm decisions about these issues to avoid a total fiasco at the hearing. We had no choice but to concentrate the first part of the hearing on proof of community discrimination and housing segregation; that was the only part of the case that was ready. Such evidence might also serve as an interesting foil to the primary defense of the school authorities, i.e., that school authorities imposed no racial restrictions on school assignments because families freely chose the neighborhood in which they wished to live and send their children to school. If we could show that the housing segregation resulted from racial discrimination and was part of a community custom of racial caste, then we might be able to move any judge to see that school authorities should not get off scot-free by arguing that they only incorporated residential segregation through an allegedly neutral system of neighborhood pupil assignments. It would not take much proof of school board manipulation designed to take advantage of, or to exacerbate, such housing segregation to show that school authorities were willing partners—not neutral observers—in the process of segregation.

Our theory of the case could then be built around the theme that school authorities worked hand in glove with other community actors to contain blacks in separate schools and to protect whites, for as long as possible, from having to attend school with any substantial number of minority children. The specific links between housing and school segregation in this theory would have to be developed as the trial progressed. Perhaps most critical, this tack would also allow Lucas and Caldwell to finish investigating and documenting the proof of intentional actions by school authorities. In any event, because we had no other choice, we convinced ourselves that the strategy made sense.

We also agreed that evidence on disparities of educational resources should not be used independently to suggest that school segregation, regardless of its cause, was "inherently unequal." None of us, including Lucas, was convinced that a black child could only learn while sitting next to a white child. We did not view desegregation as an opportunity for whites to rub off some intelligence on blacks: to us that was just another racist myth. Instead, the proof of disparities in educational resources between virtually all-black and all-white schools would be included as a part of our case of intentional segregation primarily to show how authorities identified schools as "black" or "white."

One other problem loomed. From Lamson's colorful 1940, 1950, 1960, and 1970 census maps graphically depicting the pattern of racial segregation in Detroit, it was apparent that there had long been two small black pockets (in the southwest corner and near the middle of the northern boundary) and a rapidly expanding black core in the center of the city. By 1970 the black core virtually enveloped both pockets, leaving only two receding all-white areas in the northwest and northeast areas of the city. The racial composition of the school district had increased from 45.8 percent black in 1961 to 63.8 percent black in 1970. Our "containment" theory would have to deal with a constantly shifting racial boundary and the vast expansion of the black core. In order to rebut the inference that the pattern of housing segregation was, in the final analysis, beyond the control of any school authority, we would have to show that intentional school actions contributed to the expanding pattern of housing segregation.

Some of the attorneys for the Detroit school board thought plaintiffs' counsel faced a more fundamental dilemma. They did not see how we could ever prevail in court if the result were a predominantly black school district. They asked, "What's the point of talking about desegregation when racial balancing of all the schools will just result in a system with predominantly black schools?"

That issue was not troublesome to us as a matter of ethics or constitutional law. There is nothing wrong with majority-black or all-black schools per se; to be black is not to be inherently inferior, as the question seemed to assume. The meaning of the Constitution cannot vary with the racial composition of the school district; there cannot be one law for an 80 percent black district and another for an 80 percent white district if the courts are to avoid the assumptions of inherent white superiority and black inferiority that *Brown* squarely rejected.

Nevertheless, the racial data in Detroit did present a real problem. The world of segregation did not begin or end at the Detroit city limits. Surrounding the city was an expanding ring of all-white population and schools (dotted by several small and historic blacks-only pockets). If "containment" meant anything, it included the segregation of Detroit's expanding black core from these all-white suburban havens, as well as from the remaining all-white enclaves in Detroit's northwest and northeast corners. To take on the issue of metropolitan desegregation at this stage, however, was beyond the existing state of the law and our resources. Lucas would soon be trying just such a metropolitan case in Richmond, Virginia, before a sympathetic trial judge that would involve only those local jurisdictions which, arguably, were already under an affirmative duty to take all steps necessary to eradicate Virginia's state-mandated system of dual schooling root and branch. The Richmond case would provide a better vehicle for raising the metropolitan issue and, if successful, might eventually provide the legal building block necessary to raise the issue at a subsequent stage in the Detroit case. Equally important, if plaintiffs did beat the Detroit school board on the issue of segregation in the city, Lucas was confident that Bushnell and the Detroit board would then join us in an attack on the areawide process of segregation. Thus, we all hoped that active consideration of the metropolitan issue in Detroit was at least a few years away.

Chapter 3
The Trial of Judge Roth,
April to September, 1971

The Opening Bell

At the start of the trial, Judge Roth took one last swipe at the NAACP counsel when defense attorneys complained about the swift pace of preparation for hearing such a complex case: "Mr. Lucas has kept me and everybody busy going to Cincinnati [the site of the Sixth Circuit]. I've been concerned with that. . . . But the Court of Appeals has issued an order. I abide by it as any little soldier does." But all the pretrial skirmishing had been worth the effort: Judge Roth took notice of plaintiffs' claims. For forty-one trial days, from April 6 through July 22, he listened to the evidence and evaluated the legal arguments.

In his own way Judge Roth had come to respect Nate Jones, Lou Lucas, and their band of lawyers and researchers. As an accommodation to counsel, Roth allowed us to use his jury room to house and work on our growing number of exhibits. He was impressed with the extent of the work product and the length of our workday. He also enjoyed many aspects of plaintiff counsel's unexpected adversary surprises. For example, when assistant attorney general Krasicky argued that the state board was just an advisory body with no power over the Detroit school district, Lucas responded by reading a brief filed by Krasicky in state court claiming that the state board was the omnipotent parent that could not even be sued by its dissatisfied child, the Detroit board. Krasicky complained that it was unfair for Lucas to dredge up the attorney general's arguments from another case and then argued ruefully that the state board's conflicting arguments could not be wrong in both courts. Judge Roth retorted, "It's a cruel world, Mr. Krasicky." Perhaps chastened by the Sixth Circuit's direction to hold a full hearing, Stephen Roth had made up his mind to *judge* all the relevant testimony.

As the courtroom opened on April 6, 1971, a ten-by-twenty-foot map of the city prepared by Bill Lamson dominated the wall behind defense counsel. This exhibit displayed, in vivid color, the almost complete residential segregation of Detroit: there was not much territory that was other than virtually all-black or all-white. Overlays showed high school boundaries that neatly coincided with the underlying racial divides. As one opposing counsel remarked after the trial, "Who could look at the map for four months and not realize that Detroit was segregated?"

We placed the map to Judge Roth's right where he often stared when contemplating an issue or looking away from a witness, rather than placing it above the jury box in Roth's line of sight to the witness stand: we wanted to focus the judge's gaze on the map when he was thinking abstractly, *not* to divert his attention when he was concentrating on the testimony of a witness. George Bushnell also complained that plaintiffs placed this map behind defense counsel for purposes of intimidation. Although the map hung over their heads, Lamson graciously assured that his handiwork was stable and would not fall down on anyone.

Lou Lucas introduced the first witness, Roy Stevens, a white school board member from 1959 through 1966, to provide an overview of the school portion of our case. While on the board, Stevens lived in the far northwest corner of Detroit, but his son traveled daily on the public transportation system to the technical school, Cass High, in the center city. From 1961 through 1963 the board appointed a Citizens' Advisory Committee on Equal Educational Opportunities. Stevens recounted the conclusion of the committee's report concerning boundary manipulation: "The allegation that purposeful administrative devices have at times been used to perpetuate segregation in some schools is clearly substantiated." Stevens also testified about "optional attendance zones" that existed "only in certain areas . . . between [pairs of] black . . . and white schools . . . [I]n many instances students who were white would select the predominantly white school and students who were black would . . . go to a school that was predominantly black." Stevens concluded by describing how the board then adopted a system of "open enrollment" which allowed any student in the system to transfer to designated schools. At the time, these "open schools" were generally white; many white children from predominantly black schools "utilized this option" to transfer to white schools. With this mild opening, Lucas demonstrated that the Detroit board, with full knowledge of the segregative consequences, had long utilized at least three of the classic devices of intentional segregation—gerrymandering, optional zones, and open enrollment.

The Housing Case

Lucas then left the courtroom to continue preparation of the school case with Caldwell, while Flannery, Pressman, and I put on the proof of housing segregation and community discrimination for the next ten trial days. I opened with a request that Judge Roth admit into evidence copies of the many Michigan Supreme Court cases enforcing racially restrictive covenants in real estate contracts, right through to the day of the United States Supreme Court's decision in *Shelley v. Kramer* (and its companion case from Detroit, *Sipes v. McGhee)* holding state court enforcement of such community apartheid unconstitutional.

Bushnell objected. He argued that such proof of housing discrimination was irrelevant under the Sixth Circuit's ruling in *Deal* and that recent fair housing laws now guaranteed every minority family an equal opportunity to choose a neighborhood and school. Bushnell added testily that plaintiffs' counsel sought to bring attention to these cases only as a personal insult because his father had written one of the state court opinions. I conceded the irony in the authorship but argued to Judge Roth that these state court cases were but the first link in a chain of evidence that would show that Detroit was a community divided along racial lines by racial discrimination *and* that the Detroit board, far from being immune to such community hostility to association with blacks, intentionally built upon and promoted this racial separation.

As there was no jury to protect, Judge Roth advised the parties that he would follow the rule of a simple justice of the peace: to hear everything that the opposing parties wished to present but to separate the wheat from the chaff when making his final decision. To placate Bushnell on the state court opinions, however, Judge Roth agreed to take judicial notice of state court enforcement of racially restrictive covenants prior to the time of *Shelley* without cluttering the record with the actual opinions.

We proceeded to introduce a 1947 map from the *Sipes* case itself showing that racially restrictive covenants blanketed those areas of Detroit that were still all-white. An officer of the largest title company in Detroit testified that such restrictive covenants also blanketed all of the city's suburbs that had been platted by 1950 and continued to appear in all subsequent deeds, abstracts, and title insurance policies of his company until 1969. At that time, the Justice Department forced title insurance companies to stop listing racial restrictions under the Fair Housing Act of 1968.

Richard Marks, longtime research director for the Detroit Commission on Community Relations, testified about the development of racial segregation in Detroit. Utilizing Bill Lamson's census maps for 1940, 1950, 1960, and 1970, he described the "basic containment pattern" of blacks. Blacks were "contained" within an expanding but clearly delineated and prescribed core in the inner city, with isolated pockets in the southwest "dog leg" and along Eight Mile Road, the northern border of the city. Over time, "all we saw happening was simply the relaxation of a previous [racial] line-restricting barrier and . . . the beginnings of . . . new line[s]."

Marks added that the pattern of racial containment over time could not be explained by economics: "there was plenty of range of economic level in the black community" and in the price of housing in the exclusively white areas, right down to "what might be called a rural slum." Marks then described the many racial "screens which sift out people [and] which have historically prevented blacks from living where choice might suggest": rock-throwing mob action; realtor and neighborhood association "point systems," "codes of ethics,'' and discriminatory marketing of homes and apartments to exclude ''undesirables,'' particularly blacks; FHA promotion of racial restrictions and whites-only housing; racially dual public housing with black projects in designated black tracts and white projects in neighborhoods reserved for whites.

Alex Ritchie, the attorney for the intervening white neighborhood associations, sought to cross-examine Marks about just what he meant by the word ''containment.'' Marks responded:

> Well, when a piece of property is not freely available to any person who has the desire to purchase [and] the money to purchase, . . . we would view that as an example of individual restriction, that's a refusal to consummate a deal on a piece of property that is available on the market with a person who is desirous of purchasing.
>
> When that pattern, when evidence of a pattern, not just of individual refusals, but a pattern . . . exists throughout a total area, we call that containment. It is just as effective a barrier as if a wall were built in the community.

Marks then recounted that on the edge of the historic black pocket near the northern boundary of the city, the white builder who had title to adjacent property ''actually put up a cement, . . . mortar and brick wall, which for years was a symbol of the way in which the Negro was an undesired neighbor.''

Although the answer struck a hard blow to Alex Ritchie's sense of basic decency, Judge Roth was skeptical. The judge had lived his life believing that racial segregation was just an ethnic phenomenon common to many new immigrant groups to the nation, particularly to northern industrial cities like Flint and Detroit:

> *The Court.* [A]s I see some of the pattern of housing in the most distant past, not 1940 but well before that time, . . . pockets of immigrants came here and settled, and they did it for their own protection because they didn't know the language for one thing nor the customs nor the ways. . . . [W]asn't it natural for them to collect in a group so they might better conduct their business and social intercourse?

> *A.* True.

> *The Court.* But passing from those ethnic groups are there pockets of, concentrated pockets of people who have in their communities concentrations of those who have, for example, followed a segregated pattern in other parts of this country and who have come here?

A. I'm afraid I don't know—give me an example.

The Court. Let's put it bluntly. Are there big pockets historically or present now of people who have come up from the South?

A. No. The reality of all of the groups that you have mentioned, the ethnic groups, the Poles, Italians, Germans, all of the ethnic groups, have been, as you described, first to hit a city and to have a primary area of occupancy but as that population group matures over time, say ten years, and people get involved in the life of the community, get jobs, as they begin to get jobs and their families grow they have the need to move on. They want to have a bigger house or need a little more room or want a new house. That is part of the American ethnic too.

All of the groups you described, including the Southern white, of course he has an initial point of entry, and then there is a period in which he gets his roots down but as soon as those roots are down he is established as part of the community and he begins to move. He moves where his job and his emerging status takes him which has been to housing elsewhere and so it was really this period of the post-war where we were so clearly able to see the movement of every one of the ethnic groups through the screen that historically kept them in a central city. We watched persons of Italian, German, Jewish, Russian and other extractions, watched those people move to secondary concentrations but through the screen to newer housing and watched the Negro make the effort to cross the line only to be in fact held in as a contained population.

Jim Bush, an assistant to Marks on the Community Relations Commission, filled in the details. For example, during the war years, the board of education had insufficient space for classrooms; to meet this need, the board leased space in the public housing projects for schoolroom use. The pictures in the public housing authority annual reports revealed that the classrooms mirrored the one-race composition of the officially segregated public housing projects. The 1946 "red book," the real estate license law and rules and regulations of the Michigan Corporation and Securities Commission Real Estate Division, included the suggestion that "brokers and salesmen *ought* to observe a code of ethics":

• *Article 34.* A realtor should never be instrumental in introducing into a neighborhood a character of property or occupancy, members of any race or nationality, or any individuals whose presence will clearly be detrimental to property values in that neighborhood.

- *Article 35.*   No instructions nor inducements from any client or customer relieve the realtor from his responsibility strictly to observe this code of ethics.

In 1960 the new head of this state real estate commission, Lawrence Gubow, investigated the resulting pattern of racial marketing. He found a pervasive pattern of explicit "point" systems and other discriminatory practices by which state-licensed realtors excluded prospective black purchasers from white areas. For the first time, the commission promulgated regulations under its statutory mandate to define "unfair dealing" by licensed brokers in order to protect black citizens against such racial sorting in housing. At the behest of real estate brokers, however, the Michigan Supreme Court overturned this regulation as beyond the intended scope of the real estate statute outlawing "unfair dealing." Thus did the Michigan Supreme Court deny blacks equal protection by authorizing state-licensed real estate brokers to enforce by covert means the very types of overt racial restrictions on residency which the United States Supreme Court had previously held could not be enforced in any state court.*

Bush also explained how Community Relations Commission hearings and investigations revealed a long-standing pattern of white intimidation and even violence against prospective black entrants to a white neighborhood, and the police failed to provide protection to these black families. Bush also described the various covert steering mechanisms that still prevailed in Detroit's real estate market in the spring of 1971. He concluded, "Black home seekers were invariably channeled into the areas in which black families already resided and . . . there were efforts to channel all white home seekers into areas in which black families did not reside."

Karl Taeuber, the soft-spoken professor of sociology and student of the census, took the stand. He described the pervasive extent of racial segregation as a statistical matter from the United States censuses of 1900 through 1970 for the nation and for Detroit. On a scale of 0 (meaning no separation) to 100 (complete separation), Taeuber described the current national range for black vs. white as 70 to 90 and for any European ethnic group vs. the rest of the population as 10 to 50. While the high racial segregation index had long persisted, the "nationality segregation measures diminished very rapidly" from their peak levels in the early years of the twentieth century to the current levels. Thus, segregation was *not* a common *ethnic* phenomenon.

Taeuber then debunked another popular myth—that racial segregation results primarily from "free choice" or "economics." For example, in 1960

---

*Subsequently, Gubow was appointed a federal judge and was a close friend of Roth on the bench. All parties stipulated to the basic facts of Gubow's findings and left the drawing of any inferences to Roth.

the median monthly rent for blacks in Detroit was $76 and for whites $64. At each family-income and housing-cost level, Taeuber demonstrated from the census data how blacks and whites alike in all characteristics save race were still almost completely segregated. Economics did not account for the residential segregation by race. Based on data from many opinion surveys and the continuing black efforts to seek genuinely open and integrated housing, Taeuber added, "I don't think the choice factor is very relevant."

As one of the country's foremost sociologists, Taeuber then reviewed "the considerable evidence in our society, for the past as well as for the current situation, of various types of [racial] discrimination in the housing market." Of the range of possible explanations for racial segregation in housing, Taeuber concluded that the evidence suggested that racial discrimination was a primary cause.

Nick Flannery brought Dr. Taeuber's testimony home to Judge Roth, who had emigrated from Hungary as a young boy. Because Detroit claimed one of the largest and most tightly knit Polish ethnic communities, Flannery asked Taeuber to compare the segregation index for persons of Polish ancestry as compared to blacks in the city. Judge Roth questioned the relevance of this inquiry. Flannery, in his deferential manner, stated that it would provide evidence to refute the myth that racial segregation was a matter of ethnic choice rather than official discrimination. Judge Roth seemed startled by the answer: the black/white segregation index in Detroit of 86.5 more than *doubled* the Polish/other segregation index. Dr. Taeuber then explained that the Polish/other segregation index was probably substantially overstated because it did not exclude the general white/black segregation; it would be substantially lower if calculated solely on the basis of the separation of Poles from other whites.

Judge Roth pondered Taeuber's testimony during the desultory cross-examination. As the judge turned to his right, he confronted the huge map showing the stark *racial* division in Detroit. It would have been difficult for any justice of the peace listening to this testimony to overlook the extent of the racial segregation and the probability that the condition would long endure because it resulted primarily from racial discrimination, not "ethnic choice" or the general "ethnic difficulties" experienced by many immigrant groups. As Karl Taeuber was about to leave the witness stand, Judge Roth said that he had one more question. After a long pause, however, the judge said that he should not ask the question and excused the witness. The quandary of a man testing his own lifelong beliefs was apparent. The content of the question, however, died with Judge Roth too few years later.

Martin Sloane followed with a discussion of the extensive federal support of housing segregation. The FHA had long endorsed racial segregation and supported *only* exclusively white developments protected from "adverse influences" by racially restrictive convenants. Sloane also drew a major connection between the evidence of community segregation and school segregation as he read section 951 of the 1938 FHA underwriting manual: to insure the exclusive character of any whites-only housing, the FHA required that the children have access to whites-only schooling rather than being assigned to a school "where a considerable number of the pupils represent . . . an incompatible racial element."

In Sloane's view, the "FHA had done so much to sow the seeds of housing discrimination and to lay the foundation for racial separation in metropolitan areas, to harden the patterns of residential segregation that exist, to harden the practices of the real estate industry, that even today, some thirty-five years after FHA began, we are still [living with] the results of what FHA did in [its] first [two] decades of existence, and that is a real problem." Sloane added that the Veterans Administration, Federal Public Housing Agency, Home Loan Bank Board, Controller of the Currency, Federal Reserve Board, and Federal Deposit Insurance Corporation also initially supported discrimination, and had since become oblivious to practices of community segregation and discrimination. Together these federal agencies had been involved in approximately 80 percent of the housing built in the United States since the mid-1930s. Sloane concluded that "the federal government bears a large responsibility" for the pervasive residential segregation and the continuing housing discrimination.

Alex Ritchie, the attorney for the white antibusing group, asked Sloane whether school desegregation limited to Detroit would be an exercise in futility. The remaining white residents in the northeast and northwest corners of the city could then just flee to the remaining all-white sanctuaries in the suburbs beyond. Judge Roth interrupted:

> *The Court.*   Well, taking [Mr. Ritchie's question] in that light and applying what you know about a city, any city in the United States with the same problem and the same color makeup, do you have an opinion as to what would happen to what are depicted there on the [big] map [of the City of Detroit] as now white areas? Would they, as Mr. Ritchie suggests, lead really to an abandonment in large numbers by white folks so that when you ended up with the city you'd have a city that was no more integrated than it was when you started. Do you have an opinion on that?

Sloane responded by suggesting metropolitan integration as a solution.

> *A.*   The same principle has been discussed . . . with respect to residential population. Experience in Washington is perhaps instructive. The Washington metropolitan area has not changed by more than one percentage point in terms of the percent white and percent black in the last seventy years. It's always been roughly 75 percent white, 25 percent

black. The distribution of the population by race in the Washington metropolitan area has changed very dramatically to the point where the Northern Virginia suburbs has something like 6 percent black and 94 percent white. The Maryland suburbs and suburb of Montgomery County has something like 4 percent black and 96 percent white, whereas 60, 70 years ago there was an even distribution.

But talking about integrating the schools of Washington, of course Washington Public Schools are now in excess of 90 percent black, and it's very difficult to talk about achieving school integration with that kind of percentage. But if you think in terms of the metropolitan area as a whole, the problem becomes a good deal less difficult because then we're dealing with a school population as well as a residential population which is roughly 75 percent white and 25 percent black.

I think in a situation like that you have to talk in terms of metropolitan-wide desegregation, residentially as well as in education. And it is, in fact, I think an exercise in futility to think in terms of integrating a school system which is already so predominantly black as to make racial integration an impossibility. It is, however, not an impossibility if you talk in terms of the metropolitan area as a whole.

Now I feel rather uneasy about—

The Court.   Well, I don't know whether fortunately or unfortunately this lawsuit is limited to the City of Detroit and the school system, so that we're only concerned with the city itself and we're not talking about the metropolitan area.

As Sloane was leaving the witness stand, Flannery reminded Judge Roth of the relevance of the proof of racial restrictions in housing: "neighborhood schools" may not be invoked as an "excuse" where Negroes are excluded on the basis of race from the "neighborhood"; by such housing segregation proof, plaintiffs were simply putting the officially imposed segregation truth to the "racially neutral neighborhood school" lie. Flannery continued:

I [would also] like to note for the record that other courts as a matter of relief have addressed themselves to the viability of metropolitan solutions, and if this record should disclose that school children in the City of Detroit can not be afforded equal protection of the laws . . . [by city-only desegregation], we have the State as a defendant in this action. We are not prepared to concede, your Honor, that a metropolitan solution would not be viable or would be inappropriate.

Mr. Von Ende [Bushnell's co-counsel for the Board].   Your Honor, I simply ask the purpose of the oral argument that Mr. Flannery has given today. Am I to understand that there is a pending exhibit which this argument is germane to? Or was this simply a position statement that we were favored with sua sponte?

Mr. Flannery.   Not sua sponte, Mr. Von Ende.

The Court.   I took a long lead off first base and as a result he is making motions. . . . I hope, Mr. Flannery, that [your statement] is not a threat because I am having enough to do with my limited jurisdiction in this case, and I am not one for expanding it.

Mr. Flannery.   Well, we want to see what the record will show, your Honor.

The Court.   Yes.

Mr. Flannery.   Probably it's neither a promise nor a threat at this writing.

Nevertheless, the metropolitan issue now hung over the case. Plaintiffs could only hope that it would not be entirely forgotten nor emerge too quickly, before counsel and the courts had time to prepare for the issue.

John Humphrey, a longtime real estate broker, took the stand. In age, demeanor, and stature in the community, he resembled Judge Roth in many ways, except he was black. Humphrey began by explaining that he had long been a "realtist," a member of the "Detroit Real Estate Brokers Association," an all-black group. Humphrey had never been a "realtor": "When I joined the [black] Real Estate Brokers Association, the 'realtors' was a white organization that did not allow black membership."

Humphrey gave other examples of the discriminatory practices that he confronted in his chosen profession. At first, "all the practices were simple. Blacks had areas that we were limited to, that we could buy and operate in." Humphrey also described the vandalism visited on the first black buyers introduced into any white neighborhood: broken windows, harassment, burning of houses. In one instance, white neighbors "even threw snakes in the basement and frightened [my black clients] . . . while the policeman [just stood] there." In contrast, during Humphrey's business visits to white neighborhoods, police threatened him with arrest and worse. On one such occasion, "a policeman grabbed for his gun":

And I think I came as close to getting shot as I have been in my life. . . . I stuck [my hands] up in a hurry and he patted me—and all type of harassment.

Such testimony might have seemed melodramatic, but John Humphrey had a power to his physical presence and a tone of resignation in his voice that compelled sober attention.

Humphrey then explained the inside mechanisms of housing discrimination practiced by the white realtors. Realtor listings of houses for sale were marked "x" for whites, "xx" for blacks. Realtors excluded blacks from their cooperative areawide multiple-listing services, and black realtists had to form their own list to have any chance of providing service to their customers. White realtors cobrokered cooperatively with black realtists only in the already black or changing areas, but not in white areas. Humphrey even had sympathetic whites check back with realtors to document the continued availability of housing after he had been told the white listing was already sold or withdrawn. "We've had [so] many instances like this until it's a waste of time. . . . In fact, [I have] given up on it out of disgust and knowing that I can't keep a business if I continue to try to work in the predominantly white neighborhoods, to try to find that one [person] that's brave enough to let me have his property and try to sell it for him."

In a voice that began haltingly and then quickened with emotion, Humphrey continued:

> I started out thinking that I could help to correct the situation by putting all of the effort that I could and giving people an equal opportunity in the housing market. [But] there are so many evasive ways that people can use to avoid, even though the law says that you can't do it, until it's a loss of time and money. And you just can't make a living doing it. For every one of these incidents, and I've got lots of them, they cost me a wad of money because of them. Police harassment was the biggest one, taking my license and trapping me. And every time I get one of these [requests to speak out against segregation], and my name goes [in] the paper, I start getting tickets for doing the same things I'm doing right now, and it's no coincidence.

John Humphrey then described his own difficulty in finding a large lot and a one-story home for his family in Southfield and Bloomfield Hills, two suburbs close to Detroit.

> It was rather comical some of the experiences that we had.
>
> I'd like to point out that I would not take my children with me. My wife and I were conditioned on what we were going to run into and the treatment that we were going to get, and we got just about what we knew we were going to get.
>
> We went out in Bloomfield Hills. They advertised in the paper a

piece of property that was for sale. We had no idea that we were going to buy it but just look at it. My wife just said, "See what it is." $85,000.00.

We go there and the salesman on the scene comes in and he speaks to us, and he said, "Well, I don't know why you'd want to buy this house because it floods every time it rains, a good heavy dew and things flooded all over." And he said, "It's in bad shape, bad location, the sewers, the water—" and he gave us any number. And all he did was follow us around and we were laughing because we knew.

Now, this should have been embarrassing for me because he didn't know if I could afford to buy it, but the idea was to try to prevent me from wanting to buy it.

Another [time] I looked at a house in Southfield, and I asked the gentleman who had an open house there if we could come in and look at it. He said, "Help yourself. Go ahead."

We looked around, and I asked him, I said, "What's the price on this house?"

He said, "$65,000.00."

Well I knew that was high, knowing a little about housing. So I said, "Well, we think we like it and might be interested in it."

He said, "Well, [the owner is] in Florida now and I've had two other people who might already decide to take it and then they might take it off the market."

Two blocks away I went, another company. . . . I went in and looked at his [listings]. And I thought he was the most honest of all that I had gone around. He showed me a house, and he also had his listing book there laying on the table, and I know what they are. I know what to look for.

Q.   Would you describe what a listing book is?

A.   [A] listing book is where they have the listing of these properties with the photo and with the information and the price on them.

I asked him about the one that we had just looked at.

He turned the page over there and it was $45,000.00 not $65,000.00.

And these are the kind of things that is a waste of time and effort for me to try to go in a white neighborhood because it's too costly.

Q.   What year was this?

A.   1968

Q.   Were you able eventually to get a house in Southfield?

A.   Yes. I went in to look at a house. A company showed it to me. . . .
And I made them an offer on the house. Everybody thinks he's paying too
much, so I made an offer. Being in the business, I thought I could see if I
could get it cheaper. We were going to buy it even at the [asking] price,
but we made an offer. We submitted an offer.

Three days later I get a telephone call from the owner who recognized me; I had sold some fifteen years ago some commercial property for
him and didn't remember him, didn't remember his name. And he asked
me if I had shown any interest, submitted an offer.

I said, "I [gave] an offer on your place."

And so he said, "Well, they haven't submitted the offer to me. The
company didn't submit the offer."

I said, "Well, they got an offer and $1,000.00 deposit."

And he said, "Well, if I don't get the offer, you can deal directly
with me."

Well, this would have been the most unethical thing that one could
do, even though I asked [the seller's brokers] to . . . share the commission with me, which they refused to do. But even at that . . . , I wouldn't
[deal] directly with the [seller].

I called [the realtor] and told [him] the conversation, . . . I said,
"Now, this man has called me and asked me if you didn't present it that I
could bring him an offer direct. Naturally, I'm not going to do anything
like this." And so my offer was accepted.

Q.   Had that company previously made any representations to you about
whether the offer had been made?

A.   They told me the offer had been turned down.

I then asked John Humphrey whether he still confronted these forms of
housing discrimination in his business. Humphrey answered slowly, placed
his glasses on the podium, and turned to Judge Roth:

I stay away from them. I've been—I've been licked, and I just don't like
wasting my time and my effort. And I don't like taking people like a
doctor I took out in Livonia . . . able to buy and pay cash for a piece of
property and walk to the door and the man is there and when you start to
go in he comes out, closes the door and said, "we're closed."

And I said, "Well, I've got some customers here and I'm a real
estate broker and they want to see the model because they're interested in
buying."

He said, "I told you we're closed," and he walks on around.

And this kind of thing was not bad for me because I'm immune to it, but it was so embarrassing to [the doctor], until I asked him to let me initiate a case for him, and he says, "I wouldn't want to be connected with it, you know, I'll find some place else."

He ultimately, subsequently purchased in Palmer Woods [in Detroit]. But he was—he was embarrassed.

As John Humphrey spoke about giving up in his struggles with housing segregation, he appealed directly to Stephen Roth to confront the continued racial segregation in Detroit. Judge Roth's penetrating gaze never once strayed from John Humphrey's eyes. It seemed as if the Hungarian immigrant might be ready to accept the responsibility his black brother could no longer bear.

No attorney cross-examined John Humphrey. George Bushnell conceded that the proof revealed an unconscionable "tale of horror . . . degradation and dehumanization." Although he did not in any way condone this sorry history, Bushnell argued that the board was not responsible for racial discrimination in housing. The response rang hollow. It undercut Bushnell's earlier and oft-repeated argument that Fair Housing laws guaranteed equal access for blacks to homes and "neighborhood schools." And George Bushnell himself had been visibly moved by John Humphrey's "tale of horror." Like the liberal board and superintendent he had so long represented, he believed in integration as a matter of policy and, deep down, felt that segregation in America's urban areas was, in part, a legacy of racial discrimination.

Alex Ritchie, the defender of white neighborhood schools, was also shaken. Within days he rose at the start of a court session and made a startling announcement. Standing directly in front of the big map of Detroit, Ritchie said:

The white citizens of the City realistically recognize the significance of this map. I don't think I, on their behalf, would deign to argue that we do not have a segregated city in Detroit. . . . It is quite possible for any litigant to lose a case.

Ritchie announced his intention to press for a metropolitan remedy by cross-examining every witness with any knowledge about the subject. Whether or not his motivation related in any degree to fears of white flight from city-only desegregation, Alex Ritchie, the antibuser who intervened in the case to fight integration at all costs, had undergone a deep personal conversion. Ritchie later said: "A lot of us discarded all our old slogans during this case. I don't know anyone who sat through the trial who was unmoved. It was an education in what kind of world we live in."

Unfortunately, not many other members of the white community sat through the trial. With the exception of Bill Grant of the *Detroit Free Press*, who covered every day of the trial and occasionally got his editors to print some stories on the case, the Detroit media did not pay much attention. Perhaps the media assumed that Judge Roth would just continue to find a way to thwart the plaintiffs and make the case go away. In this respect, most of the Detroit media defaulted on their much-heralded duty to support the public's right to know.

We supplemented Humphrey's testimony with a parade of black "realtists" who described similar tales of "degradation." We followed with local, state, and federal officials who explained how the racial exclusion of blacks from all-white areas within Detroit did not stop at the city boundaries but extended throughout the white suburbs. Alex Ritchie also cross-examined the head of the housing section of the Michigan Civil Rights Commission and learned that twenty thousand minority employees worked in the burgeoning plants of Warren, a suburb contiguous to Detroit on the north; but only five to seven black families resided in Warren, with only *one* black school teacher among the almost thirteen hundred instructors in the Warren public schools.

Robert Tucker, a respected black lawyer from Chicago in charge of the Equal Opportunity Division of the HUD region responsible for Detroit, testified that applications for federal housing assistance in Detroit's white suburbs had been challenged because of the "incidence of high minority employment and low incidence of minority residency." After extensive field investigations, HUD determined that the large number of black suburban workers resided largely in Detroit and had been effectively excluded from residence in the white suburbs as a result of pervasive racial discrimination. Tucker conceded, however, that HUD failed to secure any redress against racial discrimination in the local communities. For example, Warren thumbed its nose at HUD secretary Romney rather than open its housing to the twenty thousand black workers who toiled in its industrial plants. The real estate taxes from these plants, of course, helped pay for the construction and operation of all-white schools that served Warren's growing all-white pupil population.

That ended the proof for plaintiffs' "housing case." In one sense, we had not even begun to prove that school authorities intentionally segregated schools. In another sense, however, we had already won because of the dramatic conversions that had already taken place. Ritchie, the attorney for white antibusing groups, had virtually conceded defeat and was pushing for consideration of metropolitan relief much faster than plaintiffs wanted. Bushnell could no longer argue that neighborhood schools were fundamentally fair because they allowed free choice of schools by racially unrestricted choice of residence. In the face of the evidence, Judge Roth appeared to drop his long-held defense that racial segregation was just another ethnic phenomenon. Near the end of his life, he seemed moved by ten electric days of proof to consider that racial segregation was the product, in substantial part, of the white community's racial discrimination, public and private, to contain blacks in distinct areas separate from whites throughout the metropolitan area. Judge Roth was listening intently to plaintiffs' case and asking questions concerning "how to accomplish effective desegregation." Finally, Judge Roth was becoming increasingly impatient with the Detroit board's attorneys for refusing to stipulate to much of the housing proof while continuing a parade of needless objections and interruptions.

Yet the case was not over: we still had to prove that the Detroit and state school authorities participated actively in the system of community discrimination to segregate schools. For a plain justice of the peace concerned about basic fairness, it *might* be enough to argue that school authorities may not incorporate the larger community's discriminatory system of racial containment into the schools. But we intended to show more, that school authorities also manipulated their neighborhood zoning policy to fuel the system of racial ghettoization. That was the only way to secure our position with Judge Roth and to stand any chance on appeals to the Sixth Circuit and then to the Supreme Court.

The Developing Law

Two legal developments during the trial aided plaintiffs' cause. First, on April 20, 1971, the Supreme Court announced its unanimous opinions in two Legal Defense Fund cases from Charlotte-Mecklenburg, North Carolina, and Mobile, Alabama. These rulings applied the affirmative remedial duties imposed by *Green v. School Board of New Kent County* on rural dual systems to urban school districts: there must be actual desegregation in urban areas too, at least to dismantle dual systems in the South formerly mandated by state laws. There was a chance that the Sixth Circuit might now apply a national standard of desegregation to all schools in the states within its jurisdiction— Michigan and Ohio, as well as Tennessee and Kentucky. That would represent an ironic reversal from its previous stance of justifying segregation in Tennessee and Kentucky schools because of its refusal to desegregate Cincinnati, Ohio schools. This concern for uniformity might now work to make the Sixth Circuit more sympathetic to review of plaintiffs' claims of intentional school segregation in Northern cases.

Chief Justice Burger's opinion in *Swann v. Charlotte-Mecklenburg* also seemed to credit the two-way causal interaction between intentional school and housing segregation found by district judge James McMillan in his trial court ruling:

The construction of new schools and the closing of old ones are two of the most important functions of local school authorities and also two of the most complex. . . . The result of this will be a decision which, when combined with one technique or another of student assignment, will determine the racial composition of the student body in each school in the system. Over the long run, the consequences of the choices will be far reaching. People gravitate toward school facilities, just as schools are located in response to the needs of people. The location of schools may thus influence the patterns of residential development of a metropolitan area and have important impact on composition of inner-city neighborhoods.

Yet the opinion was ambivalent on any duty to avoid incorporating residential segregation fostered by other governmental actors' discrimination into the schools if school authorities had previously engaged in no overt acts of discrimination. At one point the Court suggested that holding school officials responsible in such circumstances was not constitutionally required: in school desegregation cases, the courts should not be concerned "with myriad factors of human existence which can cause discrimination in a multitude of ways on racial, religious, or ethnic grounds. . . . One vehicle can carry only a limited amount of baggage." This represented a curious perspective in view of Judge McMillan's findings that federal, state, and local action contributed to an interlocking web of discrimination in schools, housing, and community life that operated in lockstep to cause the current condition of segregated schools. The Court, however, closed its opinion by authorizing judicial intervention even *after* the long process of implementing a final remedy dismantling a dual school system had been completed upon a showing that "the school authorities or some other agency of the State has deliberately attempted to fix or alter demographic patterns to affect the racial composition of the schools."

Other parts of Burger's opinion extolled neighborhood schools, criticized judicial attempts to achieve "racial balance," and warned against judicial intervention in local school affairs in the absence of a constitutional violation. Rumors abounded, later credited in Woodward and Armstrong's account of *The Brethren,* that Chief Justice Burger originally attempted to secure a majority to curtail busing. Woodward and Armstrong reported that Burger's original draft argued that court-ordered school desegregation remedies should end where residential segregation began, as the Nixon Justice Department had argued to the Court. When the other justices objected, the original draft opinion was patched with various suggestions and finally came to read like the committee exercise that it was. As Lou Lucas fumed, the opinion "is no rosetta stone—it gives everyone something to argue."

The ultimate irony, however, was that Richard Nixon's appointees to the high court approved busing as a means to remedy unconstitutional school segregation in urban areas. In the early 1960s the Legal Defense Fund had parted company with the NAACP general counsel's office when the LDF determined to invest its limited resources primarily in cases seeking to dismantle dual systems in the South rather than challenging school segregation in the North. After the Court's decision in *Green*, President Nixon countered with an appeal to woo southern votes by opposing "forced busing."

Patrick Buchanan, the president's speech writer, summarized the reasons for this appeal:

> The second era of Re-Construction is over; the ship of integration is going down. . . . [W]e ought not be aboard. For the first time since 1954, the national civil rights community is going to sustain an up-and-down defeat. . . . For the foreseeable future, it is all over for compulsory social integration.

Buchanan recognized, however, that the "logic and decisions" of the Supreme Court would require "trying to integrate the schools of the entire nation—an impossible task." So he recommended that the administration get the Court to "back off from compulsory integration to a posture of freedom of choice." Thereafter, the Justice Department advocated an approach to achieve this goal: limit any school desegregation remedy to the precise extent to which a "school-by-school" examination showed that active discrimination by school authorities increased school segregation beyond the "normal imbalance" resulting from "neighborhood separation in housing." With the presumed "free choice" of any black family to move into any white neighborhood, "forced busing" could then be halted by using pervasive housing segregation to legitimize the remaining school segregation.

With the Supreme Court's decision in *Swann*, however, the LDF's "Southern strategy" appeared to bear more fruit than that of the president. The careful work of LDF attorneys and sensitive findings of district judge McMillan concerning the causal interrelationship between intentional school and housing segregation in Charlotte apparently persuaded the entire Court that dual schooling persisted and must be dismantled by actual desegregation in all southern school districts. It was also a credit to the independence of the judiciary and to personal integrity that Nixon's appointees, Warren Burger and Harry Blackmun, were persuaded to join in sinking dual schooling rather than "the ship of integration."

The second fortunate turn of events for the Detroit plaintiffs came when a panel of the Sixth Circuit on May 28, 1971, affirmed Judge Keith's desegregation order in the Pontiac school case. Judge Wade McCree, at that time the only other black judge ever to sit in the federal trial and appellate courts in the Sixth Circuit, distinguished *Deal*.

[T]he obvious regard for race in assigning faculty members and administrators is a factor which may be considered in assessing motives underlying past [pupil] assignment decisions which resulted in segregation. . . . [S]chool location and attendance boundary line decisions for the past 15 years more often than not tended to perpetuate segregation. Attempted justification of those decisions in terms of proximity of school buildings, their capacity, and safety of access routes requires inconsistent applications of these criteria.

But the decision did not bind the entire circuit nor directly overrule *Deal*'s "neighborhood free choice" justification for most school segregation, and only one of the appeals court's nine regular judges ruled on the appeal in the Pontiac school case.* The neighborhood school defense of *Deal* was nevertheless under attack: from the outside by proof that official racial discrimination caused housing segregation; from the inside by proof that school authority manipulation of and deviation from neighborhood schools promote segregation; and from around the corner by proof that school and housing segregation are interrelated and that racial identification of schools promotes housing segregation. Nate Jones had stated the goal: stretch the common perception of segregation as de facto into understanding the reality of segregation as de jure. Judge Roth provided the first test for Jones's strategy.

The School Case

Bob Green, the dynamic dean of urban affairs at Michigan State University, opened plaintiffs' school evidence. In the vein of the old equal educational opportunity cases, he described the racial disparity in achievement test scores between black and white schools and the community perceptions about the relative quality of schools based on their racial identifiability. The most persuasive aspect of this testimony was that the Detroit public schools were not performing particularly well for any of their students, black or white: there was no educational justification for preserving the existing system of segregated schooling. During the lengthy trial, a battle between various expert witnesses ensued over the relevance and impact of disparities in diverse educational "inputs" and "outputs" for black as compared to white schools. Plaintiffs used this testimony only as additional evidence that school authorities inten-

---

*Courts of appeal hear cases in panels made up of three judges. In the Pontiac case, the panel included a senior judge of the Sixth Circuit, a judge visiting from another circuit, and Sixth Circuit Judge McCree.

tionally identified schools as black or white, not to argue for desegregation as an educational panacea.

Dr. Green also testified to the far-reaching and enduring harm of segregated schooling, North or South, for the entire society and for succeeding generations: in this society, segregated schools have taught youngsters, black and white, that black is inferior and white superior; that lesson, in turn, teaches them that segregation is the American way of life that they should expect and perpetuate as adults. As an example, Dr. Green gave his capsule history of the Detroit public schools:

> We did not educate the white adults who went to the Detroit Public School system who are now living in Livonia. We did not educate young whites who were educated at Central [High School]. I can remember when Central was predominantly white. . . . All the whites have fled. Northwest Detroit has fled to Oak Park, Livonia, Bloomfield Hills. I see that flight being significantly related to what we have not done in our public schools. If we did a head count, we would find a good number of those residents today, and another good example, the fact blacks can't buy houses in Warren is a failure of the Detroit Public School system. Livonia was sticks and woods when I was a kid. That suburban community was built because the Detroit Public School system did not perform its functions. It was built because we had all white elementary schools, all white junior high schools and all white high schools.

Bushnell retorted:

> Do I understand this answer of yours, Doctor, to be that the catalogue of discrimination and horror that you have testified to is the responsibility of the Detroit Public School system in this metropolitan area?

Green answered:

> I would say a major share of the responsibility must be placed at the foot of the Detroit Public School system. I can never move away from the fact that in downtown Detroit today in the so-called financial district, you will find that these men were educated in the Detroit Public School system. My only position is that the public educational system can go a long way in offsetting these kinds of negative attitudes. [But] the [segregated] way our schools have been structured, it hasn't happened.

Bill Caldwell and Lou Lucas proceeded over the next month of the trial with Bill Lamson and Gordon Foster to painstakingly reconstruct the incidents of school authority intentional segregation.

- In the 1950s through the early 1960s, in violation of normal neighborhood zoning principles, at least eight optional zones affecting twentyone schools were created in the ring of changing areas around the expanding black core to allow white stragglers to escape the identifiably black schools.
- Thereafter, the board substituted open enrollment policies once the original optional zones had succeeded in flushing out two generations of white children to allow yet another generation of white pupils to avoid the next ring of black schools.
- Throughout the entire period, strict attendance boundary lines were drawn and redrawn in scores of instances on the sharp but shifting racial divides between all-white and all-black areas to contain black and white children in separate schools when feasible desegregative alternatives were available under consistent application of geographic zoning criteria.
- To relieve overcrowding, the board bused blacks away from closer white schools and whites away from closer black schools with available space.
- The board also bused all-black classes ''intact'' into totally segregated units (which featured separate instruction, lunch, and recess) in otherwise all-white schools.
- Despite thousands of administrative decisions, the board (with the exception necessitated by the burning of a white school and the ill-fated April 7 plan) refused to reassign a single white child to a black school, even when the consistent application of neighborhood zoning criteria would ordinarily have led to that result on numerous occasions.
- The board built schools to a certain size, in a particular location, with strict attendance boundaries, with the specific intent to serve racially designated, segregated public housing and federally assisted projects which inevitably resulted in one-race schools.
- The board built and located new schools and additions in a consistently segregative pattern in one-race residential areas that opened as one-race schools. A substantial program to construct twelve virtually one-race schools continued during the pendency of the lawsuit despite Bushnell's express representation to the contrary at the preliminary hearing.
- Despite a large number of boundary and grade structure decisions, the board intentionally rejected suggested reorganizations that would have accomplished substantial desegregation of contiguous pairs of opposite race schools until the ill-fated April 7 plan.
- Until the mid-1960s, faculty had been assigned on a racial basis because of white community hostility to having their children taught by black teachers; faculty continued to mirror the pupil racial composition

of the schools despite belated affirmative efforts to "balance" staff.
- In all these respects, the board intentionally built upon the residential segregation to create, maintain, and magnify school segregation, which in turn identified residential areas as well as schools as black or white and thereby encouraged racial discrimination and segregation in housing and schools throughout Detroit and the metropolitan area.

This evidence was based on thorough examination of the Detroit board's own records and the several-day, pretrial depositions of the board's chief school planner, Merle Henrickson. Gordon Foster's testimony was highlighted by Bill Lamson's school boundary overlays placed over the colorful census maps. The graphics unmistakably demonstrated the segregative nature of the board manipulations of "neighborhood zoning." The sheer number of the segregation incidents was magnified by the visual clarity of the demonstrative exhibits.

The testimony of plaintiffs' experts was validated by the similar findings of board-appointed study commissions and the honest admissions of Merle Henrickson and other board administrators. For example, Charles Wells, an assistant superintendent at the time of the trial, recounted the board's creation of the "Center District":

> In effect this District, with a few minor exceptions, created a segregated school system. It accomplished with a few marks of the crayon on the map, the return of the Negro child from the few instances of an integrated school exposure, to the traditional predominantly uniracial school system to which he had formerly been accustomed in the City of Detroit.

Assistant Superintendent Wells opposed the board's "policy of containment, an example of which is the Center District." He described its boundaries as "look[ing] like the coastline of the eastern United States where the Negro population is on one side and the white population on the other."

Perhaps the most striking segregation incident related to the Higginbotham School. The board located the school in the middle of the small black residential pocket near the city's northern border. The board built the school to a size that could serve only this isolated black community and fixed its boundaries to coincide precisely with the actual physical walls erected by adjacent whites intent on keeping blacks hemmed in. As Richard Marks had already described this barrier, "it was a symbol of the way in which the Negro was an undesirable neighbor" in Detroit.

The thrust of our school proof was to show a pattern of conduct that "naturally, probably and forseeably" resulted in segregation in the face of available desegregation alternatives. We hoped that this evidence would persuade Judge Roth to find that school authorities acted with a segregative purpose not only in the many incidents of school boundary manipulations and optional zones in racial pockets and fringe areas but also in the systematic location of one-race schools in all-white or all-black residential areas. Our goal was not to prove that Detroit school authorities were subjectively motivated by racial animus, but that objectively they were not immune to the community custom of racial segregation and discrimination.*

Plaintiffs closed their proof of the intentional segregation of schools with the state defendants. Under the Fourteenth Amendment, we argued that the ultimate responsibility for affording equal protection of the laws to Detroit's black school children rested with the state of Michigan; the state's failure to afford protection against the racial discrimination by its Detroit school district subdivision represented a breach of the state's obligations.

In addition, under Michigan law education is a state function, and the Detroit school district is merely an agent of the state subject to the state's "plenary power" and to the supervisory control vested in the state superintendent and state board of education. We therefore argued that the intentionally segregative acts of the Detroit board were the acts of the state and the direct responsibility of the state defendants. Moreover, the state directly financed the Detroit board's intentional segregation of schools, and the state defendants, in defiance of their own published guidelines, also approved the Detroit board's massive program of racially dual school construction. Finally, the state affirmatively exercised its "plenary power" over the Detroit school district by unconstitutionally preventing the implementation of the limited April 7 plan in order to reimpose segregation and by creating eight segregated "regions" wholly within the Detroit school district rather than considering the types of metropolitan decentralization proposed by the Detroit board president as a desegregative alternative.

Insofar as possible, we continued to avoid taking any position on metropolitan relief. When pressed by Judge Roth, however, we relied on a "remedy theory": as the state was responsible for public education, including the segregation of black students in one-race schools in Michigan, the state was responsible for effective desegregation in mixed schools. There were three legal problems with this approach. First, following *Brown*, plaintiffs had sued individual school districts rather than the southern states as a whole in the

---

*On occasion, we also pressed the legal theory that a historic pattern of substantial racial separation in schools shifted the burden of proof to defendant school authorities to justify any continuing school segregation as necessary to promote important state interests. We posed this "no-fault" theory in this case as a justifiable constitutional shorthand for an intent standard given the history of racial discrimination and underlying segregation in the country. But we urged Judge Roth to make specific fact findings and to apply tough legal standards that would stand up under *Deal* in the Sixth Circuit on appeal.

hope of achieving some success and the least resistance. As a result, there was relatively little case law on state responsibility. The Supreme Court's subsequent desegregation decisions spoke only of desegregation within districts as requested by the plaintiffs. *Brown II,* however, did provide some support for our remedy theory because it noted the need for "revision of school districts," as well as "school attendance areas" and "other local laws and regulations," in converting from a racially dual to "a nondiscriminatory system of schooling."

Second, the exact nature of the violation that would call for any areawide remedy for Detroit-only segregation was not clear. Although our theory of the wrong had always been the official containment of blacks in blacks-only schools, that description left open the nature of the remedy (free choice or actual pupil reassignment) and its geographic extent (the first, second, or tenth ring of white schools).

Third, the suburbs had neither been joined as parties nor heard in the trial. Although we did not want to retry the entire case again, an increasingly wary Supreme Court would be unlikely to permit cross-district desegregation if the suburban districts had not even been heard in court. Yet there was case law suggesting that school districts have no constitutional right to a hearing and need not be made parties if they are not necessary for providing relief. In our preliminary thinking, the state board could provide all necessary relief, including supervision of transfers across school district lines.

We also knew that actively initiating the metropolitan issue was more than we could handle in this already unique case with enough other landmark dimensions. Yet, we could see that Judge Roth and Alex Ritchie might not permit us the luxury of incremental development in the law and the proof in this or other cases. Our hope remained that any full development of metropolitan issues on the basis of areawide liability or suburban wrongdoing would await the filing of an amended complaint and another hearing on cross-district violation at some later date. As a result, Judge Roth would be limited in this proceeding to state responsibility and containment theories as bases for any evaluation of the propriety of metropolitan desegregation to remedy the segregation of the Detroit public schools.

Plaintiffs rested their case with a motion that the court immediately enjoin all of the Detroit board's continuing school construction pending conclusion of the case. We asked for this preliminary relief for three reasons: to test our growing conviction that we were converting Judge Roth to the view that school segregation in Detroit was the result of official racial discrimination; to remind the court that board attorney Bushnell had misstated the facts when he denied the existence of such a continuing school construction program almost a year before at the conference on a temporary restraining order; and to begin to build a nest egg of unexpended construction funds to assist in defraying the expense of any actual desegregation that might be ordered.

On June 8 and June 9, Judge Roth ordered a halt to the construction of additional facilities pending final ruling. He held that plaintiffs' proof "established a prima facie case of segregation" and that new school construction should be enjoined to prevent the board from "eat[ing] up the new capital improvement funds now available to it." Roth also recited the school board counsel's earlier representation that there was no school construction program and tartly contrasted the proof showing "that the Board has been proceeding apace on site acquisitions, planning new facilities, contracting for architects' plans, asking for bids and letting construction contracts for new school facilities."

The Defense

A heavy burden of proof now rested with the Detroit board to demonstrate that the segregation of the Detroit public schools was not the result of unconstitutional action. The facts were difficult enough; the personal dynamics of the trial made the board's burden even greater. First, Bushnell had lost Judge Roth's sympathy in refusing to stipulate to any of the basic facts. Roth had suggested that Bushnell could go "halfway" by admitting the extent and causes of housing segregation and the basic facts of school boundary decisions, while arguing the legal irrelevance of the housing discrimination proof and explaining the racially neutral basis for school board action. Instead, Bushnell demanded that plaintiffs prove every detail of their case and then continually objected to the introduction of evidence that Judge Roth had already ruled that he would hear.

Bushnell made plaintiffs dot every *i* and cross every *t* in the increasingly bitter contest. By the time plaintiffs rested their case, the voluminous evidence spelled "intentional segregation." As one co-counsel for the Detroit board conceded later, "by the time the NAACP had rested its case, we were finished. There was nothing we could do or say. The judge was convinced." Nevertheless, Bushnell mounted a vigorous, even creative defense, based on (*a*) the affirmative efforts of the board since the mid-1960s to grapple with the reality of extreme housing segregation; (*b*) the absence of any current school segregation resulting from prior board discrimination rather than shifts in residential patterns beyond the board's control; and (*c*) the presence of some black teachers or students in almost all schools in the district by the time of trial.

Second, the board's chief witness, school planner Merle Henrickson, had been the source of much of plaintiffs' proof, including the incidents of segregation and the available desegregation alternatives that the board frequently rejected. Henrickson's testimony confirmed major elements of plaintiffs' proof of intentional segregation. For example, in testifying about optional zones, he noted that one optional zone had been created in "an attempt acted out . . . to separate Jews and Gentiles within the system." That left little doubt that optional zones between opposite-race schools had been adopted with a similarly segregative, albeit racial, purpose. Henrickson also admitted that in 1959 some of the optional areas "frustrated integration and continued over the decade. . . . Western [High] appears to be still the school to which white students escape from predominantly Negro surrounding schools."

Third, Alex Ritchie, the supposed white defender of segregation, kept pressing for metropolitan desegregation. His conversion could not go unnoticed by a judge who had long associated with and represented Ritchie's white, blue-collar constituency.

Finally, the state defendants insulted the court. Upon filing a perfunctory motion to dismiss all state defendants at the close of plaintiffs' proof, Assistant Attorney General Krasicky announced "we are on behalf of the state defendants . . . going to rest. We are not going to offer any proofs. . . . Unless the Court wishes us to be here further, we would like permission to leave." Judge Roth, a former attorney general for the state of Michigan, was visibly appalled at his refusal to come forward with any meritorious defense, legal or factual, and the attorney general's decision to cease all further participation in representing the state's interests on the issue of segregation. He responded acidly to this state default: "You may leave. That is a matter entirely within your judgment."

On June 25 Judge Roth in open court denied the state defendants' motion to dismiss in the self-imposed absence of their counsel. Judge Roth continued:

> I think that those who are involved in this lawsuit ought to be preparing for [all] eventualities, the maximum and minimum, so that if the time comes for judicial intervention . . . , it would be well for all parties to be prepared. . . . If the Court in this case finds that the situation calls for some judicial action, the School Board ought to be preparing themselves to meet that eventuality. But the State Defendants too. I don't think the State Defendants should hide, put their heads in the sand and avoid considering what may happen if certain developments already made plain in this case take shape. Mr. Ritchie has made some points along this line, and I have. . . . "How do you desegregate a black city or a black school system." . . . Now State Defendants . . . ought to be thinking in these terms indeed if that's what develops.

Judge Roth then asked the Detroit board attorney to notify counsel for the state board of his ruling and comments.

On July 16, 1971, Ritchie filed a motion to join the other school districts in the tricounty area, some eighty-six in all, as parties defendant and attached the startling racial statistics showing the extent of all-white schools, pupils and teachers, with a few all-black pockets, beyond the borders of the Detroit school district. The white neighborhood intervenors from Detroit charged that these were "white segregated school districts." Plaintiffs, however, still wanted to delay full consideration of metropolitan issues. We argued that the motion related to relief and should be deferred pending the liability ruling and submission of desegregation proposals by the parties. We reiterated that the presence of the state defendants insured that all aspects of relief could be fully considered and, if ordered, fully implemented without adding suburban school districts as parties.

We were, however, sufficiently supportive of metropolitan relief to update the school racial statistics for all districts in the area and to submit striking Lamson maps and overlays showing both the crazy quilt pattern of local school districts and the overriding specter of complete racial separation in schools and housing throughout the entire metropolitan area. Detroit, with its 70 percent black pupil population and 40 percent black faculty, stood in stark contrast to the general pattern in the suburbs where the pupils and teachers were virtually all white. A few isolated suburban pockets of all-black schools with heavily black staffs only added to the metropolitan picture of complete racial identification of schools. Looking to relief, we offered an exhibit showing thirty heavily black Detroit schools that were contiguous to all-white suburban school districts and schools immediately across the Detroit border. Surely, walk-in desegregation of these de jure black schools across school district lines would offer a more convenient and practical remedy than crosstown busing within the Detroit city limits.

During its defense to plaintiffs' claims of intentional segregation, Bushnell also began to hedge the Detroit board's bets. He supplied evidence that the state had discriminated against Detroit relative to the suburbs in the financing of educational opportunities and in the provision of transportation funds. While long denying transportation assistance and full bonding authority for school construction to the Detroit school district, the state subsidized extensive busing and school construction in the suburbs. White families seeking homes and schools were thereby assured by the state that bright new schools would be available and convenient to their children in the sprawling, and virtually all-white, suburbs.

The operation of the state/local tax structure and the state education aid formula also identified Detroit as a disfavored school district compared to many of its suburban neighbors. For example, the total tax rate (city and school) for Detroit residents totaled 84.27 mills, compared to 60.57 in Grosse Pointe Farms, 40.65 in Birmingham, and 32.75 in Dearborn. Meanwhile, the equalized value of property in Detroit was $22,838 per student, compared to $44,740 per student in Grosse Pointe Farms, $45,517 per student in Birmingham, and $68,873 in Dearborn. In short, Detroit families taxed themselves much higher on a much lower tax base but could spend only a smaller percentage of their local tax dollars on schooling—generating fewer local dollars per pupil than many of their more favored suburban neighbors.*

The trend over the previous decade suggested worse trouble in the years ahead for Detroit as compared with its favored suburbs. From 1960 to 1970 Detroit lost 22.5 percent of its labor force, while its suburbs gained 61.5 percent additional workers; Detroit's share of metropolitan jobs dropped from 56.7 percent in 1960 to 38.6 percent in 1970. In 1971 the Detroit school district was on the verge of fiscal collapse. Yet, because of the pervasive housing discrimination, black families were generally confined to the identifiably black schools and residential areas, while white families continued to avoid what they perceived as the expanding and disfavored black ghetto in favor of burgeoning white suburban havens. In such circumstances, the Detroit board's primary education expert, Robert Guthrie of Stanford University, opposed desegregation limited to the city boundary: in his view, there was *no* educational or fiscal reason for keeping black children confined to tax-starved, one-race schools in the center city on the basis of state-imposed school district lines.

Ruling on Issue of Segregation

On July 22, 1971, the hearing on the segregation issue concluded after forty-one trial days. The parties worked feverishly to submit proposed findings of fact and conclusions of law. On September 27, at a housekeeping conference among counsel, Judge Roth casually announced that copies of his "Ruling on Issue of Segregation" were available in the clerk's office.

After describing the prior proceedings in the case and the overall demographic trends in the city, the ruling evaluated the proof of community segregation and housing discrimination:

> The City of Detroit is a community generally divided by racial lines. Residential segregation within the city and throughout the larger metropolitan area is substantial, pervasive and of long standing. Black citizens are located in separate and distinct areas within the city and are not generally to be found in the suburbs. While the racially unrestricted choice of black persons and economic factors may have played some part in the development of this pattern of residential segregation, it is, in the main, the result of past and present practices and customs of racial discrimination, both public and private, which have and do restrict the

---

*The figures cited in text are only representative and refer to periods from 1970 through 1975.

housing opportunities of black people. On the record there can be no other finding.

Judge Roth added, "Governmental actions and inaction at all levels, federal, state and local, have combined, with those of private organizations, such as loaning institutions and real estate associations and brokerage firms, to establish and to maintain the pattern of residential segregation throughout the Detroit metropolitan area."

Judge Roth then evaluated the interrelationship between school and housing segregation:

While it would be unfair to charge the present [school officials] with what other governmental officers or agencies have done, it can be said that the actions or the failure to act by the responsible school authorities, both city and state, were linked to that of these other governmental units. When we speak of governmental action we should not view the different agencies as a collection of unrelated units. Perhaps the most that can be said is that all of them, including the school authorities, are, in part, responsible for the segregated condition which exists. And we note that just as there is an interaction between residential patterns and the racial composition of the schools, so there is a corresponding effect on the residential pattern by the racial composition of the schools.

As to the school proof, Judge Roth found that the defendants' racially discriminatory implementation of a number of administrative devices contributed to the existing school segregation:

- *Optional zones.* "During the decade beginning in 1950 the Board created and maintained optional attendance zones in neighborhoods undergoing racial transition and between high school attendance areas of opposite predominant racial compositions. . . . The natural, probable, foreseeable and actual effect of these optional zones was to allow white youngsters to escape identifiably 'black' schools."
- *Transportation.* "The Board, in the operation of its transportation to relieve overcrowding policy, has admittedly bused black pupils past or away from closer white schools with available space to black schools. This practice has continued in several instances in recent years despite the Board's avowed policy, adopted in 1967, to utilize transportation to increase integration."
- *Attendance boundaries.* "The Board has created and altered attendance zones, maintained and altered grade structures and created and altered feeder school patterns in a manner which has had the natural,

probable and actual effect of continuing black and white pupils in racially segregated schools. The Board admits at least one instance [Higginbotham] where it purposefully and intentionally built and maintained a school and its attendance zone to contain black students. Throughout the last decade . . . school attendance zones of opposite racial compositions have been separated by north-south boundary lines, despite the Board's awareness (since at least 1962) that drawing boundary lines in a east-west direction would result in significant integration. The natural and actual effect of these acts and failures to act has been the creation and perpetuation of school segregation.''

- *School construction.*   School authorities planned, approved, financed, built and operated new schools and additions in an unmistakably dual pattern, with one set of virtually all-white schools and another set of virtually all-black schools that ''contains the black population and perpetuates and compounds the school segregation.''
- *Perpetuation of black schools.*   ''With one exception (necessitated by the burning of a white school), defendant Board has never bused white children to predominantly black schools. The Board has not bused white pupils [from overcrowded white schools] to black schools despite the enormous amount of space available in inner-city schools. There were 22,961 vacant seats in schools 90% or more black. . . . There has never been a feeder pattern or zoning change which placed a predominantly white residential area into a predominantly black school zone or feeder pattern.* Every school which was 90% or more black in 1960, and which is still in use today, remains 90% or more black. Whereas 65.8% of Detroit's black students attended 90% or more black schools in 1960, 74.9% of the black students attended 90% or more black schools during the 1970–71 school year.''

    As a result, Judge Roth concluded that plaintiffs had proven all elements of their claim that black families and pupils had been contained in a basically separate set of blacks-only schools and housing. Pupil and residential ''racial segregation are interdependent phenomena.'' In the construction of new schools and additions, the Detroit board ''built upon'' the forced segregation in housing to segregate schools. In the drawing of school attendance zones, the board shaped boundaries to conform to the shifting ''racial residential dividing lines.'' In fringe, pocket, or transition residential areas, the board

---

Feeder pattern refers to the assignment (or ''feeding'') of elementary school attendance zones to junior highs and junior high attendance zones to high schools. *Zoning change* refers to an alteration of a school attendance zone to take account, for example, of a new school or addition opening or a disparity in utilization of the capacity in nearby schools resulting from changes in the numbers of pupils in the area.

gerrymandered attendance zones or imposed optional zones to allow white families and pupils to avoid or to escape black schools. And, in turn, found Judge Roth, all of this intentional school segregation contributed to further segregation in housing.

Judge Roth did, however, exonerate the Detroit board and the teachers' union from claims of current intentional segregation of faculty and praised their "exemplary" course in adopting and implementing a "balanced staff concept." Many attributed this particular ruling to the legal craftsmanship of the Detroit Federation of Teachers' attorney, Ted Sachs. But we believed that this finding failed to apply the controlling legal standards applicable once a showing of prior racial assignment of staff had been made. Nevertheless, this aspect of Judge Roth's ruling served to highlight the heavy burden of proof imposed on plaintiffs in prevailing on all pupil segregation issues. Indeed, one month after Judge Roth's ruling, HEW refused to give the Detroit board any assistance to plan for desegregation on the ground that faculty were illegally segregated, a view subsequently affirmed by the United States Court of Appeals for the District of Columbia.

The violation findings concluded with a discussion of the state's liability: "The State and its agencies, in addition to their general responsibility for and supervision of education, have acted directly to control and maintain the pattern of segregation in the Detroit schools." Judge Roth then ticked off the state's affirmative violations:

- The state's various financial arrangements and aid imposed a disfavored status on the Detroit school district relative to its suburbs.
- The state's role in approving all school construction was "in keeping, generally, with the discriminatory practices which advanced or perpetuated racial segregation."
- Act 48's rescission of a desegregation plan, imposition of segregative pupil assignment criteria, and reorganization of the Detroit district into eight regions "had as their purpose and effect the maintenance of segregation."

To these findings of fact, Judge Roth applied the legal test that the state can be found guilty of unconstitutional conduct only if its agents (including state and local school authorities) "have taken . . . action . . . with a purpose of segregation" that creates, aggravates, or otherwise causes "a current condition of segregation." Judge Roth found "that both the State of Michigan and the Detroit Board have committed [intentionally segregative acts] which have been causal factors in the segregated condition of the public schools of the City of Detroit." Recognizing that "causation in the case . . . is both several and comparative," he concluded that "state and local government actions, including school board actions, have played a substantial role in promoting segregation.''

Judge Roth deferred consideration of Alex Ritchie's motion to join the suburban school districts as defendants until the submission of alternative desegregation plans by the parties and invited Ritchie to submit a more definite metropolitan plan. Roth announced that on October 4 he would hold a conference with counsel in open court to determine how to proceed on submission of remedy plans and hearings to consider appropriate relief.

Judge Roth concluded his opinion by discussing the responsibility of blacks to confront the "evil . . . [of] racial segregation in our public schools":

> In the most realistic sense, if fault or blame must be found it is that of the community as a whole, including, of course, the black components. We need not minimize the effect of the actions of federal, state and local governmental officers and agencies, and the actions of loaning institutions and real estate firms, in the establishment and maintenance of segregated residential patterns—which lead to school segregation—to observe that blacks, like ethnic groups in the past, have tended to separate from the larger group and associate together. The ghetto is at once both a place of confinement and a refuge. There is enough blame for everyone to share.

In the end, Stephen Roth asked the black community in Detroit to join with him in an unprecedented effort to challenge segregation for all of the children rather than accept either white domination or community control of segregated schools. He was pleading with John Humphrey, and Coleman Young, to keep the faith.

In a conversation with Bill Grant of the *Detroit Free Press* months later, Judge Roth confided, "We all got an education during the course of the trial. It opened my eyes. . . . I would never have known or understood the meaning and history of racial discrimination and segregation. . . . I hope I get a chance before this case is over to say publicly, from the bench, why I think [integration] has to happen. . . . We took this country away from the Indians and put them on reservations. We uprooted the Chinese and made them build railroads. We got the Irish, the Italians, and the rest and shoved them into the mills; but they could become a part of America because their own efforts were not held back by opposition to their skin color. Now I guess we are reserving the ghettoes for the blacks." Referring to the Detroit riot, he continued, "Everybody seems to have forgotten 1967, but I have not. Black people will not take being locked up in the ghettoes without a fight. If we don't work together to end this segregation thing now, there is just no telling what will happen to this nation in the years ahead.''

In the yearlong battle over the segregation of the Detroit public schools initiated by Act 48, we had witnessed a dramatic conversion. We saw a man—who only eight months before had invited us to leave—listen and hear and think and feel for forty-one trial days. In the course of the drama in his courtroom, Judge Roth came to know the color line of racial ghettoization in his own state: he found that an interlocking web of public, community, and private discrimination contributed to the containment of black families and children in segregated housing and schools separate from whites-only housing and schools. He viewed schools as a focal point of community life and determined that school segregation must be declared unconstitutional so that all people would finally come to grips with the continuing color line in American life. In 1954, another plain man, Earl Warren, had made a similar decision for the Supreme Court. Whether Roth's ruling would have the same impact on the national conscience depended on forces beyond his control.

Chapter 4
Metropolitan Conversion in the Lower Courts, October, 1971, to June, 1973

Reaction

The September 27, 1971, ruling on Detroit public school segregation came as a shock to most of the people of Detroit and the rest of Michigan. The media, with the exception of Bill Grant, had failed to cover the case in any depth. As a result, the public was unprepared. The *Detroit News* issued an editorial calling the ruling "unreasonable." The white neighborhood papers in the city and the suburbs generally followed the lead of the anti-integration *Detroit News*. In contrast, Grant's *Free Press* said that it was "impossible to challenge [the court's] findings." The *East Side Shopper* tried to take a neutral and informative position but, because of pressure from readers and advertisers, its owners eventually sold the newspaper to a conservative chain opposed to "forced busing."

Initially, the state central committee of the Michigan Democratic party adopted a resolution supporting busing, albeit as an "imperfect and temporary mechanism," to remedy segregation. But within days white congressmen and state legislators (Democratic and Republican) with white constituencies began to speak out against "forced busing." Most Democrats soon renounced the party's original resolution or sought to avoid comment on the issue altogether. Ironically, defendant attorney general Frank Kelley signed the original Democratic party resolution but then spent his next campaign explaining away his signature as he personally led the attack on Judge Roth's decision in the appellate courts. The state and local defendants immediately appealed the violation ruling to the Sixth Circuit rather than await a final remedy order.

At the October 4 conference, the courtroom was packed with local and national reporters, black and white spectators, and attorneys monitoring the proceeding on behalf of white suburban interests. Judge Roth would never again hold a press conference after his earlier fiasco. But his public notice of the October 4 hearing showed that he was not unaware of the human drama that was unfolding before him. Surveying the assembled crowd and the attorneys for all parties, including the state defendants, he stated from the bench:

> As I indicated at the close of my opinion recently rendered, I thought it would be advisable for me to get together with counsel on this occasion so that we might chart our course from here on in these proceedings.
>
> The Court has made its determination of things as they are, or as it

found things in the public school system of the City of Detroit. Our concern now—to take a thought from Aristotle—is of things as they might be, or ought to be. . . .

As the court indicated during the course of the taking of proofs, it entertains serious reservations about a plan of integration, which encompasses no more than the public schools of the City of Detroit. It appears to us that perhaps only a plan which embraces all or some of the greater Detroit metropolitan area can hope to succeed in giving our children the kind of education they are entitled to constitutionally. And we note here that the metropolitan area is like a giant jig-saw puzzle, with the school districts cut into irregular pieces, but with the picture quite plainly that of racial segregation. . . .

I would sum up our endeavors in developing a metropolitan plan as an embarkation on an uncharted course in strange waters in an effort to rescue disadvantaged children. It behooves us to take proper soundings and proceed with care. To use the vernacular, ''Right on!'' but steady as we go.

Judge Roth concluded the conference by ordering the Detroit board to submit within thirty days an evaluation of the so-called magnet plan that he had previously ordered and ''a plan for the desegregation of its schools within sixty days.'' He also ordered the state defendants to ''submit a metropolitan plan of desegregation within 120 days'' and gave the other parties ''an additional thirty days in which to submit objections and/or alternate plans.'' Judge Roth again deferred ruling on Alex Ritchie's motion to join the suburban school districts as defendants:

We haven't come to that pass yet. . . . [But] I do not propose to stop the voice of anybody who is apt to be affected by the plan. So this is a matter of mechanics . . . when the time comes.

The superintendents of suburban schools immediately met in groups to confer with their attorneys. Scores of white rallies to oppose Judge Roth sprang up. Within a week thousands signed antibusing petitions. The *Detroit News* blasted consideration of cross-district plans as ''casual justice.'' The *Free Press* stated that ''the barriers between the races have to be broken down [in order to avoid] another 100 years of racial separation and hostility.'' The NAACP and the rest of Detroit's black leadership supported the decision.

Within three days, Michigan's Republican senator Robert Griffin introduced a constitutional amendment to ban busing. He was quickly joined by most of his Michigan colleagues from both parties, including Democratic congressmen like Bill Ford and James O'Hara who had been crucial supporters of the Civil Rights Acts in the 1960s but who were elected from virtually all-white suburban districts. When the challenge to school segregation moved from the South to their own backyards, most of Michigan's congressional delegation switched sides. The notable exceptions to this political backlash included Michigan's black congressmen and its senior senator, Phil Hart, who came to be known as the conscience of the Senate for just such action in the face of political heat.

Much of the press and many politicians soon dubbed the Detroit school case "the Roth Case." Thousands of bumper stickers appeared on cars deriding "Roth" as a "four-letter word," "Pith on Roth," and "Roth is a child-molester." Federal marshals protected Judge Roth in Detroit, and the local police guarded Roth, his family, and his home in Flint. Even a federal judge appointed for life could not avoid hearing the political outcry and feeling the personal vilification. This was the price that Judge Roth had to pay for crossing the color line in his own mind and in his judicial rulings.

The Remedy Plans

In December, 1970, Judge Roth had approved magnet schools as a preliminary remedy for the state's nullification of the Detroit board's start at desegregation. The board's report on the magnet school program showed that it was a failure as a desegregation aid in Detroit. The "regular" schools from which magnet school students transferred remained as segregated as ever. In addition, a number of transfers allowed whites to use the "magnet" schools as an escape hatch to flee heavily black "regular" schools. For a substantial extra cost per pupil, this magnet program had exacerbated school segregation. Nevertheless, the Detroit board submitted two city-only "free transfer" plans designed to expand magnet programs and to include some "part-time desegregation" for two half-days per week for students in a few grades. The plans promised no relief from pervasive school segregation.

Plaintiffs objected and submitted an alternative that proposed (a) redrawing school attendance boundaries (similar to the April 7 plan) and (b) pairing and clustering of schools to eliminate any substantial racial disparity between the existing all-white and all-black schools within the approximately 70 percent black district.*

The state board of education filed six approaches to metropolitan remedy.

---

*Pairing involves joining two schools of opposite race; for example, two kindergarten to grade six schools may be paired, with *all* students attending one school for kindergarten to grade three and the other for grades four to six. Clustering involves joining three or more schools in similar fashion with all children, for example, attending one school in kindergarten to grade two, another for grades three and four, and another for grades five and six. The paired or clustered schools can be treated as one for purposes of administration, curriculum, and/or home activities to insure continuity.

One proposed remedial education as an alternative to any desegregation; others proposed one-way (only black students to suburban schools), "free choice," "magnet," and "part-time" approaches. A final alternative suggested reorganizing thirty-six of the eight-six school districts in a fashion similar to the plan proposed by former Detroit board president Abe Zwerdling in 1969. On behalf of the intervening Detroit white citizen's group, Alex Ritchie filed a proposal, affecting sixty-six school districts, with mandatory desegregation after the fourth grade between existing suburban districts and all eight of the Detroit district's regions. The Detroit board filed an alternative proposal that included almost all districts in the tricounty area. Eventually, the NAACP plaintiffs countered with a more limited proposal that included a smaller area. All of the proposals presented basic conceptual alternatives, but none had been fleshed out.

On February 23, 1972, a panel of the Sixth Circuit granted plaintiffs' motion to dismiss the appeals of the Detroit and state defendants from the segregation ruling and planning orders. The court of appeals held that such liability rulings and preliminary orders could not be appealed. Until some meaningful injunctive relief was either granted or denied, there was nothing concrete to review. The Sixth Circuit refused to give any advisory opinions.

There was one other legal development of note. In January, 1972, federal district judge Robert Mehridge ordered metropolitan desegregation of the city of Richmond and Henrico and Chesterfield County schools. Lucas and Chachkin had tried the case on behalf of the Legal Defense Fund and local black plaintiffs who sought complete relief from Virginia's historic system of dual schooling. There was no certainty, however, that it would be affirmed on appeal in the Fourth Circuit court, an appeals court that had begun to display little sympathy for desegregation in school cases.

Most of the suburban districts and two white suburban parent groups asked to intervene in the Detroit case pursuant to Judge Roth's invitation at the October 4, 1971, conference. Other suburban districts, on the advice of their counsel, refrained from participating on two grounds: first, their interests in opposing *any* cross-district pupil assignments would actually be represented by the suburban intervenors; and, second, the entire case might have to be retried because of their considered absence. On March 15, 1972, Judge Roth granted the petitions of the suburban school districts and a suburban white citizens' group to intervene on the condition that they not relitigate legal or factual issues already decided.

One attorney, Bill Saxton, represented forty of the suburban school districts. Saxton was a tough, sometimes pugnacious trial lawyer, experienced in defending corporations, insurance companies, and school districts for one of Detroit's oldest law firms. He led the suburban defense from the outset and objected to the conditions placed on intervention. He argued that it was improper to consider metropolitan plans based on prior hearings and rulings to which his clients had not been party. He also claimed that no suburban district could be included in any desegregation plan unless and until proof showed that it had engaged in independent acts of segregation.

After the ruling on segregation, the Detroit board also tried to hire a new and relatively inexperienced attorney to watch over their regular counsel's work in the case. George Bushnell understandably withdrew himself and his law firm from any further representation of the Detroit board. The board then hired George Roumell, an accomplished labor lawyer and arbitrator, as a replacement. Although some questioned his depth and style, Roumell could rise to make a forceful, even moving, argument.

From March 14 through March 21, 1972, Judge Roth held hearings on the Detroit-only plans. On behalf of plaintiffs, we urged that substantial Detroit-only relief be granted pending hearing and resolution of the more complex metropolitan issues. City-only relief, although inadequate, was far better than leaving the existing school segregation in place for years while waiting for metropolitan relief. We also argued that Supreme Court decisions foreclosed giving any weight to "white flight" and other fears of white community resistance as a reason for delaying or limiting city-only desegregation. We put on proof to show that there was nothing educationally or legally unsound about majority-black schools per se: the constitutional wrong was not blackness but state-imposed segregation. The Detroit board urged that any mandatory Detroit-only plan of actual desegregation would only facilitate white flight and the creation of an all-black school district walled off from virtually all-white suburban districts; the Detroit board urged that metropolitan relief was preferable. We countered by arguing that the board preferred metropolitan relief only because it allowed them to put off any remedy indefinitely.

On March 24, Judge Roth issued a "Ruling on Propriety of Considering Metropolitan Plans." He held "it necessary to proceed apace with resolution of the issue . . . [of] the legal availability of metropolitan remedy for segregation . . . in accordance with the mandate of the Court of Appeals that [the entire case] be concluded at the earliest possible time." Judge Roth rejected the state's contention that local school districts were sovereign powers that "may not be disturbed by either the State or the Court":

> This we cannot accept. Political subdivisions of the states have never been considered sovereign entities, rather "they have been traditionally regarded as subordinate governmental instrumentalities created by the state to assist it in carrying out state governmental functions." . . . Perhaps the clearest refutation of the State's asserted lack of power to act in the field of education is Act 48 of 1970 [rescinding the Detroit Board's

April 7 plan]. The State cannot evade its constitutional responsibility by a delegation of powers to local units of government.

Judge Roth conceded that Saxton's argument that the suburbs could only be included to the extent of their own intentionally segregative conduct had never been ruled on directly by the Supreme Court:

[A]ccordingly, we can only proceed by feeling our way through its past decisions with respect to the goal to be achieved in school desegregation cases. *Green v. County School Board,* . . . teaches us that it is our obligation to assess the effectiveness of proposed plans of desegregation in the light of circumstances present and the available alternatives; and to choose the alternative or alternatives which promise realistically to work now and hereafter to produce the maximum actual desegregation. . . . Substance, not semantics, must govern.

Roth felt the Supreme Court's remedial ruling in *Brown II* offered guidance:

The courts may consider problems related to *administration,* arising from the physical condition of the school plant, the school transportation systems, personnel, *revision of school districts* and attendance areas into compact units to achieve a system of determining admission to the public schools on a nonracial basis, and *revision of local laws and regulations* which may be necessary in solving the foregoing problems.

Judge Roth concluded that it was proper to consider metropolitan plans to desegregate the Detroit public schools.

On March 28, 1972, Judge Roth issued his ruling on Detroit-only plans of desegregation. Noting the failure of the "interim Magnet Plan" touted just sixteen months before, he summarily rejected the board's "magnet" and "part-time" plans. Judge Roth found that plaintiffs' plan would accomplish more desegregation than the board's proposed plans or its current segregated assignments. He also found, however, that the plan "would clearly make the Detroit public school system racially identifiable as Black," that it would "not lend itself as a building block for a metropolitan plan," and that it would "increase the flight of Whites from the city and the system." Judge Roth concluded:

[U]nder the evidence in this case, [it] is inescapable that relief of segregation in the public schools of the City of Detroit cannot be accomplished within the corporate geographical limits of the city. The State, however,

cannot escape its constitutional duty to desegregate the public schools of
the City of Detroit by pleading local authority. . . .

That the court must look beyond the limits of the Detroit school
district for a solution to the problem of segregation in the Detroit public
schools is obvious; that it has the authority, nay more, the duty (under the
circumstances of this case) to do so appears plainly anticipated by *Brown
II,* seventeen years ago.

Having sat through forty-one days of trial and having learned how the
color line in Detroit had shifted over time and the blacks-only ghetto had
expanded virtually all the way to the city limits, Roth was not about to make
the boundary of the Detroit school district the new racial divide by virtue of a
federal court decree. The school district boundary would have to be breached
in order to eradicate the color line. Consideration of the metropolitan issue
would be deferred no longer. Judge Roth would have none of plaintiffs'
incremental strategy when the right of Detroit black children to be rid of state-
imposed segregation was at stake. As he confided to his wife, Evelyn, "I
wonder how many minority children have, during the pendency of this case,
forever lost their right to attend a nonsegregated school" (Grant 1975, 866).

In March, 1972, in response to white opposition to the rulings of Roth and
Mehridge and the actual desegregation flowing from the Supreme Court's
unanimous ruling in *Swann v. Charlotte-Mecklenburg Board of Education,*
President Nixon proposed a moratorium on court-ordered busing, asked for
legislation to restrict busing, and sent the attorney general to intervene in the
Detroit case to oppose cross-district relief. Nixon suggested these actions as an
alternative to an antibusing constitutional amendment which, he told the nation
on television, has "a fatal flaw—it takes too long." When the local U.S.
attorney asked to intervene in the case, Judge Roth denied the request but
invited the U.S. attorney to appear as a "friend of the court." But his disdain
for the Nixon administration, its program of segregation, and its political
opposition to "forced busing" was apparent in the judge's terse manner.

Hearing on Metropolitan Plans

The hearing on the various metropolitan concepts began on March 28. Bill
Saxton focused his defense to any cross-district desegregation on the language
from *Swann* that the "nature of the violation determines the scope of the
remedy." He argued, repeatedly, that this rule meant that the geographic
extent of the violation determined the territorial limits of any remedy; as the
violation found extended only to school segregation within the Detroit public
schools, the remedy must be limited to the Detroit school district. Saxton also
argued that segregation was educationally sound and desegregation educa-

tionally harmful. The state defendants refused to express a preference for any plan and avoided assisting the court in resolving the complex issues before it.

Attorneys for the plaintiffs, the Detroit board, and the original white parents' group attempted to address the planning issues that could be resolved in view of the skeletal nature of the remedial and reorganization concepts submitted. These issues included:

- the appropriate metropolitan area within which to accomplish desegregation of the Detroit public schools
- the appropriate clusters of Detroit and suburban schools within which to plan for actual desegregation
- the nature of further planning for faculty desegregation, pupil transportation, new school construction, areawide school district reorganization or administration of transfers across existing districts, and other ancillary relief
- timing of further planning and eventual implementation
- creation of a responsible and effective process to conduct the further planning necessary for actual pupil reassignments and implementation and operation of any areawide desegregation plan

As plaintiffs' counsel, we became increasingly concerned that the remedy theory of state responsibility for metropolitan desegregation might need some additional support if it were to have any chance of success on appeal. Although our legal vision was not clear, we offered additional evidence showing that the pattern of one-race school construction and faculty assignments did not stop at the city limits but extended throughout the metropolitan area. We introduced state board computer printouts showing the massive program of new construction of all-white schools in the suburbs since 1950. We provided the current statistics on the racial composition of student body and staff in suburban schools. Coupled with the proof and findings of state discrimination, direct state responsibility for school construction and the operation of public schools, and metropolitan housing segregation and community discrimination, we hoped that this additional evidence would demonstrate that the "containment" violation did not end at the boundaries of the Detroit school district.

Our legal dilemma was not resolved by Judge Roth in his June 14 "Ruling on Desegregation Area and Development of Plans." He opened his opinion by noting that

> the task before this court . . . is now, and since September 27, 1971, has always been how to desegregate the Detroit Public Schools. . . . The court has taken no proofs with respect to the establishment of the bound-

aries of the 86 public school districts in the Counties of Wayne, Oakland and Macomb; nor on the issue of whether, with the exception of the . . . Detroit school district, such school districts have committed acts of de jure segregation.

The ruling did, however, gut Saxton's argument that educational considerations justified continued school segregation: "the issue, despite efforts of the intervenors to suggest a new rationale for a return to the discredited 'separate but equal' policy, is not whether to desegregate."

> In the main [Mr. Saxton's] proof entirely misses the point: the violation here found has to do with school segregation caused in substantial part by force of public authority and action; yet [his] questions and offer of proof speak mainly to educational theory and recent and sometimes contradictory research about narrowly measured educational effects. . . . Citation to such research, either in support or rejection of school desegregation, misses the primary point: insofar as pupil assignments are concerned, the system of public schooling in every state must be operated in a racially non-discriminatory, unified fashion; until that objective is met, the very system of public schooling constitutes an invidious racial classification. The adoption of an education theory having the effect of maintaining a pattern of de jure segregation is therefore clearly impermissible.

Judge Roth had determined to stick with constitutional interpretation and leave educational theorizing to others.

Judge Roth also responded to Saxton's argument that the geographic limits of the Detroit-only violation mandated a Detroit-only remedy. Roth first recited that the state had the ultimate responsibility to remedy the violation, de jure segregation of the Detroit public schools, by providing the injured students with desegregated schools now and in the future. Given his prior finding that no Detroit-only plan could provide this remedy, local school district boundaries could not be interposed to deprive the plaintiff schoolchildren of an effective remedy.

Second, Judge Roth held that segregative effects of de jure school segregation within Detroit, the areawide custom and usage of housing segregation, state discrimination against the Detroit district in favor of suburban schools, and massive construction of virtually all-white schools in the suburbs, combined to contribute substantially to the pervasive pattern of school segregation throughout the metropolitan area:

  • [The] deliberate setting of residential patterns [in the metropolitan area] had an important effect not only on the racial composition of inner-city schools but the entire School District of the City of Detroit. Just as evident is the fact that suburban school districts in the main contain virtually all-white schools. The white population of the city declined and in the suburbs grew; the black population in the city grew, and largely was contained therein by force of public and private racial discrimination at all levels.

- Between 1950 and 1969 in the tri-county area, approximately 13,900 "regular classrooms," capable of serving and attracting over 400,000 pupils, were added in school districts which were less than 2% black in their pupil racial composition in the 1970–71 school year. The precise effect of this massive school construction on the racial composition of Detroit area public schools cannot be measured. It is clear, however, that the effect has been substantial.
- People gravitate toward school facilities, just as schools are located in response to the needs of people. The location of schools thus influence[d] the patterns of residential development of [the] metropolitan area and [had] important impact on [the] composition of inner city neighborhoods.
- Unfortunately, the State, despite its awareness of the important impact of school construction and announced policy to control it, acted "in keeping generally, with the discriminatory practices which advanced or perpetuated racial segregation in these schools."

In passing, Judge Roth also noted that children in Michigan had long crossed school district boundaries to receive educational services. In addition, he observed that secondary school children from the all-black Carver Elementary School District just north of the Detroit border and the black Higginbotham pocket were "for years . . . assigned to black schools in the inner city because no white suburban district (or white school in the City) would take the children." In the few suburban districts with any number of blacks, the "black children often remain isolated in predominantly black schools." Unmistakably, the color line extended throughout the Detroit metropolitan area.

Finally, the June 14 ruling held that the very nature of the violation—the forced containment of black children in a core of all-black schools—would not allow any equity court to impose the boundaries of the Detroit school district as the limit of desegregation relief. For Judge Roth, "the legal effects of racially discriminatory confinement to a school district are not different from the effects of such containment within a district."

Although the tricounty area proved to be a relevant civic and economic community, Judge Roth held that schools could be excluded from any remedy if they were already racially nonidentifiable (compared to the metropolitan racial composition) or if they were too far away from Detroit for convenient transportation. Consistent with his view that the constitutional decision in *Brown* concerned racial discrimination, not educational policy, Judge Roth refused to include any other schools just to raise the average "socio-economic" status, as the Detroit board had proposed. As a result, the ruling limited the tentative desegregation area to fifty-three of the eighty-six school districts in the tricounty area and included some 780,000 students, 25.3 percent of whom were black.

Judge Roth added that segregation, not busing, was the real issue:

> Throughout the state approximately 35–40% of all students arrive at school on a bus. In school districts eligible for state reimbursement of transportation costs in the three affected counties, the percent of pupils transported in 1969–70 ranged from 42 to 52%. In comparison approximately 40%, or 310,000, of the 780,000 children within the desegregation area will require transportation in order to accomplish maximum actual desegregation. Hence, any increase in the numbers of pupils to be transported upon implementation of a complete desegregation plan over the number presently transported, relative to the state and the tri-county area, should be minimal. Indeed, any increase may only reflect the greater number of pupils who would be transported in any event but for the state practice, which affected the segregation found in this case, and which denies state reimbursement to students and districts wholly within city limits regardless of the distance of the child from the school to which assigned.

Noting that the state education authorities routinely funded busing of students for rides of more than an hour, Judge Roth found that "for school authorities or private citizens to now object to such transportation practices raises the inference . . . of racially motivated hostility to the desegregated school at the end of the ride." Nevertheless, Judge Roth used a maximum forty-minute ride as the guideline to limit the desegregation area.

To aid in further planning for actual pupil reassignments, Judge Roth approved the division of the area into a number of clusters or regions whose overall racial composition ranged from 20.5 percent to 30.8 percent black. Within these regions or clusters, students could be reassigned on a fully desegregated basis by grouping schools and then reorganizing their grades.* In that process, faculty would have to be reassigned and facilities restructured: "Normal administrative practice should lead to schools with substantially like facilities, faculty and staff, and equipment. . . . [Moreover,] in order to make

---

*As an example two white elementary schools could be grouped (or clustered) with one black elementary school, with all pupils in grades one and two assigned to one school, all pupils in grades three and four to another, and all pupils in grades five and six to the last.

the pupil desegregation process fully effective, the court finds that it is essential to integrate faculty and staff.'' There was more than one way to secure staff desegregation; a finding of intentionally segregative faculty assignments apparently would not be a precondition in all cases.

Judge Roth also added a provision concerning racial equity in the reassignment of pupils to desegregate schools:

> Although the number of black and white children transported and reassigned at the outset will be roughly equal, it is inevitable that a larger proportion of black children will be transported for a greater proportion of their school years than white children, if transportation is minimized. To mitigate this disproportion, every effort should be made at the outset to randomize the location of particular grade centers [between black and white schools].* In the short term, full utilization of vastly undercapacity inner city schools may also help to mitigate the disproportion for some black children; and, in the long term, new school capacity . . . should be added in Detroit in relative proximity to concentrations of black student residence.

Turning to the issues of financing and administering the operation of desegregated schools on an areawide basis, Judge Roth found that the necessary pupil, staff, and equipment transfers ''may be made, on an interim basis, by contractual agreements or otherwise among and between the existing school districts.'' However, Judge Roth ordered the state defendants to make a complete evaluation and to submit a report on ''those governance, financial and administrative arrangements which are necessary and essential to the successful implementation of a plan of desegregation on an interim *and* continuing basis.'' Wary of the state's previous default and concerned over the time that had already slipped by, Judge Roth ordered the state superintendent to submit a ''progress report'' within fifteen days and ''*one* appropriate interim arrangement to oversee the immediate implementation of a plan of desegregation'' within forty-five days. The judge also ordered other relief to assist in the transition to a genuinely nondiscriminatory system of schooling: biracial councils of parents and staff at each desegregated school; in-service training for faculty and staff on multiethnic studies and human relations; racially diverse curriculum; and avoidance of resegregation by classroom assignments, testing, or counseling within schools.

Finally, Roth appointed a desegregation panel made up of representatives of the various parties to develop a plan within forty-five days for the actual pupil reassignments, transportation routes, and the like. The workhorses of

---

*This meant that the former black schools should not be used primarily as centers for students in grades four and six; black schools should also be used as early elementary, junior, and senior high grade centers.

this panel would be Merle Henrickson and Gordon Foster, the two school planners whose honesty and no-nonsense practicality impressed the court. Judge Roth provided a foundation and set in motion a process to permit development and implementation of a plan to break the color line in public schooling.

Further Reaction

The response of the white community in the Detroit area and throughout the nation to Judge Roth's vision was swift and hostile. George Wallace's anti-busing political stock rose considerably when he captured 51 percent of the vote in Michigan's Democratic presidential primary. In June, Congress passed and President Nixon signed Michigan Representative Broomfield's bill seeking to postpone implementation of all court-ordered busing until all appeals were completed, an attempt to contradict the Supreme Court's command in 1969 to desegregate now and litigate later in dismantling dual systems. Due to its wording, however, Broomfield's amendment applied literally only to orders requiring "racial balance," not to orders requiring desegregation to remedy unconstitutional segregation.

In this frenzied atmosphere, the suburban intervenors, state defendants, and Detroit board immediately appealed Judge Roth's June 14 ruling to the Sixth Circuit and sought a stay of all desegregation planning. Nonintervening suburban districts also filed a petition in the Sixth Circuit seeking to prevent Judge Roth from ordering any remedy because they had not joined in the hearings. At the same time, however, a broad coalition of religious, civic, and labor groups, suburban and city, black and white, began to meet and formed the Metropolitan Coalition for Peaceful Integration to support whatever Judge Roth might finally approve.

On July 5 the desegregation panel filed a report with Judge Roth detailing the need for immediate acquisition of 295 additional buses in order to implement any interim plan in September, 1972. On July 11 Judge Roth added the state treasurer as a necessary party defendant and ordered him to exercise his authority under state law to issue the funds to purchase the buses. The state defendants sought a stay of this order which the district court promptly denied but the Sixth Circuit granted on July 13. On July 17 the Sixth Circuit continued its stay on the purchase of the buses "until entry by the District Judge of a final desegregation order or until certification by the District Judge of an appealable question."* The Sixth Circuit, with the reputation of a defender of segregation in the North and South and one of the most conservative of the

---

*"Certification" is a procedure whereby district courts can state important questions of law for appellate review before entry of appealable orders, in order to advance the final resolution of cases in the appellate courts and to avoid unnecessary proceedings in the trial courts.

courts of appeal, was not about to allow Judge Roth to implement the nation's first substantial cross-district desegregation plan before any appellate review.

As the NAACP attorneys evaluated the Sixth Circuit's ruling, there was little choice. Further delay of appeals would only delay any desegregation and increase the risk that plaintiffs would offend the court of appeals. Moreover, there was no actual desegregation plan yet; as a result, the two primary legal issues on any immediate appeal would be whether the finding of intentional segregation was correct and whether any remedy could go even one inch beyond the limits of the Detroit school district. We were resigned: we had to try to convert the Sixth Circuit on appeal as we had Judge Roth at trial.

On July 20 Judge Roth, with the agreement of all parties, certified his major rulings for appeal. The Sixth Circuit immediately expedited briefing, stayed all proceedings in the district court except further planning, and invited the attorney general of the United States to intervene and defend the constitutionality of the Broomfield busing moratorium. The Detroit school case had become the notorious "Roth case" and had been converted into a metropolitan—if not a national—issue.

The Appeals in the Sixth Circuit

Pursuant to Sixth Circuit practice, the panel of Chief Judge Phillips and circuit judges Edwards and Peck would hear the appeal. Peck and Phillips, who had participated in the *Deal* decision that had found school segregation in Cincinnati legal, seemed unlikely candidates to affirm Judge Roth's segregation ruling much less the proposal for metropolitan relief. Although the panel's unanimous ruling against the state's nullification in Act 48 of local desegregation efforts offered some hope, the vote on the issue of segregation remained in doubt. As counsel for plaintiffs, therefore, our first task was to sustain the violation ruling against attack by the state and the Detroit board. In our brief, we focused on the proof and findings of intentionally segregative conduct on the part of the state and the Detroit defendants. We downplayed, but did not omit, the housing proof that had played such a critical role in the trial court; we wanted to avoid a direct confrontation with *Deal* which had held such proof irrelevant and inadmissible.

This tactical judgment meant that we had to rely primarily on the theory that the state bears the primary responsibility for remedying the de jure segregation of the Detroit public schools; to support metropolitan relief, the appellate court would have to conclude that effective desegregation could not be provided within the confines of the Detroit school district. This limited remedy theory, in the long run, appeared to run the least risk: even if we did not ultimately prevail on this narrow legal principle, the Sixth Circuit (or even the Supreme Court) would be likely to leave open other avenues for metropolitan relief and might even suggest examples of interdistrict violations requiring appropriate cross-district remedies.

Yet we also had an obligation to Judge Roth and the Detroit school-children to try to win the metropolitan case now, not later. Unfortunately, the straight remedy theory played directly into Bill Saxton's defense: as the geographic extent of Judge Roth's intentional school segregation finding could be read to start and stop within the confines of the Detroit school district, so might the remedy. To avoid this contention, we tried in our briefs to articulate the alternative containment theory of the violation that could not be neatly cabined within the Detroit school district. But we failed to draft a compelling constitutional argument because of our preoccupation with the other issues in the case.

At the oral argument, Attorney General Frank Kelley challenged the district court's segregation findings against the state. Judge Edwards would not have any of it. From the first word, he pounced on his old friend and political ally with Judge Roth's findings, the constitutional theory of state responsibility, and the overwhelming evidence of state default in the face of massive and long-standing segregation.

George Roumell did not seek to defend the Detroit board so directly against the intentional segregation findings. Instead, he argued that Judge Roth erroneously applied a "no-fault," de facto standard for judging unconstitutionality; if the Detroit board was liable, so were all the suburbs. Roumell included in the Detroit board's brief a lengthy discussion of the subordinate status of local school districts under Michigan law and the major role played by the state agencies with supervisory authority over school district mergers and annexations; he alluded to these points in his argument. His strategy was clear: if you must affirm the constitutional violation, then give us a metropolitan remedy.

In contrast, Bill Saxton argued that the court could not approve relief beyond the geographic scope of the Detroit-only violation: it was the Detroit board, not the suburban districts, that had been found to violate the constitution. The suburban districts had not even been given their day in court.

Assistant Attorney General Dave Norman, in charge of the Civil Rights Division of the Justice Department, made an appearance to defend the Broomfield busing moratorium but argued the impropriety of metropolitan relief based on violation findings limited to the city of Detroit. Chief Judge Harry Phillips chastised Norman for the late filing of the government's brief and then ripped the United States for defending segregation; it seemed to us that only a Southerner who had finally determined to embrace *Brown*'s verdict on dual schooling and apply it full force throughout the land would have rejected the attorney general's arguments in this fashion.

Lucas, Flannery, and Jones all argued for the plaintiffs in defense of

Judge Roth's ruling. Lucas recited the evidence of intentionally segregative conduct by the board. Flannery, in his measured style and tone, sought to weave a mosaic of state liability, state responsibility, practical desegregation, and areawide violation to support metropolitan relief. Judge Edwards was so impressed by this single argument that he subsequently recommended Flannery to be dean of the Cincinnati Law School when a vacancy arose. It was not clear, however, whether Edwards or Flannery had comprehended the import of the powerfully stated argument: we still had not articulated our basic conception of an areawide violation with clarity. Jones closed with a ringing plea for justice: the black community had placed its faith in the courts, rather than in more riots, to end the frustrations of segregation.

As we left the courtroom, we were confident that at least two of the three judges would become members of our growing brigade of judicial converts. We were less confident that their conversion would extend to a majority of the judges on the Sixth Circuit or to the United States Supreme Court. The rumors of sharp division on the Supreme Court over *Swann* and Chief Justice Burger's attempts to mold a majority to sharply curtail busing and desegregation gained considerable credence when the chief justice issued a remarkable opinion denying a school board's plea for stay of desegregation. The opinion cited those portions of *Swann* that inveighed against "racial balance" and long distance transportation; Burger complained that lower courts were ignoring those "plain" limitations on equitable relief. The chief justice also took the unprecedented step of delivering personal copies of the opinion to federal judges.

On November 4, 1972, with the Detroit case awaiting decision from the panel, the nation elected a new president. Judge Roth spent the day "riding the circuit" on his courtrooms in Detroit, Bay City, and Flint. He also voted against the Nixon segregation program. Then Judge Roth drove to see his wife, who was recovering from surgery in Henry Ford Hospital in Detroit. The early election results began to trickle in. The Nixon sweep would be personally heartbreaking to Roth.

Yet Roth had never lost his humor. In the face of the private and public slurs, his brother had once jokingly threatened a name change because he got so many angry calls intended for the judge. Judge Roth replied "That's all right . . . I'll change my name to 'Nixon.' Then newspaper headlines will say 'Nixon orders busing.' " On this day, however, his humor was about all that would sustain him: he suffered a massive heart attack at Ford Hospital.

The reports of Judge Roth's coronary hit the news service at the same time as Nixon's overwhelming defeat of McGovern. Thousands of Detroit area residents took time to send cards, letters, and telegrams and make calls to the stricken judge. There were many that wished him well, but some tried to kick him while he was down: many callers to Ford Hospital said, "I hope the bastard dies." In his intensive care unit, Judge Roth was not receiving any calls, messages, or visitors. When he was finally able to see his wife, she encouraged him that dozens of phone calls were pouring into the hospital switchboard to wish him well. Pale and tired, Judge Roth whispered his first words to her: "Any nasty ones?" Evelyn Roth lied as only a mate for life can: "None."

The Sixth Circuit panel delayed issuing its opinion until Judge Roth recovered sufficiently to return home for convalescence. On the day the opinion was released, the circuit judges provided a copy to Judge Roth's closest friend, senior district judge Thomas Thornton, so that Roth could receive and read the opinion before it hit the press. In a lengthy opinion, the panel unanimously affirmed Judge Roth's findings of intentional segregation of the Detroit public schools by the Detroit board and the state, as well as his finding that desegregation relief limited to the boundaries of the Detroit school district would be inadequate. Reviewing the subordinate status of school districts under Michigan law and the supremacy of the Fourteenth Amendment, the panel declared that "the district court in the present case is not confined to the boundary lines of Detroit in fashioning equitable relief."

The panel did, however, vacate portions of Judge Roth's decree to permit the legislature an opportunity to frame a remedy voluntarily, and required the district court, if the state refused to act, to hear *every* suburb against whom relief might be sought before ordering any interdistrict remedy. The panel also vacated the remaining portions of Judge Roth's ruling on the appropriate desegregation area because of this procedural error. But the ruling enunciated the very standards for fashioning equitable relief already articulated and applied by Judge Roth.

Finally, with respect to the Sixth Circuit's prior decision in the case ratifying segregation in Cincinnati, Ohio, public schools, the panel ruled *Deal* "is not controlling. There the district court made findings of fact that there had been no unconstitutional conduct on the part of the Cincinnati Board of Education. This court held that these findings of fact were not clearly erroneous." As the findings of fact and evidence showed something different in Detroit, the Sixth Circuit simply said it would distinguish *Deal* and refused to consider the relevance of the proof of housing discrimination at all. Yet, for judges Phillips and Peck, who had approved and written the *Deal* ruling, such statements only served to obscure the quite different conception of the legal and factual issues they had come to embrace in affirming Judge Roth's ruling.

Roth was elated. While convalescing, he could not wait to get back to work on the case. Plaintiffs and their attorneys were gratified but concerned: the Fourth Circuit had just reversed a metropolitan remedy in the Richmond case on the ground that the three local school districts involved were separate and autonomous, had already completely dismantled three separate dual systems, and could not be restructured by federal courts because of the authority reserved to the states by the Tenth Amendment. The Fourth Circuit also held that the metropolitan school segregation between the core city of Richmond and its suburbs resulted primarily from de facto housing segregation. The Fourth Circuit wrote that the "root causes of the concentration of blacks in the inner cities of America are simply not known."

On behalf of the Legal Defense Fund and black plaintiffs in Richmond, Lucas and Chachkin petitioned the Supreme Court to review this judgment, but there was great fear about how the Supreme Court would finally rule on the case. If the Supreme Court affirmed the Fourth Circuit in Richmond, it would probably control the Detroit case and prevent meaningful consideration of metropolitan relief; but if the Supreme Court reversed the Fourth Circuit and affirmed the propriety of cross-district desegregation in Richmond, we would have a fighting chance in Detroit.

The defendants in the Detroit case sought review of the panel's opinion by all nine judges of the Sixth Circuit rather than immediate hearing by the Supreme Court. On January 16 the entire appeals court agreed to review the Detroit case. The oral argument before the full court included several new developments. First, although George Roumell for the Detroit board spoke as an appellant—supposedly seeking reversal of Judge Roth—he stunned the parties and the court:

> Four distinguished judges of this Circuit—Judges Roth, Phillips, Peck, and Edwards—have reviewed the segregation findings against Detroit and the State. Although I may not be happy with their judgement, I do not intend to argue any further on that score. Instead, I want to explain the compelling reasons supporting a metropolitan remedy in this case.

George Roumell then issued an impassioned defense of Judge Roth's metropolitan ruling based on the power and authority of the state and the state board over their agents, the local school districts, and the practical facts of the metropolitan community and areawide segregation in the Detroit area.

Second, former chief judge Paul Weick, who authored *Deal* and long led the Sixth Circuit's opposition to all desegregation, visibly quaked. His questions were perfunctory or sneering; he had lost control of his court.

Third, new circuit judge Wallace Kent sat immediately behind Judge Edwards on the bench and screamed at Nick Flannery about the rights of innocent suburban districts and suburban children over which he claimed Judge Roth had run roughshod. Judge Edwards winced at the decibel level of the attack. Flannery, ever unruffled, quelled Judge Kent by explaining the state's responsibility for segregation and its remedy, as well as the state's presence throughout the hearings to represent the interests of all people of Michigan.

Finally, Judge Wade McCree, the author of the panel's opinion in the Pontiac school case, asked Bill Saxton whether the Fourteenth Amendment required a finding of wrongdoing against every person and subdivision included in plans to remedy constitutional injury to others. Saxton paused. The erudite black graduate of Boston Latin and Harvard Law School who would later become solicitor general of the United States was not one who asked offhand questions or who could be given a facile answer about the geography of violation and remedy. Judge McCree, sensing Saxton's concern, continued:

> Take, for example, a reapportionment case where the people of Detroit have less than one-man, one-vote but its immediate suburbs are not malapportioned. In providing a remedy for the injured Detroit voters by redrawing election districts, the suburbs are not immune, are they? In fact, in the normal course of reapportionment both suburban and Detroit election boundaries would ordinarily be redrawn along with the boundaries of the overrepresented areas, say rural ones to the west.

Saxton was taken aback; but he argued that the nature of the segregation violation was different.

As we left the courtroom, we counted four firm votes for plaintiffs (Phillips, Peck, Edwards, and McCree) and only two votes against (Weick and Kent). We were hopeful that the remaining judges (former HEW secretary Celebrezze and former moderate district judges Miller and Lively from Tennessee and Kentucky, respectively) would follow the low-key but determined lead of Chief Judge Phillips. As we awaited the decision, an eight man Supreme Court (Justice Powell, a former Richmond school board president, did not participate) split four to four on the Richmond case. That was an ill omen: it meant that one of the five remaining members of the Warren court, probably Justice Stewart or Justice White, had joined the Nixon appointees in rejecting cross-district relief in Richmond. Just the year before, Stewart had written an opinion for the five Warren holdovers, including White, to reject a proposed splintering of existing school districts that would have hindered desegregation. But the Burger faction had since gained a swing vote in Richmond. Under the rules of the Court, however, no opinion issued, the votes of the justices were not released, and the affirmance of the Fourth Circuit applied only to that specific case and was precedent for no other.

In view of the four-to-four split in Richmond, we were left to wonder whether the swing members of Sixth Circuit would reject the opinion of the three-judge panel and Judge Roth in order to avoid a probable reversal in the Supreme Court. On June 12, 1973, the court of appeals with a six-member majority (including Celebrezze and Lively) reissued the panel's opinion with only minor revisions. Judge Weick dissented with vitriol by accusing Judge Roth of being an unbridled social engineer of radical ilk. Weick attributed all school segregation to private housing choices insulated from judicial scrutiny by *Deal,* denounced the denial of ''due process'' to the suburbs, and proclaimed the sovereign immunity of the state and its school districts against any federal court interference. In less strident tones Judge Kent argued that, because there were no findings of cross-district segregation violations in the drawing of the Detroit school district boundary or findings of segregation against the suburbs, remedy must be limited to Detroit proper; for Kent this substantive defect could only be attributed to the fatal procedural error of not including *all* of the suburbs in the hearing on *all* of the issues, including Detroit-only segregation and remedy. Judge Miller refused to reach the merits; he argued that the case should be remanded for a new trial on all issues with the full participation of all the suburbs.

The majority's opinion was notable for what it refused to review. With respect to the proof of areawide discrimination and housing segregation, the court said:

> This record contains a substantial volume of testimony concerning local and State action and policies which helped produce residential segregation in Detroit and in the metropolitan area of Detroit. In affirming the District Judge's findings of constitutional violations by the Detroit Board of Education and by the State defendants resulting in segregated schools in Detroit, we have not relied at all upon testimony pertaining to segregated housing except as school construction programs helped cause or maintain such segregation.

As a result, the court refused to rely on one of the three legs upon which Judge Roth finally rested cross-district relief in his ruling on desegregation area. Thus, the full court of appeals had merely distinguished the factual findings of intentional segregation by school authorities in Detroit from the findings of racially neutral action in *Deal;* the Sixth Circuit thereby refused to reverse *Deal*'s holding that private racial choices and public discrimination in housing were irrelevant to judicial review of the constitutionality of school segregation.

With respect to the state's discriminatory actions, however, the majority appeared to adopt another of the still nascent theories of areawide violation formulated by plaintiffs and Judge Roth: the state discrimination not only caused segregation *within* the Detroit school district, but also promoted segregation *of* the Detroit school district from its suburban neighbors:

> The clearest example of direct State participation in encouraging the segregated condition of Detroit public schools, however, is that of school construction in Detroit and the surrounding suburban areas. Until 1962 the State Board of Education had direct statutory control over site planning for new school construction. During that time, . . . the State approved school construction which fostered segregation throughout the Detroit Metropolitan area. Since 1962 the State Board has continued to be involved in approval of school construction plans.

> In the instant case the only feasible desegregation plan involves the crossing of the boundary lines between the Detroit School District and adjacent or nearby school districts for the limited purpose of providing an effective desegregation plan. The power to disregard such artificial barriers is all the more clear where, as here, the State has been guilty of discrimination which had the effect of creating and maintaining racial segregation along school district lines.

Yet understanding how such actions contributed to segregation across school district boundaries necessarily required consideration of the causal interaction between school and housing segregation and the proof of discrimination in housing throughout the metropolitan area, circumstances the Sixth Circuit refused to consider. The seeming dead letter of the *Deal* decision still restricted the vision of the court of appeals.

Finally, the Sixth Circuit adopted the rationale, at least in part, that further containment of blacks could not be legalized by the mere existence of the borders of the Detroit school district:

> This record reflects a present and expanding pattern of all-black schools in Detroit (resulting in part from State action) separated only by school district boundaries from nearby all white schools. We cannot see how such segregation can be any less harmful to the minority students than if the same result were accomplished within one school district.

> Like the Detroit Judge, we see no validity to an argument which asserts that the constitutional right to equality before the law is hemmed in by the boundaries of a school district.

> If school boundary lines cannot be changed for an unconstitutional pur-

pose, it follows logically that existing boundary lines cannot be frozen for an unconstitutional purpose.

We therefore conclude that the District Court in the present case is not confined to the boundary lines of Detroit in fashioning equitable relief.

The majority concluded that there was a "compelling basis for the District Court's crossing artificial boundary lines to cure the State's constitutional violations. The instant case calls up haunting memories of the now long overruled and discredited 'separate but equal doctrine' of *Plessy v. Ferguson*. . . . If we hold that school district boundaries are absolute barriers to a Detroit school desegregation plan, we would be opening a way to nullify *Brown v. Board of Education* which overruled *Plessy*."

The ruling agreed with the panel decision that affected suburban districts are necessary parties, all of whom must be joined and heard, except on the issues of the Detroit segregation ruling and the inadequacy of Detroit-only relief. The court therefore vacated Judge Roth's areawide remedy orders and remanded the case to the district court for further proceedings to consider an appropriate remedy. The court concluded:

> the plaintiffs and other parties shall be permitted to amend their pleadings to conform to the evidence . . . to add additional parties and to ask for any additional appropriate relief.

Plaintiffs filed such an amended complaint forthwith that conformed to the evidence already of record and to Judge Roth's findings. The complaint asked for the relief contemplated in the ruling on desegregation area. The amended complaint also joined all affected suburban districts.*

As Nate Jones looked back on the *en banc* decision, the conversion in the Sixth Circuit was, in its own way, as complete if not as dramatic as that experienced by Judge Roth. The appellate court's former perception that segregation was de facto had fallen; the evidence and findings proved that segregation in Detroit was the result of intentional discrimination and a custom of segregation every bit as invidious as state-mandated Jim Crow. In the words of Chief Judge Phillips, writing for the court of appeals, "even if the segregation practices [displayed in the Detroit record] were a bit more subtle than the compulsory segregation statutes of Southern States, they were nonetheless effective."

Although Judge Roth and the Sixth Circuit in approving the concept of

---

*Rule 15 of the Federal Rules of Civil Procedure provides liberally for such amendment of pleadings.

metropolitan relief had embarked on an uncharted course, the Supreme Court had not yet approved the new direction. Despite this major problem, Jones gained strength by reminding himself how far the case had come over such troubled waters, against all odds, and over so many obstacles: it was not impossible to hope that the NAACP could persuade just one more swing vote on the high court to join. For Judge Roth, still recovering slowly from his heart attack, there were no such doubts. As he told Bill Grant privately, "I'm a bit apprehensive, I guess; but the Supreme Court cannot miss seeing the logic and the right of it all."

One hope of Stephen Roth and Nate Jones, however, had already been dashed by the Sixth Circuit. Whatever meaningful school desegregation relief they had hoped might begin in the fall of 1972, then in the fall of 1973, and then in the fall of 1974, had been put off for several more years. Judge Roth was not idly musing when he privately confided to his wife his deep concern that thousands of children had lost their right to attend nonsegregated schools—forever—during the pendency of the case. Although the Supreme Court in 1969 had said that the transition to unitary schooling must be completed "now," it would come "later," if ever, for the 180,000 black pupils contained in separate schools in Detroit. Whether relief from this segregation would be further delayed or denied altogether now depended on the United States Supreme Court.

Chapter 5
The Detroit Case in the Supreme Court, June, 1973, to July, 1974

Narrowing the Issues

Nate Jones believed that the Supreme Court would review the Detroit case in order to resolve the four-to-four split in the *Richmond* case. He feared, however, that another landmark issue would have to be decided at the same time as the metropolitan issue: What is the legal standard for judging the constitutionality of school segregation within Northern school districts where dual schooling has not been mandated by state law or local ordinance? It was a major threshold issue that had to be reached before confronting multidistrict concerns.

The Supreme Court, however, reached the issue in the Denver school case before review of the Detroit case. The Legal Defense Fund, in a rare foray into a school case outside the South, had challenged segregation in the Denver public schools as intentional and as a denial of equal educational opportunity. The trial judge found intentional segregation in only one portion of the Denver district (Park Hill), but ordered systemwide desegregation including "the [black] core city schools" on the theory that truly equal educational opportunity could be provided to minority children only in integrated schools. On appeal, the Tenth Circuit affirmed only the findings of intentional segregation with respect to Park Hill but disapproved the educational theory and desegregation of the inner city schools. The Supreme Court eventually agreed to review this judgment.

The LDF decided to focus its brief and oral argument on the legal standards for judging intentional segregation. The school board, with the support of the Nixon Justice Department, countered that any violation and remedy should be limited to those specific schools directly segregated by school board misconduct; this school-by-school analysis also posited that incorporation of residential segregation in neighborhood schools was no violation.

In an opinion for the Court (in which Justices Marshall, Blackmun, and Stewart joined), Justice Brennan "emphasize[d] that the differentiating factor between de jure and so-called de facto segregation . . . is *purpose*, or *intent* to segregate." Without specifying what proof would ordinarily trigger a finding of intentional segregation, the Court found that essential elements include "a current condition of segregation resulting from intentional state action." Justice Brennan held that the Denver board's long-standing, intentional segregation of the schools in the Park Hill section through racial departures from neighborhood school concepts made it more likely that segregation in the remainder of the district had similarly discriminatory underpinnings. In such circumstances, Brennan held that the burden of proof should shift to school authorities to show that the impact of the Park Hill segregation did not extend elsewhere *and* that the racial motivation underlying the Park Hill practices did not contribute at all to other school board decisions resulting in racially separate schools in other parts of the district.

Building on the chief justice's opinion for the Court in *Swann*, Justice Brennan added that discriminatory practices earmarked schools according to their racial composition. In conjunction with the location and construction of one-race schools, this racial identification "may have a profound reciprocal effect on the racial composition of residential neighborhoods within a metropolitan area, thereby causing further concentration within the schools." The Court vacated the parts of the Tenth Circuit decree concerning the core city schools and remanded the case for further proceedings in the trial court where the Denver school board would have to meet the heavy proof burdens imposed. If the board failed, the opinion directed the trial court to find that the entire Denver school system was dual and to order "all-out desegregation" of all schools within the district consistent with *Swann*.*

Chief Justice Burger concurred in the remand to the trial court, but did not join the opinion. Justice Douglas concurred in a separate opinion. Justice White did not participate in the case at all.

Justice Powell, the former school board president from Virginia and Nixon appointee, wrote an opinion "concurring in part and dissenting in part." He expressed his disagreement with prior decisions imposing affirmative duties on Southern schools not shared by their Northern counterparts. He, therefore, discarded the de jure/de facto distinction in favor of a national right to an "integrated school system." Justice Powell defined this "right," however, as a system of "neighborhood education . . . neutrally administered [without] compulsory transportation." Powell defended neighborhood schools as the bastion of public schooling, parental choice over their children's upbringing, and school and community ties. He argued that the "fundamental problem [is] residential segregation." Powell asserted, however, that this "geographical separation of the races . . . resulted from purely natural and neutral non-state causes," some unnamed "socio-economic influences." Thus, Powell sought to constitutionalize *all* school segregation at the

---

*The majority's focus on discrimination by local school officials left open whether the requisite "intentional state action" contributing to a "current condition of segregation" could be found in other governmental actors' discriminatory support for housing segregation, which would be incorporated into the schools under most neighborhood zoning policies. The heavy reliance on wrongdoing by particular sets of school officials within a local school district, however, did not offer a broad perspective on this issue.

level of current residential segregation. He argued for reversing the *Swann* decision by limiting any affirmative duty to dismantle dual systems to the sparsely populated rural areas at issue in *Green v. County School Board*. Although Powell would provide a semantic right to be free of segregation, he would withdraw any meaningful remedy for segregation in urban areas.

Justice Rehnquist, who had participated in framing the school-by-school analysis while an assistant attorney general in the Nixon Justice Department, was apparently dissatisfied with Powell's approach to stopping busing. He directly attacked both the affirmative desegregation obligations imposed by *Green* and the majority's assumption that intentionally segregative acts in a limited group of schools had wide-ranging consequences. For Rehnquist, any uncertainties on the causation issue should be resolved against plaintiffs seeking judicial intervention in the affairs of local officials. Findings of "dual schooling" and the affirmative duty to desegregate should *not* be extended, in Rehnquist's view, to school systems without any recent history of rigid segregation mandated by formal law. Unlike Powell, therefore, Rehnquist sought to label most Northern segregation de facto before applying the same rationale to reopen the issue for Southern schools. Together, the separate opinions of Powell and Rehnquist read like the opening judicial moves in the administration's continuing program to develop rules of decision that would implement the antibusing strategy of "free choice" and neighborhood schools to justify school segregation.

The decision in the Denver case meant that Judge Roth's findings of intentional segregation by the Detroit and state defendants would not be subject to serious attack. We would only have to defend those aspects of the case that provided for relief beyond the limits of the Detroit school district. The defendants came to the same conclusion: the Detroit board did not petition the Supreme Court to review the segregation ruling. The state and suburban defendants in their petitions for Supreme Court review challenged any relief beyond the Detroit school district but raised no objection to the finding of intentional school segregation by Detroit school authorities within the city limits.

The Briefs

On November 19, 1973, the Supreme Court agreed to review the case. All of the suburban and state defendants in their opening briefs stressed Bill Saxton's original statement of the defense. The procedural unfairness of Judge Roth's supposed leap from Detroit-only pleadings, evidence, and violations to metropolitan relief without the full participation of the potentially affected suburban districts only served to highlight that Judge Roth's original finding of intentional segregation was limited to the Detroit school district. As a result, the geographic scope of any remedy must be just as limited. To drive home the point, the suburbs portrayed Judge Roth as a "racial balancer" who believed that black schools were inherently inferior and used "innocent" white schoolchildren and suburban districts to implement his beliefs. In addition, the state defendants argued that the findings of discrimination against the state were wrong. One suburban district also added a belated challenge to the violation findings against the Detroit school authorities.

As plaintiffs' counsel, we recognized the need for sharper focus in our theory of violation to support a cross-district remedy against Saxton's straightforward attack. In the Richmond case, plaintiffs had not prevailed on a theory of state responsibility for desegregation of de jure black schools across school district lines, under federal equal protection analysis and state law, even though such local districts were arguably subordinate to the state. We believed that the Fourteenth Amendment should be interpreted to require the states to afford just such affirmative protection to black persons rather than to interpose state-created boundaries as barriers to meaningful relief. The Detroit board, however, argued for metropolitan desegregation on this remedial approach. As a result, there was no need for us to duplicate that effort.

Our own areawide violation theories—based on pervasive housing discrimination, segregative school construction, and the effects that practices within Detroit had across district lines—were not sufficiently compelling to persuade any swing member of the Court. We needed a beacon light, not a series of flashlights. We tried to envision just what it was that persuaded Judge Roth not to limit relief to the Detroit school district. That led us back to our original characterization of the violation as the containment of blacks in a set of separate, de jure black schools. During forty-one trial days on violation and sixteen more on remedy, Judge Roth had seen how a core of blacks-only schools had expanded dramatically over a twenty-year period but always within a state-created racial line of containment.

On one side of this barrier, all-white schools and whites-only housing always beckoned any white stragglers but excluded black families. On the other side, a variety of racially discriminatory devices and the custom of segregation confined blacks. From the testimony and graphic exhibits, Judge Roth saw that, by the time of trial, this black core and its racial border had expanded at many points to the limits of the Detroit school district: the latest racial line of containment was fast becoming the boundary of the Detroit district itself, within which blacks would shortly be sealed up in all-black schools, still walled off from a burgeoning set of all-white schools.

By 1970 Detroit's black core had 133 virtually all-black schools containing 133,000 black pupils surrounded by virtually all-white school districts housing 626,000 pupils, 99.13 percent of whom were white. No federal judge sitting in equity could provide relief from such confinement of plaintiff black schoolchildren by limiting "desegregation" to the latest area of black containment. Judge Roth had seen that the only remedy that would fit the violation was to breach the color line itself—here, the Detroit school district boundary: "the legal effects of racially discriminatory confinement to a school district are not different from the effects of such containment within a district."

With this understanding we sought in our brief, as Felix Frankfurter once advised, "to think things not words." Nick Flannery, Bill Caldwell, and I spent six weeks researching, drafting, rewriting, revising, and editing the brief. Nate Jones added the finishing touches and we went to press. Our brief began:

> Since *Brown*, and in direct violation of their constitutional rights, black children in Detroit have been intentionally confined, by various *de jure* devices, to an expanding core of black schools always separated by a line from immediately surrounding white schools. Because of the continuing nature of that constitutional violation, reflected in the expansion of the state-imposed core of black schools, [State and suburban defendants] seek to interpose as the new dividing line the existing boundaries of the Detroit School District. If that dividing line is permitted to stand without breach to perpetuate the basic dual structure, the intentional confinement of black children in schools separate from whites will continue for the foreseeable future. The violation of constitutional rights will continue without remedy. Such a result [would] repeal *Brown* and return these children to *Plessy*.

We concluded:

> The State of Michigan [may not constitutionally] continue the intentional confinement of black children to an expanding core of state-imposed black schools within a line, in a way no less [offensive] than intentionally drawing a line around them, merely because . . . an existing school district boundary [is fast becoming] the latest line of containment.

All of the proof about areawide housing segregation, the racial identification of a set of separate schools for blacks, segregative school construction, and the discriminatory process of racial ghettoization was marshalled in the brief to inform this vision. We wove into the brief one view of the Fourteenth Amendment promise to black citizens of full protection from any customary caste, including ghettoization.

In this context, we also defended Judge Roth against defendants' attack that he was an advocate of "racial balance": as the school district boundary "was fast replacing attendance zone manipulation as the vehicle of apartheid," Judge Roth properly viewed defendants' proposals to limit relief to

Detroit only "as tantamount to judicial validation of the essence of the violation . . . , the State intentionally confin[ing] blacks to [separate] schools."

Our approach ran two risks. First, we had not steadfastly and consistently presented our case to either Judge Roth or the court of appeals with this signal clarity. In the trial court, we originally avoided the cross-district aspects of the case and then watched in awe as Judge Roth tried to articulate the reality of containment within the expanding color line that he had come to recognize. In the Sixth Circuit, we were so concerned about prevailing on the legal standard and proof of intentional segregation in the North that we failed to focus on this understanding of the violation and downplayed some of its important supports, particularly the proof of areawide community discrimination and housing segregation.

Nevertheless, Judge Roth had made many findings of fact and particular conclusions of law that supported his vision; and the court of appeals had affirmed Judge Roth's judgment, even if they had been less successful in stating the case. As a result, we briefed our school district containment theory from the point of view of the victims of the violation, the black schoolchildren, who had always provided the focus for the case. They were entitled to complete relief from intentional confinement by the state within an expanding core of blacks-only schools. Much as the NAACP plaintiffs in *Brown* attacked the doctrine of "separate but equal," we tried to burst through the school district boundary by focusing on the need to pierce the latest racial divide in order to provide a meaningful remedy for the containment violation suffered by Detroit's black children. The Sixth Circuit had aided our position by vacating Judge Roth's ruling to include some fifty-four school districts within the desegregation area: in the Supreme Court, the legal issue would be whether a single black child could cross the Detroit school district line to escape *this* form of state-imposed segregation.

There was, however, a second risk. If the Supreme Court directly addressed and rejected this vision of the nature of the violation, it would license school systems to use district boundaries to segregate blacks from whites. In contrast, the straight remedy theory of state responsibility would leave open for future challenge a variety of cross-district violation theories and proof. Jones determined that this risk must be run if we were to have any chance of persuading the swing votes on the court.

In their reply briefs, defendants did not seek to rebut directly our school district containment argument. Instead, they argued that such a case had never been presented or tried below: plaintiffs' claim of metropolitan containment was an after-the-fact fabrication. State and suburban defendants argued that plaintiffs pleaded and proved only a segregation violation within the Detroit public schools. Judge Roth had leaped without legal precedent from Detroit-only segregation to metropolitan racial balance. The Detroit-only violation authorized a remedy only *within* the borders of the Detroit school district.

In a friend-of-the-court brief, the United States government added that the case, on the existing rulings and pleadings, involved segregation only within Detroit. The government, suggesting hypothetical examples of proof (e.g., gerrymandering school district boundaries) that might be introduced in another case to show an interdistrict violation, tried to highlight the impropriety of granting interdistrict relief in *this* case. If plaintiffs still wanted an interdistrict remedy, there should be a remand for a hearing on any interdistrict violation.

In view of the positions taken by the parties, the issue of metropolitan relief in this round of the Detroit school case could be decided by which version of the lower court proceedings and violation findings a majority of the Supreme Court would choose to adopt. If the Court chose to understand the nature of the violation as a color line of containment, we would prevail. If the Court chose to define the violation as limited to specific incidents of intentional school segregation affecting only public schools within Detroit, our chances were slim.

Oral Argument

On February 27, 1974, each side had its last chance to convince any of the nine justices who would listen. Although there had been months of highly charged contact with Judge Roth in the trial proceedings and numerous briefs and extended oral arguments in the many bouts with the Sixth Circuit, each side had only one thirty-minute oral presentation to convert the swing votes on the high court. Although our opposition faced the same constraints, we feared that it would be more difficult for us to breach the color line of urban segregation than it would be for defendants to rationalize it as the unintended result of Michigan's arguably neutral boundaries for separate local school districts.

The makeup of the audience present in the Supreme Court to hear the oral arguments was no more comforting to us. The courtroom was packed. National and Detroit media jammed the seating reserved for the press. The wives of the justices even sat in their private boxes to watch how the increasingly bitter divisions on the high court over the Fourteenth Amendment, racial discrimination, segregation, states' rights, and federalism would be resolved in this landmark case. Black and white faces filled the spectator section, leaving little room for the high school visitors who regularly rotate through the seats to witness the pinnacle of American justice.

In the section reserved for official dignitaries sat the antibusing congressmen from Michigan and elsewhere who had already introduced constitutional amendments to legitimize almost all school segregation by banning busing should the Court dare to rule in plantiffs' favor. These congressmen responded to their white constituents' opposition to integration with all variety of public display and legislation designed to limit compulsory pupil assignments to walk-in schools and to immunize school district boundaries from judicial breach. The president and the Congress stood united against "forced busing" and judicial usurpation of local prerogatives. No Court could be blind to this political backlash to what had become the Roth Case.

In the back row of the courtroom sat Judge Roth's law clerk. Judge Roth would not have attended the oral argument under any circumstances as a matter of propriety. On February 27 he could not as a matter of health. He was recuperating slowly from complicated surgery to repair some of the damage inflicted by the massive heart attack on election night in 1972 and a second attack suffered a year later.

Michigan's attorney general Frank Kelley rose and faced the Court. He looked self-assured. He spoke from a prepared speech for only five minutes. His voice was clear and his message simple: plaintiffs, three years after the case started, had invented a theory of "intentional confinement" that had never been pleaded, proven, nor found in the courts below. "General" Kelley argued that "this is a classic case of a remedy in search of a violation." He then reiterated the defendants' view:

> The case was pleaded and tried and decided by the District Court on the theory of a single district violation. . . . However, the District Court, at the remedy stage, candidly revealed what we feel is a self-assumed role to pursue a social goal [because it] became preoccupied with the majority black character of the Detroit school district. . . . My clients [the state defendants] are being used as the predicate for a multi-district remedy, when it is not warranted by the facts.

Kelley concluded his march by requesting that the Court dismiss the state and suburban defendants in order to let Detroit solve its own problems: "This Court has never said that a predominantly black school district can't meet the test of *Brown*. . . . [W]e can have a unitary solution within the City of Detroit." Unlike the Sixth Circuit, the Supreme Court deferred to this solid-sounding attorney general from the state of Michigan. Frank Kelley escaped not only unscathed but triumphant.

Bill Saxton took up the attack in clipped tones. He recited that no suburban school district was even charged with "an act of *de jure* segregation. . . . There is no claim in this case, there is no evidence in this case, that any school district in the State of Michigan was established or created for the purpose of fostering racial segregation in the public schools. . . . There has been no gerrymandering of school district boundary lines." In Saxton's view the only violation related to segregation *within* Detroit: "[Violation] findings, which are limited in scope and effect to operation of the Detroit School District, may not be used like a rubber band to snap in all the [suburban] school districts in a so-called metropolitan remedy [to] desegregate the Detroit school system.'' Only a few questions relating to minor procedural points interrupted his monologue.

In a rising voice, Saxton concluded:

> In *Swann* this court said that the task is to correct the constitutional violation by balancing the individual and collective interest. That means that the interest of those one million parents and children who live outside Detroit, who have paid taxes to support their school districts, who have considerable investments in homes, who have input into their local school, who desire to continue the concept of local schools, also have an interest in this case, equally as well as plaintiffs. And if these interests are to be balanced, the rights of these [suburban] people may not be sacrificed on the altar of racial balance in order that their children may be judicially conscripted and interchanged with students in Detroit.

Solicitor General Bork then spoke for the United States in support of the state and suburban defendants. He cut an odd figure in his formal tails, flaming red hair and beard, and booming voice. But the conservative constitutional scholar lent the full weight of the United States government to the defendants' version of the facts:

> [T]he unique aspect of this case is that an extensive interdistrict remedy is contemplated . . . , supposedly [as] a remedy for racial discrimination found to have occurred so far only within the City of Detroit. The government believes that a remedy so disproportionate to the violation found is an improper exercise of judicial power. . . . [A] remedy confined to Detroit is completely adequate to meet the law's command that the unconstitutional school system be dismantled and converted to a unitary system. The interdistrict remedy here contemplated by the court below is not tailored to the constitutional violation shown. . . . [R]ather, it is designed to interfere with the consequences of demographic shifts. The redesign of demographic patterns, I think, is not a proper function of the federal courts.

The solicitor general, however, did hold out the prospect that interdistrict relief would be appropriate if the intentionally segregative acts of the state, or even of a single district, substantially affected the racial composition of schools in another district. He suggested that a remand to the trial court for initial consideration of any such interdistrict violation issues was warranted.

In view of the Sixth Circuit's remand of interdistrict remedy issues to Judge Roth already, expanding the remand hearing to include areawide violation issues seemed reasonable.

As Nate Jones surveyed this scene, he knew that plaintiffs faced an uphill struggle in their battle against a color line that was coming to coincide with the boundaries of the Detroit school district. He learned an old adage as a young lawyer: "If the facts are on your side, argue the facts. If the law is on your side, argue the law. If the court is on your side, argue to the court. If none of them are on your side, then just argue like hell for everything you are worth." Jones learned this lesson well: he chose Nick Flannery to make the substantial response to Kelley, Saxton, and Bork at oral argument. Flannery argued the facts, the law, to the court, *and* he argued like hell for everything he was ever worth.

Flannery comprehended our vision of the case. While not agreeing with the solicitor's "cramped" view of the "affirmative reach of the Fourteenth Amendment," Flannery nevertheless used it as a fulcrum for his argument. The solicitor's view of the circumstances warranting interdistrict relief "has a virtue in this instance. . . . [It] fits the facts of this record [as found] by two courts below, a total of ten federal judges." Flannery then summarized the "conventional segregation practices" aimed at the black schoolchildren in Detroit, as well as the similarly intentional school "segregation practices by the State of Michigan."

Flannery attempted to make the Court *see* the nature of the containment violation:

> There were a variety of other governmental, private and quasi-govern-mental practices which caused housing and school segregation to be mutually supportive, mutually interlocking devices. With the result— may it please the court, if you can perceive the tri-county area in your mind's eye—with the result that black families and black children were confined to a small portion of the tri-county [area]. . . . [This] confine-ment of black children to an identifiable . . . core of black schools inev-itably created on the fringe of Detroit and beyond the border of Detroit, without regard to its permeability or impermeability, a corresponding reciprocal ring of white schools.*

---

*Flannery's verbal imagery was aided by Lamson photo-maps demonstrating in vivid color the racial pattern being described. The clerk of the Court inadvertently provided copies of these 9'' × 16'' photo-maps to each justice, many of whom appeared to refer to the maps during Flannery's presentation. The parties had previously agreed to withdraw these maps because of a claim of minor error rather than engage in an unseemly dispute about their accuracy before the court. When Saxton finally regained the podium for his rebuttal, he raised the point. All the nine justices then handed the maps to the clerk with the sheepish look of a child caught with his hand in the cookie jar.

Flannery proceeded to discuss the segregative school and housing practices that confined blacks to this inner core, and the resulting reciprocal effects
on the creation and maintenance of a surrounding white ring; he referred the
justices to the specific findings of the courts below that supported this understanding of the facts. With his hands and with verbal imagery, he showed how
the boundaries of the center district and the drawing of attendance zones along
north-south lines furthered "a policy of containment" and "served to confine
black families to schools and neighborhoods designated" for their use. He
then illustrated how schools were built "to contain students" and how this
containment had "a segregative effect on neighborhoods throughout the Detroit metropolitan area." Flannery continued, "It wasn't the State's role in
isolation today and the Detroit Board's role in isolation tomorrow. All of
these factors, especially the segregated school practices, operated in lockstep
with an area-wide metropolitan policy of confining by housing discrimination . . . black families to an identifiable core in Detroit."

Flannery concluded his analysis of the state school violations with Act
48: the state intervened directly to impose segregation when

> for the first time the state's local educational agency practices affecting
> segregation had begun to falter. [When Detroit] proposed an ameliora-
> tion . . . of segregating black from white children, the State intervened
> promptly and decisively. . . . The message was imparted, to all the cit-
> izens of Michigan and to the citizens of Detroit, that Detroit was not an
> autonomous school system, but the State would manage the school affairs
> of Detroit in the most vital day to day sense when the objective was the
> retention of segregation.

Flannery then answered defendants' charge that the containment violation
was "an eleventh hour consideration." Flannery referred the Court to the trial
court record for the testimony of eight witnesses who repeatedly spoke "of
the containment pattern, housing and schools, that was coming to characterize
the metropolitan area," not merely the city of Detroit. With specific references to those portions of the lower court opinions that adopted this testimony, Flannery emphasized "that, more importantly," containment was the
"finding of both lower courts." Flannery then cited the initial colloquies
between Judge Roth and plaintiffs' counsel "during the first week of trial"
suggesting that the record as fully developed might show that more than a
Detroit-only remedy would prove necessary to remedy the larger violation.
The containment violation and the propriety of metropolitan relief were "not,
in the minds of the lower courts or in the minds of plaintiffs, a Johnny-come-
lately objective."

At precisely 12:00 noon the Court adjourned for lunch in the middle of

Flannery's argument. At precisely 1:00 P.M. the Court reconvened and Flannery lit in where he left off:

> District Judge Roth's mind-set, in our judgment, was that "after school and housing segregation had caused this containment, this confinement, should those phenomena be allowed to perpetuate the pattern of dual schools if that [can be] practically avoided?" That was the nub of his [remedial] inquiry.

That, argued Flannery, was the spirit in which Judge Roth confronted the Detroit school district line: can such an areawide pattern of dual schooling be perpetuated by erecting school district lines as "impermeable, jurisdictional barriers to practical relief"? The answer must be "no" in this case where "the State is responsible constitutionally and in Michigan practically" for both the containment violation and an effective remedy.

Substantive questions finally interrupted. Justice Blackmun, "just as a matter of curiosity," raised "the same question" he asked plaintiffs' counsel, William Coleman (former president of the Legal Defense Fund and subsequently President Ford's secretary of transportation), in the Richmond case: "If instead of the city of Detroit, this were greater Kansas City, with an artificial state line in between, I take it like considerations would flow?" Flannery, like Coleman, distinguished local school districts and their boundaries from state borders and the sovereignty "ceded to [the states] by the Constitution." But, unlike Coleman, Flannery added that if two states authorized a similar areawide violation, the federal court, "given an appropriate forum, a resolution of the jurisdictional question, . . . would have to vindicate the rights involved." Blackmun recognized that here was an answer that responded to rather than sidestepped his question.

Chief Justice Burger, however, took exception to Flannery's suggestion that the Constitution "ceded" or "conferred" sovereignty upon the states. Burger argued that the states, instead, "retained" sovereignty. Flannery responded:

> With respect to matters of constitutional philosophy, I defer to the Court. [But] in my view, *all* of the rights emanated from the people, some conferred upon the States, some conferred upon the federal government. So I don't view the States as setting up the central government and retaining some powers. But I did not mean to imply [in my answer to Justice Blackmun] that it was a matter of noblesse oblige. Those are State jurisdictions, different from that of local school districts, to be sure.

The chief justice, taken aback, said only, "Very well."

Nate Jones then argued the issue of administrative practicality of cross-district segregation. When various justices pressed questions concerning how the lower courts dealt with the specifics of governing and financing an inter-district remedy, Jones parried:

> There's no answer to that for the reason that there is no plan before the Court. All that is before the Court now is the narrow question of whether or not these [school district] boundaries are impermeable or whether they may be crossed. . . . There is no plan of government [or] finance; these are the matters that are poised for determination by the [district] court based upon the remand of the Sixth Circuit.

The general counsel for NAACP reiterated the primary issue in the case:

> [T]he nature of the violation . . . led to the containment of 133,000 black children in 133 core [black] schools surrounded by a ring of white schools. . . . [In considering remedy], the [district] court concluded that the ratification or acceptance of any of the [Detroit-only plans] would have led [to] the perpetuation of a black school district [still] surrounded by a ring of white schools.

On rebuttal, Saxton responded to the turn of the debate established by Flannery's argument:

> As I listened to Mr. Flannery, I thought of an old lady trying to knit a sweater without any thread; it just wouldn't stretch that far. . . . If the violator determines the scope of remedy then all remedies [involving state defendants] will always be coextensive with the border of any state. . . . If, however, the Court is going to adhere to previous principles, the violation will determine the scope of remedy, this remedy must stop at the boundary lines of the Detroit school district.

As the rebuttal wound down with a series of questions concerning technical issues of federal court jurisdiction, the chief justice thanked the parties and moved on to the next case. The courtroom emptied. There was nothing more to do except wait for the decision.

The wait proved hard for Judge Roth. As the days dragged by in June without a decision, the heat and humidity of an early Michigan summer became oppressive and his slow recovery from surgery seemed even more tortured. He confided to Bill Grant: "I'm not worried about reversal by the Supreme Court, but I feel terrible." He was impatient for the decision to come down and for his health to return so that he could get back to work.

On July 8, the date the Supreme Court heard argument on the Nixon tapes, there was still no decision on the Detroit case. On July 10, Stephen

Roth suffered his third and last heart attack. He died the next day at 5 P.M. at the age of 66. Lawyers, judges, reporters, and friends attended his funeral. The Reverend David E. Molyneaux in his eulogy, prepared with Mrs. Roth, said, "there is a divine moving that puts our lives in the place of specific usefulness." For Roth, the Detroit school case was the "culmination of a lifetime of preparation . . . to give a voice to the human race." To the private reception at the judge's home after the burial, Mrs. Roth invited only his personal and court families (including his law clerks, bailiffs, secretaries, guards, and a few fellow judges), close family friends, Bill Grant, and the attorneys for plaintiffs. In the end, plaintiffs' cause had consumed her husband: but Evelyn Roth blessed us and encouraged us to continue in the struggle that Judge Roth had come to lead in the last years of his life.

The Decisions

On July 24, in a unanimous decision (Justice Rehnquist not participating), the Court sealed President Nixon's fate by ordering him to turn over the Watergate tapes. The next day, in a bitterly divided five-to-four decision, the Court reversed the judgment of the Sixth Circuit that had approved relief beyond the Detroit school district. The high court remanded the case, but only for "prompt formulation of a decree directed to eliminating the segregation found to exist in Detroit city schools, a remedy which has been delayed since 1970." There was no mention of plaintiffs' amended complaint alleging an areawide pattern of containment, nor of Bork's suggestion that the case be remanded for hearing of such interdistrict violation claims.

The majority opinion of Chief Justice Warren Burger, joined by Justices Blackmun, Powell, and Rehnquist, just adopted Saxton's view of the facts and prior proceedings and ignored our view of the violation:

> The record before us, voluminous as it is, contains evidence of de jure segregated conditions only in the Detroit schools; indeed, that was the theory on which the litigation was initially based and on which the District Court took evidence. With no showing of significant violation by the 53 outlying school districts and no evidence of any interdistrict violation or effect, the court went beyond the original theory of the case as framed by the pleadings and mandated a metropolitan area remedy.

As a result, Burger ruled, the remedy must also be limited to Detroit:

> To approve the remedy ordered by the courts [below] would impose on the outlying districts, not shown to have committed any constitutional violation, a wholly impermissible remedy based on a standard not hinted

at in *Brown I* and *II* or any holding of this Court. . . . The constitutional
right of the Negro [children] residing in Detroit is to attend a unitary
school system in that district.

The Court did reject the belated challenge to Judge Roth's rulings concerning intentional segregation by Detroit school authorities: "Under the
decision [in the Denver case] last term, the findings appear to be correct."
The Court also discussed the violations committed by the state defendants and
the state. While refusing to overturn these findings, Burger reframed each so
as to relate only to segregation *within* the Detroit school district: "This
underscores the crucial fact that the theory upon which the case proceeded
related solely to the establishment of Detroit city violations as a basis for
desegregating Detroit schools and that, at the time of trial, neither the parties
nor the trial judge was concerned with a foundation for interdistrict relief."

With respect to the areawide housing proof (and, hence, the interaction
with and the reciprocal effect of school construction and various school violations containing plaintiff black families in a separate core in the central
city), the majority ducked. The chief justice wrote, "in its present posture,
the case does not present any question concerning possible state housing
violations" because the court of appeals refused to review such proof of
community segregation. This ruling directly contradicted traditional Supreme
Court practice which permits the party that prevails in the lower courts to urge
any ground in support of the judgment, including those either rejected or
ignored below.*

Ironically, the Court's opinion nevertheless made the causal interconnection between school and housing segregation a key element in future cases.
Burger ruled that the school desegregation remedy is "necessarily designed,
as all remedies are, to restore victims of discriminatory conduct to the position
they would have occupied in the absence of such conduct." That led plaintiffs
and defendants in subsequent cases back into the battles over whether school
authorities could incorporate residential segregation into the schools, the

---

*If the Supreme Court feels that the alternative ground has not been adequately developed
in the lower courts, it may send the case back for full consideration. The high court, however, is
not free just to ignore such a critical issue altogether in ruling against the party that prevailed in
the courts below. In sharp contrast to the Burger majority's refusal to consider the proof and
finding of areawide discrimination in housing and community affairs, Burger's opinion recited at
length the extent of the remedy originally contemplated by Judge Roth. But the Sixth Circuit had
specifically vacated the trial judge's areawide desegregation ruling. Thus, Burger's discussion of
the difficulties of interdistrict desegregation of some fifty-four school districts seemed only a
rationalization to justify his restrictive view of the violation. Similarly, Burger's conclusion that
local school districts in Michigan were totally separate and autonomous from state control seemed
to stretch Michigan law in order to add further support to restricting any violation within the
bounds of the Detroit school district.

quandary about the extent to which school and housing segregation had reciprocal effect, and the proof that public and private discrimination rather than nonracial choice, economics, or happenstance caused residential segregation.

A former law clerk to Justice Powell, sympathetic to limiting busing, was offended by the majority's sleight of hand: "Victimization could not be understood or genuine restoration attempted without looking at housing. . . . In failing [to consider the] past housing violation, . . . the Supreme Court failed to address the foremost cause of metropolitan segregation: precisely what [the case was] about" (Wilkinson 1979, 223). When Lewis Powell read Burger's draft opinion, Woodward and Armstrong (1979, 284) also report that he confided, "If an associate in my law firm had done this, I'd fire him." As it turned out, however, Powell eventually concurred in the chief justice's tricks. By thus ignoring housing, the majority simply sought "to lift from white America responsibility for the ghetto" (Wilkinson 1979, 242) *and* to halt court-ordered desegregation at the school district line.

Throughout the opinion, Warren Burger also maligned Stephen Roth. For example, the chief justice accused the district judge of "making abrupt announcements" and "sua sponte, abruptly altering" the theory of the case from Detroit-only to metropolitan relief without any support. Burger charged Roth with arbitrarily "equating racial imbalance with a constitutional violation calling for a remedy" of a "particular racial balance." Burger continued: "it seems clear that the District Court . . . shifted the primary focus from a Detroit remedy to the metropolitan area only because of [its] conclusion that total desegregation of Detroit would not produce the racial balance which [it] perceived as desirable." Citing the substantial alteration of public education that might be entailed in any interdistrict remedy, Burger also accused Judge Roth of trying to become, "first a de facto 'legislative authority' . . . and then the 'school superintendent' for the entire area."

The majority ruling, however, did suggest some examples of "interdistrict violations" that would support "interdistrict relief." Burger cited the intentionally discriminatory drawing of school district boundary lines or purposefully discriminatory state acts in one district that "produce a significant segregative effect in another district. . . . In such circumstances an interdistrict remedy would be appropriate to eliminate the interdistrict segregation directly caused by the constitutional violation. Conversely, without an interdistrict violation and interdistrict effect, there is no constitutional wrong calling for an interdistrict remedy."

The majority's cramped view that any remedy must "fit the violation" ignored another traditional principle of equity that broad and flexible relief is appropriate to root out all of the consequences of long-standing institutional wrongdoing. In addition, the Court's view of the nature of the violation did not even begin to address the state's responsibility for the wrong of containment, the color line of racial ghettoization and whites-only protection in metropolitan Detroit. Instead, the Burger majority seemed bent on insulating the state from such duty by viewing any violation narrowly as cabined *within* separate school districts.

Potter Stewart filed an even more troubling concurring opinion. In 1968 he had authored the Court's opinions applying the 1866 Civil Rights Act to private housing segregation. He had then written for the Court, "Just as the Black Codes enacted after the Civil War to restrict the free exercise of [fundamental] rights were substitutes for the slave system, so the exclusion of Negroes from white communities became a substitute for the Black Codes. And when racial discrimination herds men into ghettoes . . . then it too is a relic of slavery."

By 1974 Stewart spoke from a different perspective. Although he purported to examine the evidentiary support for plaintiffs' description of the areawide nature of the containment violation, he wrote: "no record has been made in this case showing that the racial composition of the Detroit school population or that residential patterns within Detroit and in the surrounding areas were in any significant measure caused by governmental activity." Only a justice intent on ignoring the substantial proof and the trial judge's express findings could purport to make such statements based on a review of the extensive record of housing discrimination. To Stewart, it was as if plaintiffs' overwhelming housing evidence, which converted even an unsympathetic judge and hostile adversary counsel in the trial court, vanished.

To add insult to this injury, Stewart conceded that "an interdistrict [school segregation] remedy of the sort approved by the Court of Appeals" would be "proper . . . even necessary . . . [if] it were shown, for example, that state officials had contributed to the separation of the races by purposeful, racially discriminatory use of state housing or zoning laws." One was left to wonder what proof and findings he had in mind. We had shown in Stewart's own words from his 1968 opinion revitalizing the 1866 Civil Rights Act that "racial discrimination" did "herd men," women, and children into an expanding and unmistakably black "ghetto" in the inner-city core of the Detroit metropolitan area; and the trial judge had so found, expressly and repeatedly.

Potter Stewart, however, had lost his vision since 1968. As reported by Woodward and Armstrong (1979, 267), he had already decided to "get off" the bus at the school district line in the Richmond case. Parroting the Fourth Circuit's apology for urban segregation, Stewart found:

[N]o factual showing was made [before Judge Roth] that . . . segregative acts within the city alone produced an increase in the number of Negro students in the city as a whole. It is this essential fact of a predominantly Negro school population in Detroit—caused by unknown and perhaps

unknowable factors such as in-migration, birth rates, economic changes
or cumulative acts of private racial fears—that accounts for the "growing
core of Negro schools," a "core" that had grown to include virtually the
entire city.

Justice Douglas dissented: "When we rule against the metropolitan area
remedy, we take a step that will likely put the problems of the blacks and our
society back to a period . . . of separate [and unequal]." Douglas added
tartly, "it is conceivable that ghettos develop on their own without any hint of
state action. But since Michigan by one device or another has over the years
created black school districts and white school districts, the task of equity is to
provide a unitary system for the affected area where, as here, the State washes
its hands of its own creations."

Justice White (joined by Douglas, Brennan, and Marshall) dissented on
the straight remedy theory:

> I cannot understand, nor does the majority satisfactorily explain, why a
> federal court may not order an appropriate interdistrict remedy, if this is
> necessary or more effective to . . . eliminate all vestiges of state-
> imposed segregation. . . . As the Court unanimously observed in *Swann*:
> "Once a right and a violation have been shown, the scope of a district
> court's equitable powers to remedy past wrongs is broad, for breadth and
> flexibility are inherent in equitable remedies." In this case, both the right
> and the State's Fourteenth Amendment violation have concededly been
> fully established, and there is no acceptable reason for permitting the
> party responsible for the constitutional violation to contain the remedial
> powers of the federal court within administrative boundaries over which
> the transgressor itself had plenary power.

Justice Marshall (speaking for Douglas, Brennan, and White) was livid:
"After 20 years of small, often difficult steps toward [providing black school-
children equal protection], the Court today takes a giant step backwards.
Notwithstanding a record showing widespread and pervasive racial segrega-
tion in the educational system provided by the State of Michigan for children
in Detroit, this Court holds that the District Court was powerless to require the
State to remedy its constitutional violation in any meaningful fashion."
Marshall continued:

> The rights at issue in this case are too fundamental to be abridged on
> grounds as superficial as those relied on by the majority today. . . .
> Those children who have been denied [the] right [to equal protection] in
> the past deserve better than to see fences thrown up to deny them that

right in the future. Our Nation, I fear, will be ill served by the Court's refusal to remedy separate and unequal education, for unless our children begin to learn together, there is little hope that our people will ever learn to live together.

Nor could Marshall stomach the majority's attack on Judge Roth. The majority "has conjured up a largely fictional account of what the District Court was attempting to accomplish. With all due respect, the Court, in my view, does a great disservice to the district judge who labored long and hard with this complex litigation by accusing him of changing horses in mid-stream and shifting the focus of this case from the pursuit of a remedy for the condition of segregation within the Detroit school district to some unprincipled attempt to impose his own philosophy of racial balance on the entire Detroit metropolitan area."

Marshall, the man who brought *Brown* and its progeny to the Supreme Court as Jones's predecessor, understood the wide-ranging impact of the basic color line at issue:

The State's creation, through de jure acts of segregation, of a growing core of all-Negro schools inevitably acted as a magnet to attract Negroes to the areas served by such schools and to deter them from settling either in other areas of the city or in the suburbs. By the same token, the growing core of all-Negro schools inevitably helped drive whites to other areas of the city or to the suburbs. . . . The rippling effects on residential patterns caused by purposeful acts of segregation do not automatically subside at the school district border. With rare exceptions, these effects naturally spread through all the residential neighborhoods within a metropolitan area.

Marshall continued: "The most essential finding [of Judge Roth] was that Negro children in Detroit had been confined by intentional acts of segregation to a growing core of Negro schools surrounded by a receding ring of white schools. . . . Under a Detroit-only decree, Detroit's schools will clearly remain racially identifiable in comparison with neighboring schools in the metropolitan community. Schools with 65% and more Negro students will stand in sharp and obvious contrast to schools in neighboring districts with less than 2% Negro enrollment. . . . It will be of scant significance to Negro children, who have for years been confined by de jure acts of segregation to a growing core of all-Negro schools surrounded by a ring of all-white schools, that the new dividing line between the races is the school district boundary."

Marshall concluded by warning of the political realities of the color line in America:

Desegregation is not and was never expected to be an easy task. Racial attitudes ingrained in our Nation's childhood and adolescence are not quickly thrown aside in its middle years. But just as the inconvenience of some cannot be allowed to stand in the way of the rights of others, so public opposition, no matter how strident, cannot be permitted to divert this Court from the enforcement of the constitutional principles at issue in this case. Today's holding, I fear, is more a reflection of a perceived public mood that we have gone far enough in enforcing the Constitution's guarantee of equal justice than it is the product of neutral principles of law. In the short run, it may seem to be the easier course to allow our great metropolitan areas to be divided up each into two cities—one white, the other black—but it is a course, I predict, our people will ultimately regret.

Reaction

That same month, Congress banned Legal Services offices, including the Center for Law and Education, from participating in any future school desegregation litigation. Coupled with other congressional bans on HEW desegregation action and the refusal of the Nixon-Ford Justice Department to initiate any challenge to school segregation, it was difficult to see how private organizations and lawyers would be able to gather the resources even to continue the fight.

Yet, as Nate Jones surveyed the wreckage of the Supreme Court majority's decision, he refused to concede defeat. Others might look back and second guess what could or should have been done differently. Instead, Jones determined to look forward to continue the challenge:

Even though we have been shot down on metropolitan school relief at this time in Detroit, the entire Supreme Court validated the theory and proof, the reality of segregative intent and de jure causation within the Detroit school district. We will just continue to pursue the intradistrict track in the many places where it will provide some relief. And we will support the metropolitan cases that meet the loopholes set by the majority. In time, as with the challenge to the inherent inequality resulting from the dual schooling of *Plessy*, we can show the Court, and the nation, that the loopholes represent the rule not the exception. In the meantime, we shall continue to challenge the color line in housing, employment, the military, all aspects of community life.

These were brave words from a man who had been deeply wounded by losing, for black children and their parents, the first school segregation case decided on the merits by the Supreme Court in a full opinion since long before *Brown*.

In subsequent proceedings in the Detroit case, Judge Edwards of the Sixth Circuit wrote: "Conscience compels me to record how deeply I disagree with the [Supreme Court's] decision. . . . [It] imbued school district boundaries . . . with a constitutional significance which neither federal nor state law had ever accorded them." Noting that the Supreme Court majority sanctioned the growth and maintenance of one set of all-black Detroit schools immediately surrounded by another set of virtually all-white suburban schools, Judge Edwards continued, "Unless the thrust of [the majority's decision] is altered by further Supreme Court interpretation or overruling—or by action in the area of racial integration by Congress or the Presidency—it can come to represent a formula for American Apartheid." Judge Edwards concluded: "I know of no decision by the Supreme Court of the United States since the *Dred Scott* decision which is so fraught with disaster for this country."*

Lou Lucas was already girding for his next argument in a federal district court challenging areawide segregation across school district lines in Wilmington, Delaware:

> The Detroit decision is like a telescope. If you look through one end, it seems like metropolitan desegregation is a minute prospect. But if you look through the other end, you see that the Supreme Court may have established a detailed roadmap to proving an interdistrict violation and securing cross-district relief. The Detroit decision will one day become a landmark: it will serve as the precedent authorizing area-wide school desegregation across school district lines in Northern Delaware.

Lucas tempered his optimism with a caveat: "It will all depend on which end of the telescope the Supreme Court wants to use. Unfortunately, in the Detroit case, I don't believe that the Burger majority looked at the record, our arguments or Judge Roth's conversion through either end of the telescope; they just relied on the suburb's closed view of 'Detroit-only violation, Detroit-only remedy.'"

---

*In *Dred Scott v. Sandford* (1857) the Supreme Court had ruled that any black person, free or slave, was in the eyes of the Constitution only a chattel, incapable even of bringing suit in a federal court as a citizen; the Court added that Congress lacked all power to limit the spread of slavery in the country because it violated the Master's constitutional rights to his property, namely the slave, without due process of law. It took a Civil War and the Thirteenth and Fourteenth Amendments to overturn this judgment.

For Alex Ritchie, the defender of white neighborhoods who had been converted by the evidence to the goal of ending the areawide color line of racial ghettoization and white protection, the Supreme Court's decision was stunning: "I'm sad and disappointed. I really thought Judge Roth made a sound statement of law. I believed in it." The president of the Detroit school board, Cornelius Golightly, remarked, "It's very possible for [black] people to now say that if we're going to have a segregated system—then let's control it ourselves. It may be that we will have two or three generations of black and white children doomed to segregated schools."

Except for the many areawide, county school districts in the South, the Court seemed to be sanctioning the segregation of most black children in urban areas in separate schools: over two-thirds of the nation's 3.5 million black schoolchildren were already assigned to virtually all-black schools within the one hundred largest school districts. The *Washington Post* headlined that "High Court Draws Final Line" at the "city line": the Court's opinion "says that this Northern, urban racial isolation may be beyond the power of the courts."

The *Detroit News* crowed about the decision, and many suburban white Detroiters revelled in the Court's assumption that they bore no responsibility for racial segregation and ghettoization. In contrast, the *Detroit Free Press* reminded that "the problems remain. . . . The State has burned up a lot of energy over the past few years saying 'no' to busing and other such solutions. What we will have to see now is whether there is any interest at all in saying 'yes' to other . . . attempts to solve the problem of racial isolation in Southeastern Michigan. The problems, we can be sure, have not been waved away by the magic wand of the Supreme Court decision."

Bill Grant stopped in to see Evelyn Roth to console her after the Supreme Court's ruling. She responded with the same iron resolve that had come to grip Judge Roth in the face of personal vilification and public outcry:

> I can't know for sure what Stephen would have thought, but I know how I feel. I'm proud and I'm sad. My heart is heavy but I'm very proud of my husband's dedication to the law and the courage he displayed in defending the Constitution. Someone must now step forward and continue my husband's efforts. How sad it is that our troubled times demand such sacrifices.

III
"Avoiding an Education": The First Round in the Dayton School Case, July, 1972, to June, 1977

Chapter 6
The Trial of Judge Rubin, July, 1972, to December, 1972

The Michigan-Ohio Connection

The NAACP local branches and general counsel Nate Jones had not limited their challenge to school segregation in Michigan to Benton Harbor, Pontiac, and Detroit. Cases also emerged in Kalamazoo, Grand Rapids, and Lansing. Except in the Grand Rapids case, the NAACP eventually prevailed in the lower courts in showing that the school segregation within these districts resulted from racial discrimination, not happenstance, choice, ethnicity, or economics. In time, these cases spurred HEW and the Department of Justice into action against the Flint and Ferndale school districts. Belatedly, the Michigan Department of Education also adopted guidelines for redressing "racial imbalance" within districts, and the Michigan Civil Rights Commission began compliance reviews of the nature and cause of school segregation within other districts in the state.

Even so, all of these actions left hanging any further challenge to school district boundaries. Only the Benton Harbor case, as amended at mid-decade, seriously contemplated any challenge to metropolitan segregation. As the decade drew to a close the Detroit case was still mired in largely procedural wrangling over Detroit-only remedies and the conduct of the new trial judge, Robert Demascio, while the district court in Benton Harbor was just beginning to grapple with the difficult interdistrict violation and causation issues left open by the Supreme Court majority's opinion in the Detroit case. In addition, the appropriate legal standards for evaluating the unconstitutionality of segregation and propriety of desegregation even within a single district in northern cases remained unsettled in the lower courts and were subject to review by a Supreme Court that was growing increasingly sensitive to the antibusing furor.

Of the second round of NAACP cases in Michigan, the most instructive involved Kalamazoo. In the spring of 1971, after three years of planning and community input, a closely divided Kalamazoo Board of Education adopted a plan to desegregate its public schools in the fall. Over the summer the balance of power shifted on the local board with the election of new board members who campaigned vigorously on a platform which promised the nullification of the integration plan. The new school board at its first meeting rescinded the plan, reinstated the segregated attendance zones, and provided for "voluntary open enrollment." The local branch of the NAACP asked Nate Jones to assist in protecting its three-year community effort to end segregation from such frustration.

On August 12 Jones filed a complaint on behalf of the black school-children and the local branch in Kalamazoo. He requested a temporary order restraining the new board's rescission of the integration plan. District judge Noel P. Fox, an aging but still fiery liberal long committed to the American dreams of opportunity and equality, responded. He immediately issued an order forbidding the school board from resegregating the schools, pending a preliminary hearing.

On August 24 and 25, Judge Fox received evidence on whether he should require fall 1971 implementation of the integration plan, pending a full hearing on the plaintiffs' claim of de jure segregation. In an opinion issued from the bench, Judge Fox noted that in the Kalamazoo school district, with a 17.6 percent black racial composition, the five predominantly black elementary schools contained 92.3 percent of all black pupils while the other twenty-four elementary schools served only 7.7 percent of the black pupils. Judge Fox also contrasted the careful consideration leading to adoption of the integration plan in the spring with the racial hostility of the June campaign and the new board's precipitous rescission of the desegregation plan. Relying on the Sixth Circuit's original opinion in the Detroit case holding the state's reversal of the Detroit board's minimal April 7 plan unconstitutional, Judge Fox ruled, "state action cannot be interposed to delay, obstruct, or nullify steps lawfully taken for the purpose of protecting rights guaranteed by the Fourteenth Amendment." Fox held that the Kalamazoo board's original adoption of an integration plan constituted such constitutional steps and that the July rescission represented such unconstitutional nullification. He ordered the new board to implement the integration plan for the fall. Five days later the Sixth Circuit affirmed in a summary order.

Following detailed discovery by all parties, Judge Fox began a trial on the issue of segregation in February, 1973, that lasted for six weeks. Once again, the peripatetic Lou Lucas was plaintiffs' chief trial counsel. On October 4, 1973, Judge Fox issued a lengthy opinion finding both the state and local school authorities guilty of instituting a "purposeful pattern of racial discrimination by intentionally creating and maintaining" segregated schools. He found, for example, that the board had "deliberately rigidified the boundaries of schools attended by a majority of black students in order to contain black students and to preserve other schools for whites," while routinely redrawing boundaries between all-white schools. At the same time, optional zones between schools of substantially disproportionate racial composition allowed whites to escape identifiably black schools. The board also located and built new schools on a racially segregated basis, in cooperation with racially exclusive real estate development; and the racial assignment of faculty to mirror the pupil racial composition of schools further evidenced the board's segregative intent. Judge Fox also described the long-standing history of segregation in the Kalamazoo community and the pervasive racial discrimination in housing. He concluded:

> When the action of many state agencies other than school authorities contributes to the creation and maintenance of segregated housing, and when the school authorities deliberately set attendance zones along "neighborhood" lines, then . . . we are faced with *double* discrimination.

On December 9, 1974, the Sixth Circuit affirmed Judge Fox's ruling over circuit judge Weick's bitter dissent. Weick, the author of the *Deal* opinion, stuck by his assumption that racial separation resulted from the choice of black folks to segregate themselves: "the Board of Education cannot be faulted for the concentration of black people in certain areas of the city. The black people voluntarily moved into these areas long after the school district and attendance zone lines had been established." The Supreme Court declined to review the Sixth Circuit's affirmance of Judge Fox's ruling.

In contrast, another panel of the Sixth Circuit affirmed the denial of pupil desegregation relief in Grand Rapids the same week that the circuit court ruled in the Kalamazoo case. Relying on *Deal*, this panel affirmed district judge Albert Engel's findings that plaintiffs failed to prove segregative intent was a motivating factor in the school board's pupil assignment practices and that, in any event, pupil "imbalance" resulted primarily from private residential choice. Although Judge Engel found intentional faculty segregation and ordered staff desegregation, the appeals court panel held that the trial court did not err in concluding that the local school authorities evenhandedly implemented a "color-blind" neighborhood school policy except when acting affirmatively to protect some "racial balance" in certain schools in the face of "white flight."

The apparently conflicting decisions of the Sixth Circuit during the same week in the Kalamazoo and Grand Rapids school cases gave rise to the troubling speculation that the court of appeals might simply defer to *whatever* findings a trial judge might make concerning the segregative intent of school authorities. It was difficult to see how the underlying facts and evidence were significantly different in the two cases. Nate Jones declined to seek Supreme Court review of the Grand Rapids case because he preferred uncertainty in the Sixth Circuit for the time being rather than running the risk of a potentially devastating Supreme Court affirmance.

Michigan was not alone among the Northern states in facing Nate Jones's legal challenges to segregation. Jones would, eventually, file cases on behalf of local branches and parents in Columbus, Cleveland, Cincinnati, and Youngstown. But the initial focal point was Dayton. There, demands of the local black community and the NAACP branch spearheaded another community effort to end school segregation. In addition, HEW in 1969 found "racially motivated assignment of teachers" and "substantial duality in terms of race and color with respect to the distribution of pupils in the various schools" in Dayton and then compelled integration of faculty in 1971. Pursuant to the Nixon administration's antibusing policy, however, HEW dropped the compliance review of pupil segregation. President Nixon had announced, and enforced, his rule of law: integrate faculty but do not threaten busing of pupils to desegregate schools.

Yet in April, 1971, the Dayton board created a diverse biracial citizens' committee to study the problem of pupil segregation in the public schools. In June, 1971, the Ohio Department of Education urged Dayton to desegregate its schools immediately to correct the segregated "conditions that offend the Constitution." In the late fall, during the course of a school board election marked by the vigorous campaign of the "Save Our Schools" opposition to "forced busing," the citizens' "Committee of 75" called for immediate integration of the Dayton public schools. In an emotional plea describing the process of personal conversion of each committee member when confronted by the harsh facts, the report adopted the school board president's admission that "the district is guilty of practices which have led to the racial isolation of school children" and called on the board to tear down the resulting color line. The school board election suggested a different consensus, however, as the S.O.S. antibusing forces prevailed. On January 3, 1972, the antibusers would assume firm majority control of the board.

Emboldened by its lame-duck fate, and the continuing entreaties of Superintendent Wayne Carle, the moderate majority of the still duly constituted Dayton board voted on December 8, 1971, to seek joint action to end segregation in education, housing, and employment in the metropolitan area; to secure state assistance in desegregating Dayton area schools; and to desegregate the Dayton public schools beginning with the fall 1972 term. In an attempt to protect these resolutions from rescission by the S.O.S. board come January, the board majority:

- cited the 1956 Ohio attorney general's opinion which provided that the state board of education had the primary responsibility for enforcing *Brown* in Ohio and should withhold funds from any noncomplying school district;
- admitted that racial segregation existed in Dayton schools because of the segregative actions and inactions of the Dayton board;
- admitted that school and housing segregation were causally interdependent phenomena in Dayton;

- recognized the board's legal duty to disestablish the school segregation resulting from its unconstitutional conduct;
- abrogated the existing segregated attendance boundaries effective September 1, 1972; and
- directed the superintendent to develop and adopt forthwith a plan for the reassignment of pupils to desegregate all Dayton public schools by September, 1972.

In drafting these resolutions for the board, Superintendent Carle secured the input and advice of many parties and experts, including the Ohio Department of Education and Lou Lucas. With the assistance of Gordon Foster, Carle promptly drew up and adopted a plan of pupil reassignments for September, 1972.

The newly constituted S.O.S. board majority responded on its first day in office. On January 3, 1972, the Dayton board rescinded the December 8 desegregation resolutions, reimposed the segregated attendance zones and "Freedom of Enrollment" pupil assignment policy, and refused to consider Superintendent Carle's pupil assignment plan. The new board impressed on the superintendent that he would not be permitted to exercise his independent authority under Ohio law to assign pupils in a desegregated manner. The state board issued no more denunciations of segregation nor calls for integration of the Dayton public schools.

Shortly after the *Brown* decision in 1954, the Dayton branch of the NAACP had formally requested the school board to "give due consideration to plans that would end the un-American school segregation" prevailing in Dayton schools. Miley Williamson, the executive secretary of the local branch, signed this letter. When she called on the general counsel of the NAACP seventeen years later to assist in challenging the S.O.S. program of continued segregation and the state board's default, Nate Jones could not refuse. He had seen Dayton's system of segregated schooling while stationed in the segregated barracks of the nearby Wright-Patterson Air Force Base. It also presented a case where the perception of school segregation as de facto or innocent could be peeled away to show the stark de jure reality of long-standing discrimination by local school authorities and official neglect by the responsible state officers. Unfortunately, the jurisdiction of federal district judge Noel P. Fox did not extend across state lines.

Pretrial Skirmishes

The first issue was the trial judge. In the NAACP complaint, both state and Dayton school authorities would be named defendants. The case could therefore be filed in the federal district court in Columbus, the home of the state school officials, or in Dayton. An aging and conservative judge, whose opinions suggested that he would probably defend the status quo of segregation, sat in Dayton. In Columbus sat a judicial moderate and a new Nixon appointee with no record on race issues. In consultation with Lucas, Jones determined to file the case in Columbus in order to get the best chance at a blind draw. This tactic would also minimize any Dayton community pressures on the trial judge and impress on the state officials from the outset their responsibility for unconstitutional school segregation in Ohio and for the provision of an adequate desegregation remedy.

Working with local counsel Richard Austin in Dayton, Jones and Lucas filed the complaint on April 17, 1972, on behalf of black parents and school-children and the Dayton branch of the NAACP. The complaint sought:

- the immediate reinstatement of the December 8 integration program and implementation of the Carle/Foster desegregation plan by the fall semester as originally scheduled pending a full hearing;
- speedy hearing on the claims of unconstitutional segregation; and
- submission of a plan for metropolitan desegregation and a decree enjoining the state defendants from making available any funds or approvals that would support the perpetuation of unconstitutional racial containment in the greater Dayton area.

As luck would have it, the case was assigned to the new Nixon appointee. Carl Rubin had served as Cincinnati's city attorney and recently as the newly elected Republican senator's campaign manager. Judge Rubin represented an unknown quantity. The defendants promptly moved to transfer the case to the Dayton district court. On June 22, however, Judge Rubin denied these motions on the basis of the claims made against the state defendants. Ironically, the district judge shortly thereafter limited any initial hearing on violation to whether "acts by the School Board of Dayton have created a segregated school system." Judge Rubin deferred all questions concerning the state defendants' responsibility and metropolitan segregation until any clarifying decisions might issue from the Supreme Court.

At a pretrial conference on July 24, Judge Rubin also refused to rule on plaintiffs' request for a preliminary hearing to consider reinstating the original desegregation program for the fall. Judge Rubin was not moved by plaintiffs' deposition of Wayne Carle in which Dayton's superintendent testified that the desegregation plan could and should be implemented in the fall. Under Ohio law Carle was the officer responsible for assigning pupils to schools in Dayton, but Rubin ruled: "Frankly, I do not think it is possible to put this [plan] in operation this September." Instead, he scheduled a two-to-three-week hearing beginning November 13 limited to the issue of the Dayton board's responsibility for Dayton-only school segregation. He stated unequivocally, however, that if the school board were found guilty, it would have to implement "the Foster plan or an equivalent" at the start of the second semester.

At subsequent pretrial conferences, Judge Rubin sought to narrow the disputed issues. Plaintiffs filed extensive requests for admissions of fact with the state and local defendants that would summarize the creation and development of the color line in Dayton's brand of dual schooling—from the overnight conversions of Garfield, Willard, and Wogaman to blacks-only schools through the creation of the citywide blacks-only Dunbar High School, the maintenance of optional zones between opposite-race schools, the one-race school construction and racial assignment of faculty until caught by HEW, and the continued racial assignment of administrators and nonteaching staff. At trial, these facts would form the core of the testimony of Ella Taylor Lowrey, Phyllis Blackburn Greer, and John Harewood. After reviewing these requests, Judge Rubin informed all of the parties that if defendants did admit these facts, then the limited hearing on Dayton board violations should not "take more than 15 minutes."

Jones received this comment warily. He felt that Judge Rubin was more concerned at the pretrial conference about the proper arrangement for seating the attorneys than in administering justice. Lucas was even more skeptical. He feared that the trial judge's refusal to consider preliminary relief and his subsequent limitation of the November hearing to the acts of the Dayton board left open the distinct possibility that he would take a narrow view of proof of intentional segregation. Lucas also feared that the pervasive reach of the Dayton dual system at the time of *Brown* would give Judge Rubin the opportunity to find that Dayton school authorities did not engage in many affirmative acts of intentional segregation after the 1954 decision.

In preparing for the hearing, Jones and Lucas prevailed on me to serve as cocounsel in light of Richard Austin's heavy time commitments to his local practice in Dayton. Once again we worked closely with Bill Lamson, Gordon Foster, Bob Green, Marty Sloane, Karl Taeuber, and local volunteers to discover the facts and prepare the case, the demonstrative exhibits, and the expert overview. Superintendent Wayne Carle, a named defendant represented by counsel separate from the S.O.S. board majority, also cooperated by making school board records and personnel available to us upon request. Carle was a Mormon in the process of rethinking segregation as well as the social implications of his religion. As a visible leader in the Dayton white community and his church, he increasingly became a target for white hostility to association with blacks as he moved from opposition when he first arrived in 1967 to support of pupil desegregation. Working for the S.O.S. board majority, therefore, was no easy task. The price was at least nonrenewal of his contract; but Carle fought to stay as long as he could to keep the Dayton schools running and to see the integration fight through. For his personal conversion to integration, however, he would pay more—social ostracism and pressure for his family, fear and loathing from many potential state and local school employers, and questions from the members of his church and eventually excommunication.

Through Wayne Carle's cooperation, however, we began to piece together Dayton's history of dual schooling beginning with the separate all-black Garfield Annex. School authorities claimed that no racial records existed prior to 1967, except for a onetime survey conducted by the Ohio Civil Rights Commission in 1963. Without accurate racial statistics that dated at least back to 1950, it would be difficult to prove conclusively that Dayton school authorities operated an explicitly dual system of schooling both before and after the *Brown* decision. By formal and informal discovery, we pressed for such racial statistics. Ralph Curk, the longtime architect of school planning decisions from the 1940s through the 1960s, claimed there were no such statistics concerning pupils. Homer Royer, head of personnel from 1950 through 1968, claimed that racial records of staff were not kept during his tenure and that he could not recollect what happened to the prior records.

Wayne Carle came to the rescue. He personally searched Curk's old research files at the central administration building. Carle found racial statistics for students and staff in Curk's own handwriting for all schools from 1947 through 1951, including records on four, separately identified, 100 percent "Negro" schools. Carle's secretary, Mary White, reported that when she worked in personnel, she kept separate racial codes for substitute teachers and separate stacks of applications for full-time employees by race at Royer's direction. Carle's chief desegregation aid, Phyllis Greer, reviewed all of the faculty directories to identify each black staff member and the clear racial assignment of faculty from 1922 through the 1968–69 HEW investigation. Carle also found the contemporaneous superintendent reports and statements from 1951 through 1958 showing that Dayton followed an explicit policy of never allowing black staff to teach any white pupils until 1951; thereafter the district's staff assignment policy continued to cater expressly to the hostility of the white community to black staff and of white staff to black pupils.

Finally, Carle's investigations also uncovered a 1952 report from Curk's research shop describing two "alternative" plans for redistricting of "West Side schools" to deal with increasing enrollment and the "all negro [*sic*]" schools. The subjective motivation underlying the two "alternative plans" was not clear, and the superintendent who implemented the plan subsequently called it an "experiment in integration." But the objective intent and foreseeable result of the plan was unmistakable:

- to continue the four all-black schools as blacks-only schools;
- to assign black pupils from these schools to the next ring of four "mixed" schools with the highest proportion of black pupils;

- to open an elementary school adjacent to the black public housing project and to assign a virtually all-black student body and staff;
- to allow whites to continue to escape the all-black schools and the next ring of "mixed" schools through the creation of optional zones, as a substitute for "free transfers," in the remaining areas of white residence on the near West Side;
- to continue to assign virtually all-black staffs to the traditional "blacks-only" schools; and
- to assign black teachers for the first time to other schools, but only to the "mixed" schools in transition, *not* to the thirty virtually all-white schools.

In sum, the "West Side Reorganization" just added another ring of four blacks-only schools to the original core of separate schools. As a result, in 1954 over 75 percent of Dayton's seven thousand black pupils attended five schools already all-black and another four in the process of conversion to being designated "black schools."

We therefore determined from the outset of the case to argue that *Brown* imposed an affirmative obligation to dismantle this basically dual system, which the Dayton board failed to meet and the responsible state officials failed to enforce through the time of trial. In our pretrial statement, we framed the first issue: "whether the defendant school authorities have complied with their . . . affirmative constitutional duty to operate a public school system without 'Negro' and 'white' schools." Other issues asked even more pointedly "whether defendants have eliminated, root and branch, all vestiges of the dual system inherited in the 1950–51 school year" and "whether, in the face of a history of dual schooling, a policy of neutrality . . . with respect to pupil assignments satisfies the [constitutional] obligations of the defendants." Under this theory the current segregation in Dayton public schools could be seen as the product of the Dayton board's failure to dismantle the basically dual school system that it inherited at the time of *Brown*.

But we were not satisfied to rest our case on this view. The Supreme Court did not fully articulate such an "affirmative duty" until 1968 for rural areas and 1971 for urban areas of the South; and the Supreme Court had yet to hold that the same affirmative obligation applied to intentional segregation by northern school officials undertaken without the benefit of a state segregation statute. So we pressed on with discovery in the hope that we could uncover evidence showing that more recent discrimination by Dayton school authorities also contributed to the current segregation. But Lucas had foreseen the difficulty with this approach: Dayton's dual structure was so firmly entrenched by the time of *Brown* that it would not take *any* overt acts to perpetuate almost complete segregation for decades to come. Blacks had been herded into the west side and a core of nine blacks-only schools. If housing discrimination allowed blacks to move only to the fringes of this core, the set of blacks-only schools would slowly expand on the perimeter unless school authorities acted to dismantle the ongoing dual system. Existing neighborhood attendance boundaries would operate as successive gates to keep the growing black core in schools separate from whites. Worse, there were no isolated, one-race pockets scattered throughout the city where we might be able to show overt manipulation of neighborhood zoning policies to contain nearby blacks and whites in separate schools.

Nevertheless, we did discover substantial evidence that the Dayton school authorities were not simply content with maintaining the original dual system. Instead, the board assigned new teachers and transfers on a racially dual basis. For example, even in the 1968–69 school year, 95 of 135 such new black teachers were assigned to black schools, while 223 of the 287 new white teachers were assigned to white schools. As Superintendent Carle testified at the limited trial in November, 1972, ''it is obvious in terms of new hires and transfers [that] the predominating pattern was the assignment of black teachers to black schools and white teachers to white schools.'' Pursuant to an explicit color code, the central administration long assigned substitute teachers on the same racially dual basis. We also lined up numerous black staff who could describe their own interviews and conversations with Dayton's personnel chief; racially segregative hiring and assignment through the 1960s became unmistakably apparent. By the time of the HEW investigation in 1969, the racial composition of staff clearly ''mirrored'' the racial composition of pupils at schools throughout the district.

Board records also revealed that optional zones were often maintained at the fringes of the expanding core of identifiably black schools and residences to allow white pupils to escape ''mixed'' schools in transition from white to black. As our expert witness Gordon Foster recounted at trial, the short-term effect was ''to allow whites to move out of a school assignment'' that was ''becoming black''; the long-term effect was to identify ''an unstable situation'' and ''to accelerate and precipitate further segregation.'' In contrast, in areas where school boundary lines had long separated opposite-race ''neighborhoods,'' school authorities steadfastly maintained rigid boundaries.

With respect to school construction, the pretrial discovery revealed a systematic pattern of building new schools and additions in the core of the black residential areas and in the far-flung areas of white residential expansion from 1950 through 1968. Of twenty-four new schools, twenty-two opened virtually all-black or all-white; seventy-eight of eighty-one additions opened virtually one-race. This school construction proof was not premised on subjective racial choices between alternative sites. Instead, there was an objective pattern of building white schools for white areas and black schools for black areas. Although the S.O.S. board majority would defend this segregative construction as the result of "building schools where the children are," we could show that the board *intended* these schools for use by one race or the other: it assigned staff to new schools and additions tailored to the race of the pupils assigned. By thus stamping a racial identity on each school, the board revealed its segregative purpose. We capped this post-1954 history with evidence of the white community's racial hostility to desegregation that led the new S.O.S. board to rescind the desegregation program and to reimpose segregation systemwide.

As a result, in the 1971–72 school year, 75.9 percent of Dayton's twenty-three thousand black pupils attended twenty-one schools over 90 percent black in their racial composition, separate from white pupils in twenty-eight schools more than 90 percent white in their racial composition. At the time of trial a year later, fully 80 percent of the district's classrooms were virtually one race.

The final prong of our case would be to demonstrate, as we had to Judge Roth, that housing segregation resulted from public and private racial discrimination, not economics, free choice, or ethnic clustering. With this proof we hoped to show that the color line pervaded Dayton's community life and provided the context within which the Dayton board had always operated. In this context, the board's intentionally segregative conduct identified "neighborhoods" as well as schools as "black" and "white" and thereby influenced the development of housing and school segregation over time. From the way in which Judge Rubin sought to limit the November 1972 hearing to the acts of the Dayton board, however, we were concerned that he would refuse to hear this proof. Unless we could develop the proof of the context of community segregation and the two-way causal interaction between schools and housing over time, we ran the risk that the trier of fact would merely assume that residential segregation caused, and justified, most of the current school segregation in Dayton, as the Sixth Circuit had ruled in the *Deal* case from neighboring Cincinnati.

Rubin's administration of the local rules of his court heightened Nate Jones's fear that the judge was preoccupied with form rather than substance. Although Rubin permitted Lucas, Jones, and me to represent the plaintiffs and named Lucas "chief trial counsel," he demanded that a member of the local bar sit with plaintiffs' counsel at all times at all hearings and conferences. Given Richard Austin's previous commitments, that directive imposed a substantial barrier, but Jones prevailed on his aging mentor, Maynard Dickerson, to join us at the counsel table.

The Trial Strategy: Testing Judge Rubin

We determined to test Judge Rubin from the beginning of the trial on November 13, 1972. First, Lucas opened by moving that the burden of proof shift to defendants based on their admissions of fact that revealed the existence of a basically dual system in the 1951–52 school year, which had never been remedied and had only recently been completely reimposed by the S.O.S. board. Rubin disregarded his earlier comment that the hearing should take only fifteen minutes if these factual requests were admitted. He ordered plaintiffs to proceed with their proof.

Second, we sought to introduce the housing proof to set the context for evaluating school board conduct and defenses. Dave Greer, counsel for the Dayton board, argued that such evidence was inadmissible because it was irrelevant under *Deal*. Judge Rubin seemed inclined toward this view. After introducing various school board records showing the racially dual pattern of pupil and staff assignments over time and the Lamson demographic maps and school boundary overlays, Lucas therefore called a witness from the regional HUD office who had failed to respond in a timely fashion to a request under the court's authority to produce documents. We hoped that Judge Rubin would be sufficiently offended by this affront to the office of his court that he would be somewhat more sympathetic to hearing the housing proof. Although Judge Rubin ordered the HUD official to produce the documents forthwith, he carefully reserved ruling on their admissibility.

Lucas then described for Judge Rubin the substance of the testimony of the next series of witnesses: representatives of the Dayton Public Housing Authority would testify that projects were officially designated for either blacks or whites only; that school authorities cooperated in the development of these racially designated projects and the location of racially segregated schools mirroring the racial identity of the project; and that school authorities even leased space in these public housing projects for classroom use and then assigned pupils *and* staff of the same race as the project to the classes. Judge Rubin reserved ruling on the admissibility of such evidence until the actual testimony developed but pointedly inquired whether the school board participated in the housing authority decisions as to the location and race of the housing projects. Lucas, thinking he could show more direct school board action in causing *school* segregation than that, responded, "We have evidence that the school board . . . made the decision as to where they would locate the schools for such [public housing] projects." Judge Rubin appeared dissatisfied with this response.

I called to the witness stand Hubert D. Poore, director of the Dayton Public Housing Authority. Poore previously served as manager of the black DeSoto Bass Courts project on the west side of Dayton from January, 1945 until June, 1971. Poore started by identifying a number of the applications for assistance to build housing projects:

> *Q.*   With respect to the DeSoto Bass application, does it appear in that document the project is designated to serve black or white occupants?

Greer objected: "This would be an appropriate time [to question] the witness to see if we aren't going afield here." Judge Rubin chimed in, "I'm inclined to agree." I responded:

> With the permission of the Court, I will rapidly connect this particular project up by showing that the Dayton School authorities leased space in this project and assigned thereto a black teacher and an entirely black pupil population for the DeSoto Bass Courts.

> *The Court.* I will not assume that to be true, Mr. Dimond. I don't think you are over the hurdle of nexus. In my interpretation nexus is something more than that and at this time I do wish to ask the witness some questions. During the time that these four projects were under consideration, are you aware of any discussions that were had with members of the Board of Education of the Dayton School District?

> *Poore.* I was not with the Authority then.

> *The Court.* You are not in a position to testify as to what, if anything, the School Board might have contributed to the determination of these projects, is that correct?

> *Poore.* I was not with the Authority at that time.

> *The Court.* Mr. Dimond, I am going to permit you to have this witness identify these documents, and I think that is all that I will permit him to testify to.

I protested that the evidence would show that the school board built one-race schools specifically to serve one-race public housing projects. Judge Rubin countered:

> *The Court.* Mr. Dimond, I am aware that for a substantial period of time so-called public housing, financed by agencies of both the Federal Government and local Government, were specifically designated, some were white and some were black. This is insufficient for our purposes.
> If you wish to present this evidence as to these projects, I am sure that it will state therein for whom the occupancy was intended.
> If the School Board at that time took that area as it found it and provided school accommodations, that is not a nexus with the determination that a specific project would be white or black, and until and unless you can demonstrate that participation or a similar participation, the fact that the School Board rented space, provided schools, was aware of the

fact that a specific project was white or black, I am going to rule that this is not admissible.

Poore then identified the DeSoto Bass project as designated for Negroes. I asked him, "While you were at DeSoto Bass, [was it] used for school purposes?" Poore answered, "yes."

Q.   And what was the race of the children and the faculty?

The Court.   Now, Mr. Dimond, at this point we are going beyond what the Court will permit. You may interrogate this witness as to these documents and that is all, unless you can show a connection, as I have indicated before, as to the action of the School Board in segregating the projects.

Mr. Dimond.   I guess that particular piece of testimony would be admissible for another purpose, your Honor, in that you have already admitted [the document exhibits showing] the fact [that] there were black students and . . . black faculty . . . assigned [to various schools]. . . . [T]hat was admissible under your view. You seem to have no problem with that. All I am establishing through this witness . . . is that there was a black pupil population there which had a black faculty member assigned thereto.

The Court.   Mr. Dimond, the assignment of students and the assignment of faculty is an action by the School Board and that is admissible. The actions by anybody else in creating what we now refer to as a segregated development is not the responsibility of the School Board and I will not permit testimony as to that.

I was baffled by Judge Rubin's rulings: he would allow testimony concerning the racial identity of the projects, a fact which he considered "insufficient"; he had previously agreed that the race of faculty and students assigned to classes by the Dayton Board was relevant; but then he would not allow Poore to testify about the school board's assignment of faculty and pupils of the same race to classroom space leased by the school board in the projects. After some additional skirmishing, Mr. Poore identified the official designation of each project from the initial applications for federal financial assistance. Judge Rubin then refused to listen to evidence concerning the racial "compatibility" of the residents in the areas surrounding the designated "black" or "white" project.

I then asked Poore to focus on the "school contracts" negotiated by the school board "to lease space in various projects for classes." Before board counsel Greer could object, Judge Rubin interrupted: "I am going to sustain the objection." Rubin then admonished: "Mr. Dimond, until you can establish that the School Board participated in some fashion with the original determination that this would be a white or black project, whatever else the Board might have done, they have taken the area as they found it. They did not participate in the creation."

As I asked permission to withdraw Poore from the witness stand, Lucas stalked to the podium and confronted Rubin. Although they were separated by twenty feet of carpet, a lectern, and Judge Rubin's bench, they stood eye to eye:

Mr. Lucas. May it please the Court, I would like to be advised, if I can, what the Court's position is with respect to why this proof, that the Dayton School Board leased space and assigned black pupils and black teachers to that school, is not admissible in a trial where the issue is whether or not the Dayton School Board knowingly, as even the Defendants' briefs said, they say it has to be knowing, that the School Board deliberately made a school a black school or a white school?

Judge Rubin. It is the Court's position that the School Board may take an area as [it] found [it] and if that area happens to be 100 percent black and if the School Board has erected a school to service that area, absent some other showing, that fact alone does not create a segregated school.

Now, I am content to have you offer any and all evidence as to activities by the School Board, but in the case of housing you will be required as a prerequisite to show a participation in the original endeavor.

If the School Board, faced with a hundred percent black housing authority, stated, "We will not provide a school for this area," I suspect that they could be mandamused by any court in the State.

Now, I do not propose to debate this issue. I am aware that counsel does not agree with the Court. That is what Courts of Appeal were created for.

Lucas then pressed Rubin for an immediate adjournment to permit an emergency appeal to the Sixth Circuit to determine the admissibility and relevance of such proof: "[It] is absolutely of no point [to continue the trial] if I cannot introduce evidence that the School Board leased [space] knowingly in this black housing project and put in black teachers [and] black children." At first Judge Rubin flatly refused to certify this issue for immediate review by the court of appeals. But as Lucas pressed, Rubin began to waver. Finally, the judge told Lucas that plaintiffs could have their emergency appeal but with no guarantee that the trial would thereafter be resumed at an early date. For emphasis, Rubin added, ''Mr. Lucas, the choice is yours.''

Lucas, Jones, Dickerson, and I retreated for the evening from Rubin's visible wrath. There was no question in our minds that the judge's understanding of the limited relevance of proof showing the interaction between public housing segregation and school segregation did not bode well for us. The chance that we might get the Sixth Circuit to educate Rubin through an early appeal seemed to offer more hope than continuing the trial. We decided to take the option of adjourning the hearing and certifying the question of the relevance of the excluded evidence for review by the Sixth Circuit. Jones commented wryly that the hiatus might also have ''the added benefit'' of keeping Lucas and me ''out of the hoosegow reserved by Judge Rubin for his least favored lawyers.''

At the opening of court on November 14, Jones addressed Rubin in solemn tones:

> May it please the Court, I am Nathaniel Jones, General Counsel for the NAACP and one of the counsel for the Plaintiffs.
>
> At this time, Your Honor, on behalf of the Plaintiffs, I would like to move to adjourn these proceedings and request the Court to certify two questions to the Sixth Circuit Court of Appeals.

Judge Rubin, however, backtracked on his rulings of the previous afternoon. He refused to allow an immediate appeal, but permitted plaintiffs to place in evidence ''information regarding any contact that [Mr. Poore] may have had or that his department may have had with the School Board of Dayton.''

In too short order Hubert Poore and I were back on the firing line without any sign that Judge Rubin had changed his mind at all in making this tactical retreat. Poore proceeded to identify the housing assistance applications, to recite their official racial designation, to recount the dual policy of locating ''black'' projects only in areas of black residency and ''white projects'' in exclusively white areas, and to describe the separate tenant application offices for blacks and whites. Poore also identified and described the lease agreements negotiated by the Dayton school board with the housing authority to rent space in the projects for ''school purposes'' and the fact that all-black staff and pupils were assigned to the classrooms in the officially designated, blacks-only DeSoto Bass project.

When Poore's testimony shifted to the continuing identification of DeSoto Bass as a black project, Judge Rubin warned:

> *The Court.*   Mr. Dimond, I think you are going very far afield in your interrogation, and I am relying on your professional word that you are

going to connect this up, because at this point the Court sees no relevance, no relevance whatsoever in the last series of questions.

Mr. Dimond.   As I stated earlier, I was going to connect this up and I am going to do it through other witnesses.

The Court.   Mr. Dimond, I am relying upon you to do so, and I expect you to do precisely that.

Mr. Dimond.   I will try.

The Court.   You understand that you have made such a representation to the Court.

Mr. Dimond.   I understand that.

The Court.   All right. You may proceed.

I thought seriously about Jones's reference to the "hoosegow," but swallowed hard and moved on to another subject.

I asked Hubert Poore about his own family's experience with the Dayton board's conversion of Wogaman into a blacks-only school. Judge Rubin refused to allow Poore to testify on this subject because it was not included on the witness list as a specific area of Poore's questioning. I noted that Mr. Poore, if permitted, would testify that the board transported white children out of the Wogaman area following its conversion to a blacks-only school. Judge Rubin remarked crossly, "You have proffered into the record." Discretion being the better part of valor, Hubert Poore and I retired.

With subsequent witnesses, Judge Rubin expressed his reluctance to hear about prevailing customs of segregation in Dayton, even in the schools, unless the result of an express "policy of the Dayton Board." Rubin said that "social customs, unless influenced, assisted and encouraged by the Dayton School Board, are not before the Court." It was manifest that proof of the color line that divided the Dayton community would not impress Judge Rubin even as a demonstration of the racial context and pressures within which the Dayton board had to operate.

Nevertheless, when Marty Sloane detailed the segregative federal housing policies and practices, Lucas focused his testimony on the "nexus" between school board action and the initial location of racially designated housing projects. Federal officials approved the location of the one-race housing projects only upon certification by the local school authority that suitable school space would be provided for project children. As a result, school authorities held an absolute veto over the location of public housing and were inextricably involved in the initial public housing application. Incredibly, after all the dispute, debate, and veiled threat of contempt, Judge Rubin in his liability ruling made *no* findings concerning this "nexus" or the Dayton board's leasing of space and assignment of one-race classes and staffs to the racially designated projects.

As the third part of our trial strategy to test and to budge Judge Rubin, we started the school proof with the district's personnel director from 1950 to 1968. We felt that Homer Royer would either have to admit the segregative nature and racial mechanisms of staff assignments during that period or feign ignorance. We were prepared for each of these alternatives; a string of black staff members and Royer's own former secretary were ready to fill in any gaps in his memory. Lucas started by asking questions in a straightforward fashion. When Royer responded that personnel records were kept or marked separately only for the "first year or two" after his arrival in 1950, Lucas pounced by asking Royer whether he kept substitute teacher records pursuant to a racial code. Royer claimed to know of no such practice after "the early days of [his] administration." Later in his testimony, Royer relied on one of a series of self-serving reports on "faculty integration" to claim that "as of 1958, we no longer keep any records of staff by race." He did concede, however, that "when I came to office [in 1950], frankly, there were no black teachers teaching white children . . . anywhere in the city."

Royer then claimed that he followed what one black board member had described as a policy of "dynamic gradualism" to "integrate" faculty slowly and without fanfare over time. Royer characterized the introduction of even one teacher of the opposite race from the remainder of the faculty in a school as "integration to some degree." Royer also refused to admit that he implemented this staff assignment policy so that black teachers were "introduced" primarily to "mixed schools" being converted to black schools and to new schools opening primarily for blacks, while continuing to assign virtually all-white staffs to identifiably white schools.

Board attorney Greer in his questioning focused on "dynamic gradualism": Homer Royer made it sound like an affirmative policy of integration. Greer continued with Royer:

Q. In your opinion, based upon your experience in this area, did the placing of white or black teachers one way or another in the school system have anything to do with parts of the Dayton community becoming black or white?

A. Comparatively little, I should think. I presume some people fled from a community because of approaching integration, but I don't think assignment of staff was a basic decision in that regard.

Q.   And to what do you attribute the changes in communities?

A.   Well, of course, we discussed many, many times the matter of housing, which is such a difficult one for everybody to solve, was the important factor in the change in communities. I don't know if that is a part of this court case discussion or not.

Q.   Did the composition of the student bodies in the various schools in the Dayton System reflect, in your opinion, anything other than the composition of the neighborhoods in which those schools were located?

A.   That was basically what they reflected I would assume.

When Royer claimed that the policy of "dynamic gradualism" operated effectively to "integrate" staff right through his retirement in 1969, Lucas could take no more. His redirect examination brought Royer back to the objective facts. School by school, Lucas asked Royer to compare the racial composition of staff and students in the 1968–69 school year. After tediously working through ten schools, the pattern of almost all-white schools with virtually all-white staff and black schools with black staff was painfully clear. Rubin interrupted: "Mr. Lucas, I do hope you don't propose to go through this line by line."

Mr. Lucas.   No, sir.

The Court.   Because I am not going to permit it. I think you have made your point and I think it is quite clear what your point is, and I recognize it. Would you go on to something else.

As with other points that were "quite clear" to Judge Rubin when he wished to cut off arguably cumulative questioning, he did not mention these facts when he subsequently issued his ruling.

Nevertheless, the trap had been set. We followed with a number of black staff members who had been given the racial runaround by the Dayton school administrator. For example, Herman Brown, superintendent of the nearby Jefferson Township School District at the time of trial, testified that he sought employment in 1955 with Royer after graduating with honors in biology from a southern black college, securing a high school teaching certificate, and teaching a year in Alabama. Royer indicated there were no jobs available, but allowed Brown to substitute teach for a year in Dayton schools. After this year of additional experience, Royer informed Brown there was a vacancy at the white Kiser High School in biology. He asked whether Brown "could teach white children." Brown answered, "Yes, I [don't] see where the color of one's skin [should] change the terminology of the course. I . . . [will] teach [whites], Indians, Eskimos, or anyone. It [doesn't] make any difference. I just [want] a job.'' Such straightforward honesty was too much; Homer Royer filled the Kiser vacancy with a new white graduate with *no* experience and told Brown to get an elementary teaching certificate. After Brown complied with this additional requirement, Royer finally hired him on a full-time basis. Royer assigned Brown, however, to teach a fifth grade class at Miami Chapel, the all-black school opened just two years before to serve the blacks-only DeSoto Bass housing project.

Phyllis Greer then began her compelling personal presentation that described the objective facts of continued faculty segregation and its long-term impact in earmarking schools as designed primarily for blacks or whites. John Harewood described his meetings with Royer in the 1960s and the separate stacks of applications for blacks limited primarily to jobs in black schools. Mary White, Royer's unmistakably white secretary, told of the racial codes and the racial mechanisms (blue dots for blacks) used to assign substitutes and (with minor exceptions) full-time teachers on a dual basis in the 1960s.

Bob Green, Gordon Foster, and Wayne Carle rebutted the apparent claims of Homer Royer and Dave Greer that the segregative effects of such long-standing faculty segregation and resulting racial identification of schools were minimal or had been cured by actual faculty desegregation alone. All three testified that the long history of faculty segregation earmarked schools as "black" or "white" and substantially contributed over time to the racial identification of nearby residential areas on a reciprocal basis. Perhaps Phyllis Greer said it best: the constant assignment of black staff only to "schools with predominantly   black   student   bodies . . . identified   [them]   as   black schools. . . . Assignment of staff to go along with 'neighborhood change' was the kind of thing that gave the impression of the schools designed to be black.''

Wayne Carle added still further evidence of the racial identification of Dayton Schools resulting from racially dual staff assignments: "there is [still] an almost perfect correlation between the race of the principal and the predominating race in the school. All black high schools, for example, have black principals. All the other high schools have white principals. . . . That considerable vestige of segregation still has not been eliminated.'' In addition, although teachers had been substantially desegregated pursuant to the agreement with HEW, faculty racial composition was still "weighted . . . in the direction of the previous discrimination.'' Carle concluded, "It is very difficult, I think, to understand the depth of segregation. It is so pervasive that its vestiges are difficult.''

We relied on one final evidentiary tactic. Lucas always said that one way to win a judge's mind was to win his law clerks. At the very least if a lawyer persuaded the clerks, even a hostile judge would be stripped of one of his primary personal, intellectual, and legal supports; and any adverse decision and opinion would not come easily. The law clerks told us a story about Judge Rubin that may only have been apocryphal but nonetheless was instructive. As a high school student in the 1940s Carl Rubin attended a "mixed" high school in Cincinnati and participated in a vote of his classmates to determine whether black students should be permitted to use the swimming pool; Rubin raised his hand along with the overwhelming majority of students to exclude blacks and felt guilty about the decision ever after.

As a result, every local black witness in the Dayton case testified about the segregated or whites-only swimming pools, locker rooms, plays, and school proms, as well as other "back-of-the-bus" pupil assignment practices within "mixed" schools during this era. We hoped this evidence of brutal human stigmatization would move Carl Rubin to see that the objective fact of pervasive racial discrimination and separate schooling in Dayton at the time of *Brown* cried out for just as much affirmative relief as the state-mandated segregation of southern dual schooling.

The Continuing Trial of Judge Rubin

Throughout the trial, Wayne Carle provided a counterpoint for Judge Rubin. Carle shared John Harewood's perception of segregation as a continuing result of racial discrimination. When Carle recounted, for example, how tuition, hardship, or emergency transfers reflected the basic dual pattern of whites assigned to white schools and blacks to black schools, Rubin seemed more interested in finding plausible nonracial explanations.

When Carle described, on the basis of maps locating every affected pupil by race, the creation of middle schools in the late 1960s as another opportunity for desegregation consciously rejected, Rubin seemed more interested in fitting this decision into a "neighborhood school" concept. It did not appear to matter to Rubin that the Ohio Department of Education contemporaneously described the middle school organization as "only add[ing] one more action to a long list of state-imposed activities which are offensive to the constitution." When Carle painted "freedom of enrollment" as a discriminatory one-way ticket which took very few blacks to white schools, no whites to black schools, and many whites away from black schools, Rubin seemed unmoved.

Carle sought to describe his own deeply personal conversion to ending segregation as a matter of conscience, finally coming to grips with his growing perception of historic discrimination in Dayton and the pressing educational need to break the color line in public schooling. In his cross-examination, board counsel Greer pounced on Carle's public statements in the first years of his superintendency in support of both "neighborhood schools" and the various claims of "integration" made by former superintendents to challenge his credibility. When Carle sought to explain that he subsequently came to understand that the claims of "integration" and "neighborhood schools" were cover-ups for policies of intentional segregation, Rubin seemed unimpressed.

Despite all of the evidence from black eyewitnesses and contemporary board records showing the actual racial mechanisms, segregative impact, and human harm of Dayton's style of dual schooling, it was apparent that Rubin came to view Carle as an unabashedly biased plaintiff. In contrast, the board's retired school defenders, including Homer Royer, were treated as objective observers.

When Greer tried to implicate Lucas in Carle's alleged "scheme" to manufacture constitutional violations by the lame-duck board's adoption of a desegregation program just before the S.O.S. takeover, Rubin cut Greer off: "Let's assume that this [desegregation program] was [adopted] in direct defiance, if I may use that word at the moment, of the will of the electorate. Does all of that have any significance, in view of the fact that they were the legally constituted Board and they did have authority to do precisely that?"

Greer conceded that "they certainly have the right to adopt any appropriate resolutions. . . .[But] I think it's important to show the context in which they arose as an eleventh hour effort that was precipitous. It wasn't the result of a long deliberation of the body. It was merely an attempt to do something before the situation changed." Rubin countered, "Is it any the less the legal action of a duly constituted Board of Education?" Greer answered, "No, your Honor, I would say that it is not."

Judge Rubin apparently tried to confine every issue to a narrow legal box; on this occasion, he hamstrung Dave Greer's defense. At the same time, however, Judge Rubin refused to hear plaintiff's proof showing the invidious segregative intent of the S.O.S. election campaign and of the new S.O.S. board majority's rescission of the desegregation program and reimposition of segregation.

During the trial Judge Rubin engaged me in a theoretical discussion about the act of judging. He suggested that the judicial mind should be governed by the technical application of the narrowest possible legal rules. I countered that the process of judging was a considerably more complex task and that the best judicial minds informed their legal judgments with a broad understanding of constitutional history and the human striving for equal justice under law. Rubin retorted that he not only would not be governed by emotions but would not allow any emotional pleas to be made in his courtroom. I resolved to make the judge feel this case in his gut during the trial; but Carl Rubin, in foreclosing any evidence dealing with the community custom of segregation and the subjective motives of the responsible actors, did his best to ban *all* such "emotional pleas" from his courtroom. Nevertheless, Judge Rubin could not remain aloof from the intensity of the attorneys and witnesses on all sides throughout the hearing.

The trial proceedings were often electric. The defenders of segregation in Dayton believed in the propriety of continuing segregation as much as plaintiffs believed that segregation had to be ended immediately. The S.O.S. board majority defended the case frontally on the theory that residential separation was not the responsibility of the school board and that a neutral neighborhood school policy explained all of the school segregation in a community where racial separation in housing was complete. The school board had simply acted in a color-blind fashion, except for the assignment of faculty, which had only recently been completely desegregated. The battle between counsel was therefore over two conflicting views of reality. The views clashed against each other again and again and again. Even though Rubin tried to shut his ears to the din, some sound had to get through.

Gordon Foster summed up plaintiff's case. He described the history of the dual system of schooling, inherited in the 1951–52 school year, through the time of trial. He detailed the diverse segregation devices used in the West Side Reorganization that continued the four "black" schools, constructed and opened a fifth, and converted the four "mixed" schools in the next ring to "black" schools. He concluded that "the effect was clearly one of locking in and freezing the configuration including these schools in an all-black school situation." The law clerks expressed their appreciation at seeing the basic facts as Gordon Foster's picture of intentional segregation visually unfolded through the comparison of Lamson's school boundary overlays with the underlying census maps. The West Side Reorganization was no "experiment in integration" as the Dayton superintendent had suggested in 1954: it was as unmistakable evidence of continuing segregative intent as the contemporaneous faculty segregation policy based on white hostility to association with blacks.

Judge Rubin was not impressed. To the contrary, he was peeved when Foster testified that even superficially nonracial alternatives that were available to the board at the time of the West Side Reorganization would have failed to dismantle the pervasive dual system already extant in Dayton. Foster responded, "the problem as I see it in this type of situation, is essentially one of diddling around piecemeal with desegregation instead of attacking the problem wholesale and making clear that you are desegregating the entire system . . . I think the only secure solution . . .is to disestablish a dual structure in the entire system."

Foster then described the segregative impact of racially identifiable faculty assignments, as well as racial optional zones and the citywide blacks-only option of Dunbar High School. With respect to the optional zones, statistics on choices gleaned from a search of individual pupil records supported Foster's testimony: Substantial numbers of white children used the optional zones to transfer from "blacker" to "whiter" schools. In Dayton, however, optional zones also existed between white schools in all-white areas. Foster explained that optional zones are a common political response to local community pressure, racial or nonracial, which favors or disfavors attendance at a particular school. The optional zone (like the gerrymander) is just another boundary decision, but one that is antithetical to any evenhanded application of supposedly neutral neighborhood school assignment criteria. In Dayton, optional zones served both racial and nonracial purposes and proved that "neighborhood" was not the motivating factor in the assignment of pupils.

Foster also recounted the board's massive program of segregative construction of new schools and additions. He found that the pervasive pattern of one-race school construction "by and large . . . took the place of changing zone lines in terms of maintaining existing racial patterns and compacting them." The board just added school capacity on a segregative basis to contain blacks and whites in separate schools rather than constantly shifting attendance boundaries to meet enrollment changes. The segregative purpose infecting this school construction was underscored by the dual "pattern . . . of assigning faculty by race according to the race of the school" at opening.

Nor was the post-*Brown* board just the innocent victim of housing segregation or even of the dual school structure it inherited. For example, from 1958 to 1962, the board converted Roosevelt High into an all-black school (*a*) by siphoning off the remaining whites through the maintenance of the optional zone to Colonel White High School, (*b*) by assigning the other white areas to the newly constructed Roth school, and (*c*) by assigning increasingly black staff to Roosevelt. During the same period the board located, constructed, and opened Meadowdale High School with an all-white staff and student body and opened an addition to Belmont High of the same character. In 1962 the board capped its imposition of high school segregation and rejection of available integration alternatives by locating, constructing, and opening a new Dunbar High "neighborhood" facility at the far southwest corner of the school district, well removed from white population concentrations on the north and east sides. Not surprisingly, the new Dunbar opened to a virtually all-black student body to which the board assigned a black staff. At the same time, the board closed the blacks-only Willard and Garfield schools and assigned their all-black staff and student bodies to the old blacks-only Dunbar High School building, converting it into the "new" blacks-only McFarlane Elementary School.

This systematic pattern of one-race construction, in the words of Dr. Foster, "managed to lock in and compact both the school population and the residential population in the inner city, and at the same time promote housing segregation and school segregation in the far-flung suburbs.'' Whites moved to areas closest to their designated schools, while blacks were confined to the black schools and housing. Foster concluded that this one-race pattern of school construction, with ''locked-in black schools,'' as well as white schools ''in the area of the white suburban expansions which are farthest'' from black areas, created ''a loaded game board . . . [in] the Supreme Court's language'' from the *Swann* case.

School board attorney Greer defended Dayton's public school segregation with the same surgical precision, and the same broad and unproven assumptions, with which he cross-examined plaintiff's witnesses. The board's case consisted mostly of retired administrators from the pre-Carle regime who testified that, whatever the discrimination prior to *Brown*, the Dayton board had voluntarily ceased pupil discrimination by 1951 and moved gradually thereafter to integrate staff, finally ''racially balancing'' all faculty by the time of trial. Greer's defense assumed that any vestiges of segregative faculty and pupil assignments in the past had thereby been removed and long since overwhelmed by the forces of housing segregation and shifts in residential patterns. For Greer, the affirmative proof of the nonracial motive of the Dayton board rested with the relatively few boundary changes in the face of the expanding black residential core. As to the segregative construction of new schools and additions, the board was only ''building schools where the children are'' on a ''color-blind'' basis. As to optional zones, they were only nonracial anomalies scattered throughout the district; and any racially segregative effects of any suspect options had largely run their course by the time of trial. Finally, for Greer, Lamson's colorful maps of the underlying demography supported his case: if racial separation in housing was almost complete, it was plain that school segregation would be just as thorough under *any* neighborhood school policy, no matter how administered.

On cross-examination, Lucas attempted to pin the board witnesses on the overriding patterns of segregation rather than engage in technical debates over specific administrative decisions. For example, Lucas went at the chief school construction planner's claim of ''color-blindness'' with the undeniable fact that the Dayton board assigned staff of the same racial composition as pupils at the opening of new schools. The witness conceded this correlation and admitted it was then board ''policy.'' As a result, the racial identity of the new schools intended by the board was unmistakable. Similarly, this same witness admitted on cross-examination that ''when you put an addition to a school, that as far as that space is concerned, you determine the boundaries and they are coextensive with the original boundaries of the school. . . . So that if a school is already 100 percent black and you are making an addition to that school, you in effect have determined the boundaries to be . . . creating a 100 percent black school unit.'' Thus, as Gordon Foster had testified, segregative school construction practices can be just as effective as gerrymandering in intentionally segregating schools.

The battle lines had been drawn. Yet Judge Rubin had prohibited introduction of much of the evidence concerning community discrimination, board intent, and the interaction between school and housing segregation over time which might have illuminated the path to decision. On December 1, 1972, Judge Rubin closed the evidentiary hearing that he had limited to the issue of whether the acts of the Dayton board ''have created segregated educational facilities in violation of the Equal Protection Clause.'' All parties worked feverishly to submit detailed findings of fact and conclusions of law to the court. Then we all waited for Judge Rubin's decision. Jones, Lucas, and I were not confident of *any* favorable ruling. Although we had tried to inform Judge Rubin from as many angles with as much evidence as possible, he had done much to avoid an education.

Chapter 7
The Skirmishes between the Sixth Circuit and Judge Rubin, January, 1973, to September, 1976

The Trial Court Rulings

As 1973 opened without an opinion, Judge Rubin's promise of second semester relief if he found a constitutional violation lapsed. His refusal to hear the state responsibility and metropolitan issues and his limitation of proof of intent, community discrimination, and the interaction between school and housing segregation gave additional warning that Judge Rubin was not persuaded by the plaintiffs' claims. Even so, we had created a substantial and, in many respects, uncontradicted case that long-standing dual schooling had been perpetuated by board action right up to the eve of trial. In the interplay between the attorneys and the judge, Lucas had also protected his flanks with Rubin's series of inconsistent evidentiary rulings. If ever there was a school case in which the Sixth Circuit might consider reversing a trial court decision excusing segregation, Dayton was it.

On February 13, 1973, Judge Rubin issued his opinion. He found that "racially imbalanced schools, optional zones, and recent Board action [in rescinding the previously adopted desegregation program] . . . are cumulatively in violation of the Equal Protection Clause. . . . The totality of these findings require intervention by this Court under the mandate of *Brown*."

He found that "the great majority of all schools in the Dayton System today have student populations which are racially imbalanced, consistent with the black-white population and geographical distribution thereof as shown by the 1970 census." With respect to the optional zones, Rubin noted that they "are dual or overlapping attendance areas which allow children residing within them a choice among two or more schools. . . . An optional attendance zone is a limitation upon [the neighborhood school] concept and if carried to an ultimate conclusion effectively destroys it." While finding that several optional zones had racial significance in the past, only two affecting three high schools "today have any significant potential effects in terms of increased racial separation." With respect to the S.O.S. board's overturning of the lame-duck board's desegregation program, Rubin held, "The right of the majority to override protected minority rights has clear limitations in our constitutional democracy. . . . The rescission in early 1972 of the resolutions adopted by the 1971 school board constituted an independent violation of the Equal Protection Clause rights enjoyed by the black minority of Dayton.''

With respect to the proof of a history of dual schooling prior to *Brown*, Judge Rubin equivocated. Although noting ''isolated but repeated instances of failure by the Dayton School Board to meet the standards of the Ohio law mandating an integrated school system,'' Rubin found that ''prior to *Brown*, physical isolation of black students ended, swimming pools were no longer restricted, and black athletic teams competed on an equal basis with all other Dayton High Schools.'' Rubin added that the mistreatment ''of black children during this period was at least inhumane and by present standards reprehensible.'' But Rubin concluded, ''Both by reason of the substantial time that has elapsed and because these practices have ceased,'' the pre-*Brown* discrimination ''will not necessarily be deemed to be evidence of a continuing segregative policy.'' Similarly, Judge Rubin found that ''Dunbar High School was intended to be and did in fact become a black high school until it closed in 1962.'' He did not analyze whether such proof showed a dual system of schooling at any time nor, if so, whether the board ever had acted, or had refused to act, to eradicate all vestiges of the dual system.

With respect to faculty, Judge Rubin adopted the views of Homer Royer and Dave Greer: ''In the 1951–52 school year, the policy of assigning black teachers only to black schools ended and black teachers were gradually assigned to white or mixed schools. By 1963, under a policy designated as one of 'dynamic gradualism,' at least one black teacher had been assigned to all eleven high schools and to 35 of the 66 schools in the entire system.'' Judge Rubin added, ''By 1969 each school in the Dayton system had an integrated teaching staff consisting of at least one black faculty member. . . . Pursuant to the agreement with HEW, the teaching staff of the Dayton Public Schools [thereafter] became and still remains substantially integrated.'' Rubin made no mention of any continuing racial identification of schools arising from the long-standing faculty segregation.

Judge Rubin also ignored the proof that staff assignments long mirrored the racial composition of pupils at the opening of new schools and additions. As a result, Judge Rubin found that ''no evidence has been presented that school construction was segregative in nature other than to provide schools in white neighborhoods which remain predominantly white and schools in black neighborhoods which remain predominantly black.'' Judge Rubin did note, however, that ''other sites could have been selected'' to open the five new high schools and fourteen high school additions on a substantially integrated, rather than segregated, basis.

By ignoring the interconnections between racially identifiable faculty assignments, segregative school construction (particularly the use of additions rather than boundary changes to perpetuate segregation in the face of population growth), and the continuing impact of any historic dual system, Judge Rubin analyzed "attendance zones" in a vacuum. Ignoring that "optional zones" are just another type of boundary manipulation, Judge Rubin found no "gerrymandering" or other irregularity in attendance boundaries.

The heated, intense, sometimes bitter confrontations at the hearing had moved Judge Rubin a little. But his findings of fact read like a series of small capsules shaped in isolation. His legal reasoning was similarly constrained:

> An examination of the decisional law of this circuit does not provide an identifiable category for the Dayton Public School System. Ohio law, unlike the law of many Southern states, has never mandated the separation of the races in public school; to the contrary, since 1887 it has specifically prohibited this practice. . . . The Dayton system is a square peg for the round holes of Memphis, Knoxville, and other Southern cities. It is, however, also a round peg for the square hole that is Cincinnati in *Deal v. Board of Education*. In *Deal*, which dealt with an urban school system organized under the laws of Ohio, there was no finding that the actions of the school board had contributed in *any* fashion to the segregation of the Cincinnati public schools.

Rubin ordered the Dayton board to submit a plan within sixty days "to abolish all optional attendance zones," to "restate the priorities for high school attendance . . . in order that no student of a minority race will be denied attendance at any high school," and to insure "that transfers for the purpose of improving racial balance take precedence over curriculum transfers." Judge Rubin added that "the plan submitted by the defendant Board shall in all other respects conform" to the Supreme Court's decision in *Swann*.

Judge Rubin closed his opinion:

> Irrespective of the determination of this Court, there will remain in the city of Dayton a substantial black population entitled as a matter of law to equality in education, housing, and job opportunity. No peaceful community can consist of two separate societies viewing each other with mistrust and suspicion from ever higher walls of separation. Education has been historically in our country, and remains to this day, one of the primary means of overcoming barriers of class, status, and occupation.
>
> A court can only enjoin upon a school board its legal duty. It cannot reach the infinitely more sensitive moral obligation that defies legal measurement. We commend to the School Board of the City of Dayton its

moral obligation to provide the highest possible level of education equally for all children entrusted to its care, without distinction or bias or
partiality.

Given Judge Rubin's opposition to emotion in the judicial process, it was not
easy to assess whether this plea was anything more than an attempt to substitute rhetoric for the connective sinews that were missing from his opinion.

Lucas called me to discuss the ruling. He was surprised by how much we
had won from Judge Rubin and how little he had hurt us on appeal with his
disjointed findings. I asked Lucas what remedy he thought Rubin would
approve. He answered:

> Not much. But he's made a crucial mistake. He thinks that a school
> system can be just a little bit pregnant with discrimination. On the law,
> we can get him on appeal—the remedy will have to be actual desegrega-
> tion, not tinkering, because he found the rescission of a system-wide plan
> unconstitutional. On the facts, we can get him on appeal—the proof
> shows a pervasive violation. Rubin's wrong. You can't be a little preg-
> nant with discrimination without delivering an actual desegregation baby.

I was not as confident. I read Rubin's opinion as requiring only the elimination of optional zones and minor modification of transfer policies. We would
have to get the Sixth Circuit to reverse Judge Rubin on appeal, at least on the
legal implications of the undisputed facts showing a systemwide violation, if
we were to obtain a meaningful desegregation. I feared that a minor violation
finding could lead to inconsequential relief.

Nevertheless, we continued to battle on the issue of remedy in the district
court. The S.O.S. board majority proposed a "plan" that eliminated optional
zones, provided for free transfers at the high school level, and promised biracial
"learning experiences" to a few elementary pupils. Superintendent Carle and
the minority board members countered with an update of the Carle/Foster plan
of systemwide desegregation. We filed objections arguing that the board's plan
did not utilize the desegregation techniques approved in *Swann* and failed to
place the students in the situation of systemwide desegregation that they would
have occupied but for the unconstitutional rescission of Carle's desegregation
program by the S.O.S. board. We also criticized the board majority's plan with
its provisions for "part-time cultural association," including biracial "singing
and dancing" at a "musical stereopticon." We supported the alternative plan
of actual desegregation submitted by the defendant superintendent.

On July 13, 1973, Judge Rubin issued a supplemental opinion and order
approving the board's plan with minor modifications. Rubin claimed that his
remedy opinion had been "delayed pending study of the decision of the

Supreme Court'' of June 21 in the Denver case. Curiously, however, Rubin relied solely on the *dissenting* opinion of Justice Powell and its identification of an ''integrated school system'' with ''neighborhood schools.'' Rubin refused to reevaluate the evidence and his violation findings pursuant to the legal standards announced by Justice Brennan for the Court. As a result, Rubin approved the S.O.S. board's plan and extolled the ''neighborhood school concept . . . which often represents the bedrock strength of the public school system.''

To cap the remedy opinion, Rubin suggested that his Dayton-only plan ''appear[s] to moot the metropolitan question and to require the dismissal of [the state] defendants.'' Judge Rubin had previously limited the November, 1972, hearing by seeking to exclude all evidence concerning metropolitan issues *and* the responsibility of the state defendants for Dayton-only segregation. Now he wanted to dismiss these issues and the state defendants without any hearing.

The First Set of Appeals

Plaintiffs immediately appealed Judge Rubin's ruling, and the Dayton board cross-appealed. In our briefs and oral arguments for plaintiffs, we made several basic points based on the record evidence and the decisions of the Supreme Court in Denver and of the Sixth Circuit in the Pontiac and Detroit cases. First, we argued the district court erred when it failed to assess the legal significance of the proof of overt discrimination at the time of *Brown*; the Dayton board was then operating a dual system in every practical sense. Under the Court's ruling in *Brown*, the board had an affirmative obligation to disestablish its segregated system, and the board's post-*Brown* conduct should be judged not by its racial motivation but whether its effects converted Dayton to a unitary system or perpetuated the dual system. Under this legal standard, the Dayton board did not meet its affirmative duty: it *never* assigned white children from a ''white school,'' by transfer, attendance boundary, or otherwise, to a ''black school''— once a ''black school'' in Dayton, always a ''black school.'' The board therefore had an unfulfilled duty to dismantle the continuing dual system.

We called this our *Brown* argument. Its potential weakness rested with the difficulty of proving that the current segregation was directly caused by the long-standing dual system. But this was a weakness that was just as troublesome for the defendants: they could not prove that the current conditions were *not* shaped by the continuing impact of the system of dual schooling that flourished in Dayton at the time of *Brown*. Thus, the strength of this argument rested with the constitutional value at stake. In the face of a history of systemic discrimination, we argued that responsible public officials today should bear affirmative responsibility to afford full protection to the victims of any such caste system: the burden of any uncertainty over proximate cause should rest with the official defendants, not the plaintiff class.

Second, we stressed that the district court erred in evaluating the board's post-*Brown* conduct when it failed to consider the legal significance and interconnections between (*a*) the pre-*Brown* discrimination, the express policy of faculty segregation through at least the 1969–70 school year, and the dual overlapping or optional zones that affected segregation at some twenty-five schools over time and (*b*) school construction, attendance boundary, middle-school reorganization, and various pupil transfer practices that also resulted in segregation. We argued that these practices, when considered in their overall context, actively augmented the historic system of segregation through the eve of trial. We therefore asked the Sixth Circuit to reverse and to supplement Judge Rubin's ambiguous violation findings by applying the correct legal standards to the evidence of the board's long-standing, pervasive, and continuing system of segregation. The only proper remedy for such a continuing, systemwide violation was systemwide desegregation.

We dubbed this our de jure argument. Its weakness rested with Judge Rubin's findings of no discrimination following 1954, except for optional zones. Unlike our *Brown* theory, therefore, this argument would require the court of appeals to examine the evidence independently and to reverse Judge Rubin's factual findings directly.

Third, in this context, we argued that the S.O.S. board's unconstitutional rescission of a systemwide desegregation program and reimposition of systemwide segregation was an independent cause of the current segregation in the Dayton public schools. In January, 1972, such action amounted to a mandatory ordinance that segregated schools throughout the district as effectively as the old-time Southern segregation statutes. But for this unconstitutional act, the Dayton schools would be substantially desegregated pursuant to the Carle/Foster plan. The only suitable remedy was to order "all-out desegregation."

We called this our rescission argument. Its weakness rested with its contingent aspect: unless the historic context were understood as showing a pervasive violation, it would be difficult to demonstrate that the rescission itself had been motivated by segregative intent based on the truncated record on that issue permitted by Judge Rubin.

Finally, we challenged Judge Rubin's suggestion that the state defendants should be dismissed, particularly because he had expressly deferred consideration of their conduct for a later hearing. The brief summarized the existing proof of state responsibility:

• failure to enforce state nondiscrimination law

- refusal of the state board to meet its responsibility under state law to enforce *Brown* by refusing to withhold state funds, accreditation, and school charters from any local school district engaged in segregation
- default in the face of the state board's own affirmative findings in 1970 and 1971 of unconstitutional segregation by the Dayton board

We argued that Rubin's attempt to dismiss the state defendants was a symbol of Rubin's erratic supervision of the entire case. We asked the court of appeals to direct Judge Rubin to keep the state defendants as parties and to hear the case against them.

School board attorney Greer countered by arguing that the district court's novel doctrine of a "cumulative constitutional violation" based on racial imbalance, optional zones, and a recent rescission could not withstand scrutiny. Racial imbalance standing alone was not unconstitutional. The optional zones were at most happenstance administrative devices whose segregative effects, if any, were of a short-term nature, affected relatively few students, and had long since been dissipated by changing residential patterns. The recent rescission was only unconstitutional if the board had a preexisting constitutional duty to desegregate; as the only duty under the trial judge's own findings related to isolated optional zones of no real segregative consequence, no violation inhered in the rescission. In sum, Greer argued, the Dayton board had long operated a racially neutral system premised on the nonracial implementation of the "neighborhood school concept"; any isolated instances of discrimination predating *Brown* had long since been abandoned voluntarily by the board. Judge Rubin, said Greer, may have been well meaning, but there was *no* call for judicial intervention. Even under the most expansive reading of the case law, the board's plan eliminating optional zones represented the outer limits of any court-ordered remedy, as held by Judge Rubin.

The strength of Greer's argument rested with the trial court's unequivocal finding that school segregation mirrored residential segregation in Dayton. As Rubin had foreclosed consideration of evidence showing the causes of housing segregation and its interaction over time with school segregation, Greer was free to argue that school authorities acted constitutionally any time they did no more than incorporate residential segregation. But this strength was also a weakness: if the appeals court concluded that the Dayton board had ever operated a dual system of schooling, Greer could point to no evidence demonstrating the current school segregation was not affected by such pervasive discrimination in the past.

Chief Judge Phillips, the author of the Detroit decision and concurring member of the *Deal* panel, presided over the Sixth Circuit panel hearing the case. He was joined by Judge Peck, the trial judge in *Deal* and concurring member of the Detroit panel, and Judge Miller, the author of the Grand

Rapids decision. While the panel was pondering its decision in the spring and then summer of 1974, the Supreme Court issued its long-awaited decision in the Detroit case. Although the high court reversed the metropolitan remedy, it affirmed the Detroit-only findings of violation. As the evidence of intentional segregation within Dayton based on the acts of the local board was probably more intensive and surely of longer history than in Detroit, the Detroit decision might help us. Judge Rubin's findings, however, presented a mixed bag, closer to the findings of no pupil assignment violation in Grand Rapids than the findings of systemic segregation in Detroit. We could not guess how the Sixth Circuit would measure Rubin's factual determinations against the evidence.

Also, the Supreme Court's restrictions on remedy and obvious concern with causation might provide some support for Greer's argument if the Sixth Circuit accepted Rubin's findings. How Chief Judge Phillips would react to the Supreme Court's narrow reversal of his opinion in the Detroit case was a final concern. In all events, the Sixth Circuit's pending decision in the Dayton case represented an immediate test for Nate Jones's strategy of pushing within-district cases following the Detroit decision. If Jones could not win in Dayton before an appeals court that he had invested four years converting, the old de facto perception would likely prevail over the awakening judicial awareness of the underlying de jure reality of urban school segregation.

On August 20, 1974, the Sixth Circuit issued its ruling. The opinion, authored by Chief Judge Phillips, went off more like a cap pistol than a cannon. Although it traced in more detail than the trial court the pre-*Brown* history of discrimination, it did not assess the legal significance of this evidence in any considered way beyond a single reference to "other alleged constitutional violations . . . which purportedly maintained and expanded the basically dual school system inherited at the time of *Brown*." In the subsequent portion of the opinion on remedy, the panel adopted an "affirmative duty" legal standard, "once plaintiffs have shown that state-imposed segregation existed at the time of *Brown* (or any point thereafter)." Even so, the court did not expressly apply this standard to evaluate whether the Dayton board had dismantled or perpetuated the dual system following *Brown*. Whether the Sixth Circuit had ruled on our *Brown* argument remained unclear because the panel noted that the board did not challenge "the historical determination."

The opinion also discussed at some length the evidence that staff assignments, school construction, middle school reorganization, and pupil transfers either perpetuated any preexisting violation or amounted to independent violations. For example, Phillips noted that "prior to 1952–53 . . . the Dayton Board assigned [faculty] pursuant to an explicit segregation policy. In 1951–52, the Board introduced a new policy ostensibly to integrate the faculties, but which effectively continued in practice the racial assignment of faculty through the 1970–71 school year.'' The opinion did not, however, evaluate the interconnection between the segregative school construction and the racial assignment of faculty at the opening of new schools and additions. Nor did the appeals court assess the impact of any of these ''other alleged constitutional violations'' on continuing or dismantling ''the basically dual system inherited at the time of *Brown*.'' Instead, the Sixth Circuit concluded that plaintiffs ''have raised serious questions with respect to whether the District Judge's failure to include these . . . school practices within the cumulative violation was supported by substantial evidence.'' The court of appeals refused to determine whether to affirm, reverse, or supplement Rubin's findings and thereby left our de jure argument in limbo.

As to our rescission argument, the panel refused to examine the racial context, motivation, and independent segregative impact of the S.O.S. board's recent reimposition of segregation. Instead, the chief judge talked of the rescission in the vague terms of ''cumulative constitutional violation'': was rescission an independent constitutional violation in the absence of a preexisting duty to desegregate or only part of a ''cumulative violation''? Having raised the issue, the court refused to give an answer.

The court of appeals compounded the uncertainty by redefining, without expressly reversing, the trial court's findings concerning ''racial imbalance'' and ''optional zones.'' ''Racial imbalance'' was almost complete separation of pupils into one-race schools from 1951 through trial; ''optional zones'' were classic segregation devices that in the short term allowed whites to escape from blacker to whiter schools and in the long term promoted instability, racial transition, and further segregation.

The ruling affirmed only Judge Rubin's findings of ''racial imbalance,'' ''optional zones,'' and ''rescission'' as ''cumulatively in violation of [plaintiffs'] rights guaranteed by the Equal Protection Clause,'' while failing to assess the legal implications of our *Brown*, de jure, and rescission arguments. Nevertheless, the panel held that ''the remedy ordered by the District Court is inadequate, considering the scope of the cumulative violations.'' Without describing the extent of the violation, the panel remanded the case to Judge Rubin to formulate a plan, ''consistent with the remedial guidelines outlined'' in the Denver and *Swann* cases, that would eliminate ''all vestiges of state-imposed segregation.'' As a result, the appropriate scope of remedy remained as unclear as the nature and extent of the violation. The only straightforward direction was the last: After detailing the state involvement in Dayton's school segregation, the Sixth Circuit directed Judge Rubin ''to keep the State defendants as parties to the action.''

Neither plaintiffs nor the board could be jubilant over the ruling because no one could gauge its meaning. The appellate court told the district judge to do more; but there was no statement of why or how much. Only further hearings before Judge Rubin and subsequent appeals could clarify the result.

Further Proceedings in the Lower Courts

Following a number of conferences between the attorneys and the trial judge, Judge Rubin on January 7, 1975, ordered the parties to prepare and submit new plans by February for his review. Although advising that "no known desegregation device should be overlooked," Rubin said that the "coercive solution [of busing] is the least satisfactory. The Court will consider transportation of students only as a last resort and only after careful inquiry has established that no other solution exists." Rubin referred to "the tragic events of the past three months in the city of Boston," the racial violence accompanying school desegregation there, similar in kind but sustained for a longer time and spread over a much wider area than was the violence in 1958 at Central High School in Little Rock, Arkansas. Local segregation politics and express presidential opposition to "forced busing" had fueled the violent reaction to breach of the color line in Boston. Rubin's opinion, however, seemed to suggest that "busing" was the *source* of the problem.

Such thinking diverted attention from the hard reality: if Dayton schools were unconstitutionally segregated, most "black schools" and most "white schools" could be integrated only by the enrollment of students, through voluntary choice or more traditional board assignment, beyond normal "walk-in" distance. It would be a cruel joke to assign the pupils on such an integrated basis without providing the busing necessary to make attendance at school convenient as required by Ohio law. It would be a crueler hoax to suggest that such assignments and such busing might not be necessary to integrate the schools. The real issue, then, was whether the extensive segregation of schools in Dayton violated the Constitution.

The Dayton board proposed a series of part-time "magnet programs" and "learning centers" to attract some students from their segregated home schools for a portion of the school day or school year. Plaintiffs submitted a systemwide plan of desegregation providing for the pairing and clustering of schools to eliminate the pattern of one-race schools. Following three days of perfunctory hearings in February, 1975, Judge Rubin issued another supplemental ruling on remedy. With minor modification, Rubin approved the board's plan for fall 1975 implementation and rejected the plaintiffs' plan based on his reading of the latest congressional antibusing statute, "The Equal Education Opportunities Act of 1974." This was a strained reading because even President Ford had expressed his reservations about the effectiveness of its antibusing provisions: By the statute's own terms, its prohibitions on assignments beyond the next nearest school were only advisory and were not intended to restrict the authority of the courts to enforce the Fourteenth Amendment.

Rubin did require the board to prepare an alternative plan of undefined scope and content to become effective in September, 1976, if the board's voluntary, part-time programs failed to achieve their projected results. Judge Rubin conceded that "it is entirely possible the [board's] proposed program will not attract . . . black and white students and might instead further segregate the Dayton school system." Rubin defended this delay:

> To postpone yet again the ultimate determination of this matter may appear to plaintiffs to be a further delay of their rights. . . .While this [case] is hardly a model of speed and dispatch, it is consistent with the magnitude of the problem that must be solved.

Rubin characterized delay in the final resolution as following a "rule of moderation." He counseled "patience" in the effort "to become a people without any motivation borne of our differing racial beginnings."

Judge Rubin continued to express confusion over use of the term "dual school system." In the Denver case the Supreme Court had applied the phrase to any district, North or South, in which the racial separation of students throughout the district was intended by school authorities *or* resulted from continuing effects of official racial discrimination. This notion escaped Judge Rubin's analysis:

> The State of Ohio does not now, nor has it since 1887 mandated a dual system of public education. To the contrary, 84 Ohio Law 34, dated February 22, 1887, specifically required a unitary public school system. . . . The defendant School Board of the City of Dayton had engaged in activities which were segregative in effect and which did impinge upon the Constitutional rights of students. . . . At no time, however, did defendant maintain a dual system of education. . . . Overt evidences of such segregative activities have been eliminated both by action of the Board of Education and by previous Order of this Court but the effect thereof may not.

The March 10, 1975, ruling did nothing to clarify the nature of the violation. What relief would finally be considered adequate to remedy the violation also remained in doubt.

Plaintiffs appealed to the Sixth Circuit for a summary reversal. We felt constrained to attack Judge Rubin directly: Whether confused or recalcitrant, he was an obstacle to any hope for actual desegregation. For example, Rubin's views on the applicability of the antibusing statute were directly contradicted by the express language of the legislation and its debates. The "Equal Education Opportunities Act of 1974" was not "intended to modify or diminish" the court's power to order remedies "to enforce fully the . . . fourteenth amendment." Rubin's understanding of the phrase "dual school system" was also plainly wrong. We therefore asked the appellate court to reverse with specific directions as to the scope and timing of the remedy: We requested systemwide desegregation, now.

Wary that the "three-part cumulative violation" as ill-defined by Judge Rubin and the court of appeals might not support systemwide relief, we argued in our brief that the prior appeal established four pervasive aspects of the continuing violation:

- Overt acts of segregation created, in the Sixth Circuit's words, a "basically dual system . . . at the time of *Brown*" that imposed on the Dayton board an equally "affirmative duty . . . to eliminate all vestiges of state-imposed segregation."
- The resulting pattern of one-race schooling continued without any break through the time of trial; the Dayton board did not even purport to meet its affirmative duty because, except for the rescinded 1971 resolution, it neither recognized nor acted upon such obligation.
- Instead, some fifteen optional zones had racial implications over time, directly caused racial separation among some twenty-five schools, and precipitated further segregation of even broader scope; and the Dunbar blacks-only high school long operated as a citywide dual overlapping zone causing the segregation of all high schools.
- In the context of this failure to dismantle a continuing dual system, exacerbated by the substantial additional discrimination of many optional zones and a citywide overlapping high school zone with wideranging and long-enduring consequences, the board in December, 1971, "was acting in a manner consistent with its [constitutional] duties" in adopting a program of systemwide desegregation; and the S.O.S. board's rescission of that program and reimposition of the prior segregated assignments intentionally resegregated the entire system.

In sum, we asked the Sixth Circuit to articulate, in a fashion not inconsistent with its prior ruling, a reasonable basis for ordering systemwide relief and to state in no uncertain terms that the nature of the violation was systemwide, de jure segregation. In our brief, we also urged that the court finally decide the constitutionality of the other post-*Brown* practices that had been discussed but not ruled upon in the panel's previous opinion. At the oral argument, however, I stressed the need for clear remedy instructions and detailed a step-by-step procedure to secure systemwide desegregation. Judge Peck finally interrupted my monologue: "Mr. Dimond we appreciate your suggestions on how and when we should order system-wide desegregation. But our basic issue is still whether to order such desegregation at all." School board attorney Greer seized on this opening to argue that Rubin had been generous to plaintiffs in ordering a remedy that exceeded the limited findings and proof of violation, i.e., optional zones minimally affecting segregation at three high schools.

On June 24, 1975, the panel of Phillips, Peck, and Miller issued its ruling. The court again found the plan approved by Judge Rubin inadequate: "[T]he basic pattern of one-race schools will continue largely unabated. . . . The District Court's plan fails to eliminate the continuing effects of past segregation." Noting that summary reversal would be appropriate "except for the time factor," the Sixth Circuit instead directed that the lower court "adopt a *system-wide* plan for the 1976–77 school year that will conform to the previous mandate of this Court and to the decisions of the Supreme Court" in *Swann* and the Denver case. The panel pointedly added, "We direct that this plan be adopted not later than December 31, 1975 so that it may be placed in effect at the beginning of the new school year in September 1976."

The board had won a reprieve from actual desegregation for another year; but the time for remedy had finally been fixed, along with its systemwide scope. What remained unclear in the opinion of the court of appeals was the extent of the violation. Although noting "segregative acts . . . both before and after the decision of the Supreme Court in *Brown*," the ruling did not reverse, supplement, explain, or otherwise disturb the limited and ambiguous "cumulative violation" finding previously affirmed. Although holding that the "Dayton school system has been and is guilty of de jure segregation practices," the panel failed to reach the reserved issues or to explain in any way the extent to which this "cumulative violation" caused or contributed to the current condition of segregation. The Sixth Circuit still avoided reversing or otherwise supplementing Judge Rubin's ambiguous and limited findings of violation.

Plaintiffs now had a mandate for systemwide desegregation beginning by September, 1976, but we had failed to get the court of appeals to explain its decision. Perhaps in our briefs and arguments we had stressed the timing and scope of remedy too much. In any event, the appeals court failed to evaluate the nature and extent of the violation. As a result, Greer had a target for review by a Supreme Court that was growing increasingly wary of school desegregation in the midst of the continuing antibusing clamor in Congress. Only a few Southern politicians, either weary of the debate or satisfied with the grudging acceptance of actual desegregation in their home schools, joined with senators like Mansfield (D., Montana), Scott (R., Pennsylvania), Hart (D., Michigan), Kennedy (D., Massachusetts), and Brooke (R., Massachusetts) to prevent the Congress from engaging in a direct confrontation with the Court. The Congress did impose further restrictions on the already beleaguered HEW compliance program by adopting antibusing amendments proposed by Senators Byrd (D., West Virginia), Eagleton (D., Missouri), and Biden (D., Delaware) that validated *all* assignments to the *nearest* school for purposes of Title VI of the 1964 Civil Rights Act.

Greer, in his petition to the Supreme Court for review of the case, stressed that the Sixth Circuit failed to tailor the remedy to any identified discrimination. There was no warrant to direct systemwide desegregation to remedy some limited "cumulative violation" that had a current impact on at most a handful of schools and a few students. On December 2, 1975, however, the Supreme Court declined to review the case.

Judge Rubin appointed Charles Glatt as an expert to assist in the development of a plan. Glatt had previously worked on the plan approved in the *Swann* case, assisted the Ohio state board in documenting the Dayton board's segregation actions and desegregation alternatives in 1970–71, and worked with Wayne Carle and Phyllis Greer in preparing for desegregation of the Dayton public schools. He immediately began to develop a new plan in the old federal courthouse in Dayton. But a racial extremist, who had recently showered random rifle fire at blacks on the streets of Dayton, killed Charles Glatt in the midst of his work in Judge Rubin's chambers. This was the low ebb of Phyllis Blackburn Greer's commitment to the seemingly interminable judicial struggle to desegregate Dayton's public schools. The gains achieved in what would become an eight-year round of appeals, hearings, and rulings lost whatever meaning the passage of time had not already obscured. For the next two days, Charles Glatt's widow stayed with Phyllis Greer, but there was no consolation. Even if the killer was only an aberration, the shooting made Mrs. Greer question why so many good people had to die while the color line endured. Judge Rubin responded by keeping a handgun close at hand and by ordering the General Services Administration to finish his office suite in the new federal building ahead of schedule with armored doors, closed circuit TV monitoring, and intruder alarms.

On November 5, 1975, Judge Rubin appointed John Finger, the chief architect of the plan approved in *Swann*, as an expert for the court and directed the parties to submit systemwide plans. Following two days of evidentiary hearings on two plans submitted by the parties and a third submitted by friends of Dr. Glatt, Judge Rubin appointed Dr. Finger as a master to work with the board to develop a systemwide plan. Rubin's order gave priority to walk-in desegregation and sought to minimize the time and distance of transportation so long as the result would be schools substantially proportionate in their racial composition to the districtwide racial ratio. Because of Dayton's relatively compact nature and the efficiency of its thoroughfares, witnesses for all sides agreed that such complete desegregation could be accomplished without "long-haul transportation." Nevertheless, Judge Rubin allowed for exceptions to the desegregation requirement to avoid any bus ride exceeding twenty minutes.

On March 15, Finger submitted his comprehensive plan developed in conjunction with the Dayton school administrators. Dr. Finger estimated that "the longest travel time should not much exceed twenty minutes." The Dayton board proposed several minor modifications and a three-year phase-in at the elementary level. Denying this latest gambit for delay, Judge Rubin in his final order of March 23, 1976, otherwise gave the board the discretion to implement Finger's plan or the proposed modifications. The district court invited the board to submit additional modifications and granted five more upon request of the local school authorities. The Dayton board asked Judge Rubin to stay implementation of September, 1976, desegregation to permit time for an appeal. But Carl Rubin was no obstructionist: he denied the request in order to enforce the Sixth Circuit's mandate.

School board attorney Greer immediately appealed to the Sixth Circuit to preserve what he perceived as a "very limited hope for review by the Supreme Court." He also applied for a stay of implementation pending disposition of the appeal. The court of appeals denied the stay but ordered expedited briefing and oral argument. Greer again argued that the "nature" of a comprehensive, systemwide remedy exceeded the limited "scope of the violation"; he added an attack on what he called the "racial balance" aspect of the plan.

We responded by reiterating the four parts of the continuing violation that we wanted the court of appeals to articulate as the basis for its previous judgment. We also argued that the nature and extent of this four-part violation was intentional, continuing, and systemwide. The appropriate remedy for such violation was that of systemwide desegregation under the decisions of *Swann* and the Denver case. In response to Greer's claim of a fixed racial balance, we pointed to the flexibility provided by Judge Rubin in formulating the decree. In addition, we noted, the board had failed to offer any proof to meet its burden under *Swann* to show why any school or student should not be included in the final plan.

Greer, however, was aided somewhat by an opinion from the Supreme Court in the Pasadena school case. Following a 1970 trial court finding of intentional school segregation in the United States government's second foray into nonstatutory school segregation, the Pasadena board implemented a desegregation plan in September, 1970, pursuant to a court order prohibiting any school from continuing "with a majority of minority [race] students." Four years later the Pasadena board sought to modify the plan, but the district judge denied the request and stated in a fit of pique that his 1970 order "meant to me that at least during my lifetime there would be no majority of any minority [race] students in any school in Pasadena.'' The Supreme Court in an opinion by Justice Rehnquist rejected the district judge's apparent perpetual ''racial balance'' requirement.

Recognizing that the violation findings justified the systemwide remedy imposed in 1970, Rehnquist noted that even the parties to the initial decree had never read it to mandate a fixed racial limit over the years nor annual adjustments in assignments to account for demographic shifts unrelated to the original or any continuing violation. The Supreme Court remanded to the court of appeals for further proceedings, as ''it may well be that [the Pasadena board has] not yet totally achieved a unitary system.''

The Pasadena ruling, however, also provided support to us: it recognized the propriety of the systemwide remedy initially ordered in Pasadena, including a strict racial limit that was considerably less flexible than the broad range and potential modifications provided by Judge Rubin's proceedings and decree. If anything, Rehnquist's opinion seemed to indicate that school boards could not cry ''forbidden racial balance'' when an initial systemwide plan used almost any kind of percentage racial range as a guideline for remedying a systemwide violation.

We again invited the panel to decide all reserved issued concerning the nature and extent of all alleged segregation practices in order to protect the systemwide desegregation from any conceivable challenge in the Supreme Court. At the oral argument, both Lucas and I stressed the nature and extent of the violation and requested the appeals court to clarify and to supplement its earlier rulings, including its decision on the various violation issues ''reserved'' in its first opinion.

On June 7, 1976, the Supreme Court, in an opinion by Justice White, over the dissents of Justices Brennan and Marshall, ruled that the equal protection clause, as applied to the United States by the due process clause of the Fifth Amendment, does not prohibit a law or official act ''*solely* because it has a racially discriminatory impact.'' The case involved a challenge to alleged racial discrimination against blacks in employment tests by the District of Columbia police department. The case was tried and argued upon the theory that the ''disproportionate impact'' standard for evaluating whether employment tests violated the antidiscrimination provisions of the 1964 Civil Rights Act also applied to actions brought under the 1866, 1871, and 1875 civil rights and jurisdiction acts to enforce constitutional rights. Almost no attention had been paid to possible constitutional issues or the legislative history and reach of the enforcement acts of the First Reconstruction.

Nevertheless, the Supreme Court not only held that the 1964 act standard was inapplicable to constitutional cases but also proceeded, without so holding, as if the earlier Reconstruction Acts did not inform the meaning of the

Fourteenth Amendment. The Court held that, under the equal protection clause, the "invidious quality of a law claimed to be racially discriminatory must ultimately be traced to a racially discriminatory purpose." Although Justice White went on to note that disproportionate impact is relevant evidence and may support an inference of intent, the Court's opinion failed to consider the legality of "neutral" or "blind" incorporation of community discrimination, official perpetuation of prior discrimination, or public failure to afford protection to minorities against the continuing effects of customary discrimination.

As a result, White's opinion did not stand as a beacon illuminating the meaning of the equal protection clause and other Reconstruction legislation. But, as a signal to practicing lawyers trying to win cases and to stretch the judicial perception of the de jure reality, White's opinion was significant: prove the intent of the public officials by as much and as diverse circumstantial, direct, objective, and subjective evidence as possible; prove a pattern of overwhelming segregative effects and show that racial considerations or a context of community discrimination contributed to the official decisions; try to encourage lower courts to avoid loose or ambiguous findings concerning "cumulative violations." Subjective malevolence by the defendants and judicial name-calling might not be required, but exhortations to do "right" would not be supported by gentle findings that failed to affix blame. No wonder Jones, Lucas, and I hoped that the Sixth Circuit would expand upon its prior opinions in the Dayton case in some meaningful fashion.

On July 26, 1976, the panel (with Judge Lively of Kentucky replacing the late Judge Miller) issued a short opinion affirming the systemwide plan. The opinion offered no further explanation of the nature and extent of the "cumulative violation" and did not reach the reserved issues. The panel distinguished the Pasadena case by noting that the Dayton plan was an initial remedy and did not contemplate any fixed racial balance over time or annual readjustments in pupil assignments.

Greer asked the Sixth Circuit for a stay pending disposition of his petition for Supreme Court review. The panel denied the request on August 16. The next day Greer, arguing that a systemwide remedy far exceeded the limited violation found by Judge Rubin, filed his request for stay with Potter Stewart, the Supreme Court justice with authority over the Sixth Circuit. We responded the following day by explaining the extensive nature of the continuing violation arguably upheld by the court of appeals and the other evidence of additional violations which showed systemwide intentional segregation. On August 19, 1976, Justice Stewart denied the stay.

School opened peacefully in the fall of 1976 on a desegregated basis, four years and many struggles after originally scheduled by Wayne Carle and the old board majority. Yet the feeling was not one of triumph. Wayne Carle had already been released by the S.O.S. board. Phyllis Blackburn Greer and John Harewood feared that the new regime cared more about complying with the letter of the law than using desegregation as a creative process to raise the expectations and to join the hands of all schoolchildren. For Miley Williamson, Richard Austin, and the local NAACP branch, school desegregation represented a beginning, not an end. But the S.O.S. board and its new superintendent, who developed and implemented the plan without disruption, did not appreciate the historic break it could mark in all aspects of the color line or the spur it might provide to challenge other racial inequities. And Charles Glatt had been murdered.

For Nate Jones, the rolling of the buses represented a substantial but disconcertingly hollow achievement. The court of appeals rulings only proved that the Sixth Circuit might eventually reverse a district judge without even saying so. The opinions failed to provide a reasoned explanation of the law or facts that might help others to stretch their perceptions to understand the underlying de jure reality of urban segregation.

At least the protracted legal struggle over Dayton-only violation seemed at an end with actual desegregation. That should have been some relief. Dave Greer was filing motions against the state defendants to assist in paying for the desegregation, while we were preparing applications for the award of fees and expenses as the ''prevailing party'' against the Dayton board, pursuant to the statutory authorization from Congress in such cases. These money disputes had to be resolved before considering whether and how metropolitan issues should be joined and if Dave Greer and the Dayton board could be enlisted in the effort. Greer seemed resigned; he had fought a tough but losing fight. Although he filed a petition for review by the Supreme Court, Greer conceded that it would now ''take a miracle'' even to get a hearing in the Supreme Court.

Chapter 8
The Supreme Court Sounds Retreat,
December, 1976, to June, 1977

Bad Omens

By the end of November, 1976, I was becoming concerned. Judge Rubin had scheduled a hearing on the board's motion against the state for financial assistance and asked that plaintiffs present their fee application at the same time. The date for the hearing approached, however, without the expected denial of review by the Supreme Court. I suggested to Dave Greer that we postpone the hearing, even if it was unlikely that the high court would overturn a desegregation plan already in operation and thereby resegregate the schools. I felt it might be presumptuous to seek payment for a legal victory while the Dayton board's petition to review the entire case was still pending in the Supreme Court.

On December 6, 1976, the Supreme Court vacated Judge Wisdom's ruling for the Fifth Circuit which had found unconstitutional school segregation against Hispanic Americans and ordered systemwide, triethnic desegregation in Austin, Texas. Although Judge Wisdom's opinion sought to blur the distinction between de jure and de facto standards, the evidence and findings included many examples of classic segregation devices. Without briefs or arguments from the parties, the Court remanded the case, over the dissents of Justices Brennan and Marshall, to the Fifth Circuit for reconsideration in light of the "intent" requirements recently established by the Court in the case involving alleged employment discrimination by the District of Columbia police. Such a summary disposition was troubling. At best, it was a less than subtle command to Judge Wisdom not to extend the verbal net of de jure or intentional segregation beyond the limits developed by the Supreme Court. At worst, it meant that a majority of the Supreme Court was girding for a retreat from decisions such as *Swann* and the Denver case.

A separate opinion filed by Justice Powell (joined by Chief Justice Burger and Justice Rehnquist) was even more troubling. It made clear that these three Nixon appointees had set aside their conceptual differences to advance housing "imbalance" as an excuse for virtually all school segregation:

As is true in most of our larger cities with substantial minority populations, Austin has residential areas in which certain racial and ethnic groups predominate. Residential segregation creates significant problems for school officials who seek to achieve a nonsegregated school district. . . . The principal cause of racial and ethnic imbalance in urban public schools across the country—North and South—is the imbalance in residential patterns. Such residential patterns are typically beyond the control of school authorities. For example, discrimination in housing—whether public or private—cannot be attributed to school authorities. Economic pressures and voluntary preferences are the primary determinants of residential patterns. . . . The tendency of citizens of common national or ethnic origins to form homogeneous residential patterns in our cities is a familiar demographic characteristic of this country.

Powell added a theory of causation that could lead to a wholesale retreat: "I merely emphasize the limitation repeatedly expressed by this Court that the extent of an equitable remedy is determined by and may not properly exceed the effect of the constitutional violation. Thus, large-scale busing is permissible only where the evidence supports a finding that the extent of integration sought to be achieved by busing would have existed had the school authorities fulfilled their constitutional obligations in the past."

Powell's view, of course, did not present a uniformly accepted view of reality. In many cases, trial judges had found that the evidence demonstrated (*a*) a two-way causal interrelationship between school and housing segregation over time and (*b*) racial discrimination as a primary cause of segregation. Powell nevertheless posited that racial segregation in America was just a "natural ethnic phenomenon" by which blacks chose to segregate themselves. He argued that school authorities were free to incorporate such voluntary, self-imposed, residential school segregation in neighborhood schools. This "ethnic diversity" and "cultural pluralism" rhetoric had become fashionable among neoconservatives and even some black intellectual pundits. It was the bedrock of President Nixon's program of continued racial ghettoization under the "benign neglect" banner as articulated by Pat Buchanan's memo, "The Ship of Integration is Sinking."

In adopting this new "ethnic diversity" banner, Powell dropped any aura of dispassionate compromise that might have accompanied his curious dissent in the Denver case calling for a right to "integrated schools" but providing segregated neighborhood schools as the only remedy. Powell now said that, presumptively, most school segregation was de facto; as a consequence, little school desegregation and less busing would ever be required. Powell switched from all violation and no remedy in Denver to little violation and almost no remedy in Austin. He gave every appearance of searching for five votes on the Supreme Court to end busing.

The Sixth Circuit's opinion affirming an ambiguous three-part "cumulative violation" provided a perfect launching pad for the limiting principles announced by Powell, Burger, and Rehnquist in their separate opinion in the Austin case. The violation "findings" in Dayton could be reduced, under one plausible reading, to two optional zones affecting three high schools—hardly a sufficient predicate to support systemwide desegregation. On January 17, 1977, the Supreme Court granted the board's petition to review the Dayton school case. There would be no final resolution of plaintiffs' case for years to come. Greer had his miracle.

The Briefs

Nate Jones's first problem was to prepare a brief. Earlier in the term, the Court had accepted the Detroit school case for review a second time on two critical questions: the propriety of relief ancillary to actual pupil desegregation (e.g., in-service training, nondiscriminatory testing and counseling, remedial reading) designed to begin to overcome the continuing harm of unconstitutional segregation and to smooth the transition to desegregated schooling; and the authority of federal courts to order such relief (including paying the substantial dollar tab) against unconsenting states.

At least, these were the two issues Jones chose to brief and argue in the Supreme Court. In the district court, the new trial judge, Robert DeMascio, had sought to desegregate only the white schools and to exclude from any reassignment plan the black schools in the inner core of Detroit that had been the primary target and result of the intentional segregation found by Judge Roth. On the novel theory that the "adversarial phase" of the litigation was over, DeMascio then excluded plaintiffs' counsel from further "judicial proceedings" involving "negotiations" with the Detroit board concerning the scope of the supplemental relief finally ordered.* On appeal, however, the Sixth Circuit overturned exclusion of the core of black schools from consideration for desegregation, while affirming the ancillary relief and the order that the state share in paying for the substantial costs of implementing remedy. Although Jones feared that Judge DeMascio ordered the ancillary relief as a substitute for (rather than as a supplement to) actual desegregation, the Sixth Circuit's judgment eliminated that question.

The fundamental issue in the Supreme Court case involved the growing doctrinal dispute between Justices Rehnquist and Brennan over the meaning of "our federalism": To what extent can the courts and the Congress provide meaningful relief under the enumerated federal powers (particularly those of the Fourteenth Amendment) against states? What are the appropriate guidelines for federal courts providing equitable relief against state and local offi-

---

*DeMascio also stayed consideration of plaintiffs' amended complaint seeking interdistrict relief until final resolution of a dispute over costs.

cials? What are a state's rights and immunities under the Tenth and Eleventh Amendments against such federal intervention? Even Rehnquist had retreated somewhat from a restrictive view of federal power and expansive view of states' rights, at least in cases where federal courts sought to enforce personal rights guaranteed by Congress against invasion by state officials. Where the balance would come to rest on these critical institutional issues, however, remained in doubt. Rehnquist, even while beginning to concede federal power in some circumstances, still seemed intent on sharply limiting federal court intrusion on an inchoate theory of "equitable limitations" somehow "inherent in our federalism."

Jones had already asked me to draft the Detroit brief with the assistance of Bill Caldwell; he therefore asked Caldwell to take primary responsibility for drafting the Dayton brief, with my assistance and input from Lou Lucas. Jones determined to make the oral argument in Detroit (which would be split with George Roumell for the Detroit board) to support the propriety of ancillary relief and the power and authority of the federal courts to include state wrongdoers in Fourteenth Amendment equitable remedies. He also decided that Lucas should make the oral argument in Dayton to defend the systemwide desegregation plan already in operation against attack from the limiting view of causation and remedy trumpeted by Rehnquist in his dissent in the Denver case and by Powell, Burger, and Rehnquist in their separate opinion in the Austin case.

Our brief in the Detroit case attempted to show that under established case law, settled constitutional history, and Rehnquist's own decisions, the Detroit judgment should be affirmed. The Fourteenth Amendment would, for all practical purposes, be repealed if any state were granted immunity from providing prospective relief for its own violation of the Fourteenth Amendment. The brief was a surgical legal analysis. It summarized several additional arguments supporting Brennan's adoption of the radical Republican's hopes for the Reconstruction amendments and enforcement acts; consideration of these points could be avoided by the Supreme Court only if it adopted our main thesis. These additional arguments continued our effort in a series of cases to challenge Rehnquist's attempts to rework "our federalism" to suit his personal vision of appropriate intergovernmental relations.

In contrast, the Dayton brief had to turn, again and again, to the underlying facts of the case and the record evidence of official discrimination if we were to prevail. Given the mood and drift of the Court and the express goal of at least three of its members, it would have been folly to make a technical defense of the propriety of ordering systemwide relief based on a narrow reading of the lower court opinions. "Racial imbalance," "optional zones," and "recent rescission" may amount to a constitutional violation of some sort, but the extent of their segregative impact was not clear and had never been determined by the courts below. In the seventh year of Nate Jones's litigation program to "stretch the *de facto* perception to fit the *de jure* reality," the lower court opinions presented the Supreme Court with the opportunity to do exactly the opposite. Our best hope was to convince the Court that the record evidence showed a long-standing and continuing pattern of pervasive, intentional segregation. Our problem was that the Supreme Court sits to review the law, not to evaluate masses of evidence.

Our legal argument therefore had two prongs. First, under *Brown I* and *II*, we contended that the Dayton board never fulfilled its affirmative duty to dismantle its historic dual system until it was ordered by the courts below to implement the systemwide desegregation plan in the fall of 1976. Alternatively, under the decision in the Denver case, we argued, the Dayton board failed to rebut the post-*Brown* proof of intentional segregation which affected a much more substantial portion of the district and its operations than did the segregation in Denver's Park Hill section. The Dayton board, therefore, was properly ordered to implement a plan of "all-out desegregation."

Neither prong of the legal argument had been explicitly adopted by the Sixth Circuit. Under Supreme Court rules, however, we were entitled to argue any grounds in support of the judgment below. Each factual and legal point of our argument could be found and was directly supported somewhere in the Sixth Circuit's opinions. We were more concerned, however, about defending the record evidence of intentional segregation than defending the opinions of the Sixth Circuit. The critical factor was that each factual point stood virtually *undisputed* in the record: only the legal significance of the undisputed facts needed to be resolved by the high court.* As we noted in the brief:

> There are interstices in the decisions and orders entered below. But we find it considerably easier to fill in these gaps than do [the defendants]. The *settled* portions of the record bring the remedy flush with the constitutional violation and make constitutionally unassailable the determination below that plaintiffs are entitled to system-wide relief from the extensive *de jure* segregation of the Dayton Public Schools.

---

*In an appendix to the brief, we also summarized the evidence relating to the issues on which decision had been "reserved" by the court of appeals—school construction, grade structure reorganization, and pupil transfers and transportation. We noted that the Court need not reach these issues if it agreed with either our *Brown* or Denver arguments; but if it disagreed with both, then the Court must either reach these "reserved issues" itself or remand to the court of appeals for initial review. (We included "staff assignment" in our main argument because the court of appeals' "reservation of decision" on this issue related to whether faculty remained segregated after HEW intervention, *not* whether staff assignments were made on a racially discriminatory basis prior thereto.)

The United States, speaking through a brief authored by the new attorney general Griffin Bell and the new assistant attorney general Drew Days, among others, supported our view of the undisputed record evidence and the controlling legal principles. For the first time since the Johnson administration, the government actively supported plaintiffs in a school desegregation case. President Carter, with his election campaign praise for "ethnic purity" and "neighborhood cohesiveness," and Attorney General Bell, with his Fifth Circuit opinions in support of "equi-distant zoning" and in opposition to busing, hardly seemed likely supporters for our case. Carter had, however, defused the antibusing campaigns of George Wallace and Scoop Jackson in the Florida primary; and he personally supported integrated education and said that he would enforce court orders and oppose antibusing constitutional amendments despite his preference for "free choice."

Attorney General Bell made more than a symbolic gesture in appointing Drew Days to head the Civil Rights Division and Sixth Circuit judge Wade McCree solicitor general. Days had long served as head of the Legal Defense Fund's highly successful Florida school desegregation effort before becoming a law school professor. Days was joined in drafting the government's brief by Joel Selig, a "lawyer's lawyer" who independently reviewed the entire record with his eagle eye for puffery and discrimination; Selig had previously worked at the Lawyer's Committee for Civil Rights under Law with Flannery, Caldwell, and me, but had specialized in cases of employment discrimination. McCree withdrew from participating in the case because of his previous service on the Sixth Circuit; but Judge McCree's leadership in the judicial awakening to the de jure reality of Northern school segregation in the Pontiac and Detroit cases was well known to Griffin Bell and the solicitor's staff who worked on the brief.

The government's brief supported systemwide desegregation on the basis of the *evidence* of wide-ranging intentional segregation:

> This case presents as clear an example of pervasive discrimination prior to *Brown* as the Court is likely to find in a State in which discrimination was not required by statute. . . . Only one conclusion is possible: in 1954 the Dayton School Board operated two school systems; one primarily for whites and another primarily for blacks. The district court should have made such a finding. . . . [The evidence of record] establishes pervasive racial discrimination with persistent effects.

Dave Greer's brief for the Dayton board pulled no punches:

- It accused plaintiffs of three times unsuccessfully begging the court of appeals to reverse Judge Rubin's unambiguous findings of (a) racial neutrality in the operation of a lawful neighborhood school concept with respect to school construction, attendance zones, transfers, grade structure, and reorganization, (*b*) complete faculty integration prior to the time of trial, and (*c*) school racial imbalance consistent with (and hence, resulting solely from) residential separation.

- It argued that the lower court violation findings of racial imbalance, optional zones, and rescission did not include any discussion of segregative intent and that the Sixth Circuit leaped from at best limited and ambiguous findings to systemwide relief without analysis of their causal impact on the school segregation existing at time of trial.
- It put the "cumulative violation" findings through a verbal ringer and a close microscope to show that "racial imbalance" and "rescission" were not constitutional violations and that the lower court findings on optional zones concerned at most two zones affecting three high schools at the time of trial.
- It argued that the Sixth Circuit was intent on achieving "racial balance" and should be sternly rebuked.
- It noted that the optional zones had been eliminated by the Dayton board in 1973 pursuant to the district court's order and prayed that the Supreme Court reverse the court of appeals and remand the case to the district court for dismissal.

As Caldwell and I prepared Jones and Lucas for the oral arguments in Detroit and Dayton, we feared that the Supreme Court's first Detroit decision marked the beginning of the end of the struggle to bring meaningful desegregation to almost totally segregated northern schools. Yet actual, court-ordered desegregation was already in place, albeit with mixed results, in cities such as Kalamazoo, Lansing, Denver, Boston, Pasadena, and several other northern school districts, and hundreds of school districts throughout the South had long since completely desegregated in relative peace. Nevertheless, "white flight" to private schools and all-white school districts remained a serious threat even to some of the ostensibly desegregated districts. While the political cry for antibusing constitutional amendments seemed to abate with the hope that the Supreme Court would put the brakes on busing, each HEW initiative to force discriminating school districts to desegregate seemed to be met by an appropriation bill rider either hamstringing administrative enforcement or seeking to limit the 1964 Civil Rights Act. We feared that the Court would offer "ancillary relief" as a substitute for desegregation in Detroit while gutting the meaning of *Brown,* at least for northern districts, in Dayton.

The Oral Arguments

On March 22, 1977, the Court heard the arguments in the second round of the Detroit case. Once again Frank Kelley, Michigan's attorney general, spoke for the state. Several justices peppered him with the suggestion that *Brown* held that de jure segregation injured the black children and resulted in "inherently unequal education." They asked whether courts, on appropriate findings, could attempt to overcome such harm. Kelley responded that if the only violation found concerned pupil assignment, then the *only* remedy was pupil reassignment. But this narrow scope-of-violation/scope-of-remedy tautology that prevailed the first time around in the Detroit case was not in favor with the Court on this day. Nevertheless, it was apparent as Frank Kelley concluded his presentation that the only real issue in the case was whether the ancillary relief ordered redressed some effect of the violation, because the attorney general had no answer to our argument that the courts had the *power* to order the state to contribute to a suitable remedy if the state participated in the violation. In fairness to Frank Kelley, there was no principled answer under "our federalism."

George Roumell utilized his time on behalf of the Detroit board to fit the ancillary relief ordered to the effects of the "invidious segregation" violation found by the lower courts. With every question, Roumell, in his own emotional style, made his points forcefully through a spray of words. Nevertheless, the causal link between intentional segregation and lower reading and communication skills was based on broad and untested assumptions at best. Roumell sought to avoid this issue. He noted the potential racial problems in newly desegregated classes in which children have markedly different communication skills along racial lines; the reading component of the ancillary relief was designed not only to help black children to become literate but was also *necessary* to permit actual desegregation within the classroom without resegregation based on tracking. Chief Justice Burger groped for a way to defend such ancillary relief by asking Roumell:

> What would you have to say if there were a finding by the District Court that the language [earlier characterized by the chief justice as "ghetto speech"] of these Negro students was below par . . . and the further finding that it was necessary to engage in these remedial components in order to balance that out?

Roumell responded emphatically: "Five words, Your Honor. 'It was the finding.' " It did not matter that George miscounted; he did not misspeak.*

Jones started his argument on behalf of plaintiffs by noting that the city-only and metropolitan *desegregation* issues remained to be finally decided

---

*It also did not seem to matter to the chief justice that there would be relatively few classes in the Detroit school district where blacks and whites attended school together under the trial court's "desegregation" plan reserving three entire inner-core regions for blacks only.

below on the remand from the court of appeals. The Court seemed uninterested. As his argument progressed, Jones rejected the suggestions of some justices that educational components might either be "novel" or the *primary* remedy in some segregation cases. He argued that such programs had become the common but "ancillary assistance to . . . the basic remedy of pupil desegregation." Jones was then pressed on why he supported educational components at all. The NAACP's general counsel responded:

> The plaintiffs . . . insist upon, in the first instance, the desegregation of schools. [But we also] insist that some agency of the State address these secondary problems that are a part of bringing about the creation of a unitary system. In fact, we learn as we grow, and one of the lessons that has been learned through 23 years of litigation and efforts to desegregate schools [since *Brown*] is that there are certain problems in connection with creating a unitary system that have to be faced.

On April 26, 1977, the Court heard the arguments in the Dayton case. Justice Marshall's chair was vacant, indicating that he would not participate in the case. Greer opened his argument for the Dayton board with all the assurance of a ten-to-one favorite. He painted the picture of a Dayton board that may have engaged in isolated discriminatory practices in the distant past but had since operated an essentially race-neutral neighborhood system to serve all the children of Dayton, as the district judge had found. Greer spoke candidly, but without any petty asides, about the error of the Sixth Circuit in ordering "racial balance" to remedy the isolated and long since dissipated impact of optional zones affecting three high schools. With the air of a fellow club member sharing an inside joke, he joined some justices' questioning on how such a violation could be called "cumulative if there's only one" violation. He focused on the "neighborhood school" policy of the Dayton board at the time of trial: any racial imbalance was not the constitutional responsibility of the Dayton board but "merely reflected the changing racial composition of the neighborhoods." When any member of the Court began to ask Greer a question about whether some portion of the record evidence undercut this version of the facts, Greer advised the Court not to engage in its own "rewriting of the findings" as requested by the plaintiffs and the government, lest the appellate courts be set up as special "fact finding commissions in every school desegregation case that is filed." Greer expressed his "hope" that the Court "accept the facts as found by the trier of facts and adjust the remedy, rather than accepting the remedy and adjusting the findings of fact."

As Lucas approached the podium, he would have been better served by a flak vest and a foxhole than notes and a lectern. Only his native instinct for survival saved him from a debacle. Lucas tried to make the *Brown* argument by summarizing the facts from the beginning. Justices Stewart and Powell would have none of it. They expressed interest only in any overt acts of segregation that existed at the time of trial. Each time Lucas tried to respond by suggesting that the segregative effects of the violation of dual schooling in the 1950s continued largely unabated through the time of trial, Stewart became increasingly hostile. Stewart, joined by Powell, finally suggested that it was lawful for a board openly to segregate prior to *Brown* and thereafter lawful to segregate by devices such as optional zones, at least "until free choice" was "thrown out" in *Green* in 1968.

It was as if Lucas were arguing in 1967 before Paul Weick in the Sixth Circuit and his apology for segregation. Dogged as usual, Lucas kept trying to recite the litany of segregation devices by tracing their segregative roots through to the growth of a dual system. But Stewart and Powell were only interested in whether any current practices, viewed in isolation from each other and the prior history of the school district, amounted to overt segregation.

Lucas moved on to other subjects only when it became clear that arguing about the violation was not getting anywhere. He took on the straw man of "racial balance" by noting that any percentage guideline between 1 percent and 99 percent would be challenged by school board lawyers, while the school administrators went begging for *some* benchmark for developing an effective and lawful plan. Lucas then made an agile and, in its own way, dispositive move as his time ran out. In his best Southern accent, he spoke of the effective operation of the desegregation plan already in place: "What we have here is not racial balance. We have typical desegregation, and it's working in Dayton. There are no headlines. I think the school board has done a good job in trying to make it work, and there are an awful lot of people in that community with a commitment to making it work." The implication was clear: there was no equitable reason for dismantling this desegregation pending further judicial review of the plaintiff claims for pre- and post-*Brown* discrimination that had yet to be determined by the court of appeals.

Greer's rebuttal was brief and to the point. He asked for dismissal of the case. The implication of this plea was also clear: it was an open invitation to the Court to allow the Dayton board to resegregate its schools.

The Opinions

On June 27, 1977, the Court issued its decisions in both the Detroit and Dayton cases. In this second round of the Detroit case, the Court unanimously affirmed the Sixth Circuit in an opinion authored by the chief justice. With respect to the propriety of ancillary relief, the Court rejected the state's claim that since the constitutional violation found by the district court was the unlawful segregation of students on the basis of race, the court's decree must be limited to remedying unlawful pupil assignments. ''The well-settled principle that the nature and scope of the remedy are to be determined by the violation means simply that federal-court decrees must directly address and relate to the constitutional violation itself.'' Turning to the facts of the Detroit case, he continued:

> [W]here, as here, a constitutional violation has been found, the remedy does not ''exceed'' the violation if the remedy is tailored to cure the ''*condition* that offends the Constitution.''
>
> The ''condition'' offending the Constitution is Detroit's *de jure* segregated school system, which was so pervasively and persistently segregated that the District Court found that the need for the education components flowed directly from constitutional violations by both state and local officials.

This still left the causal link between intentional segregation and educational deprivation. Burger brushed this issue aside: ''In a word, discriminatory student assignment policies can themselves manifest and breed other inequalities built into a dual system founded on racial discrimination. Federal courts need not, and cannot, close their eyes to inequalities, shown by the record, which flow from a longstanding segregated system.'' The chief justice added, ''pupil assignment alone does not automatically remedy the impact of previous, unlawful educational isolation; the consequences linger and can be dealt with only by independent measures.''

Burger then applied this reasoning to the ''communication skills'' component of the ancillary relief ordered: ''speech habits acquired in a segregated system do not vanish simply by moving the child to a desegregated school. The root condition shown by this record must be treated directly by special training, at the hands of teachers prepared for that task. This is what the district judge in the case drew from the record before him as to the consequences of Detroit's *de jure* system.'' This stirring rhetoric from the chief justice sounded out of character. Burger's focus on ''speech habits'' provided a possible insight into his meaning. Perhaps it was a reflection of his own concern about understanding ''ghetto speech,'' rather than the result of an analysis of how intentionally segregated schooling itself may contribute to communication difficulties.

Burger's paean to the breadth and flexibility of equitable authority in the second Detroit decision did not square with the cramped view provided in his first opinion in the Detroit case. Perhaps Burger's unstated hope was that ''ancillary relief'' would eventually replace desegregation as the primary ''remedy'' for unconstitutional segregation. Indeed, the chief justice went out of his way to praise Judge DeMascio's limited pupil assignment plan. Although this plan had omitted the inner core of all-black schools, already had been vacated by the Sixth Circuit and remanded to the district court for further consideration, and was not at issue in the Supreme Court, Burger wrote,

> the order does not punish anyone, nor does it impair or jeopardize the education system in Detroit. . . . Indeed, the District Judge took great pains to devise a workable plan with a minimum of transportation. For example, he sought carefully to eliminate burdensome transportation of Negro children to predominantly Negro schools and to prevent the disruption, by massive pupil reassignment, of racially mixed schools in stable neighborhoods which had successfully undergone residential and education change.

That the facts belied such charitable characterizations and had never been presented nor argued to the Supreme Court apparently did not concern "the chief."

The Court also summarily rejected the state's claim of immunity under the Tenth and Eleventh Amendments and "our federalism" from paying for the "ancillary relief." With respect to the Eleventh Amendment, the "compensatory" program "operates prospectively to bring about the delayed benefits of a unitary school system." As a result, decisions interpreting the Eleventh Amendment as immunizing the states from "retroactive" money damages for past misconduct were inapplicable. The Court similarly held that Michigan's defenses under the Tenth Amendment and general principles of federalism had "no merit." The Tenth Amendment's "reservation of nondelegated powers to the State is not implicated by a federal court judgment enforcing the express prohibitions of unlawful state conduct enacted by the Fourteenth Amendment." Burger added that an order requiring the state to provide funds to pay for relief "does not jeopardize the integrity of the structure or functions of local government." The local school district would still be responsible for administering any "educational" relief.

Whatever the motivating factors, the Court's unanimous affirmance of the authority of federal courts to enforce the Fourteenth Amendment against unconsenting states and its unanimous rejection of the state's distorted view of "our federalism" was a welcome and important victory. The Second Reconstruction had survived "General Kelley's" attack in the second round of the Detroit school case. Perhaps equally important, the Court's opinion seemed to recognize that the nature-of-violation/scope-of-remedy conundrum need not be read woodenly to provide band-aid relief for institutional cancers.

That was, however, small consolation given the Court's ruling in the Dayton case. There, the Court spoke in a different tongue and with a different purpose. With pupil assignments at issue, the Court, in an opinion by Justice Rehnquist, chose to view restrictively any lower court support for complete relief and to avoid all review of the record evidence showing pervasive discrimination. Although noting the authority of federal courts to grant system-wide desegregation relief when the requisite "constitutional violations on the part of school officials are proved," the rest of the Court's opinion continued in a different vein:

> But our cases have just as firmly recognized that local autonomy of school districts is a vital national tradition. It is for this reason that the case for displacement of the local school authorities by a federal court in a school desegregation case must be satisfactorily established by factual proof and justified by a reasoned statement of legal principles.

The Court read Judge Rubin's limited and ambiguous subsidiary violations findings as Dave Greer wanted: two optional zones affecting the racial composition of three high schools. The opinion then rebuked the Sixth Circuit:

> [T]he Court of Appeals simply had no warrant in our cases for imposing the system-wide remedy which it apparently did. There had been no showing that such a remedy was necessary to "eliminate all vestiges of the state-imposed school segregation." It is clear from the findings of the District Court that Dayton is a racially mixed community, and that many of its schools are either predominantly white or predominantly black. This fact without more, of course, does not offend the Constitution. The Court of Appeals seems to have viewed the present structure of the Dayton school system as a sort "fruit of the poisonous tree," since some of the racial imbalance that presently obtains may have resulted in some part from . . . instances of segregative action found by the District Court. But instead of tailoring a remedy commensurate to the . . . specific violations, the Court of Appeals imposed a system-wide remedy going beyond their scope.

"In effect," Rehnquist said, the "Sixth Circuit imposed a remedy which is entirely out of proportion to the constitutional violations found by the District Court."

There was, however, one ray of hope for us in the recitation of errors in the Sixth Circuit. Rehnquist chastised the court of appeals for merely "discussing" and "describing" possible constitutional violations rather than "upset[ting] the findings of the District Court, revers[ing] the District Court's conclusions of law, . . . [or] engag[ing] in fact finding of its own based on [the record] evidence." Although the Supreme Court was not inviting the courts of appeals to become "special fact finding commissions," it was reminding them to perform their reviewing function with care, depth, and precision, including the making of supplemental findings where necessary.

The Supreme Court also expressly noted plaintiffs' right to a ruling of all their claims of unconstitutional conduct:

> [T]he last word has [not] been spoken as to the correctness of the District Court's findings as to unconstitutionally segregative actions on the part of the [school board]. . . . [Plaintiffs] are entitled under our precedents to urge any grounds which could lend support to the [Sixth Circuit's system-wide remedy] judgment below, and we think that their contentions of unconstitutionally segregative actions, in addition to those found by the District Court, fall into this category.

Justice Rehnquist and the Court rejected Greer's suggestion that the case be dismissed. Rather than rule on the outstanding contentions or remand to the court of appeals to decide the "reserved questions," however, the Supreme Court "remanded to the District Court for the making of more specific findings and, if necessary, the taking of additional evidence." Having barely survived Supreme Court review, Rehnquist sent us back to further trials before Judge Rubin. This was an ill omen: whereas the first hearing had been a trial of Judge Rubin, the remand hearing from the Supreme Court was sure to be a trial of plaintiffs and their attorneys, particularly Lou Lucas. The district judge would have the opportunity to make detailed findings and a reasoned statement, and finally to dismiss the case and subdue the previously indomitable will of Lucas that had stood in the way for so long.

Rehnquist added some advice to guide the proceedings on remand. The lower courts should

> first determine whether there was any action in the conduct of the business of the school board which was intended to, and did in fact, discriminate against minority pupils, teachers, or staff. . . . If such violations are found, the District Court in the first instance, subject to review by the Court of Appeals, must determine how much *incremental segregative effect* these violations had on the racial distribution of the Dayton School population as presently constituted, when that distribution is compared to what it would have been in the absence of such constitutional violations.

Justice Rehnquist concluded, "The remedy must be designed to redress [only] that difference."

Our worst fears about Powell's separate opinion in the Austin case could be read into this advice concerning "incremental segregative effect." Many, including all school board attorneys intent on defending school segregation, would argue that the phrase limited any violation and remedy to the minor extent to which current school segregation *exceeded* current residential segregation. Although the Court's opinion did not say as much, it certainly might mean as much to many lower courts, and to the next school case decided by the Supreme Court. If "incremental segregative effect" meant that the Court had determined that the nature of any school violation related only to those isolated acts of school authorities intensifying segregation in a few residentially mixed areas, then the end of Nate Jones's legal challenge to the color line of urban school segregation was near.

By proceeding in measured steps toward this result, however, Justice Rehnquist's opinion avoided any direct ruling on such substantive issues. The opinion could therefore be read as applying only to limited findings of isolated instances of misconduct, without reaching a case with findings and evidence of pervasive school authority intent to segregate schools in order to implement a community custom of racial ghettoization. The opinion even cited the Denver case for the proposition that there "may be a system-wide remedy . . . if [the violation] has a system-wide impact."

Two days later, the Court summarily enforced "the incremental segregative effect" instruction by vacating systemwide school desegregation rulings from Milwaukee and Omaha over the dissents of Justices Brennan, Marshall, and Stevens. The message seemed all too clear: Nate Jones's valiant attempt to stretch the de facto perception to fit the de jure reality was faltering in the high court at the feet of Richard Nixon's appointees. Every other school board lawyer and politician bent on defending "racial imbalance" would relish the prospect of joining in the defeat of the NAACP's initiative against northern school segregation. Others would then act to rekindle the antibusing furor of the late 1960s and early 1970s in the South, which had died down once school desegregation had actually been implemented or finally avoided.

In the Dayton case, the Supreme Court had put up a yellow caution light, if not a stop sign, for busing to desegregate schools. The Court was pointing the way to a new, constitutional standard: the color line in schools could be explained and excused by the color line in housing. The early suggestion by Lucas that the Dayton school district could "not be a little bit pregnant with discrimination without delivering an actual desegregation baby" had been squarely rejected by the Court.

There was some consolation for plaintiffs. Justice Rehnquist directed that the plan of actual desegregation remain in effect pending the further proceedings in the trial court. The court had not totally rejected Lucas's argument. The last word had yet to be heard on the nature of the constitutional wrong demonstrated by the evidence and the appropriate scope of remedy. Actual desegregation would continue in Dayton pending a final decision in the case.

In addition, Justice Brennan concurred in the judgment of the Court vacating the Sixth Circuit's ruling and remanding for further consideration. He suggested a different scenario for the remand proceedings. Systemwide desegregation might yet prove right in Dayton if plaintiffs showed either that racial discrimination still infected a meaningful portion of the district or that a historic system of dual schooling had never been dismantled. Justice Brennan, at least, was girding for further battles in the Supreme Court. In order to keep the legal challenge to urban school segregation alive, he attempted to rationalize the broad reading of equitable authority in the second round of the Detroit case with the narrow view provided in the first Dayton decision: "the courts, of course, need not, and cannot, close their eyes to inequalities which flow from a long-standing segregated system."

Although Nate Jones, his co-counsel, the NAACP, Dayton's local branch, and the black community had to nurse substantial wounds, they were not yet defeated. As long as the likes of John Harewood could keep faith, from the midst of the depression and racism in the 1930s through the many setbacks before Judge Rubin and Justice Rehnquist's rulings for the Supreme Court, then 1977 was not the time to give up on Harewood's vision of full freedom from the caste discrimination he had witnessed in racial segregation in Dayton, Ohio.

IV
Standing and Waiting: The Floundering of the Legal Challenges to Housing Segregation in the 1970s

Chapter 9
Open Housing, Closed Court, 1970–79

The Policy Failures in Housing

Nate Jones described the legal and political situation after the Supreme Court's ruling in the Dayton case in the summer of 1977: "We're in the trenches just fighting to survive. At issue is whether we can even keep the Second Reconstruction alive." Jones and the school segregation cases were not alone in that trench. Program initiatives and legal challenges seeking to breach the color line in housing were under almost as severe attack. The challenges to school and housing segregation shared a common goal: to raise an issue that the majority would just as soon ignore, whether a caste system of racial ghettoization divided metropolitan America.

For a time, it appeared that the Nixon administration might confront the issue in the context of federal housing programs. In 1969 the secretary of housing and urban development, George Romney, announced an "open communities" policy. It promised minorities real access to housing and the expanding job opportunities in the suburbs and exurbs from which they had been historically excluded. In March of 1970, President Nixon announced his support of this policy while promoting "neighborhood schools" and opposing "forced busing." Equal housing access could then serve as a program to show that the administration did not favor segregation, but just opposed busing. In this context, Nixon promised "free choice," including both "the *right* to choose, . . . and the *ability* to choose. The right to move out of a mid-city slum . . . means little without the means of doing so."

Romney then sought to use HUD funding and programs as a lever to end racial exclusion from white residential areas such as Warren, Michigan. In April, Nixon backed this rhetoric in his second annual report of national housing goals by conceding that racial discrimination was a motivating factor in white suburban opposition to subsidized housing. The president urged that "all Americans, regardless of race or economic status, are entitled to share" in the abundant land available in the burgeoning suburbs for residential use.

But when whites expressed their hostility to association with blacks in the same neighborhoods (and hence in the same schools), Nixon directed Romney to scrap the open communities policy. In December of 1970 President Nixon announced at a televised news conference: "I believe that forced integration of the suburbs is not in the national interest." He adopted as his new "basic principle" that no municipality should have federally assisted housing "imposed from Washington by bureaucratic fiat." Although he encouraged "voluntary" local efforts, he refused to withhold federal housing assistance and community development funds from all-white local jurisdictions that intended to remain that way.

Nixon conceded that this political response amounted to an abdication of federal responsibility for segregation in his next annual report on national housing goals:

> Residential separation of racial minorities was, and is, another characteristic of the social environment which has been influenced by federal housing policy. [For example,] until 1949, FHA officially sanctioned and perpetuated community patterns of residential separation based on race by refusing to insure mortgages in neighborhoods not racially homogenous. The effects of this policy have persisted for many years after its reversal and are still evident in metropolitan areas today.

While the president proclaimed HUD programs should be used to expand housing opportunities for all Americans, federally subsidized "scattered site" housing programs continued on a dual basis—white families "sited" in identifiably white areas, black families in black areas. Nixon then imposed a moratorium on all federally subsidized housing on January 7, 1973. Shortly thereafter, he announced that the urban crisis was over.

Nevertheless, Romney continued to stump the country in vain for metropolitan solutions to the problems of the "real city," the central city and its surrounding urbanized area. HUD's own administrative rules also continued to use actual "housing market areas" coincident with entire metropolitan regions as the proper measure for considering "project selection criteria," including "minority housing opportunities." HUD's areawide, open housing criteria existed only on paper, however, not in the policy and practices of the administration.

Congress responded to Nixon's default in housing by consolidating all federal housing and community development programs and funding under a "block grant" or "special revenue sharing" approach. As one of its goals, the Housing and Community Development Act of 1974 spoke boldly of two-way integration of housing on both sides of the color line. The act promised to reduce the "isolation" of poor persons through the "spatial deconcentration of housing opportunities" and to revitalize "deteriorating or deteriorated neighborhoods to attract persons of higher income." To implement such "specific objectives," the act provided that each local jurisdiction applying for HUD funding must submit a "housing assistance plan." Each plan must accurately assess "the . . . needs of lower income families . . . *residing in or expected to reside* in the community" and indicate "the general locations of proposed housing for lower-income persons" in order to promote "*greater choice* of housing opportunities and *avoid undue concentrations* of assisted persons in areas containing a high proportion of low-income persons." With its anti–race discrimination clause, the act promised that federal housing and community development funds would finally be used to overcome rather than to finance racial and economic ghettoization.

The 1974 act provided important tools to further fair housing goals of the 1968 Civil Rights Act. If read and implemented in a coordinated fashion, the act would require all-white suburban jurisdictions receiving federal housing and community development funds to provide housing for many of the low-income minorities, currently trapped in ghetto cores and isolated suburban pockets, who might reasonably be "expected to reside" in suburban communities near expanding job opportunities. At the same time, central cities would have to provide for integrated community developments to attract higher-income whites to urban amenities closer to the core city financial and corporate centers. The Nixon and Ford administrations, however, failed to implement HUD funding and programs in such a coordinated fashion. Instead, they allowed the separate applications of myriad local jurisdictions and housing authorities to subvert any "real city" linkages between individual housing project proposals, separate housing assistance plans, and actual areawide housing needs.

The 1974 act did not require local jurisdictions to cooperate with public and private developers in the construction and marketing of subsidized housing and integrated developments. Instead the act gave HUD the authority to "bypass" unwilling local jurisdictions so long as developers owned land and had the requisite local zoning and code approval. But HUD rarely invoked its bypass power, and local jurisdictions still retained the power to manipulate their land use authority to exclude developers of low-income and integrated housing.

The Ford administration continued the Nixon policy of refusing to use the fund cutoff threat or to file suits as a lever to open housing in whites-only areas to minorities. HUD often failed even to review the adequacy of the housing assistance plans of suburban and central city jurisdictions to determine whether they complied with HUD's own metropolitan "housing market area," "spatial deconcentration," and "neighborhood revitalization" criteria. In the first two years after the 1974 act, federal housing and community development assistance simply continued along the color line. These federal funds, in the main, financed segregated housing and communities rather than "majority-to-minority" moves by black families to white neighborhoods and white families to otherwise black or mixed neighborhoods.

Exclusionary Zoning, Exclusionary Court

The NAACP and many other groups, national and local, shared the broad two-way integration objectives of the 1968 Fair Housing Act and 1974 Housing and Community Development Act. They looked to the courts when the

Nixon and Ford administrations refused even to begin to implement these goals. The suit filed by Nate Jones on behalf of the NAACP to open housing and to expand job opportunities to black citizens in Oyster Bay, Long Island, was one among many brought by private parties seeking to open white suburban enclaves. The town of Penfield, immediately adjacent to Rochester, New York, was the object of another such lawsuit.

Metro-act, a nonprofit corporation formed to expand housing opportunities for minorities in the wake of Rochester's race riot in the mid-1960s, joined with two associations of home builders, poor white and minority persons, and Rochester taxpayers to challenge Penfield's exclusionary zoning ordinance. Penfield's zoning allocated 98 percent of the town's vacant land to single-family detached housing and imposed stiff lot size, set back, density, floor area, and other requirements. The scheme allocated only 0.3 percent of the land available for residential construction to multifamily structures; and low density, floor size, and other requirements limited any multifamily construction to expensive townhouses and apartments. Penfield also denied approvals and variances to individual members of the two building associations seeking to build housing open to low- and moderate-income and minority persons.

In their complaint, filed in January, 1972, the various plaintiffs charged that the purpose and effect of Penfield's zoning policies and practices "was to preclude low and moderate-income people and non-whites from living in Penfield." In addition, several minority-race plaintiffs, black and Hispanic citizens, alleged that "as a result" of Penfield's exclusionary practices they were unable, despite persistent efforts, to find housing in the town and were thus relegated to inferior housing, schools, and services, and restricted job opportunities in the inner city. One plaintiff charged that in Penfield "a black person has *no* choice of housing." Another alleged that he was first forced by such exclusion to live more than forty miles from his job in Penfield and then incurred such substantial commuting costs that he could no longer keep his job there. In sum, the nonwhite plaintiffs argued that the exclusionary zoning intentionally and effectively reserved the entire town of Penfield for whites-only occupancy and thereby herded them into minority ghettos. But they also charged that their inability to afford existing housing in Penfield was another factor in the exclusion.

The members of one of the builders' associations had constructed over 80 percent of Penfield's single family homes and over 90 percent of its private multifamily units during the preceding fifteen years. This association alleged that the town's exclusionary practices prevented its members from proceeding with planned low- and moderate-income projects and thereby caused lost profits. The association also charged that Penfield officials threatened to retaliate against its members for getting involved in the suit. One member of the other housing council actively sought Penfield's consent to construct specific low- and middle-income housing units open to persons such as the poor and minority race plaintiffs. The town refused to grant the necessary zoning approvals. Sixteen other members of this council were engaged in building subsidized housing open to minorities in the Rochester metropolitan area and stood ready to build such units in Penfield if the town would open up.

Finally, Rochester taxpayers alleged that they had to pay higher real estate taxes because Penfield's total exclusion forced Rochester to assume more than its fair share of tax-abated housing projects to meet the needs of poor persons in the metropolitan area. The taxpayer and low-income claims in the complaint made the case look as much about economics, poverty, and taxes as about race. But the complaint did include specific claims of official racial exclusion more readily cognizable in federal court under the anti-discrimination provisions and jurisdiction of the Reconstruction amendments, the Civil Rights Acts of 1866 and 1871, and the 1968 Fair Housing Act.

The trial court and the Second Circuit Court of Appeals, however, dismissed the case without giving the plaintiffs a hearing. Plaintiffs were thereby excluded from the very federal courts which the Congress had given jurisdiction to hear such civil rights claims.

The Supreme Court agreed to review the issue of whether any of the plaintiffs had "standing" to challenge Penfield's exclusionary zoning in federal court. The issue turned in large measure on whether the justices would perceive the plaintiffs' challenge to Penfield's exclusionary zoning as based on poverty or race. In a series of cases the Court had previously decided that housing was not a "fundamental interest" protected under the Constitution and that suburban communities were not forbidden by the Fourteenth Amendment from engaging in a referendum to exclude low-rent public housing projects. If the challenge to Penfield's zoning were based on wealth rather than race, it seemed likely that a Supreme Court majority might find a way to prevent federal courts from hearing such cases.

At the oral argument several justices tried to make plaintiffs' counsel, Emmelyn Logan-Baldwin, concede that the case was really about poverty rather than race, about zoning to exclude the class of persons too poor to afford high-cost suburban housing rather than about zoning to exclude non-whites. Although her previous pleadings and briefs permitted such a reading, she now expressly rejected this suggestion. She argued that Penfield's zoning practices were designed and operated "so as to exclude racial minorities." Logan-Baldwin cited a 1970 study indicating "the primary motivation for the exclusion of [low- and moderate-income] housing is to exclude blacks." She also cited the town's manipulation of its zoning policy to thwart low-income housing open to minorities. Justice Powell was skeptical: "Are you on the racial point or the money point?" Logan-Baldwin answered:

What we are talking about here are affirmative acts of the Town of Penfield to exclude minorities. Now, we have to, of course, have our day in court on those allegations. . . . What we *are* saying here is that this is racially motivated, and it's the same as the Town hanging a sign outside of the Town Penfield that [says] "minorities are not wanted here."

James Hartman responded for Penfield. He argued that none of the plaintiffs had standing because *no* specific project or application for a zoning variance was now at issue. In these circumstances, Hartman argued, no one had a concrete interest sufficient to require any hearing on plaintiffs' broad-brush economic claims which, only coincidentally, affected low-income blacks.

Justice Powell, joined by Chief Justice Burger and Justices Stewart, Blackmun, and Rehnquist, concluded that the plaintiffs and Baldwin-Logan should have no opportunity to prove their allegations in a federal court. Powell touted novel "prudential rules of standing that, apart from [the Constitutional] minimum [case or controversy] requirements, serve to limit the role of courts in resolving public disputes." He argued that his new rule was "essentially [a] matter of judicial self-governance" designed to keep the federal courts from being bothered by cases in which plaintiffs assert a claim for which the courts are unable [or unwilling] to consider judicial relief.

As to the nonwhite claimants, Powell found that they asserted "standing as a person of low or moderate income and, *coincidentally,* as a member of a minority racial or ethnic group." He similarly argued that their substantive claims were based primarily on income, not race: Penfield's practices "have had the purpose and effect of excluding persons of low and moderate income, many of whom are members of racial or ethnic minority groups."

Powell nevertheless conceded "that such intentional exclusionary practices, if proved in a *proper* case, would be adjudged violative of the constitutional and statutory rights of the persons excluded." Under his new "prudential" rule, however, only those individuals wrongly excluded from a *particular* proposed construction project under active consideration by a suburban jurisdiction would have standing to challenge their exclusion in federal court. Justice Powell suggested in a footnote that this "particular project" requirement might not be an absolute precondition for standing because "a particularized personal interest may be shown in various ways, which we need not undertake to identify in the abstract. But usually the specific focus should be on a particular project." Powell concluded by suggesting that "citizens dissatisfied with provisions of [zoning] laws need not overlook the availability of the normal democratic process." That was about all his standing opinion left open to plaintiffs, even if they alleged they had already tried but had been excluded by the application of Penfield's "democratic process."

Powell, however, had more work to do to keep the named nonwhite plaintiffs out of court. Recognizing that Penfield had only recently rejected two specific low- or moderate-income projects, he had to analyze the family and income circumstances of each nonwhite plaintiff in order to suggest that none could have rented these units had they been built. While conceding that "the matter is left entirely obscure," Powell went on to explain that "there is no indication" that any of the nonwhite plaintiffs "had the resources necessary to acquire the housing available in the projects." Curiously, Powell found that several of the nonwhite families were arguably too poor to afford the rent of the proposed projects, while another was arguably too rich to qualify. With respect to a final nonwhite plaintiff, Powell simply ignored his circumstances entirely. Powell thereby deprived all individual plaintiffs of standing.*

With respect to the organizational plaintiffs, Justice Powell relied on another technicality. The 1968 Fair Housing Act broadly defined "persons" to include corporations and associations and specifically authorized federal courts to hear suits "to provide, within constitutional limitations, for fair housing throughout the United States" based on an aggrieved person's challenge to any attempt "to refuse . . . or otherwise make unavailable or deny, a dwelling to any person because of race, color, . . . or national origin." To avoid this clear command, Powell argued that the complaint cannot "fairly be read to make out any such [racial] claim" on behalf of the builder associations. Instead, Powell again read the complaint as alleging only income but not racial discrimination. This allowed Powell "to intimate no view as to whether, had the complaint alleged purposeful racial or ethnic discrimination," the plaintiff organizations would have stated a claim under the 1968 act. This left open the possibility that more precise pleading or less restrictive reading of future complaints might enable another organization or individual to challenge racially exclusionary zoning under the 1968 Fair Housing Act, as well as under the 1866 and 1871 Civil Rights Acts.

Powell's promulgation and selective application of the "prudential" standing test to exclude the plaintiffs from any hearing in federal court operated to confirm what President Nixon had already told the whites-only enclaves: "I believe that forced integration of the suburbs is not in the national interest." Whatever Powell's intent, the opinion signaled to lower court judges that housing suits either had to challenge rejection of a specific project on racial grounds or face dismissal. As would happen in many other cases, Nate Jones's challenge to Oyster Bay's almost complete exclusion of minor-

---

*Justice Brennan, in dissent, objected to Powell's nonconstitutional "prudential" test for standing and noted that under the town of Penfield's own reading, *each* of the nonwhite plaintiffs might well qualify for either of the two projects. At the very least, these individuals were entitled to the opportunity to prove that fact at a hearing.

ities from housing and nearby jobs fell victim to the "particular project" requirement.

Justice Douglas dissented: "With all due respect, I think that the Court reads the complaint and the record with antagonistic eyes. . . . Cases such as this one reflect festering sores in our society; and the American dream teaches that if one reaches high enough and persists, there is a forum where justice is dispensed. . . . I would let the case go to trial and have all the facts brought out."

Justice Brennan, joined by Justices White and Marshall, reached much the same conclusion in his dissent:

> The [majority] opinion . . . tosses out of court almost every conceivable kind of plaintiff who could be injured by the activity claimed to be unconstitutional. [This] can be explained only by an indefensible hostility to the claim on the merits. . . . [T]he Court turns the very success of the allegedly unconstitutional scheme into a barrier to a lawsuit seeking its invalidation. In effect, the Court tells the low-income, minority and building company plaintiffs they will not be permitted to prove what they have alleged—that they could and would build and live in the town if changes were made in the zoning ordinance and its application—because they have not succeeded in breaching, before the suit was filed, the very barriers which are the subject of the suit. Understandably, today's decision will be read as revealing hostility to breaking down even unconstitutional zoning barriers that frustrate the deep human yearning of low-income and minority groups for decent housing they can afford in decent surroundings.

Lincoln Green and Village White

The Leadership Council for Metropolitan Open Communities was the "blue ribbon" response of Chicago's civic leadership to a "summit agreement" signed in 1966 with Martin Luther King. The agreement represented a truce to end Reverend King's first foray against Northern segregation, a series of "open housing" marches and vigils against exclusively white communities and real estate firms in the Chicago area. The Leadership Council built a broad program to begin to give minorities some opportunity to secure housing throughout the greater Chicago area. The council trained lawyers and matched them with clients claiming racial discrimination in the sale, rental, or construction of housing, in order to enforce the 1968 Fair Housing Act; it brought suits on behalf of local communities and individuals against real estate companies for racial steering; and it challenged exclusionary zoning and the exclusion of black brokers from major real estate companies, associations, and multilists. To increase the supply of low- and moderate-income housing in Chicago's suburbs open to minorities, the Leadership Council met with suburban officials and developers, evaluated the local Housing Assistance Plans and applications to HUD for federal funding, and developed community guides and provided technical assistance explaining the operation of available low- and moderate-income subsidies and open housing programs. The council coordinated the efforts of eight other fair housing centers in the Chicago area committed to the goal of open housing for minorities.

The Leadership Council also worked closely with Home Investments Fund to make financing available for low- and moderate-income housing and to serve the functions of a housing authority under HUD programs when no local housing agency was willing or able to perform. Finally, another arm of the Leadership Council, the Metropolitan Housing Development Corporation (MHDC), was formed to build integrated low- and moderate-income housing in the suburbs. It constructed developments in South Elgin, Palatine, and Bloomington. Under the direction of Kale Williams, a longtime fair-housing advocate of the local American Friends Service Committee, the Leadership Council tried to work cooperatively and informally to resolve problems, to build community support for open housing, and to assist in the development of low- and moderate-income housing available to minorities on a non-discriminatory basis. Lawsuits were threatened and filed only when voluntary efforts failed.

With jobs and housing moving rapidly from downtown Chicago to its northwestern suburbs in the 1960s and 1970s, the Leadership Council and other open housing groups expressed concern that minorities were being effectively excluded from this growth. For example, the population of the four-township Cook County area to the northwest increased by 219,000 from 1960 to 1970, but only 170 of these persons were black. During the 1960s, the city of Chicago lost 230,000 jobs, while the four-township area gained 100,000. Despite massive redistribution of population in Chicago's Standard Metropolitan Statistical Area, residential segregation by race remained almost complete, 91.2 on the Taeuber Index in 1970, the same as in 1960.

Seminarians Organized for Racial Justice was particularly vocal in promoting integrated housing to open such white growth areas. It persuaded the Clerics of St. Viator to devote some of the vacant land on their eighty-acre site in the village of Arlington Heights for such development.

Arlington Heights seemed a perfect target for such an integrated housing project. In 1950 Arlington Heights housed 8,768 people; according to the 1970 census, the village had grown to 64,884 residents, 99.9 percent of whom were white. Only 137 of the 13,000 persons working in the village were black; and almost all of these few black workers had to commute from

Chicago. A Cook County survey showed that the village employers' main problem in hiring minorities was the lack of adequate housing open to non-whites within a reasonable distance of their plants, offices, and stores. The percentage of low-income families in Chicago was more than ten times as great as the figure for Arlington Heights; and the median family income in the village, $17,034, was 66 percent higher than in Chicago. The village's assessed value per capita was more than four times that of Chicago, while Chicago's per capita property tax payment was twice as great as that of the village. In sum, the village of Arlington Heights was growing dramatically on an all-white basis, had far greater resources and lower tax burdens, and excluded all blacks and most poor persons, while Chicago was losing white population and jobs and taxing itself much harder on considerably lower property wealth to serve its far greater proportion of low-income and black families.

The clerics agreed to lease and then sell a fifteen-acre portion of the Viatorian property to MHDC for the express purpose of building integrated, low- and moderate-income townhouses subsidized by HUD. The rest of the site included the Viatorian High School, a three-story novitiate building, a Montessori school, and vacant land. The Viatorian property was surrounded by single-family homes, zoned for single-family use. The agreement established a bargain price for the land in order to qualify for federal subsidies and was contingent on MHDC's securing federal assistance and a zoning variance from the village for multifamily dwelling.

MHDC engaged an architect to design a two-story cluster development with considerable open space, in keeping with the visual character of the nearby homes and the remainder of the Viatorian property. The plans called for 20 two-story townhouses with a total of 190 units, each with its own private entrance. One hundred units would have one bedroom, primarily intended to appeal to the elderly, and the other units would have two to four bedrooms, for families. The plan included extensive landscaping with trees and shrubs to screen the development from the single-family homes that abutted the site on one side. In view of the visual character of the property, MHDC dubbed the proposed development "Lincoln Green." MHDC secured assurances for the necessary federal subsidy and petitioned the village planning commission for rezoning. MHDC made clear that the proposed project would be integrated and worked closely with village planning staff to assure full compliance of the design with building, fire, and other code requirements, and aesthetic considerations. MHDC also contracted for a fiscal analysis, which showed that the project would provide more tax revenues per pupil than single-family housing.

During the spring of 1971, the village planning commission held three public hearings on the proposal. Large crowds attended and vocally demonstrated against the project based on the "social issue" involved, the "undesirability" of introducing integrated low- and moderate-income housing. Thousands of white residents filed petitions objecting to the intrusion of Lincoln Green; others wrote the local newspaper objecting to the project because "it is a ploy to export blacks from Chicago to integrate the suburbs." Other opponents charged that Lincoln Green would either lower property values for neighboring homes or conflict with the village's recently adopted policy to use multifamily dwellings primarily as a buffer between single-family housing and commercial or manufacturing districts. The planning commission recommended to the village board of trustees that the particular rezoning request for MHDC's proposed project be denied, while conceding that "the need for low and moderate income housing may exist in Arlington Heights or its environs." On September 28, 1971, the village board denied the rezoning for Lincoln Green on a six-to-one vote. The board president noted that "the objections of the residents [represent] a mandate to reject this proposal."

In June, 1972, MHDC joined with several black families, who claimed they would move to the project if built, to sue the village of Arlington Heights for its refusal to rezone the property. Plaintiffs claimed that the village's refusal perpetuated racial segregation in violation of 1866 and 1871 Civil Rights Acts, the 1968 Fair Housing Act, and the Fourteenth Amendment.* After discovery and pretrial skirmishing over plaintiffs' standing, the case was tried before district judge Thomas McMillen. The trial judge and the parties sparred over whether plaintiffs had to prove a racially discriminatory intent in order to prevail. MHDC repeatedly insisted that if the refusal to rezone had the discriminatory effect of perpetuating segregation in the Chicago metropolitan area by disproportionately excluding minorities from Arlington Heights, then the village had to justify its action by showing that it served compelling interests. MHDC also offered, however, to put on proof relevant to the subjective state of mind of the village board and planning commission if the trial court disagreed with its legal position. The village countered that the plaintiffs had to prove that the refusal to rezone was undertaken with a racially discriminatory motive, but that the subjective state of mind of individual officials was irrelevant and inadmissible.

At the hearing, plaintiffs offered evidence describing the background for the proposed development, the plan for Lincoln Green, and the proceedings before the village planning commission and board. MHDC also put on proof showing that the village granted some sixty zoning changes to commercial developers, fifteen of which might have violated the village's "comprehen-

---

*The complaint also claimed that the refusal denied MHDC's purported right to use its property in a reasonable manner, a claim doomed to failure under prior case law.

sive plan'' to use the apartment or multifamily zoning classification as a buffer between single-family and industrial or shopping districts. In addition, one of the individual plaintiffs testified that he worked at the Honeywell factory in Arlington Heights and would move with his family to Lincoln Green if it were built, rather than continue to commute from twenty miles away. Throughout the presentation, plaintiffs stressed their proposed ''effect'' standard for evaluating the legality of the rezoning refusal.

The village countered with evidence showing that all but four of the rezonings questioned by plaintiffs did not violate the buffer policy for the apartment classification and that several requests to rezone to the apartment classification had been rejected or withdrawn because of their failure to comply with the buffer policy. The village also showed that the Lincoln Green proposal could not technically serve as such a buffer because there was no adjacent industrial or shopping property, only a three-story dormitory and school which represented a preexisting nonconforming use about which the village could do nothing. The defendants presented testimony suggesting that the Lincoln Green development might lower property values of abutting property. The village also demonstrated that there was an 11 percent vacancy rate in the existing nonsubsidized apartments which could serve the housing needs of any financially independent minority family that wished to move into Arlington Heights.

Thus, the village argued, plaintiffs' case once again related to income, not race, and the refusal to rezone for Lincoln Green was based on the nonracial objective to protect property values and the buffer policy. When MHDC's counsel, Bill Caruso, tried to cross-examine the village board trustees to test whether race and not such purported nonracial factors motivated their votes, however, Judge McMillen prohibited all such questioning.

On February 24, 1974, Judge McMillen dismissed the case. His opinion showed the confusion over ''effect'' versus ''intent'' that plagued so many triers of fact at that time. After having excluded evidence of motivation, he found ''there is no direct evidence by which to determine the motives or mental processes of the trustees.'' He then continued, ''the crucial fact question, however, is whether the result of the defendant trustees' action caused racial discrimination. . . . [M]otives are irrelevant if the effect is illegal.'' Judge McMillen concluded that plaintiffs had shown only an economic impact, not a racial effect: ''[H]ousing for low-earners [of all races] is scarce in Arlington Heights.'' Judge McMillen did note that ''large groups of citizens of the village . . . strongly opposed'' Lincoln Green:

> *Their* motive may well be opposition to minority or low-income groups.
> [But] the weight of the evidence proves that the *defendant* [trustees and
> village] were *motivated* with respect to [the rezoning refusal] in question

by a *legitimate desire* to protect property values and the integrity of the zoning plan.

Yet McMillen had refused to allow the plaintiffs to question the defendants' motives.

On appeal in the Seventh Circuit, Caruso continued to argue that the effect of the village's refusal to rezone, without more, amounted to an exclusion based on race that violated the equal protection clause, unless Arlington Heights could justify the decision by showing that the construction of Lincoln Green would substantially impair compelling public interests. Caruso focused on whether the rejection of Lincoln Green adversely affected minorities, "since a [relatively] greater percentage of blacks than of whites are in the low and middle income categories that are eligible for the proposed . . . development." This tactic, however, tended to support Judge McMillen's finding that the basic issue in the case involved poverty rather than race, although the very purposes of MHDC, the Clerics of St. Viator, and Lincoln Green were to promote *integrated* housing, to open the almost exclusively white village of Arlington Heights to blacks, and to insure that racial minorities were not effectively excluded from employment opportunities available in the growing white suburbs.

On June 10, 1975, the Seventh Circuit court of appeals issued its decision. Circuit judge Swygert, writing for the majority, first affirmed the district judge's finding that the village's policy of using the apartment classification as a "buffer" between single-family and industrial business property had not been racially manipulated in this case. Although noting that the "buffer" policy was not followed by the village with "absolute consistency" and that "more detailed factual findings concerning the [various] zoning changes would have been helpful," Swygert ruled that the district court's finding that the trustees "were concerned with 'the integrity of the Village's zoning plan' [rather than race] is not clearly erroneous."

Judge Swygert accepted Caruso's factual argument that the rejection of Lincoln Green had a disproportionate effect on minorities because more blacks than whites would be eligible for this lower income housing project. But Swygert held that such "racial disparity *alone* as it relates to the housing project under consideration does not amount to racial discrimination."

Swygert then analyzed the refusal to rezone "not only in its immediate objective but its historical context and ultimate effect." Such an analysis might have included this exclusive white village's place in the racially segregated Chicago metropolitan area and might have asked how the historic color line had come about and how it would only be furthered by the rejection of Lincoln Green. The case had never been fully tried nor clearly argued on that basis. Judge Swygert, nevertheless, held that Arlington Heights "has been exploiting the problem [of segregated housing of the entire Chicago area] by allowing itself to become an almost one hundred percent white community." Judge Swygert continued:

> The rejection of Lincoln Green has the effect of perpetuating both this residential segregation and Arlington Heights' failure to accept any responsibility for helping to solve this problem. . . . Because the Village has so totally ignored its responsibilities in the past, . . . Arlington Heights' rejection of the Lincoln Green proposal has racially discriminatory effects.

Finding the suggested justifications of aesthetics and neighboring property values inadequate to defend the rejection of such a model two-story townhouse development, Judge Swygert ruled that the "refusal to grant the requested rezoning is a violation of equal protection clause of the fourteenth amendment."

The opinion never analyzed the meaning and application of the Fair Housing Act of 1968. Also omitted was any consideration of the legislative history of the Thirteenth and Fourteenth Amendments as enforced in the 1866 and 1871 Civil Rights Acts. Such judicial inquiry might have supported Swygert's argument that the village could not close its eyes to customary or private discrimination that contributed to the all-white character of Arlington Heights and made the proposal of Lincoln Green such an important symbolic challenge to the color line in the Chicago metropolitan area. Instead the opinion characterized the marked racial division throughout the area as a "problem of *de facto* segregated housing," a legal code for a constitutionally permissible condition.

In sum, Swygert's opinion left the impression that race played *no* part in the development of an all-white town of some sixty-five thousand white persons or in the rejection of the *only* proposal for integrated housing in this village. Judge Swygert, in Nate Jones's terminology, merely continued "the *de facto* perception" without coming to grips with the "*de jure* reality." That was a prescription for ultimate defeat. But the Seventh Circuit knew it was dealing with a de jure reality from its confrontation with the color line of housing in a series of cases from the Chicago area involving racial location of public housing, discrimination in the sale and rental of housing, and price exploitation of the dual housing market to gouge blacks. The case should have been remanded for a full hearing in this broader context to decide whether the all-white village's rejection of Lincoln Green perpetuated the pattern of official racial exclusion of blacks from whites-only communities.

In his dissent, Chief Judge Fairchild noted that sixty tracts already zoned for apartment use in the village were "still vacant and available to" MHDC:

"the record does not contain a sufficient showing by plaintiffs that it was not reasonably possible to construct the proposed project on one of these sites." If no one was at fault for the whites-only character of Arlington Heights and if MHDC could actually develop Lincoln Green at other sites within the Village, the challenge to the refusal to rezone the Viatorian property seemed almost frivolous. In these circumstances, Supreme Court review and reversal of Judge Swygert's decision was unavoidable.

When the village petitioned, the Supreme Court agreed to hear the case. Arlington Heights argued that the case involved reasonable zoning regulations that involved questions of poverty, not race; that the buffer policy had been administered evenhandedly; and that the motivation of village trustees in rejecting Lincoln Green was not subject to judicial scrutiny. Plaintiffs' counsel Caruso seemed bent on arguing that proof of actual segregative intent was not necessary to prove a violation of the equal protection clause. In view of the recent decision by the Court in the District of Columbia employment case that proof of racially discriminatory intent was necessary to show a constitutional violation, however, such a position was no longer tenable. In addition, normal Supreme Court practice requires full evaluation and ruling on statutory claims before decision on constitutional issues and generally supports remand for additional proof relevant to full consideration of all legal issues before advisory opinions are sought. As a result, Caruso had the opportunity to argue for a remand in order to rehabilitate the case.

Caruso did modify his constitutional argument on "effects" slightly. He suggested that the District of Columbia employment case set an intent standard based on the "totality of the circumstances," which had been met by Judge Swygert's opinion. Swygert's own affirmance of the trial judge's finding that the refusal to rezone was *not* motivated by race, however, undercut the claim. Caruso failed to demonstrate how the confusion over intent/effect in the lower courts led to this "no intent" finding and that the standards announced in the District of Columbia employment case compelled a remand for consideration of the intent issue and the proof wrongly excluded. Caruso did argue, however, that the Fair Housing Act provided a legal standard independent of his racial effects argument and that, insofar as intent was relevant to the constitutional determination, district judge McMillen erred in excluding evidence questioning the motives of the village trustees in rejecting Lincoln Green.

On January 11, 1977, the Supreme Court issued its decision, in an opinion written by Justice Powell. Powell stretched his concept of "prudential" limitations on standing previously announced in the Penfield case, in order to reach the merits of Caruso's constitutional claim. Powell first sought to refine the test of the District of Columbia employment case that official action will not be held unconstitutional under the equal protection clause unless it can ultimately be traced to purposefully discriminatory conduct. In the process, Powell rejected Caruso's proposed racial effects and totality of the circumstances arguments. Powell listed a variety of factors relevant to determining whether racially discriminatory purpose was a motivating factor in the responsible public officials' decision. Under Powell's view, plaintiffs need not show that such racial bias was the "primary" or "dominant" motive. Nor is proof of racially disproportionate impact irrelevant to the intent inquiry; however, absent a "stark [racial] pattern, the Court must look to other evidence."

The intent determination "demands a *sensitive inquiry* into such circumstantial and direct evidence of intent as may be available," including:

- "the specific sequence of events leading up to the challenged decision"
- "departures from the normal procedural sequence"
- "substantive departures . . . , particularly if the factors usually considered important by the decisionmaker strongly favor a decision contrary to the one reached"
- "the legislative or administrative history"
- the testimony of the decision makers "concerning the purpose of the official action," although such "testimony frequently will be barred by privilege."

It should have been apparent that the parties and the lower courts never attempted any such sensitive inquiry into intent. They had been concerned primarily with Caruso's racial effect claim. This fact was also obvious to Justice Powell:

The [plaintiffs] proceeded on the erroneous theory that the Village's refusal to rezone carried a racially discriminatory effect and was, without more, unconstitutional. [Plaintiffs] complain that the District Court unduly limited their efforts to prove that the Village Board acted for discriminatory purposes, since it forbade questioning Board members about their motivation at the time they cast their votes. We perceive no abuse of discretion in the circumstances of this case, even if such an inquiry into motivation would otherwise have been proper. [Plaintiffs] were allowed, both during the discovery phase and at trial, to question Board members fully about materials and information available to them at the time of decision. In light of [Caruso's] repeated insistence that it was effect and not motivation which would make out a constitutional violation, the District Court's action was not improper.

Yet these defects in the lower court proceedings did not deter Justice Powell from affirming the findings of the lower courts that race was *not* a factor in the trustees' refusal to rezone for the Lincoln Green proposal. Powell concluded, "[Plaintiffs] simply failed to carry their burden of proving that discriminatory purpose was a motivating factor in the Village's decision." Apparently it did not matter that the primary unsettled issue that had plagued the case always had been whether plaintiffs bore such a burden. Having decided that they did, a fair result would have been a remand to the lower courts to allow consideration of all relevant proof. Instead, Justice Powell held MHDC responsible for Caruso's failure to predict Supreme Court opinions that were rendered several years after he filed the complaint and tried the lawsuit. Powell used Caruso's inability to prophesy the future to foreclose MHDC's equal protection claims. It seemed a stiff penalty.

For dissenting Justices Brennan, Marshall, and White, the proper result was to "remand this entire case" to the lower courts "for further proceedings" in light of Powell's intent standards and his demand for a "sensitive inquiry" into *all* relevant factors:

> The Court of Appeals is better situated than this Court, both to reassess the significance of the evidence developed below in light of the standards . . . set forth and to determine whether the interests of justice require further District Court proceedings directed toward those standards.

Such a procedurally fair disposition of the case to allow MHDC to argue and to try the case pursuant to the Supreme Court's newly developing intent standards would have been consistent with Powell's own handling of the Fair Housing Act: "The Court of Appeals . . . , proceeding in a somewhat unorthodox fashion, did not decide [this] statutory question. We remand the case for further consideration of [plaintiff's Fair Housing Act] claims." Powell, of course, chose not to note the irony: Powell's own opinion also proceeded in the *same* "unorthodox fashion" by reaching out to decide constitutional issues first.

The Court's decision in Arlington Heights did not deal a mortal blow to the Lincoln Green project nor protect the virtually all-white Village against all minority intrusions. The HUD moratorium and economic inflation would have delayed the project and required its restructuring in any event; and the claims of MHDC and Caruso under the 1968 Fair Housing Act could and would still be pressed in the Seventh Circuit. Without an affirmative decision from the Seventh Circuit at some point, however, Arlington Heights might remain virtually all-white and closed to most blacks for the foreseeable future.

On July 7, 1977, the Seventh Circuit held that Congress passed the 1968 Fair Housing Act "to provide for . . . fair housing throughout the United States . . . , to promote open, integrated residential housing patterns and to prevent the increase of segregation, in ghettos, of racial groups whose lack of opportunities the Act was designed to combat.'' If the *effect* of a zoning decision ''perpetuates segregation and thereby prevents interracial association, it will be considered invidious under the Fair Housing Act.'' Finding that ''the construction of [the integrated] Lincoln Green [project] would be a significant step'' toward breaking up the village's ''overwhelmingly white'' character, the Seventh Circuit remanded to the trial court to determine whether any other suitable sites within Arlington Heights were available. If not, ''the district court should conclude that the Village's refusal to rezone effectively precluded plaintiffs from constructing [integrated] low-cost housing within Arlington Heights'' in violation of the 1968 act.

When the Supreme Court rejected the village's petition to review this judgment, the Leadership Council and MHDC moved to seek a compromise with the village. Eight years after conceiving Lincoln Green, it was time to build some integrated housing in Arlington Heights instead of engaging in further litigation. The village trustees were also weary of the battle and recognized that MHDC had finally established a narrow legal principle that probably would open the village in time to subsidized housing anyway. To save face, however, the village fathers could not agree to construction of the project on the contested Viatorian site. After exchanging alternative proposals and negotiating at length, MHDC and the village finally agreed on a new site, a piece of land in a nearby unincorporated area, which the village agreed to annex and zone for a Lincoln Green–type townhouse development. As the decade closed, however, MHDC's development of this alternative site was still being thwarted by pending litigation—not any suit with Arlington Heights, but a suit brought by the adjacent all-white village challenging the annexation and the agreement between MHDC and Arlington Heights. The opening of Lincoln Green was still years away.

Racial Steering

Despite such frustrations, the Leadership Council was still committed to making the Supreme Court, and the people of greater Chicago, confront the issue of racial segregation in housing. In 1975 it had filed another housing discrimination suit. With the village of Bellwood in surburban Chicago and four residents of a racially mixed area, the Leadership Council sued two real estate firms for ''steering'' prospective black home buyers into and prospective white purchasers out of this mixed area. They complained that such racial steering manipulated the housing market, affected the racial composition of the area and the village, deflated housing prices in the racially mixed area, threatened to diminish the tax base of the village, and deprived blacks and whites of the "social and professional advantages of living in an integrated community . . . and the benefits of interracial associations."

Caruso filed the complaint under the provisions of the 1866 and 1871 Civil Rights Acts, as well as the 1968 Fair Housing Act. Citing Justice Powell's opinion in the Penfield case, the trial court dismissed the complaint on the ground that only the direct victims of discrimination, not third parties (such as the village and residents of the affected area) had standing to challenge the alleged discrimination. The Seventh Circuit reversed and remanded this decision for a full hearing on the charges, basing its decision on the reservation in Powell's opinion that the 1968 act might give standing to such broader claims.

On April 17, 1979, the Supreme Court, in an opinion by Justice Powell, held that Congress in passing the 1968 Fair Housing Act intended to open the federal courts to hear claims of racial discrimination in housing by all aggrieved persons, even indirect victims. Powell held that, under the 1968 act, both the village and the residents of the mixed area did have standing "to protest the intentional segregation of their community" by any racial steering practiced by real estate brokers. This ruling was consistent with the Court's previous decisions that Congress may provide for the hearing of cases despite "prudential limitations" which the Court might otherwise place on standing, e.g., a white resident challenging the racial exclusion of potential black entrants to a community.*

That left open the prospect that *some* aggrieved party might yet be successful in bringing a broad challenge to racial ghettoization in some metropolitan area. The irony was that Bellwood, a town worried about having too many blacks, had standing to challenge racial steering that would bring in more blacks; but black citizens excluded from all-white enclaves like Penfield would not be heard unless they could find a developer willing to join in the challenge to the color line with a commitment to a specific integrated project.

Justice Powell's opinion also seemed more concerned about protecting traditional suburban values than minority rights:

> The adverse consequences attendant upon a "changing" neighborhood can be profound. If . . . steering practices significantly reduce the total number of buyers in the . . . housing market, prices may be deflected

---

*Justice Powell, however, refrained from reviewing whether the Civil Rights Acts of the First Reconstruction provide similarly broad standing. Justice Rehnquist, joined by Justice Stewart, dissented. Rehnquist wrote that the 1968 act did not allow the indirect claims of discrimination of the village and area residents; and he read Powell's opinion in the Penfield case as concluding that the 1866 Civil Rights Act did not provide a cause of action for injuries resulting from private racial discrimination aimed at others.

downward. This phenomenon would be exacerbated if perceptible increases in the minority population directly attributable to racial steering precipitate an exodus of white residents. . . . A significant reduction in property values directly injures a municipality by diminishing its tax base, thus threatening its ability to bear the costs of local government and to provide services. . . . There can be no question about the importance to a community of "promoting stable, racially integrated housing." . . . If, as alleged, . . . sales practices actually have begun to rob Bellwood of its racial balance and stability, the Village has standing to challenge the legality of that conduct.

Powell also noted that "other harms flowing from the realities of a racially segregated community are not unlikely. . . . It has been widely recognized, for example, that school segregation is linked closely to housing segregation."

The Courts and Judicial Review of Housing Segregation

In a series of cases involving the sale and rental of housing, exclusionary zoning, the segregative placement of public housing, and attempts by realtors and developers to exploit the dual housing market, the Seventh Circuit Court of Appeals had confronted various faces of residential segregation and systemic housing discrimination in the Chicago metropolitan area. This appeals court eventually concluded that there was a racially dual housing market, one for whites, the other for blacks, in the region. At the fringes of ghetto expansion, from which prospective white home seekers were steered and to which blacks were not yet completely channeled in this dual market, there could be panic selling by whites and little demand from whites or blacks. But in the relatively small "Negro ghetto" to which blacks were usually restricted in their housing choices, demand could exceed supply. In these areas blacks often paid substantially more than whites did for a comparable home in the much larger, protected white areas with greater housing stocks.

So great was this disparity between the separate white and black housing markets in the Chicago area that the Seventh Circuit found that one real estate group had charged 20 percent more for housing in black areas. The Seventh Circuit found that this group's average gross profit margin for black housing was almost 15 percent greater than for its comparable developments in white areas. The Seventh Circuit held that such exploitation of the dual housing market was a violation of the 1866 Civil Rights Act. In outlawing such gouging of black home buyers, however, the Seventh Circuit also reminded that the fair housing laws prohibit the perpetuation of the basic system of dual housing.

The [Negro family's] right to open housing means more than the right to move from an old ghetto to a new ghetto. . . . The goal of our national housing policy is to replace the ghettoes with truly integrated and balanced living patterns for all races.

That was a goal shared by Kale Williams, the Leadership Council for Metropolitan Open Communities, the NAACP, and the likes of John Humphrey and John Harewood. Whether Justice Powell and four other members of the Supreme Court would ever come to share this view remained in serious doubt. Despite Powell's latest rhetoric expressing concern about racial turnover at the fringes of the ghetto, it was not at all clear that he shared this goal. His insensitivity to the deep-seated racial aspect of the exclusionary zoning of such all-white villages as Penfield and Arlington Heights suggested that Powell was still bound by the views expressed in his opinions in the Denver and Austin school cases:

Economic pressures and voluntary preferences are the primary determinants of residential patterns. The tendency of citizens of common national or ethnic origins to form homogeneous residential patterns in our cities is a familiar demographic characteristic of this country.

In so thinking, Powell chose to ignore the findings of many lower court judges when they examined all of the evidence: Racial residential segregation is not explainable as a common ethnic phenomenon nor as an economic necessity. Racial segregation has long been almost complete in major metropolitan areas; on the average, from 70 percent to 95 percent of blacks would have to relocate, compared to 10 percent to 40 percent for white ethnic minorities, to achieve a random distribution. Racial segregation also persists long after other ethnic groups have begun to integrate fully in the larger community; while white immigrants eventually escape any initial concentration after entry to this country, blacks continue to be contained within an expanding ghetto. Further, this ghettoization through racial identification and neighborhood succession cannot be explained by income differences. Whether rich or poor, and whatever the cost of housing, blacks and whites continue to live apart. Finally, in a survey of marketing practices in forty major metropolitan areas, HUD found that black home seekers had a 75 percent chance of meeting discrimination if they contacted four real estate agents. In sum, pervasive racial segregation is not caused solely by economics, ethnicity, or minority choice. Racial discrimination helped to segregate the metropolitan landscape.

Yet, after a decade of litigation in school and housing cases, the Justice Powells of the Court refused to see the segregation of metropolitan America as a problem of racial discrimination. Nevertheless, due to the technical nature of their rulings, it was still possible that the pleadings, arguments, evidence, and findings in a future case might begin to open the Court's eyes. An almost thirty-year life struggle by a black public housing tenant and her fifteen-year legal challenge to segregation in publicly supported housing would provide the occasion.

Chapter 10
Waiting for Gautreaux: The Chicago Public Housing Case, 1950–79

In 1950 Dorothy Gautreaux filed a tenant application with the Chicago Housing Authority (CHA) because she was, in her own words, "in desperate need of housing." Aware of CHA's policy forbidding her family from living in any project in a white neighborhood because they were black, she agreed to live anywhere to escape the one bedroom her family of three shared with relatives. No help from CHA was forthcoming. By 1953, when she filed another application with CHA, Mrs. Gautreaux stated that she was "in even more desperate need of housing . . . because the number of [my] children increased from one to four, and [my] family of six was still occupying one bedroom." In such circumstances Mrs. Gautreaux and her family again agreed to live in *any* project. CHA assigned the Gautreaux family to a nonwhite project in a blacks-only section of Chicago pursuant to its policy not to assign "B" (i.e., black) families to four projects reserved for "A" (i.e., white) families.

By 1966, however, Dorothy Gautreaux was no longer willing to accept public housing segregation when CHA proposed packing another thirteen hundred units in some twelve new projects in all-black areas but none in white neighborhoods. She was inspired by Martin Luther King's initial marches in Chicago against northern segregation. Dorothy Gautreaux and her compatriots protested the location of new public housing projects in the black ghetto. When federal housing officials responded by supporting CHA, Mrs. Gautreaux and several other plaintiffs filed suit in federal court on August 9, 1966. They challenged CHA's continued policy of deliberately choosing sites so as to avoid the placement of black families in white neighborhoods, thereby forcing black families in need of public housing assistance to reside within "the Negro ghetto." Simultaneously, they filed suit against the responsible HUD agency for supporting CHA's policy and practice of black ghettoization and white protection.

Alex Polikoff, a former editor in chief of the *Chicago Law Review* and an experienced partner in one of Chicago's leading corporate law firms, represented the *Gautreaux* plaintiffs on a *pro bono* basis. He framed the two complaints to secure a maximum finding of violation and left detailed consideration of remedy for another day. The two suits were assigned to federal district judge Austin, a former prosecutor with a no-nonsense manner. When Polikoff first explained the basis for the suit, Judge Austin shot back: "Where do you want [me] to put [the CHA projects]? On Lake Shore Drive?"

Judge Austin proceeded to postpone consideration of the case against HUD until the suit against CHA was resolved. CHA promptly filed a motion to dismiss the case based on the plaintiffs' own housing applications which expressed a preference for living in projects that happened to be located in black neighborhoods rather than the four CHA projects located in white neighborhoods. The gist of CHA's motion had some appeal: as the named plaintiffs got exactly the housing they requested, they had no standing to complain about the responsiveness of CHA to their wishes; and CHA merely located new projects in response to the demands of the applicants.

Dorothy Gautreaux filed a counteraffidavit explaining the circumstances compelling her application and her "willingness" to accept housing in "any project" to which CHA chose to assign her beleaguered family in 1953. Her recognition of CHA's segregation and of her need for shelter did not mean that she approved of CHA's segregative policies.

Polikoff also began to investigate whether discriminatory mechanisms caused CHA's blatantly segregated system of project location and tenant assignment. From CHA's former director of research, he learned that from 1946 to 1952 CHA refused to admit Negroes to the four whites-only projects and established a small quota of blacks for other "mixed" projects. CHA's supervisor of tenant selection from 1953 through 1961 confirmed that CHA staff first "steered" all applicants to request housing on a racial basis and then marked the applications "A" for whites and "B" for Negroes. She explained that CHA staff never assigned a "B" family to the four whites-only projects without a "specific exemption" from the CHA director.

Polikoff also needed to find the discriminatory underpinning of CHA's practice of locating almost all family projects (in contrast to elderly projects) in heavily Negro neighborhoods and locating no family projects in white neighborhoods after 1950. The community activists who had long engaged the CHA in a running battle provided a good source of information. Kale Williams, then a staff member with the American Friends Service Committee, described several conversations that he had had with the director of CHA. The director said that he had been forced in the past "to withdraw his proposals [for projects in white neighborhoods] when local aldermen would not support them. [The CHA director] stated that he would not propose any further sites outside of Negro ghettoes because it was clear that he would not be able to get the Chicago City Council to approve such proposals; and approval of the City Council was required by [Illinois] law." This evidence of white community opposition to public "family" housing projects perceived as "black" could help to demonstrate the discriminatory mechanism underlying the all-black site location pattern since 1950. HUD's response to the recent protest lent additional support: the reason for the location of CHA family projects exclusively in black areas was that "sites other than in the south or west side . . . invariably encounter sufficient opposition in the [Chicago City] Council to preclude Council approval."

Armed with these affidavits, Polikoff argued that Mrs. Gautreaux was entitled to her day in court on her charges against CHA. Judge Austin denied the motion to dismiss but held that plaintiffs, in order to prevail on the merits, had to demonstrate the CHA actually intended to discriminate on the basis of race. Faced with this burden of proof, Polikoff secured the judge's permission to search CHA records for relevant evidence. Aided by the Urban League and a half-dozen college students, Mrs. Gautreaux's counsel spent the summer and fall of 1967 rummaging through cabinets and boxes of CHA records.

Following depositions of responsible CHA officials, CHA on March 28, 1968, moved for a summary judgment based on the claim that plaintiffs' massive discovery uncovered no evidence of intentional discrimination. CHA argued that its selection of sites was dictated solely by the city council, not by its own racial considerations. As Polikoff now knew from his discovery, however, this "defense" amounted to an admission of guilt. He responded with his own cross-motion for summary judgment based on the evidence from CHA's records and the admissions of its managing agents.

- In the late 1930s and 1940s, CHA officially designated all projects as "Negro" or "white" and "would not permit a housing project to change the racial make-up of the neighborhood in which it was located." In 1942 CHA announced, "as a matter of policy, the requirement that a housing project shall be tenanted with families of the same race as occupied the site previous to its demolition."
- In 1948–49, "a principle objection of the alderman to the initially proposed sites [of CHA] was that Negroes would be moved into white areas of the city. The purposeful intention on the part of the aldermen of the City Council [was] to keep Negroes out of white areas of the city." The mayor sent an aid to CHA to resolve the dispute by "compromise," i.e., eliminate most of the proposed sites in white areas. CHA accepted.
- The CHA director resigned in 1954 because CHA would not allow her to desegregate the four original whites-only projects. As a result of CHA's continuing "quota system," these four projects remained 95 percent white. Until May 22, 1968, these four projects were listed on CHA tenant selection forms as appropriate for "A families only," that is, whites only.
- The "desire to prevent an influx of Negroes into white neighborhoods" led to the passage of the Illinois law giving the Chicago City Council final authority to approve CHA sites. As one alderman from a white ward reported to CHA, "My people . . . are strongly against colored coming

out here.'' In 1955 the new CHA director agreed (*a*) to ''pre-clear'' all proposed sites privately with the affected alderman and housing committee of the city council and (*b*) to submit ''extra'' black sites to allow the council to disapprove white sites if community opposition arose after the preclearance without losing any of the federal housing money available to CHA.

- Thereafter, 99.5 percent of CHA family units were located in areas that were or soon predictably would become all-Negro. Of 10,256 family units approved by CHA, only 30 (or less than 0.3 percent) were located in white neighborhoods; and the council rejected 99.5 percent of all family housing initially proposed by CHA on white sites, but only 10 percent of the units on Negro sites.

Judge Austin found, in his February 10, 1969, opinion, that CHA built family housing pursuant to a ''policy of eliminating white sites on racial grounds.'' The evidence was undisputed: ''no criterion, other than race, can possibly explain'' the racial pattern and process; ''there is no genuine issue as to the truth of the fact that the pre-clearance procedure was known by CHA to result in the veto of substantial numbers of sites [for white areas] on racial grounds.'' Judge Austin also observed that another result of the ''segregationist policy of protecting whites from [the] 76,000 eligible Negro families'' by locating projects only in the black ghetto was to keep 188,000 white families eligible for public housing out of CHA projects altogether. Judge Austin granted plaintiffs' motion for summary judgment and denied that of CHA. He gave the parties thirty days to ''attempt to formulate a comprehensive plan to prohibit the future use and to remedy the past effects of CHA's unconstitutional site selection and tenant assignment procedures.''

CHA publicly protested the finding of intentional segregation by proclaiming that it had simply located projects ''where the community welcomed public housing and where the need for slum clearance was the greatest.'' Even so, CHA decided not to appeal and entered into a series of discussions with Polikoff on remedy before Judge Austin in his chambers. CHA argued that it should be enjoined only in the most general terms from further discrimination. Polikoff countered that CHA should be required to build four units in white areas for every one unit in black areas until the segregative effects of the prior practice of building only in black areas had been overcome. Judge Austin solicited the views of HUD on the propriety of a specific formula but received only a noncommittal response after much delay.

On July 1, 1969, Judge Austin issued his judgment order. He permitted CHA to go forward with the proposed projects in black areas that had triggered the lawsuit, but ordered that three-fourths of future family units would have to be built in white areas and that the next seven hundred units would have to be located in white areas to "match" the black projects approved. The order also provided that one-half the tenants in any new project could be residents from the local community; in effect, this would permit projects in white areas to include at least 50 percent white families. The decree also permitted CHA to make leased dwelling units in white areas of Cook County outside Chicago available to the *Gautreaux* plaintiffs as part of the formula.

In order to prevent the development of any more "instant ghettoes," Judge Austin also prohibited CHA from building large projects with more than 120 dwelling units and three stories in height or building any projects in census tracts containing more than 15 percent CHA residents. The order also directed CHA to "use its best efforts to increase the supply of dwelling units as rapidly as possible" in conformity with the "scatter," low-rise, low-density objectives of the decree. Austin retained jurisdiction for the specific purpose of permitting any modifications of his decree that might be required for specific projects or changes in circumstances over time.

Congressman Roman Pucinski predicted that the order "dealt the death knell to public housing." The *Daily News* responded somewhat differently: the order "put[s] Chicago face to face with its most crucial issue—whether it is to be a city united or a city divided. . . . The [City] Council, under the leadership of Mayor Richard J. Daley, must act in the full knowledge that if the decision is for a divided city, that can only be a stopgap on the way to a city in social and economic ruin."

While CHA, the city council, and Mayor Daley wrestled with which course to choose, Polikoff filed for a summary judgment against HUD based on its knowing and uninterrupted thirty-year support of CHA's intentional segregation. HUD responded with its own motion for summary judgment. Judge Austin pondered the issue of HUD liability for over a year, while CHA sat on its hands, proposing no new sites to the council. On September 1, 1970, Judge Austin dismissed the complaint against HUD on numerous technical grounds that boiled down to a determination that HUD secretary Romney had enough responsibilities, problems, and good intentions without any judicial interference with the exercise of his discretion. While plaintiffs immediately appealed the dismissal of HUD, CHA determined "to find some suburbs willing to accept a portion of the proposed housing before it submitted its chosen sites to the city council for approval." Judge Austin responded to this delay by ordering CHA to submit sites to the city council pursuant to a specific timetable. Although sites for fifteen hundred dwelling units had already been selected by CHA and approved by HUD, CHA consumed another year in unsuccessful appeals before finally submitting the proposed sites to the city council on March 5, 1971.

Meanwhile, Mrs. Gautreaux continued to wait for any meaningful relief from CHA's regime of segregation that had herded her family into an institutional and social wasteland and contributed substantially to the growth of an unmistakable "Negro ghetto" in Chicago. Mayor Daley responded to the CHA submission of sites as if the court's previous findings and orders had never been entered. At a city hall press conference, he called the proposed sites "detrimental" and railed that they "should not be built." Daley argued that public housing should be built "where this kind of housing is most needed and accepted," i.e., the Negro ghetto. Over the summer, the city council moved in a desultory fashion and approved only those sites concentrated in neighborhoods "closest to the ghetto," while delaying on sites in more protected white areas.

On September 10, 1971, five days before the final court deadline for city council approval of scattered sites in compliance with its orders, the Court of Appeals for the Seventh Circuit held that HUD was also liable for CHA's long-standing discriminatory program of black ghettoization and white protection. The appeals court understood HUD's explanation for its support of CHA: "[G]iven the acknowledged desperate need for public housing in Chicago, HUD's decision was that it was better to fund a segregated housing system than to deny housing altogether to the thousands of needy Negro families of that city." But the Seventh Circuit ruled that "HUD's approval and funding of segregated CHA housing cannot be excused as an attempted accommodation of an admittedly urgent need for housing." Quoting Judge Austin's earlier ruling against CHA, the appeals court held that HUD had a duty to face up to the segregation "dilemma" and white community hostility to association with blacks, rather than continue to support "a deliberate policy to separate the races."

HUD's choice, like that of CHA, had never been limited to a choice between housing of blacks on segregated terms or no housing for blacks at all. The Third Circuit had already reached the same conclusion in a case against HUD's funding and approval of a similar program of racial ghettoization in Philadelphia's public housing program. Although the facts of the cases differed somewhat, the Seventh Circuit noted that any differences were "legally insignificant." Thus, Secretary Romney's greatest problem remained the continuing legacy of long-standing federal support for segregated housing throughout the country. While the president inveighed against "forced integration" of white communities, federal courts informed Romney that HUD itself was responsible for forced segregation of public housing. The Seventh Circuit eased Romney's dilemma somewhat by suggesting to Judge Austin that he consider only a "best efforts" instruction to HUD to assist CHA in providing a remedy.

Polikoff immediately sought HUD's assistance in withholding further financial support to Chicago until the city council approved a set of scattered sites in compliance with Judge Austin's order. When HUD declined, Polikoff asked Austin to enjoin HUD from transferring $26 million in Model Cities funds to Chicago until the city council approved scattered sites. At the hearing on this motion, the city argued that such a fund cutoff would only harm the poor families of the ghetto, like the *Gautreaux* plaintiffs, who relied on such funds for the hot lunch program. Here was the segregation "dilemma" again being posed as an excuse for continued support of racial ghettoization. Judge Austin responded: "You're telling me it's better for a child to have breakfast than to have the opportunity to move out of the ghetto. Let them have cake, but don't let them move to the Northwest side or the Southwest side." Coming from a man who had started the case by ridiculing just such moves, the statement revealed a remarkable change in perspective.

On October 1, 1971, Austin issued a blistering ruling requiring the city to approve seven hundred units on a scattered basis in order to obtain the Model Cities funds from HUD. Austin found that the city, after over two years of delay, had demonstrated no inclination to comply with his prior order. Whether there would be the "devastating effect on tens of thousands of the citizens of this city" resulting from any fund cutoff was left to the conscious choice of the city. He also compared Daley to public officials who had stood in schoolhouse doors elsewhere in the past to thwart integration. The judge decried the "anomaly that the 'law and order' chief executive of this city should challenge and defy federal law."

The city council persisted in its refusal to approve the scattered sites proposed by CHA and appealed Austin's threat of a Model Cities fund termination as a sanction for further noncompliance. On March 8, 1972, the Seventh Circuit reversed Austin's ruling on the ground that federal courts' equitable powers concerning federal funds should be confined to those specific programs for which violations have been found. As the model cities funding did not directly relate to the federal support of segregated public housing, Judge Austin had abused his discretion in using these funds as a lever to secure compliance. Circuit judge Sprecher dissented. Reciting the findings of massive violation and the long history of obdurate delay by the city and default by HUD, he argued that Judge Austin had the authority to withhold "federal funds from one program to enforce another." In Judge Sprecher's view, "the use of Model Cities funds seems to derogate the [national] policy of racial non-discrimination by attempting to enrich the ghetto instead of striving to eliminate it."

Stymied by this reversal, Polikoff returned to the district court, joined the city council as a named party defendant, and moved to suspend the state law requiring the council's prior approval to CHA project sites. Following a hearing at which the city failed to explain its default, Judge Austin ruled on April 10, 1972, that the effect of the city's failure to approve the scattered sites "has been and continues to be to thwart the correction of federal constitutional wrongs." As a result, the court suspended the state law requirement for prior city council approval, directed the city to deliver a list of vacant sites to CHA, and ordered CHA to approve scattered sites for fifteen hundred dwelling units for prompt submission to HUD for funding.

The city appealed but eventually lost before a divided Seventh Circuit panel on January 12, 1973. By this time, however, President Nixon's moratorium on all federal housing funds had already gone into effect. The wait of the *Gautreaux* plaintiffs for actual scattered-site housing in conformity with Judge Austin's July 1, 1969, remedy order would go on.

Plaintiffs filed yet another motion in district court, this one asking Judge Austin to consider what joint relief should be granted against HUD and CHA. Polikoff also asked the court to determine the propriety of considering some form of metropolitan relief for the unconstitutional ghettoization of black families within the Chicago core. Polikoff now believed that the white suburbs could assist in providing the relief so long denied in white neighborhoods within the city—housing open to the *Gautreaux* plaintiffs outside the Negro ghetto. In support of this motion, Polikoff cited Austin's first order permitting CHA to participate with the suburbs in providing housing for the *Gautreaux* plaintiffs. He also relied heavily on the recent decisions of district judge Roth and Chief Judge Phillips in the Detroit school case approving metropolitan relief to remedy the unconstitutional segregation within the Detroit public schools. Polikoff tried this new tack in order to secure some meaningful relief from HUD, and he analogized HUD's wrongdoing and areawide responsibility to that of the state of Michigan in the Detroit school case.* HUD also represented to the district judge that a metropolitan remedy was "desirable," a concept it "endorsed." This position was in keeping with HUD's own regulations concerning the actual "housing market area" and Secretary Romney's expressed concern for "metropolitan wide solutions . . . [for] problems of the 'real city.' "

On September 1, 1973, Judge Austin, however, denied that portion of the motion seeking consideration of metropolitan relief on the ground that the "wrongs were committed within the limits of Chicago and solely against residents of the City." Judge Austin could not understand why Polikoff now sought a metropolitan remedy:

[P]laintiffs should not have to be reminded that no public housing has been built in this City since my order of July 1, 1969 because the munici-

---

*Polikoff also offered an exhibit showing that the relatively few family public housing projects outside Chicago followed a familiar pattern: they were predominantly black and located in or adjacent to heavily black census tracts. Nevertheless, the fate of any extra-city relief in the Chicago housing case seemed tied to the outcome of the Detroit school case on review in the Supreme Court.

pal authorities refused to approve sufficient sites for such housing and recently because of a lack of funds. But, now that one of those obstacles has been eliminated by the Seventh Circuit's recent affirmance of my order to build housing in Chicago without City Council approval, plaintiffs have curiously raised an issue that would let the principal offender, CHA, avoid the politically distasteful task before it by passing off its problems onto the suburbs.

Judge Austin ordered HUD to use its "best efforts" to assist CHA in increasing the supply of family public housing programs within Chicago consistent with his previous orders. For Austin, it was past time to get CHA to build some scattered site housing within Chicago without further complicating the case.

Once again Polikoff appealed to the Seventh Circuit. He argued that the lower court decisions in the Detroit case authorized consideration of metropolitan relief where necessary to afford complete relief. The *Gautreaux* plaintiffs needed to look to the white suburbs as well as the remaining white neighborhoods within the city if they were successfully to escape the wrong of ghettoization in public housing located in all-black neighborhoods. The panel hearing the appeal included retired Supreme Court justice Tom Clark. Before the appeals court ruled, however, the Supreme Court issued its first decision in the Detroit school case holding that city-only violations authorize city-only, not metropolitan, remedies. HUD filed a supplemental memorandum applying the Supreme Court's holding to support Judge Austin's ruling: as the geographic scope of the violation was limited to the city of Chicago, so must the remedy be limited.

Polikoff now attempted to distinguish the very Detroit school case on which he had placed such heavy reliance for his straight remedy theory. Housing, unlike schools, he argued, did not involve all of the traditions of local control and practical problems of interdistrict relief. The affected suburban jurisdictions could be fully heard on any remand before framing relief. HUD had both areawide authority and areawide regulations concerning the overall administration of federal housing programs throughout the Chicago metropolitan area.

In his August 26, 1974, opinion for the Seventh Circuit, Justice Clark expressed dismay at the Supreme Court's five-to-four decision in the Detroit school case:

At least until [that opinion], the law was clear that political subdivisions of the states may be readily bridged when necessary to vindicate federal constitutional rights. . . . The equal protection clause speaks to the state, and the state cannot escape its obligations under that clause by delegating some of its governmental functions to local units.

Clark proceeded to read the opinion narrowly as dealing only "with equitable limitations on remedies," not basic constitutional principles. He found that public housing, unlike schools, had "no deeply rooted tradition of local control" and that HUD and CHA could build housing in the suburbs like any other landowner without "the problems of daily busing thousands of children to schools in other districts run by other local governments." Citing HUD's support for metropolitan relief and "the realities of 'white flight' to the suburbs and the inevitability of 'resegregation' by rebuilding the ghettos as CHA and HUD were doing in Chicago," Clark concluded that opening metropolitan housing to the Gautreaux victims was essential:

> We must not sentence our poor, our underprivileged, our minorities to the jobless slums of the ghettoes and thereby forever trap them in the vicious cycle of poverty which can only lead them to hells of crime and violence.

Circuit judge Tone cryptically dissented:

> The "controlling principle" [of the Detroit school case] . . . is that the remedy must be commensurate with the constitutional violation found, and, therefore, an interdistrict remedy is not justified unless the evidence shows an interdistrict violation. This seems to me to preclude metropolitan relief here. No violation outside the City has even been alleged, let alone proved, as the District Court pointed out.

The government repeated Tone's refrain in asking the Seventh Circuit to reconsider its ruling. In a supplemental opinion, Clark responded by making additional findings to try to distinguish the underlying facts from the Detroit school case:

> [D]efendants' discriminatory site selection within the City of Chicago may well have fostered racial paranoia and encouraged the "white flight" phenomenon which has exacerbated the problems of achieving integration to such an extent that intra-city relief alone will not suffice to remedy the constitutional injuries. The extra-city impact of defendant's intra-city discrimination appears to be profound and far-reaching and has affected the housing patterns of hundreds of thousands of people throughout the Chicago metropolitan area.

That, said Clark, is an interdistrict violation authorizing metropolitan relief. He therefore "reaffirm[ed the] remanding of this case for additional evidence and for further consideration of the issue of metropolitan area relief in light of this opinion and that of the Supreme Court [in the Detroit school case].''*

Polikoff sensed trouble. Once again, Solicitor General Bork would argue to the Supreme Court that plaintiffs and the lower courts had a predetermined remedy in mind and were searching in vain for some supportive interdistrict violation. Carla Hills, HUD's new secretary, requested the solicitor general to seek Supreme Court review. Bork's petition repeated a familiar refrain: City-only violations support city-only remedies; therefore HUD should not be required to participate in hearings on metropolitan remedies when the only violations were limited to the city of Chicago, as Judge Austin had found. The veiled implication of the petition was also clear—a retired justice's dissent did not make the vote on the ''controlling principle'' of the Detroit decision a five-to-five tie. Bork argued that Clark's judgment should be reversed to insure that the geographic extent of judicial meanderings did not exceed the geographic scope of any proven violations.

Polikoff thought hard about his case. He consulted widely among Supreme Court and civil rights advocates. He concluded that he could not prevail if he relied primarily on arguments concerning either areawide violations (which he had not yet alleged nor attempted to prove) or equitable distinctions between public housing and schools. Although he disagreed with the Supreme Court majority's wooden statement of the ''controlling principle'' in the Detroit case, he had to win five votes now, not complain about the past. In his opposition to Supreme Court review, Polikoff staked out a simple position to defend Clark's judgment that consideration of metropolitan relief was appropriate: There was no interdistrict remedy as to HUD. That federal agency had areawide authority, responsibility, administration, regulation, and practice. Because HUD committed a violation within its self-defined metropolitan housing market area, it could be ordered to exercise its authority

---

*Clark added, however, that ''in the meantime, intra-city relief should proceed apace without further delay.'' To this end plaintiffs had already moved in the district court for the appointment of a ''commissioner to formulate plans for the expeditious construction of new public housing units in the City of Chicago.'' With the passage of the Housing and Community Development Act of 1974, federal funds to subsidize low-income housing had finally become available. Because of HUD's primary reliance on so-called Section 8 funds for rent supplements rather than new construction, Judge Austin's remedial order would have to be expanded to include rental programs if the Gautreaux plaintiffs were to secure the maximum benefit of the newly available federal subsidies. On November 7, 1974, Judge Austin appointed a federal magistrate as a master ''to pinpoint responsibility for defendants' lack of diligence and to develop methods for achieving compliance with my orders. . . . For the past five years and four months, no public housing construction has been completed by any party. . . . For reasons entirely unclear to me, the effect and import of my orders have been avoided and frustrated for over five years. . . . The Master is directed to study and review the existing patterns of racial segregation in Chicago public housing, to determine and identify the precise causes of the five-year delay in implementing my judgment orders, and to recommend a plan of action that will expedite the realization of my various orders and judgments.''

throughout this region. In sum, the Detroit school decision did not foreclose an areawide housing remedy against HUD in Chicago because a federal agency with areawide authority had committed the violation, not a single subdivision of one of many separate and autonomous local school districts of limited geographic scope.

When the Supreme Court agreed to review the case, Polikoff again consulted widely with members of the civil rights and Supreme Court bar. Several suggested that Polikoff seek a remand to the district court for joinder of suburban jurisdictions and proof of violations or segregative effects spilling over the boundaries of the city of Chicago. This course would have conceded the error of Clark's decision, let HUD off the hook of its self-proclaimed (if rarely exercised) areawide responsibility, and inevitably prolonged proceedings in the courts below for at least another five years. Polikoff believed that this argument was only valuable as a fallback position to avoid snuffing out the prospect of metropolitan relief in the case forever. HUD's areawide authority would remain his key to distinguishing the Detroit decision. In his Supreme Court brief, Polikoff therefore continued to stress that ''housing market area relief against HUD is not 'inter-district' under'' the Supreme Court's ruling in the Detroit school case. Solicitor General Bork continued to argue in his brief that a violation limited to the city of Chicago authorized *no* remedy of broader geographic scope.

At the oral argument Solicitor General Bork opened by arguing that the rule of the Detroit school case should also circumscribe relief in the Chicago public housing case. The Seventh Circuit's remand to Judge Austin for consideration of metropolitan approaches would require HUD ''to impose obligations upon communities [outside Chicago] that are without fault in order to achieve a remedy . . . that is entirely premised upon wrong-doing in Chicago.'' Bork continued with the confidence of the sovereign authority he represented:

> [The judges on the Seventh Circuit] are not pursuing governmental action. . . . They are pursuing population and demographic shifts. . . . They are reacting to the phenomenon of ''white flight.'' . . . The remedy, in short, is directed to a predicted *de facto* segregation and not the limited, proven *de jure* segregated public housing [violation within] Chicago. . . . [The] violation took place within the City of Chicago, and it is therefore inappropriate to reframe relief in an area that encompasses three hundred other governmental units that are complete strangers to the violation.

Bork then challenged Polikoff's suggestion that an order directed solely against HUD would not be ''interdistrict.'' The solicitor argued that such relief would inevitably destroy ''the autonomy . . . of local cities and housing authorities who have no connection with the violation in Chicago." Calling Polikoff's suggestion a "rather extraordinary legal principle," Bork added sarcastically:

> HUD is to be made into a conduit, through which the impact of local violations flows outward to . . . all other governments in the area that [Gautreaux plaintiffs] or the district court think it useful to reach. . . . The faults of one locality are being made a jurisdictional predicate for area-wide social planning on communities that are in no way involved.

Bork concluded his assault by noting simply that the Detroit decision "governs" such nonsense. The only substantive question from the justices concerned whether Polikoff's fallback argument was correct even under Bork's analysis. The solicitor general agreed that if plaintiffs filed a new complaint joining all the suburbs and proved areawide violations extending beyond the city limits of Chicago, the case would be different.

Although Polikoff opened by staking out his primary position against HUD, he was soon driven by several justices' questions to his fallback position. At one point, he suggested that it was premature for the Court to consider the scope of any metropolitan relief until the local jurisdictions had been brought before the trial judge for a full hearing on all areawide violation and remedy issues. Near the close of his argument, however, Polikoff returned to his primary point, that an "order confined to HUD, even though it extended to the housing market area . . . , would not be [an] interdistrict order under" the decision in the Detroit school case. HUD could be ordered to exercise the power it already has under various statutes and regulations to provide the *Gautreaux* plaintiffs with meaningful relief throughout the Chicago housing market area. A decree could and should be entered directing HUD to use its own areawide definition of this "market area for administering the stream of federal housing subsidies flowing into Chicago." HUD itself had already made the determination that housing is not like schools: persons compete for shelter throughout a real housing market area—here the entire Chicago metropolitan area as defined by HUD itself—not within separate local jurisdictions.

In short, the nature of the violation by HUD amounted to restricting the opportunity of the *Gautreaux* plantiffs to compete for housing throughout this housing market area by confining them to projects in the "Negro ghetto." In such circumstances, the federal courts had the *duty* to order HUD to remedy its wrongdoing in order to allow "the wronged persons [to seek] housing within the housing market area." To provide such appropriate areawide relief, HUD could deal directly under its "Section 8" authority and the 1974 Housing and Community Development Act (HCDA) with developers and landlords who already owned land or buildings complying with all local zoning and building ordinances. The prerogatives of local jurisdictions could be respected by such a HUD-only order just as fully as provided by Congress in the 1974 HCDA.

At last there was some analysis of substance rather than form. Sensing this danger, Bork's rebuttal attempted to get the argument back within the rule of the Detroit decision:

> This talk about ordering HUD alone—and this not being interdistrict as to HUD—is a semantic game that really ought not to go unchallenged. . . . [It is] inevitable that local authority is going to be overridden or by-passed, and we're going to end up with effective remedies in towns that have done nothing wrong.

Justice White interrupted: "Whatever you [i.e., HUD] were found guilty of doing in Chicago, you ought to quit it and quit it in the Chicago housing area." Bork tried to object that such an areawide injunction was inappropriate under the Detroit decision because HUD's violation was limited to the city of Chicago. Justice White retorted, "Well, if [they are the] *same* people who are operating in the Chicago housing area, then we do have an issue; and I guess that's what the lawsuit is all about."

On April 20, 1976, Justice Stewart issued the opinion for a unanimous Court. Although he rejected Justice Clark's narrow reading of the Detroit decision and broader speculation about the extracity effects of the proven CHA-HUD violations within Chicago, Stewart accepted Polikoff's primary argument:

> We reject the contention that since HUD's constitutional and statutory violations were committed in Chicago, [our ruling in the Detroit case] precludes an order against HUD that will affect its conduct in the greater metropolitan area. The critical distinction between HUD and the suburban school districts in [Detroit] is that HUD has been found to have violated the Constitution. . . . Here, unlike the [interdistrict] desegregation remedy found erroneous in [Detroit], a judicial order directing relief beyond the boundary lines of Chicago will not necessarily entail coercion of uninvolved governmental units, because both CHA and HUD have the authority to operate outside the Chicago city limits.

Stewart then proceeded to adopt Polikoff's analysis of the nature of the violation:

> Here the wrong committed by HUD confined the [*Gautreaux* plaintiffs] to segregated public housing. The relevant geographic area for purposes of

[HUD's] housing options is the Chicago housing market [as defined by HUD itself], not the Chicago city limits. . . . To foreclose such [metropolitan] relief solely because HUD's constitutional violation took place within the city limits of Chicago would transform [Detroit's] principled limitation on the exercise of federal judicial authority into an arbitrary and mechanical shield for those found to have engaged in unconstitutional conduct.

Citing "well-established federal housing policy" and the specific HUD programs that respect the role of local governments in housing and community development, the Court even touted HUD's power to use federal housing programs to foster projects located in white areas throughout the Chicago housing market.

Stewart's authorship of the opinion was ironic. In the Detroit school case, there had been substantial evidence and express findings by the trial court that discrimination, public and private, including by HUD and its predecessor agencies, contributed substantially to segregation throughout the metropolitan area as well as within the Detroit city limits. The basic violation found by Judge Roth had been the containment of black families within an expanding blacks-only core of one-race schools and housing surrounded by an exclusionary whites-only ring. But, in his separate concurring opinion, Stewart had purported to review the record and said there was no such evidence. He had even suggested that the causes of the creation and expansion of the Negro ghetto in Detroit (and the protected white sanctuaries on the fringes of Detroit and in the surrounding suburbs) were "caused by unknown and perhaps unknowable factors." In the Chicago public housing case there was no proof of discrimination, public or private, outside the Chicago city limits, and there was an express trial judge finding that the violation involved only the city of Chicago.

Moreover, in the Detroit school case, the state of Michigan was a primary wrongdoer and had complete authority under state law and direct responsibility under the Fourteenth Amendment for public schooling throughout the Detroit metropolitan area; HUD's wrongdoing and areawide authority in the Chicago public housing case certainly were no greater. Yet Stewart chose to perceive that the nature of the violation in the *Gautreaux* case was the confinement of black families to segregated public housing in the Negro ghetto and authorized a remedy against HUD based on the "real" housing market area, including Chicago's suburbs.

In the Detroit school case, fears of too intrusive judicial remedies and of massive white opposition to actual areawide school desegregation seemed to obscure Stewart's vision of the nature of the wrong and the state's responsibility for the system of racial ghettoization found by Judge Roth. The easier path in the Detroit school case was to avoid seeing such systemic violation. In the Chicago public housing case, however, the specter of massive resistance did not serve to obscure the wrong. Federal housing funds would merely be redirected to allow a relatively few low-income black families to choose housing, primarily in the private rental market, outside the blacks-only core to which HUD had previously confined them.

Some newspapers hailed the *Gautreaux* decision as the new *Brown* for the nation's segregated housing. Polikoff knew better. The Court's decision represented at most another small opportunity to move one step along the long road to opening, at some unspecified future date, a limited number of dwelling units in white areas to the *Gautreaux* plaintiffs who had waited so long for relief. Further obstacles had to be overcome before even this small step could be taken. CHA still had not met its within-city obligations and had built or leased no new family units. Judge Austin was slowly dying of cancer and was physically unable to apply much further pressure. The hearings on the CHA default and a revised plan before the new master would go on for four more years before a final report fixing blame squarely on CHA and HUD would be produced. And any further hearings on metropolitan relief on remand would have to put up with the unknowns of a new judge and more delay.

After consulting with fair housing groups, black leadership and representatives of the public housing projects and black families on the waiting list, Polikoff tried another tack to secure some relief. Over drinks and frank discussion in a Chicago pub, he agreed with HUD's general counsel to a limited one-year experiment to place a few hundred *Gautreaux* families in suburban rental units subsidized by Section 8 funds, from June, 1976, through June, 1977. The agreement acknowledged that the parties needed some working experience with metropolitan relief before engaging in any further wrangling in the trial court on remand. The agreement promised to give all housing authorities in the Chicago area an opportunity to participate; but where any local housing authority was unwilling or unable to perform, HUD agreed to bypass the local authority, as specifically provided in the 1974 HCDA.

To find suburban landlords willing to accept black CHA tenants and applicants for these moves to rental apartments in suburbia, Polikoff and HUD also agreed that the Leadership Council for Metropolitan Open Communities should be retained. The Leadership Council had already performed similar search and counseling functions for the Illinois Housing Development Authority (IHDA) in a much smaller test program to provide opportunities for low-income, inner-city minorities to move out of CHA's public housing ghettos into rental apartments in the suburbs. Although the Leadership Council had some problems in finding willing landlords in the suburbs and in finding *Gautreaux* plaintiffs who wanted to risk the move, the metropolitan remedy agreement was expanded and extended. As the decade closed, 703 *Gautreaux* families had been placed under the demonstration project with HUD, over 500 through the efforts of the Leadership Council, and only 100 in newly constructed dwelling units financed by HUD, IHDA, or CHA.

Kale Williams, the director of the Leadership Council who had helped to affix responsibility for CHA's intentional segregation some thirteen years earlier, reported in November, 1979, that *Gautreaux* families were volunteering in increasing numbers and that 3,500 could be placed in the next year alone if willing landlords could be found. Williams added, however, that without the active solicitation and searches by the Leadership Council almost all participation in HUD's Section 8 program would continue on a racially dual basis, with white families subsidized in all-white areas and blacks in all-black areas.*

HUD analyzed the experience of the first 400 *Gautreaux* families moving under the demonstration project. Generally, the moves to otherwise virtually all-white suburban apartment developments were peaceful and rewarding. Complaints about lack of public transportation and social acceptance by some white neighbors were tempered by comments about new opportunities and interactions and by the overall improvement in their own lives and those of their children. These *Gautreaux* demonstration families found apartments throughout the metropolitan area, most in relatively new developments with idyllic names such as Willow Creek, Royal Meadows, and Rollinghill Manor. The difference between CHA's aging and blighted high rises of despair and the two-story apartment complexes with green meadows, amenities, and a spark of hope was dramatic. The demonstration project, however, was severely limited because *Gautreaux* tenants in the suburbs needed a car, three- and four-bedroom apartments were unavailable, and landlords with apartments in the highly competitive close-in suburbs were usually unwilling to accept either Section 8 tenants generally or *Gautreaux* plaintiffs in particular. The many CHA tenants and applicants eligible for some relief who had large families or no car were still effectively confined in their housing choices to CHA's blacks-only ghetto.

---

*Under Section 8, the local housing authority certifies the eligibility of a family to receive a HUD subsidy based on family size and income. Landlords willing to accept a certified Section 8 family and price their apartments within HUD guidelines then sign a lease with the prospective tenant *and* the local housing authority. Generally, the tenant pays 15 to 25 percent of the family income and HUD pays the remaining rent directly to the landlord. A substantial portion of all Section 8 families remain "in place," i.e., simply maintain their existing apartment with a HUD subsidy. The remainder generally play "finders keepers" with the certificate provided by each local housing authority and usually look for an apartment within the immediate area. Almost all Section 8 funds therefore subsidize housing on a racially dual basis. Under the demonstration project, however, *Gautreaux* plaintiffs break into the otherwise closed Section 8 programs because of the Leadership Council's active solicitation of vacancies in the apartments of suburban landlords and an areawide certificate of eligibility.

CHA opened only 117 scattered site family dwelling units from 1969 through 1979. Roman Pucinski had not been far wrong: for ten years Judge Austin's order did deal the "death knell to public housing" within Chicago because city politicians and HUD officials opted for the choice of *no* scattered site subsidized housing rather than threaten any encroachment into the remaining white neighborhoods. In the process, Chicago lost over $700 million in federal housing aid, as did white and black families in desperate need of shelter.

Representative Cardiss Collins, the chairperson of the Congressional Black Caucus, held hearings on September 22, 1978, for the purpose of burying the *Gautreaux* decision on the ground that it caused the loss of money for badly needed housing in the blacks-only areas she represented. Representative Collins received an earful that day from opponents of the case and from poor black families as desperate for any habitable shelter as Dorothy Gautreaux had been in 1949 and 1953. The testimony of a variety of witnesses, including Alex Polikoff, showed that responsibility for the lack of new subsidized housing in Chicago rested squarely on the city and CHA, which had failed to implement Austin's order. There was no rigidity or shortcoming in the order itself.

Representative Collins could not help but see the real problem: government and housing officials had defaulted on providing housing opportunities for all Americans because they feared breaching the color line. The truth of this reality became even more evident to all of Chicago when Polikoff agreed to a compromise formula for building new CHA units: one-half of all new projects could be built in black neighborhoods, not one-fourth as originally ordered. CHA still opened no new housing, however, despite HUD's promise of $100 million to get CHA's lagging efforts underway. The public officials in Chicago, with no sanction from HUD, still refused to build housing open to blacks in protected white areas.

As the decade closed, Polikoff reviewed his almost fifteen-year involvement with the *Gautreaux* plaintiffs. Many things had changed but some remained the same. Polikoff was still committed to Dorothy Gautreaux's original dream of open housing for blacks. With respect to the implications of the Chicago public housing case, Polikoff had a mixed view:

> We have been nearly 100% successful in stopping the construction of instant, institutional ghettoes in black and poverty areas of Chicago and, with the aid of other suits and attention, in most American cities. But from Judge Austin's first order in 1969 through the Supreme Court's decision in 1976, we were a total failure in obtaining any meaningful relief for the confinement of minorities by CHA and HUD in the ghetto. From 1976 through 1979, we began to explore the metropolitan option of

opening housing opportunities in areas outside Chicago. The number of families benefitted is small but growing. We started slowly and we are only now beginning, belatedly, to chug along. With the aid of the Magistrate's report affixing responsibility for the delays, we've also convinced the judge newly assigned to the case to order HUD to condition community development funding on the city's performance of its housing obligations under the modified order. And we're negotiating with HUD on a final consent decree for metropolitan relief. They've found that our Gautreaux demonstration project is far more effective than anything else in opening housing opportunities to minorities. As a result, we've got a chance to expand the program and totally reform HUD's administration of its subsidized housing program. What is now only at most a small trickle could become at least a sizeable stream in the years ahead if we can think creatively and work affirmatively.

Yet it was a sad commentary that HUD, charged with implementation of the two-way integration objectives of the 1968 Fair Housing Act and the 1974 HCDA, was only beginning in 1980 to recognize that *Gautreaux* demonstration projects could become a part of the rule of equal housing rather than an exception to the long-standing practice of funding continued ghettoization. Similarly, the Nixon administration's decision to accept segregation had deprived many federal civil rights enforcement agencies first of their will and then of their ability to function. The two- and three-year backlogs of complaints in these agencies and the numerous federal court rulings finding pervasive agency failure to comply with their prescribed duties symbolized the extent of the damage. When the Carter administration took over in 1977, the federal civil rights enforcement effort was in shambles.

David Tatel, director of the Office of Civil Rights in HEW, reported that he arrived to face "absolute disarray resulting from a breakdown in the federal anti-discrimination law enforcement machinery. We spent the first two-and-a-half years just trying to fix up the federal civil rights compliance shop to make it useable." Yet as the decade closed, the Carter administration had yet to provide its now "functioning" civil rights army with any new mission relevant to the issue of urban segregation. Instead, administration officials conceded that they ignored the issue of racial segregation altogether in framing a "new" urban policy. After completing an investigation of the civil rights enforcement effort for the secretaries of HUD and HEW, Harold Howe II, the respected vice president of the Ford Foundation, concluded that the government continued to default on its responsibility in the housing area:

> While President Carter has done some good and useful things so far in attacking the fiscal problems of the cities, I do not think there is any

clarity about the long-term problem of racial isolation in the major metropolitan areas. Indeed, it seems fair to think that the current policy of the Administration is to keep the core cities as they are, predominantly inhabited by blacks and poor people, and simply to provide some jobs and social services there to serve them. That is not much of a dream for the future.

Alex Polikoff could see the extent of the work that remained to be done. Although he was beginning to see some ways to open exclusively white areas to a few blacks trapped in Chicago's ghettos, he had only begun to think about how to assist in revitalizing central city neighborhoods and rebuilding minority ghettos on a nonracial basis. He had begun to work on the notion that housing near the central business district and mass transit could be attractive to both whites and blacks. He was also considering ways that HUD could link up with private developers to rehabilitate these areas and build new housing on an integrated basis, with some units open to the *Gautreaux* plaintiffs. Similarly, he pondered how the remarkable ''gentrification'' of some old and abandoned center city housing by middle income whites and enterprising entrepreneurs could be linked to building stable, integrated neighborhoods under the terms and money of the 1974 Housing and Community Development Act. Polikoff remained deeply skeptical of such development, however: ''Unlike the remedy of school desegregation, all of these housing initiatives affect only a small portion of the people and only chip away, one bit at a time, at the overall and overwhelming pattern of segregation.'' Polikoff had more than enough work to do for the next fifteen years.

Dorothy Gautreaux died three years before the Supreme Court gave credence to her dream of open housing. During the pendency of the countless hearings and appeals, her children had grown up to face their own segregation dilemmas long before a single *Gautreaux* family moved out of the CHA projects pursuant to Judge Austin's order or the HUD demonstration. Dorothy Gautreaux's legacy was her name, firmly affixed to the principle that HUD has the continuing responsibility to provide minorities with a choice of housing beyond the color line.

Whether the *Gautreaux* principle of housing opportunity would long survive remained in substantial doubt as the decade closed. Representative John Conyers, a leading member of the Congressional Black Caucus, had expressed this concern at a congressional hearing on the principle in 1978: ''[white] people don't want to live in an integrated society and they could care less what the Supreme Court says, what laws we pass, and how we go about trying to enforce it.''

A sadder fact was that most Americans refused even to consider whether an invidious system of racial ghettoization split the country. Perhaps only another spate of riots and protests could awaken the American conscience to confront the issue. Or, perhaps, a forthright ruling from the Supreme Court on the nature and extent of such a caste violation might place the issue on the front of the political agenda for action rather than reaction. The prospects for any such direct judicial challenges to urban apartheid, however, seemed dim, particularly after the Court's rulings in the Detroit and Dayton school cases. While the *Gautreaux* ruling was limited in its impact to a relatively few families, the rulings in the Dayton and Detroit school cases appeared to be designed to avoid consideration of any systemic wrongs out of concern for the opposition that would greet the larger impact of systemwide school desegregation decrees. The Columbus, Ohio, school case would provide the next opportunity for the Court, and the country, to face this dilemma.

V
The Lower Courts Answer the Supreme Court's Call to Retreat, 1976–78

Chapter 11
Judge Duncan's Trial of the Columbus
School Case, April, 1976, to October, 1977

The First Witness

On April 20, 1976, district judge Robert Duncan instructed plaintiffs to call their first witness. Helen Jenkins Davis stepped forward to take the stand in the Columbus, Ohio, school case. She was eighty-one years old. Davis was the first witness in the trial that would, eventually, test the Supreme Court's view of segregation yet one more time before the end of the decade.

As a child, Helen Jenkins heard tales from her parents of "hiding if they ever saw a covered wagon on the road to avoid drivers looking for black children to sell into slavery." They had fled to Ohio before the Civil War in the hope of avoiding that legacy. As Helen Jenkins grew up in Columbus, however, a caste system of segregation still surrounded her. She attended Garfield Elementary in grades one through eight. As the "only colored girl in the class," she said that she "hated school because [she] was so mistreated." For example, her eighth grade teacher put her in the back of the class behind even the "bad white boys" and refused to allow her to mingle with the white girls. When she went home, her mother said, "You sit right there, show that teacher you can learn no matter where she puts you." At East High, Jenkins was one of forty black students, but one of four who graduated. "The rest just couldn't take that racism," she said as she described her classmates' exclusion from the school's extracurricular and social activities, ostracism in class, and discrimination in teaching and grading. "If it hadn't been for my mother, I would have quit. . . . She was behind me all the time. She told me, 'You stick in there and do your work and show them you can learn no matter what they do to you.' "

It seemed as if the color line that she experienced in school spread throughout community life as more blacks and southern whites moved to Columbus. She remembered fondly her first experiences in a racially mixed neighborhood. She went in and out of the homes of playmates of many races and creeds freely and without racial slurs. By the time Helen Jenkins was in high school, however, the racial discrimination she had come to know in school had spread to the theater where blacks had to sit together in the "chicken roost" and to the dime stores where blacks had to sit at one end of the counter and drink their soda pop out of glasses with red bottoms. As one contemporary reporter of race relations in Columbus noted, "nothing is more repulsive to the white man than the idea of amalgamation of the races.'' In 1912 the city shifted from ward elections that provided black representation to at-large elections that would exclude all blacks from the city council for decades. Before she graduated from high school, Helen Jenkins joined the NAACP to fight such discrimination.

After high school, she attended the school district's teacher's college and graduated in 1916 with a 98.6 grade point average out of 100. Of the sixty-eight white graduates, all received teaching jobs immediately; Jenkins and her two black classmates did not. She worked for eighteen months as a store clerk to support her widowed mother and waited for a teaching job. When Jenkins applied for an elementary school position with the Columbus public schools for a third time, the assistant superintendent of schools, Miss Gugle, told her, "There's no place in Columbus for you. We're not putting any [more] colored girls in [our] school[s], but I will help get a school down South."

Helen Jenkins Davis bristled on the witness stand as she remembered her response:

> I said my parents were taxpayers here, and they didn't educate me to go down South and I had never been farther south than fifty-five miles from Columbus, and I said, "My three generations . . . to my mother lived in central Ohio before, and I repeat, before the Civil War, and my father was a businessman downtown, had a big restaurant on Long Street between Third and High before I was born, and three or four years after I was born, before he passed," and I said, "my father and my mother paid taxes and they didn't educate me to go down South."

After 1910, however, no blacks taught in any Columbus school except the blacks-only Champion Elementary.

Miss Gugle's rejection moved Jenkins to challenge the superintendent in December of 1917 to break this color line in hiring:

> I had been bitten so much by that viper called racism that I had almost become immune like the repellants for bugs, so I went back the next week [to see] the superintendent. . . . I didn't see Miss Gugle because I suppose she would have stopped me.
>
> I went in, and he said, "What can I do for you?" I told him I was in the week before and Miss Gugle told me there was no place for me in the Columbus schools. "We are not putting any colored girls in." She would send me down south to help me get a school. I said I wasn't educated to go down south. I said I didn't like it.
>
> He was sort of fat. His belly shook like Santa Claus.
>
> I said there are so many schools. I named the schools where the large

proportion of black [students] were. I said, "Now, you try me in one of those schools, and if I don't make good, I will quit."

On the Saturday before Christmas, Jenkins received a special delivery letter directing her to report on the first day of school following the holidays to the Old Spring Street Elementary School. There Helen Jenkins taught for the next two-and-a-half years. Jenkins was the only black teacher outside Champion in the entire district. She ran a disciplined class of all races and backgrounds, stressed learning, and tolerated no bigotry. Sixty years later she received a letter from one of her former white pupils from the Old Spring Street school saying "what a wonderful experience it would be if all people could be exposed to such a United Nations."

Before 1910 there had been other black teachers at a few Columbus schools, for example, "Miss Baker and Miss Nell Moffit at the Mound Street school . . . , Miss Monmouth at Fieser School [and,] Miss David at Front Street School." Then the board opened the Champion school with black staff and black pupils. The local press called it a "clever scheme to separate races in Columbus public schools." The headline, however, reported, "Negroes to have fine new school." The board assigned all the black teachers to the school, appointed Miss Baker principal, and assigned an all-black student body to Champion.

Prior to 1910, the Columbus Board of Education had sought ways to return to the explicit dual system of "colored" and "white" schools mandated by law prior to 1887. The all-black Champion school provided the answer. In 1921 the Columbus board perfected its new dual system and ended its last remaining experiment in integrated education for years to come by closing the Old Spring Street school and transferring Helen Jenkins to the blacks-only Champion school.

In the 1920s and 1930s, successive boards added ninth grade students to Champion's K–8 enrollment and instituted a "Downtown Option" to allow white students in this large area to avoid Champion. In 1925 the board created a small, all-black elementary "school," the "American Addition," out of portable classrooms to preserve nearby elementary schools as white. At the same time the board assigned the older black children from American Addition to the Champion school, even though it was farther away than the white neighborhood school.

By 1928 another school with many black students was renamed Mt. Vernon; the board then assigned an all-black staff to this latest blacks-only school to make its racial identity clear to black and white families alike. At the same time, Champion's boundaries were enlarged to contain the expanding black population. In 1932 the Columbus board converted Garfield into another blacks-only school by transferring the white staff and substituting an all-black faculty and black principal. That same year, despite protests about segregation, the board also moved a school boundary so that students from nearby white residential areas would no longer attend the previously mixed Pilgrim Junior High. In 1933 the board closed the "mixed" Eastwood school and assigned the white students to white schools and the black students to the already overcrowded but blacks-only Champion school.

By 1932 Helen Jenkins had become Mrs. Davis to her students. At that time she taught an all-black class of fifty-two children, which was much larger than classes in white schools. The board also gave white schools the new books, while the black schools "got all the old books from the white schools and the old desks. . . . [I]t was demoralizing." Mrs. Davis had come to know the reasons for the color line in the burgeoning dual system: for example, the Eastwood school closed because "there were all white people living [near the school], and they did not want colored children crossing Long [Street] to come over into their neighborhood." The color line extended to the orphanage, "the old children's home on Sunbury Road. . . . [T]he white children [walked] to Shepard. . . . They wouldn't have a colored child in that school. . . . The black children passed their neighborhood school and were sent to Champion [by bus] because it was too far to walk." In 1937 the board completed the conversion of Pilgrim into a blacks-only school. The board transferred an all-black staff to Pilgrim and made it an all-black elementary school. At the same time, the board reorganized Champion from kindergarten through grade nine into the blacks-only school to serve students in grades seven through nine who would graduate from the blacks-only elementaries— American Addition, Garfield, Mt. Vernon, and now Pilgrim.

From 1921 through 1938 Davis never taught a white child in her classes at Champion. With the reorganization, the board assigned Mrs. Davis to the now all-black Pilgrim Elementary. Yet "white children [continued to live] within the Pilgrim attendance area . . . right across the street [from the school]. White families across the street, down the street, all the way down on Taylor Avenue, and all of Greenway . . . they had restrictive covenants [and white people] on that street." Despite the proximity of white children to her blacks-only school, "they were always assigned someplace else." So for seventeen years at Champion, and for another seventeen at Pilgrim, Davis always taught in a school that was "All black . . . all black."

Throughout her career, however, she joined protests by the NAACP, the Vanguard League, and black students at Ohio State University against segregation in housing and public accommodations. Through six decades she witnessed segregation in Columbus public schools and remembered. For Judge Duncan she recounted in detail the stigmata daily imposed by the color line in Columbus schools. In 1954, after thirty-four years of teaching in the dual system of schooling in Columbus, Mrs. Davis retired. After a brief respite, she volunteered to substitute teach but was again assigned to Pilgrim and other blacks-only schools some distance from the mixed school near her home. "The [white] principal and those [white] teachers wanted no black face over in that building, and [the person in charge of assignments] would not send me over there." In 1961 she told the Columbus school officials why she would substitute no more: "I have had enough racism. I am going to quit."

As she testified in the federal district court fifteen years later, Mrs. Davis was buoyed by the knowledge that her time to challenge school segregation in Columbus had finally come. She described the overall picture, the details, the names, the places, the faces, the voices, the feelings.

After she testified, her picture was on the front page of the local paper and on the evening news; the local media reported her story and placed it in the context of this major trial. Davis received tens of warm, sympathetic letters and telegrams from former students, friends, and people she had never met in the community, black and white alike. One white person, a stranger, wrote, "I read what you went through and cried. What does color mean anyway? Nothing!" This outpouring was marred by several hate letters, including one from the new Ku Klux Klan telling her to keep her mouth "shut" or the "KKK will take care of you." But Helen Jenkins Davis was not frightened. As she recalled later, "I have been bitten by that viper called racism so much I *am* immune. You can't live on fear or hate. I am just so sorry that not everyone, white and black, has learned this lesson."

After the Columbus trial was over, she said "separate schooling survives on hate propaganda and imposes the myth and the distance of segregation. The children of all races have to come to know each other if this country is to survive. You can't have several countries within one country, one reserved for whites and another for each minority group. How can you have a great country if you keep part of the people down?" As to the white fear of sexual "amalgamation" of the races, she observed that "white men have long integrated at night with black dates, while voting to segregate during the day. Why don't we just allow our young people—men and women, black, red, yellow, white and all the variations in between—to choose their mate for themselves without regard to race or color or fear of social reprisals?"

The cross-examination of Helen Jenkins Davis at trial by the school board's attorney, Sam Porter, focused on the details rather than the broad sweep of her testimony. When Porter suggested that black students attended black schools like Champion from a specific geographic area or neighborhood, Davis retorted: "That's the only place [blacks] were allowed to live . . . [, and] that's the way [the school boundary] was designed [by the school board]." When Porter pressed that "it was the practice of the Columbus Public schools to have school attendance zones," Mrs. Davis reiterated: "They were supposed to have them, yes, but any white child that wanted to leave could leave. . . . [T]his was through some kind of an optional zone for white children, yes.'' On redirect examination by plaintiffs' cocounsel Tom Atkins, Davis was even more emphatic: the so-called neighborhood school concept never seemed to apply to white students living in attendance zones for the designated black schools such as Champion or Pilgrim where she taught for thirty-four years. The detailed facts gave credence to her understanding of the wrong of segregation in Columbus, Ohio.

The Adversaries and the Judge

Robert Duncan's success, from his first days in school with white teachers and classmates to his practice of law with white Ohio Republicans, was substantial. Whatever the reasons, he usually succeeded in making most of his white colleagues and peers forget his color. As a result, the extent to which Mrs. Davis succeeded in conveying her own quite different experience and understanding of the growth of segregation in Columbus schools to Judge Duncan would go a long way toward determining the outcome of the case.

As William Saxbe's accomplished first deputy in the Ohio attorney general's office, Duncan had earned his appointment to the Ohio state court bench. By his imposing judicial performance and political connections, he secured President Nixon's appointments, first to the United States Military Court of Appeals in Washington and then to the federal district court in Columbus. It did not hurt Duncan's rise that his mentor, Saxbe, became attorney general for Richard Nixon.

There was another side to Duncan's experience: like Nate Jones, he had started his legal career as one of Maynard Dickerson's disciples, as a lawyer for the Industrial Commission which Dickerson chaired. Nor had discrimination missed Robert Duncan. Even when he returned to Columbus as a federal judge, he secured the house that he wanted in a white neighborhood only after his realtor enlisted the aid of that community's religious leaders to convene a neighborhood meeting. During the course of heated discussion at this meeting, common decency finally prevailed on the congregation: ''We had a chance. We owe the judge a chance.'' As a black citizen in white America, Duncan knew something of racial discrimination.

Judge Duncan also knew Maynard Dickerson's other most accomplished pupil, Nate Jones, quite well. Nor could the judge's view of the Columbus school system be completely abstract or impersonal; his wife taught in, and his children attended, Columbus public schools. On the other hand, the school board lawyer, Sam Porter, was Judge Duncan's law shcool classmate, a respected attorney and friend. With this range of ties and experience, Judge Duncan provided the final test for the battle between the Nixon program of "benign neglect" and "de facto segregation" and Nate Jones's argument that urban school segregation resulted from racial discrimination and continued the color line of caste.

Throughout the pretrial discovery, the trial, and his subsequent rulings, Duncan did his best to judge the dispute fairly and fully, without playing favorites. The judge even met once with the press before trial in an attempt to assure all segments of the Columbus community that his trial and ruling would be fair. On the bench, Judge Duncan was reserved. He listened impassively to the testimony of witnesses, rarely interrupted with questions, ruled calmly on legal issues, and allowed counsel to make their case.

During the numerous pretrial proceedings, Lou Lucas and his NAACP co-counsel Tom Atkins feared that they were losing at least as many of the skirmishes with Sam Porter as they had won. Worse, the close calls seemed to be going to Porter. The judge even seemed reluctant to put pressure on Porter to disclose the historic location of the boundaries for school attendance zones over time. Perhaps Bill Lamson's reputation as the mapmaker who destroyed neighborhood school defenses with his exhibits had given the school board cause for caution. Lamson's handiwork and the trial could not proceed, however, without the basic school facts.

Finally, Atkins and Lamson found the Columbus school planner who knew the facts. Together, they pored over Lamson's half-finished maps. Still, by the first week of trial, there remained some gaps in the boundary descriptions that plaintiffs could not fill. Lucas and Lamson then discovered that the formal boundary descriptions provided by the board in answers to written interrogatories omitted many details, including optional zones, that had previously been provided to another set of plaintiffs.* As Lucas demonstrated the critical nature of the omissions in open court, Judge Duncan appeared incredulous; he refused to impose any sanctions on defense counsel, but gave Lamson all the additional time he needed to complete his maps and boundary overlays to reflect the omitted material, optional zones and all.

Porter defended the Columbus school segregation on the ground that it was the neutral result of implementing the nonracial building recommendations of the School of Education at Ohio State University. Lucas and Atkins feared that Duncan's belief in his alma mater might outweigh his understand-

---

*The other set of plaintiffs originally sought an injunction against using a new bond issue to build additional segregated schools; after they amended their complaint to seek systemwide relief, members of the Columbus black community prevailed on Nate Jones to intervene on their behalf to ensure that the case against intentional segregation would be fully made. The counsel for the original plaintiffs, Bill Davis, resented this intrusion; but his successor, Leo Ross, cooperated with the NAACP attorneys to make for a strong, joint effort with a broad base of community support.

ing of the historical development of the dual system of schooling described by such witnesses as Mrs. Davis. At one point Duncan even expressed his doubts about the current relevance of the historical proof but allowed the plaintiffs to make a complete record on the issue.

Atkins and Lucas, in their own presentations and through the testimony of witnesses, repeatedly stressed that the prior history was necessary to understand the creation, growth, and perpetuation of a basically dual system through the time of trial. In addition, the OSU school facility study defense had a soft underbelly: Columbus school authorities provided the direction and details to OSU; they studiously avoided asking for assistance to desegregate schools; they ignored OSU recommendations by using such devices as optional zones, intact busing, discontiguous zoning, and racial assignment of staff to segregate schools; and they rejected OSU advice that might lead to some school desegregation.

As the case progressed, two issues began to loom paramount: Did school authorities actually intend to segregate schools? If so, did their intentionally segregative conduct cause the current school segregation? Porter argued that school authorities did not act with any intent to segregate schools and that, in any event, residential choice caused the current racial imbalance in schools. Lucas and Atkins countered that school authorities long acted with a purpose to segregate schools and that such segregative conduct interacted over time with residential segregation to cause the current school segregation. Porter argued that school authorities chose a neighborhood school policy without regard to race and evenhandedly implemented this nonracial policy. Lucas and Atkins countered that the long-standing systemwide policy and practice of segregating faculty, deviating from supposedly neutral neighborhood practices in the fringe between black and white areas, and assigning pupils in small one-race pockets to separate schools demonstrated that segregation and not neighborhood motivated successive boards' actions. As the trial proceeded, it was impossible to know how Judge Duncan would resolve these critical factual disputes.

Throughout the trial Judge Duncan made it clear who was running the courtroom: he would brook no diversions or surprises by counsel from either side. When one scheduled witness unaccountably disappeared, Atkins attempted to substitute another witness from the list previously provided to defense counsel and the court. When Atkins suggested that the new witness be taken out of order and that Porter be allowed to cross-examine at a later date, Judge Duncan balked. Unless Porter offered no objection to the irregularity, the judge instructed Atkins to call the next witness on the list rather than pull any surprises by substituting a witness for whom defense counsel could not be prepared. Atkins hotly suggested that Duncan not sacrifice plaintiffs' constitutional rights to a procedural straightjacket. Duncan retorted that he was in charge of the constitutional rights here and that there would be a five-minute recess during which Atkins could find the next witness on his list. Atkins did not repeat this mistake; he wanted to win Judge Duncan on the merits, not lose him to procedural squabbling.

For Atkins, however, the dispute was not his first brush with authority, and the safe resolution was far from his first opportunity to move on from such a scrape to a substantive challenge. Atkins, born in 1939, attended the blacks-only elementary school in Elkhart, Indiana, through the third grade. When the black school literally fell down, the local school board assigned Atkins and the other black children to a previously whites-only school. The older blacks advised Tom to be prepared for a fight; so he loaded his pockets with rocks, beanshooter, knife, and slingshot. Fortunately, he had no occasion to use his armaments, and he could concentrate on his schooling.

Atkins's father worked in the railroad roundhouse servicing trains for twenty years, and spent another ten years as a sanitation worker for the city of Elkhart. As a minister in the local Pentecostal Church of God in Christ, he led the emotional daylong services and baptism by total body immersion. At the age of ten, Tom had asked if he could be baptized. Reverend Atkins, with a fatherly twinkle, answered, "No, not yet. You would go in a dry devil, and you would come out a wet devil." Tom's mother worked as a domestic for a leading white family and was active in the local NAACP. Both parents were fiercely ambitious for Tom: they told him he had "to do better than those who discriminate against you."

Atkins had his own ideas. He rejected the Pentecostal Church as having too negative a view of life; and he viewed the NAACP as too accommodating on the issue of race. When Atkins got his driver's license, his father asked him to pick up his mother from work. He parked in front of the big house and knocked on the front door. When the white lady of the house answered, he introduced himself and asked for his mother. The woman responded, "She doesn't come in this door. She comes in the side door. You go around, and I'll fetch her." Atkins just walked through the front door and got his mother. As they walked hand in hand out the front door, Tom informed the nonplussed mistress of the house, "My mother will not be coming in your side door." Although Mrs. Atkins never set foot in that house again, she could not scold her son for his reaction; she even gloated a bit when he was elected president of the high school student body that included the son of the woman whom she once served.

Politics and school became Atkins's life at Indiana University. For four years he organized, first the men's residence halls, then the women's residence halls, and finally all of the independents. He was elected student body president by only forty-four votes in the thirteen thousand ballots cast. Sheet-wearing, torch-bearing opponents had placed seven burning crosses on campus and planted cotton balls on the lawn of a sorority that had defected from the fraternity camp to vote for Atkins. The fraternity candidate, one of Atkins's close friends, apologized for the unseemly display but ruefully remarked that it had one benefit: there would be no call for a recount lest he too be mistaken as another racist.

Atkins used his new position to challenge racial segregation on and off campus. When the off-campus barbers refused to give haircuts to blacks, he enlisted the aid of the university president. The president called in the barbers, apologized for the "little bother" caused by IU students, and offered to resolve the dispute by building on-campus barbershops and declaring the off-campus shops off limits for *all* IU students. Within one half-hour, the barbers decided that they wanted "to be good neighbors too" and would open their shops to blacks.

Atkins graduated Phi Beta Kappa and determined to enter the foreign service after earning a graduate degree from Harvard University in Middle Eastern Studies. With his new bride he looked without success at thirty-two apartments in the Cambridge area that had been available when he called on the phone but that seemed to be always "already rented" when he arrived in person for inspection. He finally found a fourth floor walk-up in Allston.

While at Harvard, he took a political science course on organizational structure and wrote a paper on the Boston branch of the NAACP. He followed Ken Guskett, the local president, everywhere. Atkins's paper excoriated the branch for its lack of staff, organization, and direction. As a courtesy, he sent a copy to Guskett. Guskett responded by inviting Atkins to serve as acting executive secretary over the summer before returning to Harvard in the fall for a doctor's degree. Atkins accepted and, over the summer, supported a boycott of Boston schools to protest segregation, withstood thirteen emergency board meetings of the local NAACP to fire him for his audacity, and led a sit-in at the school board office of Louis Day Hicks, the prosegregation leader. Atkins was having so much fun nettling the forces of racial segregation that he stayed on for two years with the local branch.

In 1966, after a stint as professional basketball player Bill Russell's business manager, Atkins returned to Harvard to study law. Bored with law school, he ran for Boston City Council and won a seat in 1967 and again in 1969, the year he graduated from Harvard Law School. On the city council, Atkins served with Louis Day Hicks. In 1971 he ran, unsuccessfully, for mayor.

Governor Sargent then prevailed on Atkins to join his cabinet as secretary for communities and development. Atkins served until Sargent's defeat in 1975. In the midst of the furor over busing in the Boston school case, Atkins challenged Sargent not to submit to public pressure and state legislative attempts to oppose desegregation by repeal of a state antisegregation statute.

Šargent responded by promising to veto such antibusing bills and by sending state police to assist in keeping the peace when violence rocked South Boston High.

After he left state government, Atkins started a private law practice and served as president of the local branch of the NAACP. He and his family received many threatening phone calls from whites opposed to desegregation of the Boston public schools. One such call led to information permitting the redirection of a school bus away from a white mob bent on destruction. Atkins's personal experience with the massive white resistance to crossing the color line in Boston schools, housing, and beaches steeled him to work on school segregation cases for Nate Jones on behalf of the NAACP, first on remedy in Detroit before Judge DeMascio, then on violation in Cleveland, Columbus, Benton Harbor, and many other places.

Lucas and Atkins brought to the Columbus school case a deep understanding of the custom of segregation and the process of discrimination. After they proved the racial discrimination in the Columbus community through such witnesses as Helen Jenkins Davis, they spoke with considerable credibility in arguing that the school board was subject to the same racial pressures. Lucas ridiculed the school board defense that school decisions had been made on a neutral basis without regard to race: ''can anyone really believe that school officials who live in a community riven by racial discrimination walk through some magic door when they enter the central administration building and are thereby freed from all sentiments and pressures arising out of the community custom of segregation?'' As the proof mounted of historic systemwide faculty segregation policies and specific incidents of racial conversion that promoted a growing core of blacks-only schools, the school board's ''magic door'' defense would appear increasingly dubious to any fair finder of fact.

Notice and Conscience, Intent and Causation

If Helen Jenkins Davis provided the first historic insight into the Columbus school case, Barbee William Durham provided the ongoing drive and conscience. He was born in 1910 to parents from Kentucky who knew the color line first hand: the state prevented his mother from continuing at the private Berea College when the high court upheld the constitutionality of Kentucky's statute barring the teaching of black and white together. His parents returned with Barbee to a farm in Taylor County, eighty miles from Louisville, with a one-room colored school and one teacher for the forty to fifty black children of all ages in attendance. For four years, he walked three miles to this wooden building, until his parents moved to Dayton, Ohio, in 1920. There he experienced the same racial discrimination visited on his contemporary, Phyllis

Greer. Barbee Durham first attended Longfellow Elementary, where some teachers placed Negro children in the back of the class separated from whites by a row of empty seats, and then Steele High School where the few blacks could never use the swimming pool or attend social functions.

In 1930 Durham matriculated in the College of Pharmacy at Ohio State University. Durham waited tables at a whites-only fraternity and a downtown hotel to help pay his way through school. He studied hard and earned admission to an academic honorary organization, but only on the condition that he not attend the annual banquet at a hotel that excluded blacks. Durham challenged this special restriction; and, within the year, the annual banquet was held at a campus location and was open to all races. Durham was also active in an antilynching league that challenged the latest rise in overt Klan activity in Ohio.

After graduating in 1934 with honors, Durham returned to Dayton to work in a Frigidaire plant. He became active in the local branch of the NAACP but returned in 1937 to Ohio State University as a pharmacist. Again he joined the local branch of the NAACP, and in 1939 he formed a Vanguard League with seven others, all but one employed by the state, who were dissatisfied with the limited nature of the NAACP protest. The new group picketed theaters, restaurants, hotels, and other public accommodations that excluded or segregated blacks; they also filed lawsuits, no fewer than five at a time in order to maximize the impact as well as the legal costs on the defendants. The Vanguard League flooded potential white allies and newspapers with letters. They challenged separate park, recreational, and educational facilities and discrimination in hiring, assignment, and promotion by public and private employers. They attacked racially restrictive covenants and the racially dual public housing in Columbus. When America went to war, they reminded that racism was just as much the enemy at home as abroad. While blood banks announced a policy that "the blood [was] separated on the basis of race," Durham protested that blood knew no color line; with a bit of ridicule from the Vanguard League, the blood banks eventually dropped their charade. In time, however, the Vanguard League withered in Columbus. So Durham returned to energize the local branch of the NAACP, where he served as the executive director from 1951 through 1966.

Through all of these years, Durham worked full-time on the staff at Ohio State, spending his evenings and weekends for the cause of racial justice. He chronicled his contacts and his struggles with racial discrimination. He helped publish pamphlets and distribute leaflets, wrote letters to the editor constantly, and challenged every facet of segregation in the community. For example, as he testified before Judge Duncan, the Vanguard League "on a number of occasions attempted to persuade the board of education, the administration, to hire, place and promote school personnel on the basis of qualification rather than race."

Instead, the board proposed to convert another school, Felton, for blacks-only in 1943. The Vanguard League protested this telltale all-white to all-black faculty flip-flop and "asked to have an integrated staff." As Durham had come to see, "the philosophy that [the board] should have black teachers for black children . . . require[d the board] to assemble black children in [one] place so that you can put the black teachers with them. . . . [That's] the policy of separatism." When the board responded that it was "unanimous in their approval" of the racial assignment to Felton, the Vanguard League publicly protested, "What did we get? More segregation!" This conversion left a core of five blacks-only schools—Champion, Garfield, Mt. Vernon, Pilgrim, and Felton—that contained all the black teachers and a large portion of the black pupils in the Columbus school district.

After the Vanguard League surveyed other cities to prove "how integrated faculties would work" and requested nonracial assignment of staff, the board responded by "saying that recommendations or requests [of that type] would not be acted upon this September." The Vanguard League answered by publishing a booklet entitled "Which September?" As Durham testified, "When the Board said, 'Not this September,' we just took it to be more delay and, in fact, perhaps, indefinite delay." The superintendent said that "the administration and the Board could only go so far as they felt that the . . . white . . . community would accept."

The booklet challenged the board's continuing "policy that black teachers would not be assigned to schools except where there were only black children." It also described the gerrymandering of boundaries to create and maintain the expanding core of separate black schools:

> School [zones] are established in such a manner that white families living near "colored" schools will not be in the "colored" school [zone]. . . . We find the school [zones] skipping about as capriciously as a young child at play. The west side of Taylor Avenue (colored residents) is in Pilgrim elementary and Champion Junior High. The east side of Taylor (white families) is in Fair Avenue elementary and Franklin for junior high. Both sides of Woodland Avenue between Long and Greenway are occupied by white families, and are, therefore, in the Fair Avenue-Franklin [zone]. Both sides of this same street between 340 and 540 are occupied by colored familes [who] are in the Pilgrim-Champion, or "colored" school [zone]. . . .

Such attendance boundaries were not entirely "capricious"; they followed the color line exactly. Where other attendance boundaries for black schools happened to include white families, the white children were "transferred by school authorities to white schools."

Barbee Durham kept every record and every publication neatly stored in a growing mountain of filing boxes in his home. Every time he suspected discrimination, he put the responsible officials on notice and saved the clippings, notes, and correspondence that resulted. He therefore had a large quantity of information about his dealings with Columbus school officials. When Bill Davis filed suit against the Columbus school authorities, Durham contacted his old friend and civil rights lawyer Maynard Dickerson; with other black leaders in the Columbus community, they prevailed on Nate Jones to enter the case on behalf of a large group of black parents and their schoolchildren in order to prove systemwide intentional segregation. Subsequently, Durham opened his files, his contacts, his memory, and his insight, first to Lamson and Lucas, then to Judge Duncan in testimony.

On the witness stand, Durham spoke deliberately, sifting through the evidence, the masses of recorded information, probing still more, and then weighing the evidence against experience before providing an answer. Lucas and Lamson knew that they had a witness who for thirty-five years had served as the conscience of the Columbus community and repeatedly given the board notice of the segregative nature of its conduct. With his own dogged perseverance, Durham had forced the board to confront community discrimination and almost continuously had warned Columbus school authorities not to create, incorporate, maintain, build upon, or exacerbate the color line. As Atkins later described this testimony before Judge Duncan, "Barbee Durham exhumed the body of Jim Crow in Columbus and conducted an autopsy to show that its main trunk and vestiges still split the community at large and the public schools in particular."

The detail of Durham's testimony took up where that of Helen Jenkins Davis left off. After the conversion of Felton over the summer of 1943, the five blacks-only schools continued as black schools through the time of trial, identified one part of Columbus schools and housing as designated for blacks and, reciprocally, contributed to the identification of other areas and schools as reserved for whites. As of the 1950s, Durham testified, local banks and lending institutions reinforced this color line by only making mortgages available for blacks in black areas and whites in white areas; and the real estate board enforced a canon of ethics that prohibited any realtor "from introducing blacks or any other 'inharmonious groups' . . . in white neighborhoods." Durham knew this ugly scene not only because he researched it for the NAACP but also because he experienced it when he attempted to buy a house near his work at OSU.

In the 1960s and 1970s, Durham protested to Columbus school officials when they planned new schools or additions in areas effectively reserved for white or black families only. The school board did not heed his warnings, even in the 1970s, any more than they did in the 1940s. Instead, school authorities worked hand in glove with the housing developers, often purchasing sites and promising "neighborhood," i.e., one-race, schools before the first new housing unit broke ground.

On cross-examination, Porter tried to make "the point [to Durham] that you consider probably the single most significant factor in . . . dealing with racially unbalanced schools is the lack of open housing." Durham responded:

> This is sort of a chicken and egg situation. If the schools make a purchase of land even before the developers get into it, the schools have taken the first step. Secondly there are many occasions where school boards . . . [and] administrators work in conjunction with the development of new areas. . . . [Third,] boards and/or administrations have augmented the conditions produced by the segregated housing patterns. . . . [Fourth,] the school board or administration helped the process along by the manner of locating buildings and/or the way in which school boundaries are drawn.

Just as Durham had been the conscience of the Columbus community for the past thirty-five years, so every day on his lunch break he attended the remainder of the trial of the Columbus school case and watched the story unfold. He was joined by many other members of the black community, including Maynard Dickerson, who wanted to bear witness to the continuing challenge to segregation.

Durham, the Vanguard League, and the NAACP had not stood alone in giving notice to the board of its policies and practices of segregation. Other individuals and organizations—including the Urban League, the Columbus Area Civil Rights Council, the Housing Opportunity Center of Columbus, the League of Women Voters, and finally, in 1968, Ohio State University—also proposed desegregative alternatives or challenged various segregative practices. The board steadfastly had chosen the segregation alternative.

At the trial before Judge Duncan, other witnesses and exhibits filled in any gaps in Durham's testimony. For example, William A. Montgomery, a tireless civil rights researcher, recounted the results of his work. He detailed, from contemporaneous reports and newspaper accounts, the board's intent as far back as 1907 to recreate separate schools for white and black. At that time, one board member "said he was a friend of the colored people as well as the white, and he believes it is for the best interests of both that they be educated in separate schools." Contemporaneously, the local press reported, "Negroes held a mass meeting [of eight hundred residents] and [adopted] resolutions condemning the suggested plan to establish separate schools in Columbus for white and colored pupils" that were presented to the board. Montgomery detailed similar evidence of subjective intent and combined it with evidence of objective intent to discriminate—board minutes, boundary overlays, and census maps—right through the time of *Brown.*

When the board's own historian verified the picture of long-standing segregation painted by Davis, Durham, and Montgomery, and embellished it by going back even further in time to describe the nineteenth-century origins of the color line in Columbus schooling, there could be little doubt that the Columbus board operated a basically dual system at the time of *Brown* similar in many material respects to the one of its counterpart in Dayton. Other local witnesses, such as Clarence Lumpkin, head of the Education Committee of the local branch of the NAACP and the Urban League and convener of Civil Rights Commission hearings, testified how the board refused to give anything more than token responses to repeated demands to desegregate the entire system of racially segregated schooling.

Local real estate agents and expert witnesses Taeuber, Sloane, and Green detailed the community context of discrimination in which the school authorities operated. They also illustrated the two-way causal interaction between segregated schools and housing. For example, Taeuber explained that residential segregation by race in Columbus was long-standing and pervasive, ranging from 84.1 to 88.9 on the Taeuber segregation index during the years 1940 to 1970. Economics, choice, ethnic clustering, and happenstance explained little of this racial segregation. The highest index of separation for various European ethnic communities was about 50 and decreased with each generation to levels of 10 to 30. If income rather than race were the operative factor, the black/white segregation index would be "more like 5 or 10 or 15 rather 70 or 80 or 90." A familiar pattern of discrimination in housing—e.g., restrictive covenants, discriminatory marketing and steering, and racially dual federally subsidized housing—contributed to the pervasive residential segregation on which school authorities purposefully built.

In Columbus, school authorities built schools in response to, in cooperation with, and in advance of housing developments that they knew were one-race. As the school official long responsible for setting school attendance zones testified, the board itself defined "the school neighborhood, the school community" in locating new schools, adding to existing schools, and in drawing boundaries. As a result, the board's segregative conduct not only established the racial identity of the school but also stamped that "neighborhood" as "black" or "white." Persons moving to Columbus or relocating within the area relied on the racial identity of the schools to identify the areas in which they should live. Brokers steered white families away from identifiable "black school neighborhoods" and into "white school neighborhoods." This practice increased housing segregation which, in turn, exacerbated school segregation as school authorities continued to build and operate schools along the color line. The existence of one set of black schools and another set of white schools in Columbus contributed to an environment for continued segregation in housing and schools.

Sam Porter disputed Taeuber's description of this two-way interaction between schools and housing, as well as the extent of the school authorities' contribution to housing segregation. Taeuber responded by referring Porter to the concept of "*Unity* . . . the common linkage between [all forms of discrimination, including] economic discrimination and housing discrimination and educational discrimination and labor market discrimination and social discrimination." His testimony confirmed that school segregation was an integral part of a community process of racial discrimination and ghettoization that could not be viewed in isolation. In his view, it was not only impossible, but also clearly wrong on the available evidence, to attempt to distinguish that portion of school segregation caused by school board action from, for example, that caused by housing segregation. The two were interdependent. Judge Duncan listened carefully, almost in fascination. Porter failed to undercut Taeuber's testimony describing the interlocking web of discrimination that set most blacks apart in separate schools and an inferior caste.

Gordon Foster summarized plaintiffs' case against school officials. He detailed the Columbus board's active segregation practices and policies following *Brown* through the time of trial. The catalog of classic devices in Columbus was long: a continued pattern of assigning faculty on a racial basis until caught by the Ohio Civil Rights Commission in 1973; racially identifiable assignment of administrative staff through the time of trial; optional zones; discontiguous attendance areas, and other racial gerrymanders of school attendance zones; use of portable classrooms and busing to relieve overcrowding with segregative results; busing entire classes of black students and teachers into white schools intact as separate blacks-only enclaves; and a pattern of one-race school construction. In addition to the perpetuation of the dual system of schooling inherited in 1954, seventy-seven specific segregation incidents directly affecting 149 schools in every portion of the system were cited.

For example, the "Downtown Option" continued to permit the remaining white students in the center city to avoid attending black schools. East of the downtown area, the board created and maintained optional zones to allow white residents in a small enclave to avoid black schools by crossing the separate city of Bexley to attend white Columbus schools on the other side. The board imposed optional zones in many other areas between pairs of nearby schools of substantially disproportionate racial composition to allow whites to escape from black schools. As other examples, in the southern part of the school district the board created a discontiguous zone to assign a white residential area across the black Alum Crest school zone to the Moler school. Throughout the south and southeastern portions of the district, the board used similar discontiguous zoning, other gerrymandering, and specifically targeted school construction to protect whites from attending identifiably black schools and to keep blacks out of designated white schools for as long as possible. On the west side, the board utilized similar segregative boundary changes and optional zones to segregate black and white students into separate elementary schools. Similarly, as the black population grew north from the center core and the blacks-only Champion school, the board replicated the pattern of segregative manipulations with the opening of new one-race schools, gerrymandering of boundaries, and utilization of optional zones.

The pattern revealed by the string of incidents following *Brown* was unmistakable. The board implemented its "neighborhood" policy in one-race areas to incorporate residential segregation but deviated from or entirely repudiated neighborhood policy at the fringes between black and white areas and in small one-race pockets in order to avoid integration. The systemwide segregation patterns of faculty and staff assignment verified that race, not any neutral principle, undergirded school segregation in Columbus. On the eve of trial, the board even broke its 1971 promise to voters on a bond issue to construct new buildings to favor integration. To relieve overcrowding in a recently annexed area with a racially mixed school to the northeast, the board first built a school in a predominantly white portion and then rejected the superintendent's integrated zoning proposal in order to open the new school as predominantly white and convert the old building into a virtually all-black school. The consistent thread in the board's school operations was segregation, not neighborhood.

Dr. Foster concluded his testimony concerning the variety and pattern of the board's intentionally segregative conduct by describing its contribution to the racial separation of the Columbus public schools over the years. Going around the map of the Columbus school system, Foster pointed out how the "blacks in that area have been compacted and the white area maintained because of actions or lack of action by the Board." In another portion of town, board conduct "helped to keep the black community [in] . . . schools northeast of the Chesapeake Railway and the whites in isolation to the southwest of that dividing line." In other areas, the board's intentionally segregative practice "contributed in various ways to allowing whites . . . to remove themselves to whiter schools and has generally had the effect of compacting the black pupils [in separate] schools."

There could be little doubt that Columbus school authorities engaged in a pattern of intentionally segregative conduct. Although board witnesses succeeded in offering nonracial explanations for a few of the segregation incidents, they failed to explain nonracial grounds for the bulk of the board's segregative practices. While some might argue that capacity concerns justified the board's use of segregative optional zones, discontiguous attendance areas, intact busing, and other boundary changes, the proof revealed that these devices had been manipulated to serve segregative ends; and one of the board's own administrators conceded that optional zones were useless as a device to relieve overcrowding. Sam Porter could not prove that his clients generally succeeded in walking through any "magic door" of racial neutrality in a community split by race.

Having failed to limit the board's intent to segregate to isolated incidents, Porter turned to the argument that pervasive residential segregation, not unconstitutional school board action, caused the current "racial imbalance" in the schools. In essence, he argued that school authorities should not be held responsible for incorporating current residential segregation in their schools. Under this view, faculty desegregation and a "Columbus Plan" of "free choice" remedied the current effects of any prior board misconduct. But faculty desegregation did not desegregate administrators, nor did it overcome continuing racial identification of schools and neighborhoods resulting from the long-standing staff segregation. The "Columbus Plan" involved less than 4,000 students and only 584 full-day transfers for the purpose of "racial balance," and did not even purport to be a desegregation plan.

Porter was therefore left to argue that the "tremendous growth" in the geographic size and population of the school district since 1950 simply overwhelmed the board. By a series of annexations, Columbus grew from 40 square miles to 173 square miles; student enrollment increased from 46,352 to a high of 110,725 before declining to 95,998 at the time of trial; the black population grew apace, spreading out from the center of the city with isolated pockets in several outlying areas. The board built 103 new schools and made extensive renovations and building additions to almost every school in the system to accommodate this growth. But the detailed testimony of Foster, Taeuber, Durham, Montgomery, and others showed that this growth gave the board hundreds of opportunities either to dismantle the historic dual system and to integrate new schools or to impose segregation throughout the system. Far from being overwhelmed by the growth since 1954, the proof showed that the board responded with all manner of new construction, boundary manipulation, and faculty and staff assignments to further segregation.

As the trial closed, Lou Lucas and Tom Atkins were not certain that they would win Judge Duncan on all counts. They had, however, presented the five elements of Nate Jones's complete case for the de jure reality of urban school segregation:

- Pre-*Brown,* the evidence revealed a history of explicitly dual schooling with "overnight" conversion of five schools to "blacks-only," the transfer of nearby white students to other schools, and the refusal to assign black teachers to schools with white pupils.

- Post-*Brown*, the proof showed a racially dual pattern of assigning faculty on a segregated basis that mirrored the pupil segregation and the opening of new schools and additions to serve primarily black or white student bodies with the coordinate assignment of same-race staffs.
- Throughout the entire history of the school system, the proof revealed numerous manipulations and deviations from "normal" geographic zoning criteria in residential "fringes" and "pockets," including optional zones, discontiguous attendance areas, intact busing, other gerrymandering, and school capacity targeted to house only one race; this proof raised the inference that the board chose "normal" geographic zoning criteria in the large one-race areas of the city to reach the same segregative result.
- In recent years, the evidence showed that the board rejected feasible desegregation alternatives proposed by its own staff, outside consultants, and community groups.
- Throughout the entire history of the school system, the proof showed that the board operated within a community context of racial discrimination, was subject to racial pressures, and built upon and contributed to the color line of black ghettoization and white protection.

Lucas and Atkins also knew that Judge Duncan's normal silence on the bench should not be mistaken for lack of interest. Near the end of the trial, Judge Duncan revealed something about his developing judgment: he asked why the state board of education had defaulted on its own obligations under Ohio and federal law to make the Columbus board comply, thereby giving the ultimate responsibility to the federal court. As in all of the other cases tried by Nate Jones and his cooperating counsel on behalf of the NAACP, the state superintendent of public instruction and state board of education had been added as defendants, along with the local school officials. The state, through its responsible state officers, bears the duty to afford equal protection to the plaintiff schoolchildren. If the state officials default in their supervisory obligations, federal courts must supply the necessary protection.

On June 17, 1976, after thirty-six trial days, the violation trial ended. Atkins and Lucas, Barbee Durham and Helen Jenkins Davis, Maynard Dickerson and Nate Jones hoped that Judge Duncan was now ready to meet his responsibility.

The First Word

Judge Duncan wrestled with the arguments of counsel, the cases, and a voluminous record—over seventy witnesses, six hundred exhibits, and sixty-six hundred pages of transcript—to determine the facts and apply the law.

Eight months after the trial closed, he had not yet issued a decision. In the interim, the Supreme Court agreed to review the Dayton case. Jones, Lucas, and Atkins feared that Duncan would delay ruling until the Supreme Court rendered its opinion in Dayton. Instead, on March 8, 1977, Judge Duncan ruled without the benefit of the Supreme Court's decision. While noting that the "Dayton case may provide a vehicle for the Supreme Court to elaborate more fully upon some of the themes discussed by three of its members" in the Austin case, Duncan held that he had an "obligation . . . to read the binding appellate court decisions and to act accordingly."

Duncan ruled that "proof of racially discriminatory intent or purpose is required to show a violation of the Equal Protection Clause. . . . Plaintiffs must prove not only that segregated schooling exists but also that it was brought about or maintained by intentional state action." Citing Judge Weick's decision in the *Deal* case, Duncan also ruled that the requisite school board intent could not be found in "racial imbalance in a school system *solely* caused by discrimination in housing." Duncan added, however, that segregative intent of school authorities can be inferred from objective evidence and docs not require proof of subjective racial motivation or malevolence. After hearing all the evidence and listening to all the arguments about the "neighborhood school," Duncan determined that the purposeful implementation and manipulation of such a policy on segregated housing patterns with full knowledge of the racial result for schools was *one* factor among many others which may be considered by a court in determining whether an inference of segregative intent should be drawn. Duncan concluded his discussion of the applicable law: "if plaintiffs . . . prove purposeful or intentional acts or omission by defendants which have caused a meaningful part of the Columbus system to be unconstitutionally segregated, then defendants are under an obligation to show that racial imbalance in other components of the system is not the result of their purposeful acts or omissions." Duncan, citing the Denver decision, added that intentionally segregative board actions preceding *Brown* were relevant to this determination absent proof showing that they had no continuing impact of any significance.

As to the dispute between the parties over the basic facts, Judge Duncan was "firmly convinced that the evidence clearly and convincingly weighs in favor of the plaintiffs." Duncan recited the intentionally segregative conversions of Champion, Pilgrim, Mt. Vernon, Garfield, and Felton to black schools during the years 1909 to 1943, involving racial assignment of faculty and staff, gerrymandering, and segregative pupil transfers. Through the time of *Brown*, "the Columbus Board of Education maintained what amounted to an enclave of separate, black schools." This substantial duality continued through the time of trial: despite faculty desegregation in 1974, during the 1975–76 school year, "70.4% of all the students in Columbus Public Schools

attended schools which were 80–100% . . . black or white . . . 73.3% of the
black administrators were assigned to schools with 70–100% black student
bodies; and 95.7% of the 92 schools which were 80–100% white had no black
administrators assigned to them.''

As to the specific school board actions continuing the basic dual system
after 1954 in the face of tremendous growth in the geographic extent and
number of pupils and staff, Duncan found:

- continued assignment of faculty and staff on a segregated basis through
  the 1972–73 school year so that, for example, 63.3 percent of black
  elementary school teachers taught in black schools, while thirty-four
  white elementary schools had no black staff.
- a pattern of opening new schools and then maintaining them on a
  racially identifiable basis, black or white, with board knowledge of the
  segregative consequences.
- examples of building schools to a certain size in a specific location with
  particular boundaries gerrymandered so as knowingly to contain nearby
  black and white students in separate schools when feasible desegregation alternatives were readily available but rejected by the board for no
  apparent nonracial reason.
- examples of board use of optional zones, discontiguous attendance
  areas, and other boundary manipulations that contained black and white
  pupils in separate schools and further evidenced the board's wide-
  ranging segregative intent.

Judge Duncan also described the almost continuous ''notice to the Board''
given by various civil rights groups and the state board of education since
1954 ''that action was required to correct and to prevent the increase'' in
racial segregation in the Columbus public schools. The board's response to
this notice ''and to a mass of advice about alternatives has been minimal.''

As to the debate between the parties over residential segregation, Duncan
relied on Karl Taeuber, ''a University of Wisconsin Professor of Sociology
with outstanding qualifications.'' Duncan found housing segregation in Columbus to be pervasive and long-standing. He found that housing choices
were ''constrained because in reality there is a dual housing market, one for
blacks and another for whites.'' Racial discrimination by federal agencies,
local housing authorities, financing institutions, developers, landlords, real
estate brokers, restrictive covenants, zoning, and annexation contributed to
the extensive housing segregation in Columbus.

With respect to the relationship between school and housing segregation,
Duncan found, ''there is often a substantial reciprocal effect between the
color of the school and the color of the neighborhood it serves. The racial
composition of a neighborhood tends to influence the racial identity of a
school as white or black. . . . The racial identification of a school [by segre-

gative board action] in turn tends to maintain the neighborhood's racial identity, or even to promote it by hastening the movement in racial transition areas.'' To Porter's argument that housing segregation caused, and therefore legitimized, the current school segregation, Judge Duncan responded:

> School authorities do not *control* the housing segregation in Columbus, but . . . the actions of school authorities have had a significant impact upon the housing patterns. The interaction of housing and the schools operates to promote segregation in each. It is not now possible to isolate these factors and draw a picture of what Columbus schools or housing would have looked like today without the other's influence. I do not believe that such an attempt is required.

Judge Duncan had slammed the ''magic door'' on the defendants: the Columbus school authorities were inextricably intertwined in the white community's imposition of the color line of ghettoization. ''Defendants' evidence falls short of showing that the racial character of the school system is the result of racially neutral social dynamics or the result of acts of others for which defendants owe no responsibility. Defendants have not proved that the present admitted racial imbalance in the Columbus Public Schools would have occurred even in the absence of their segregative acts and omissions.'' Judge Duncan's view directly challenged Justice Powell's assertion in the *Austin* case that housing segregation resulted primarily from economics and choice and caused almost all school segregation independent of any intentionally segregative conduct by school authorities.

Judge Duncan then made his ''finding of segregative intent'':

> The Columbus Public Schools were openly and intentionally segregated on the basis of race when *Brown I* was decided in 1954. . . . [The board] never actively set out to dismantle this dual system. . . . Viewed in the context of segregative optional attendance zones, segregative faculty and administrative hiring and assignment, and the other such actions and decisions of the Columbus Board of Education in recent and remote history, it is fair and reasonable to draw an inference of segregative intent.

Judge Duncan concluded his ruling by focusing on the extent of the violation in order to provide school authorities with directions for the necessary scope of relief:

> The finding of liability in this case concerns the Columbus school district as a whole. Actions and omissions by public officials which tend to make black schools blacker necessarily have the reciprocal effect of making white schools whiter. . . . [T]hose elementary, junior and senior high

schools in the Columbus school district which presently have a predominantly black student enrollment have been substantially and directly affected by the intentional acts and omissions of the defendant[s].

Nevertheless, Duncan noted that some outlying white schools might not have been affected by the violation: "had school officials never engaged in a single segregative act or omission, the system-wide percentage of black students would . . . not be accurately reflected in each and every school in the district."

Applying the teaching of *Swann,* Judge Duncan gave the defendants the opportunity in submitting a remedial desegregation plan to prove that certain white schools result from "racially neutral circumstances [rather than] present or past discriminatory actions or omissions of defendant[s]." He cautioned, however, that "it would be extremely difficult to attempt to roll back the clock at this point and determine what the school system would look like now had the wrongful acts and omissions . . . never occurred." Judge Duncan ordered the school authorities to submit proposed plans for the desegregation of the Columbus public schools beginning with the 1977–78 school year, within ninety days. Remedy hearings on the plan and a final judgment would follow.

Lucas and Atkins had different reactions to the opinion. Although both were justly proud of the result, Atkins feared that the citation to examples rather than the detailing of each segregative incident left the extent of violation open to attack on appeal. In contrast, Lucas, apart from quibbles over the use of terms like "racial imbalance" rather than "pervasive segregation," felt that the opinion was the most persuasive rendered by any trial judge because of the clear and honest way in which it dealt with the issue of intent and causation, the "neighborhood" school defense, and the interaction between schools and housing. Both agreed that Duncan understood, accepted, found, and wrote in the Columbus school case what Nate Jones had been trying to prove from the beginning: the de jure reality of urban segregation.

Robert Duncan's personal view of the case emerged in his discussion of the history of racially dual schooling in Columbus over continuous protests by blacks. Duncan noted that complete segregation prevailed as a matter of customary law until abolished by board resolution in Columbus in 1881 in response to black protest. From that date through 1909, black teachers regularly taught side by side with whites in racially mixed schools in Columbus, but blacks continued to point out racial grievances in the schooling of their children to the board. With the building of the blacks-only Champion school in 1909, Columbus reverted to its racially dual ways. This return to segregation, however, did not go unchallenged: a black parent sued the board. As Duncan noted: "[E]ven before the turn of the century black citizens complained about the plight of black students in Columbus. In 1909, Charles W.

Smith took the Columbus Board to court in a futile effort to secure equal rights for black school children.''

In the conclusion to his ruling Judge Duncan spoke of those like Helen Jenkins Davis who had appeared before him:

> The evidence in this case harkens back to a previous era in the history of Columbus: a time fresh in the memory of some who testified at trial, when black parents and their children were openly and without pretense denied equality before the law and before their fellow citizens.

From the evidence Judge Duncan found that Columbus school officials, "since the day when Columbus and Columbus Public Schools were openly segregated on the basis of race," just "ignored" Barbee Durham and the "repeated requests and demands for an integrated educational system." The Columbus board instead "engaged in overt actions" of intentional segregation. Robert Duncan may have been appointed by Richard Nixon, but Judge Duncan would not accept the Nixon program of segregation:

> [I]t is essential that plaintiffs now be afforded relief; if they are not, their constitutional rights will not be vindicated. Each black school child in Columbus must have an opportunity for the integrated education and attendant educational advantages contemplated by *Brown I* and the cases which have followed.

The Second Word

On June 10, 1977, the Columbus board, by a four-to-three vote, submitted a plan which proposed to omit twenty-two white schools from its desegregation plan. The board minority submitted an alternative proposal to desegregate all schools in the system, and the state board submitted a plan that included all schools except four on the western edge of the city. On June 27, 1977, the Supreme Court finally issued its decision in the first round of the Dayton case limiting any desegregation remedy to the "incremental segregative effect" of identified violations.

Atkins's concern over the failure of Duncan's liability ruling to catalogue all of the board's intentionally segregative manipulations grew with the Supreme Court's decision. He worried that the "incremental segregative effect" language could be used to limit the desegregation remedy to the five blacks-only schools at the time of *Brown,* plus any additional schools still segregated by the specific post-*Brown* incidents discussed in Judge Duncan's opinion. Although these incidents had been cited as examples, Atkins feared that the Supreme Court might either view them as the sum total of the violation or limit the remedy to the "incremental segregative effect" of only those violations specifically discussed by the trial judge.

If the high court chose either course, another defeat or another trial hearing was in the offing, particularly in light of Judge Duncan's statements (a) that he did not parse the current segregative effects of schools and housing and (b) that absent the board's unconstitutional conduct all schools would not have the same racial mix. Although Jones and Lucas shared these concerns, they both felt that Duncan's opinion as written provided the best vehicle to undercut any move by the full Court to a doctrine that the current impact of each school board action should be analyzed separately and in isolation from the community custom of ghettoization and the two-way interaction between school and housing segregation.

Plaintiff's counsel, therefore, did not ask Judge Duncan to supplement his violation and causation findings in light of Justice Rehnquist's opinion for the Court. Instead, they decided to rely on the upcoming remedy hearings to provide any necessary clarification by responding to any new proof from the board suggesting that particular schools were not affected by the systemwide violation. As Lucas would have it, "Let the defendants take the lead and founder on the impossible task of calibrating the current segregative impact separately caused by the school violation. There is no such time machine or vernier caliper available to separate unconstitutional School Board conduct from housing segregation." Unless *Swann* and every other federal equity case was to be reversed, the wrongdoers could not meet their burden of showing that the current segregation at any school in Columbus was not affected by the systemwide violation.

Sam Porter seized on the Dayton decision to ask Judge Duncan for leave to file an amended desegregation plan to remedy only the "incremental segregative effect" of the specific violations in the March 8 liability opinion, based on a comparison of what the current racial distribution in Columbus schools "would have been in the absence of such constitutional violations." Duncan headed Sam Porter off at the pass. On July 7, 1977, the judge granted the motion to file an amended plan but rejected Porter's argument that the Dayton decision has "a far-reaching impact upon this litigation." Noting that Dayton merely applied the "well-settled principle that the nature and scope of the remedy is to be determined by the violation" to some ambiguous "three-part violation," Judge Duncan reiterated, "there should be no confusion concerning the scope of defendants' liability" here:

> [This] Court specifically found in the March 8 opinion that "liability in this case concerns the Columbus school district as a whole". . . . [T]his case does not rest on three specific violations, or eleven, or any other specific numbers. . . . System-wide liability is the law of this case. . . . Defendants had ample opportunity at trial to show, if they could, that the admitted racial imbalance of the Columbus Public Schools is the result of

social dynamics or of the acts of others for which defendants owe no responsibility. This they did not do.

In permitting Porter to file an amended plan, Duncan reminded that the school board had another opportunity under *Swann* to meet the burden of showing that the current racial composition of any school "is not the result of present or past discriminatory action on [the board's] part."

Porter filed an amended plan that proposed to desegregate only the 11 black schools specifically named as examples of intentionally segregative board conduct in the March 8 opinion. Of the 167 schools in the Columbus system, the amended plan proposed to continue 73 identifiably white schools and 41 identifiably black schools. At the hearing on the various plans submitted, the Columbus school authorities offered no new evidence attempting to demonstrate that these 114 racially identifiable schools, or even the 22 white schools in the original board plan, were "not the result of present or past discriminatory action" on their part as required by *Swann*.

In view of the board's refusal even to attempt to meet this burden of proof, Judge Duncan in his July 29, 1977, remedy order rejected the board's original and amended plans as "constitutionally unacceptable." Once again Duncan reiterated the nature and extent of the violation and the scope of the remedy: "The entire Columbus Public School System was unconstitutionally and intentionally segregated. The law requires, then, that the remedy have the hope of desegregating the entire system." Following additional skirmishes, on October 4, 1977, Judge Duncan finally approved a systemwide plan submitted by the Columbus board for implementation at the beginning of the 1978–79 school year.

Throughout the case, in court and out, Duncan heard the clamor of those who argued that "desegregation of our schools is not worth the trouble of doing it." The National Association of Neighborhood Schools (founded in Columbus to fan antibusing fervor throughout the North), Citizens Against Forced Busing, the Neighborhood Schools Coordinating Committee, and even the Ohio KKK publicly and privately opposed "forced busing" at rallies and meetings, in pamphlets and letters, and through door-to-door campaigns. They were joined by local congressman Chalmers Wylie, who railed that "busing should not be forced on a community to achieve racial balance." Wylie conceded that he "laid low" on the issue until it hit Columbus because, when other districts had been found guilty of fostering segregation, he thought "something must be wrong with them"; but when Judge Duncan found intentional segregation at home, Wylie changed his mind.

Attorney Robert Hammersmith sought belatedly to intervene in the case to argue that parents had a right under the due process clause of the Fourteenth Amendment to send their children to the school nearest home. When Duncan rejected that claim, Hammersmith filed a suit in state court seeking a contrary declaratory judgment based on Ohio law. After that tactic failed, Hammersmith secured the petitions of one thousand parents warning the Columbus board that they would simply ignore any reassignment under a desegregation plan. Hammersmith then requested an order from Duncan advising families of their supposed ''right'' under state law to choose home instruction, a private school, or a ''neighborhood school'' over ''racial balance.'' The district judge frustrated such mischief by issuing an opinion explaining that, under the supremacy clause of the Constitution, federal law controls over any conflicting state law.

Meanwhile, President Ford's solicitor general Robert Bork had continued to draft appeals to the Supreme Court to curtail busing sharply. He argued that the courts should be limited to rectifying the assertedly minor effects of supposedly isolated violations, even in cases of pervasive discrimination such as in Boston, where the specter of the federal government capitulating to violent white opposition to desegregation threatened the rule of law. Only the entreaties of an outraged civil rights community had persuaded Attorney General Edward Levi to halt Bork's filing such an appeal to the Supreme Court in the Boston case.

President Carter's appointment of Sixth Circuit judge Wade McCree as solicitor general ended the Justice Department's attempts to strip *Brown* of practical meaning. But Representative Ronald Mottl, from an exclusively white suburban district near Cleveland, stepped in to begin a movement in Congress to amend the Constitution to ban all ''forced busing'' by prohibiting the compulsory assignment of any child to any school other than that nearest his or her home.

For many, the first Dayton decision sounded a welcome retreat from court-ordered desegregation. But Judge Duncan, citing the Sixth Circuit's recent affirmance of Judge Fox's thorough-going desegregation decree for the Lansing, Michigan, public schools, unequivocally rejected this reading of *Dayton*: ''Arriving at such conclusions requires the rewriting of *Brown,* [the Denver ruling, and] *Swann.* . . . The United States Court of Appeals for the Sixth Circuit has not retreated from adherence to the letter and spirit of those landmark Supreme Court determinations . . . , and neither will this Court.'' Unfortunately, the Sixth Circuit's resolve was not as sure. On July 20, 1977, a panel remanded the systemwide violation finding in the Cleveland school case to the trial judge for reconsideration in light of the ''incremental segregative effect'' standard and noted that the Supreme Court's decision in Dayton formulated ''test language which the Majority [on the high court] has now declared to be critical.''*

---

*The Sixth Circuit's remand order could also be read, however, as giving the trial judge, Frank Battisti, an opportunity to clarify and to document the bases for his finding of systemwide liability.

Due to the careful and complete news coverage, however, most citizens in the Columbus community were not surprised by Judge Duncan's ruling. They had to come to know and appreciate something about the nature of the man and the case. As the *Columbus Citizen-Journal* commented when Duncan explained to the Columbus board that the Dayton decision provided no immunity, "it would be better for the city as a whole if the Board would accept the peaceful desegregation of the school system, instead of frantically grasping at legal straws to avoid its responsibilities."

Nor was Helen Jenkins Davis surprised. She saw Judge Duncan as calm but independent, a person who would meet his responsibility and had the interests of all the children and the entire community at heart. She was confident that Duncan would stand firm against the white racists who proposed, after his ruling, that federal judges be "elected in order to insure quality on the bench." In the school desegregation ruling, Davis hoped that black and white children and their parents in Columbus would finally have "the opportunity to learn to know one another rather than the hate propaganda of segregation."

The Metropolitan Columbus Schools Committee formed to assure peaceful acceptance and orderly implementation of any desegregation plan. This coalition included Mayor Tom Moody and a wide cross section of community groups, ranging from the AFL-CIO, building trade unions, UAW, Police Officers' Association, and teachers' unions to the United Way, Junior League, Catholic Diocese, Boy and Girl Scouts, YMCA and YWCA, and the League of Women Voters. With a series of full-page advertisements, slides, tapes, movies, and meetings, the committee explained the facts of the court's rulings and of desegregation to explode myths and halt rumors. One pictured clubs, rocks, and helmets in front of a "Stop Forced Busing" placard and warned that "raising hell is no way to raise our children." The ad continued: "Strong language? Maybe. But that's what it seems to take to wake up some Columbus citizens to the fact that all this overreacting, screaming, and rumor spreading is hurting our school children and community." After explaining the rumors and the facts, the committee concluded that Columbus schools could be peacefully desegregated if enough people put the well-being of the children first: "We've made up our minds to act peacefully in the acceptance of a desegregation plan." The vast majority of Columbus families, black and white, and taxpayers, large and small, seemed willing to make at least *this* commitment.

Chapter 12
The Sixth Circuit on Trial: The Columbus and Dayton School Cases on Appeal, June, 1977, to July, 1978

On the Attack

Judge Rubin read the news of the Supreme Court's June 27, 1977, ruling in Dayton not only as a call to retreat but an invitation to scuttle the desegregation plan that had gone into effect the year before. He immediately convened a conference call among counsel to schedule a hearing to ascertain whether plaintiffs had any additional evidence. Lucas received the call at his home in Memphis, where he was recuperating from minor surgery. He informed Rubin of his condition, his commitments at previously scheduled court-ordered appearances in the Columbus, St. Louis, and Wilmington school cases throughout July, and the need to review the Supreme Court's opinion and fully prepare for any evidentiary hearing.

Lucas also thought to himself that if it had taken almost four years of litigation to get a desegregation plan in Dayton, it ought to take more than a month to end it.

Over the phone, however, Lucas only described how his reading of early newspaper accounts of the decision suggested that the hearing contemplated by the Supreme Court was not a foregone conclusion and that the desegregation plan would in all probability have to remain in effect at least for the coming school year. Rubin pressed for an expedited hearing because he saw no reason to bus for another year if it would not be required thereafter. By suggesting that further debate over a ruling that no one had yet read made little sense, Lucas cut the conversation short. Rubin agreed to another conference call for Friday, July 1.

On the next call, Judge Rubin reiterated his desire to hold the hearing and make his determination before the opening of school. He offered to hold any hearing in Memphis at any time to fit with Lucas's medical and scheduling problems. Lucas reiterated his view that a complete review of the existing record and further discovery were required to prepare for the hearing contemplated by the Supreme Court remand. Rubin resisted and instructed Lucas to file a statement concerning why any hearing should be delayed.

On July 5 Lucas submitted his "Report to the Court." The "Report" described the substance of the two conference calls; it left no doubt that in plaintiffs' view Rubin had prejudged the issues left open by the Supreme

258

Court's remand. On the same day Lucas called me to draft an application to the Sixth Circuit to stay any order that Rubin might issue dismantling desegregation. On July 18, Judge Rubin reiterated his intention to rule before the fall semester and scheduled a hearing for August 8.

Lucas appeared at the August 8 hearing but only to argue for delay, not to present evidence. He stated that he needed until October to review the record and to interview witnesses for possible supplementation. In particular, Lucas cited the several offers of proof excluded by Judge Rubin at the first hearing concerning the critical issue of intent. Rubin claimed to have "no such independent recollection" of excluding such evidence but added, "Mr. Lucas, I will accept your *professional* word." Lucas also noted that many of Lamson's maps and overlays had been lost by the court clerk during the various appeals; time was needed for preparation of new exhibits. Finally, Lucas argued that the Supreme Court had, in effect, cautioned the parties and the lower court "to take your time" in order to do it right this time around.

Rubin retorted, "Mr. Lucas, I am astonished to hear a plaintiff in this type of case use the phrase 'take your time.' " Rubin then engaged Lucas in a debate over the relative merits of "busing," desegregation, and segregation. The judge suggested that the courts might be wasting the taxpayers' money for no reason if busing continued another year.

Dave Greer, the board's attorney, responded by noting sarcastically that "October 1, coincidentally, would be just after the opening of another school year under the racial balance plan." Greer was relentless. As Lucas had offered no additional evidence, Greer argued that the case should be dismissed. The trial court had already found the basic facts in the board's favor. The only conceivable issue remaining was whether a few isolated optional zones were created with discriminatory intent and whether they had any current segregative impact years later; surely such trivial violations could not support busing for another year. If the court would not dismiss the case, then Greer asked permission for the board to dismantle the systemwide desegregation plan in favor of a voluntary, magnet approach.

At the close of the hearing Rubin called Lucas forward: "The Associated Press this morning quoted you as saying that the NAACP was attending this hearing 'scornfully.' Was that word used by you?" Lucas responded, truthfully, "No, your Honor." Nevertheless, Rubin threatened Lucas that another "disparaging incident of this sort will simply force me to institute disciplinary hearings." Lucas would have none of these threats: he had no way of controlling newspaper interpretations or misquotes, but he was free as counsel to express his disagreement "with this Court and we think the Court is rushing to judgment." Once again Lucas and Carl Rubin stared at each other eye to eye. Lucas refused to blink despite Rubin's warning that "there is some evidence of an intentional disparagement of federal courts." After the hearing, the AP reporter offered to inform Rubin that the phrase ''scornfully'' had been the reporter's interpretation, not a phrase used by Lucas; Lucas declined any further ''help.''

On August 12, Lucas responded in writing with a motion to stay further remand proceedings ''pending hearing on the merits'' and with a ''Memorandum in Opposition to District Court Proceeding in Violation of Supreme Court Opinion.'' Reciting the language in the high court's ruling that criticized the limited nature and extent of the prior proceedings in the lower courts and required careful review on remand, Lucas struck back at Rubin. Quoting Rehnquist's opinion, Lucas wrote: '' 'Complex factual determinations,' not hurried, predetermined shots from the hip, are 'what must be done in this case.' '' One hour later Judge Rubin issued an opinion continuing the systemwide desegregation plan in effect for the fall semester only and scheduled an evidentiary hearing for October 10. Rubin held that ''the right of any person and all whom he may represent to demonstrate asserted deprivations must never be denied.''

Lucas took no particular satisfaction in this ruling. He felt that Judge Rubin had merely given plaintiffs ''their right of elocution prior to the termination of their constitutional rights'' for the second semester. Nate Jones, Bill Caldwell, Lou Lucas, and I discussed what evidence should be offered at the October hearing. Caldwell wanted to stand pat on the existing record. I argued that Gordon Foster and Karl Taeuber should present an analysis of the segregative impact of the various systemic violations over time; this could supplement the evidence showing the interaction between schools and housing and the current systemwide impact of the Dayton board's perpetuation and expansion of the historic dual system. Lucas responded, ''There isn't enough time to allow the experts to prepare such an extensive analysis without running some risks that Greer's cross-examination will puncture holes in a too-hurried effort; I'm satisfied their previous testimony already supports our theory of the case. On the other hand, we have to offer something; otherwise, Rubin will probably send me to jail with something quicker than 'all deliberate speed.' Wayne Carle and John Harewood can provide our picture of the case and clarify the ambiguities and gaps in their previous testimony resulting from Rubin's cutting them off or Greer's cross-examination.'' As general counsel, Jones resolved the dispute by accepting Lucas's recommendation.

The evidentiary hearing in October therefore would provide only limited evidence beyond the original record to aid in deciding the case. Judge Rubin also denied the motion of the Carter administration to appear in the trial court to support its position on the systemwide nature of the violation and propriety of systemwide relief. While Wayne Carle and John Harewood did testify, Judge Rubin repeatedly interjected his view.

- Any racial identification of schools resulting from the racially motivated assignment of staff was irrelevant because it involved "community perceptions" rather than "incremental segregative effect." Once
faculty had been desegregated, that corrected any "problem." The
former faculty segregation provided "no condition precedent for
punishment," i.e., actual school desegregation, because the Dayton
opinion refused to extend *Swann* to northern schools.
- Proof of intentionally segregative acts at one high school is "somewhat
less than significant" because that school is "no longer open." "The
incremental [segregative] effect of a non-existent school . . . is of historical interest only."
- Proof of racial manipulations (e.g., optional zones, race-based faculty
assignments) in the West Side Reorganization was irrelevant because
"the events of 25 years ago, I suspect, would not affect any student in
school at the moment and might not even have affected his parents. I'm
going to limit any inquiry to 1954."
- School authorities had the right, if not also the duty, to build schools
"where the children are," even if the foreseeable result was the maintenance and expansion of a segregated system, regardless of any preexisting board responsibility to desegregate and of any continuing board
policy of assigning staff to new schools and additions of the same racial
composition as the student body.

Rubin also prohibited Wayne Carle from testifying about the objective
evidence which demonstrated that a former superintendent's calling the West
Side Reorganization "an experiment in integration" was a sham. John
Harewood tried, once again, to make his case against segregation to Judge
Rubin. The judge, however, questioned Harewood's view that school authorities bore any affirmative obligation to avoid operation of segregated
schools if neighborhoods were already segregated by race.

Dave Greer presented a witness who argued that the largest high school
optional zone had "an integrative effect" by 1970 because substantial numbers of blacks then began to choose the whiter Colonel White school rather
than the all-black Roosevelt. On cross-examination, however, the witness
conceded that this option in 1970 still allowed 317 whites to escape Roosevelt. As a direct consequence, Roosevelt remained 100 percent black rather
than the 87 percent black it would have been without the racial option.

The intensity of the struggle between Rubin and Lucas could be felt by
everyone in the courtroom. The battles over evidentiary rulings still raged. At
one point, the dispute overwhelmed Lucas; his blood pressure soared, and he
became dizzy on his feet. Lucas approached the bench, informed Judge Rubin
of the problem, and asked for a recess. Rubin graciously adjourned the

proceedings for the day to permit Lucas to consult with a physician and to recover. In contrast, when Lucas was questioning John Harewood, Judge Rubin sustained an objection by defendant's counsel because the "time" of the event was not clear. Lucas then asked Harewood to "give us the points in time when you made those recommendations. By that I assume we don't require the hour, but just the particular day or period of time." Rubin called Lucas to the bench and said:

> I have to be extremely careful with you. . . . [I]f you make any remark of that kind that I deem to be a reflection of my response, I will take action against you, Mr. Lucas. . . . Nobody under any circumstances ever talks in terms of hours. That's a sarcastic remark, Mr. Lucas, done deliberately, and I consider it an affront. Don't repeat it.

Lucas apologized, "Your Honor, I didn't mean it as an affront to you." Rubin shot back, "It succeeded."

At the end of the hearing on November 4, Judge Rubin indicated that he did not want any more briefs or proposed findings because he would be moving to a decision with dispatch. Greer nevertheless filed a lengthy statement of proposed findings on all contested issues; he argued that school board actions had no discriminatory motivation and/or no "incremental segregative effect." Lucas filed a letter offering to submit proposed findings should Rubin change his mind.

On December 15, 1977, Judge Rubin entered his judgment, findings of fact, and conclusions of law. He dismissed the entire case. He ruled that plaintiffs bore the burden of proving not only segregative intent but also the "incremental segregative effect" of each separate board action viewed in isolation from one another, without regard to the context of community discrimination. Curiously, Rubin described "incremental segregative effect" as "the remedial portion of the [plaintiffs'] burden of proof." He read the Supreme Court's ruling as requiring the victim rather than the wrongdoer to prove whether an intended wrong had other than the intended effect. Rubin concluded that plaintiffs failed to prove that *any* intentionally segregative board action had *any* "incremental segregative effect" as of the time of the original trial.

Rubin also withdrew his previous violation findings concerning optional zones and the rescission. He held that plaintiffs failed to show that any of the optional zones had "segregative intent or effect." With respect to the rescission, Rubin recounted involvement of former superintendent Carle and attorney Lucas in the drafting of the original desegregation resolutions: "The Court does not believe that violation of the United States Constitution can be manufactured by political or legal maneuvering. Surely the gravity of school desegregation cannot turn on such intrigues.'' Rubin then concluded that the rescission of the lame-duck board's desegregation program was not unconstitutional.

As to the board's pre-*Brown* involvement in overt actions of purposeful segregation, Rubin found that plaintiffs failed to present "evidence showing their effect on 'the racial distribution of the Dayton school population as presently constituted.' " Although the core of blacks-only schools remained virtually all-black through the time of the original trial, Rubin held that plaintiffs failed to prove any current segregation was caused by the board's past misconduct. As to the board's blatant faculty segregation policies before 1969, Rubin found that "dynamic gradualism" was a "policy of integration" that had "virtually eliminated all traces of segregation" by 1969. HEW's imposition of a "racial quota" thereafter "edged the legal limit." Rubin concluded by finding that the board's faculty assignments did not identify schools by race and thus had no "incremental segregative effect."

Rubin found the West Side Reorganization an "experiment in integration." Although it preserved the original core of four all-black schools, constructed and opened a fifth, and led to the conversion of four more, he held that "its purpose was clearly integrative rather than segregative." Rubin ignored the contemporaneous proof of racially motivated faculty assignment and the substitution of "optional zones" for "free transfers" to allow whites to escape schools already black or in the process of conversion.

As to the operation of Dunbar as a citywide blacks-only secondary school for thirty years, Rubin did find "intent to segregate." He concluded, however, that any segregative effects "were totally subsumed in the effects of five to six decades of housing segregation in which the Board played no part." He did not accept our argument that the board's intentionally segregative location of a core of blacks-only schools on the west side of Dayton contributed to both school segregation and residential patterns over this time span.

But Rubin did not view the process of residential segregation as solely a matter of economics, choice, ethnicity, or happenstance. He found: "Without question, the prime factor in this concentration [of blacks on the west side] has been housing discrimination, both in the private and public sector." Rubin did not accept the neoconservatives' "free choice" justification for "neighborhood schools"—that racial segregation in housing (and hence in schools) resulted from family choice of where to live rather than discrimination. Rubin held that "the segregated housing pattern has had a concomitant impact upon the composition of the Dayton public schools."

Under Rubin's view, however, that finding immunized school authorities from all responsibility for school segregation. Rubin concluded that the Constitution authorized school boards to locate schools "where the children are." Unless plaintiffs showed that "school authorities conspired with public or private developers to make the West Side all black [or] that they intentionally established black schools to further that goal,'' plaintiffs failed to show the ''nexus'' necessary to meet their ''burden of proving that school officials intended their site selections to have a segregative effect on the school population *and* housing patterns.'' For Carl Rubin, unlike Robert Duncan, there was a magic door through which school authorities entered when they ran the schools: Rubin held school boards act on a color-blind basis so long as they incorporate pervasive residential segregation into the schools.

If Judge Duncan was leading the charge to defend *Brown* in cases of urban school segregation in the North, Judge Rubin was heading up the retreat. Rubin noted the conflict in describing his continuing battle with Lucas: ''The course of this protracted litigation has been marked by conceptual differences not only as to the facts but as to the legal significance of those facts.'' The Sixth Circuit, in the first instance, would have to resolve the fundamental disagreement that divided the two Nixon appointees before final resolution by the Supreme Court.

Columbus school board attorney Sam Porter also fought the legal challenge to urban school desegregation. From the moment of Judge Duncan's first liability ruling in March, 1977, Porter began filing with the Sixth Circuit notices of appeal, briefs, and applications seeking to reverse Judge Duncan's rulings and to stay further remedy proceedings in the trial court. Porter filed another interlocutory appeal from Duncan's July, 1977, rulings and order rejecting the Columbus board's ''incremental segregative effect'' theory and limited desegregation plans. Porter filed his final appeal from Judge Duncan's fall, 1977, ruling approving a systemwide desegregation plan.

Once again, the Columbus board applied for a stay in implementing desegregation. Plaintiffs opposed any stay in remedial proceedings but sought to extend the time for responding to Porter's piecemeal appellate forays until Judge Duncan approved the final remedy.* After all this procedural maneuvering, the Sixth Circuit denied all stays and consolidated the appeals so that plaintiffs could file one response and the court could make one decision on the entire case.

In his briefs, Porter argued that the Columbus board, ''as required by Ohio law, . . . consistently adhered to a neighborhood school policy since before 1900.'' Moreover, between 1950 and 1970, the Columbus board implemented this policy, ''without segregatory purpose'' to ''provid[e] quality educational facilities for an expanding enrollment . . . that increased at an annual rate of 3,300 students.'' Once again Porter pressed the OSU ''school building needs studies'' as the proof of his nonracial ''neighborhood school''

---

*The state board also filed separate appeals, making for a total of five appeals pending at the same time in the same case in the Sixth Circuit.

defense. He argued that the pervasive residential segregation in Columbus, not intentionally segregative school board action, caused the continuing school segregation in the racially neutral "neighborhood schools" in Columbus. Porter even claimed that "Dr. Taeuber did not list the practices of school boards as a causative factor in housing segregation."

In his statement of the facts, Porter treated Judge Duncan's discussion of specific incidents of discrimination as a "few isolated instances" of board misconduct having only minor effect on "racial imbalance." In his legal arguments, Porter charged that Duncan wrongly inferred "segregative intent from the consistent use of a non-racially motivated neighborhood school policy . . . and from isolated instances of board action that did not correct racial imbalance." Porter also claimed that Duncan erred in "attribut[ing] housing discrimination by non-parties and responsibility for segregated residential patterns to the Board of Education."

Finally, Porter argued that Duncan utterly failed to make the "determination of how much incremental segregative effect any intentionally segregative actions had on the racial distribution of the Columbus school population as presently constituted, when that distribution is compared to what it would have been in the absence of such constitutional violations," under the Supreme Court's test announced in the Dayton case.

Relying on Justice Powell's separate view in the Austin case, Porter also advised the Sixth Circuit:

> the principal cause of racial imbalance in urban public schools is the imbalance in residential patterns. These patterns are beyond the control of school authorities and cannot be attributed to their actions. . . . As the subsequent Dayton decision made clear, the jurisdiction of the district court in such a case extends only to the correction of the current incremental segregative effect of specific constitutional violations committed by school officials.

Concluded Porter, the systemwide, racial balance remedy ordered by the district court far exceeded the limited extent of the isolated violations found.

The Plaintiffs' Counterattack

On January 5, 1978, Judge Rubin denied plaintiffs' motion to keep the systemwide desegregation plan in effect pending the appeal to the Sixth Circuit. On the same day the Dayton board voted to end the desegregation plan at the close of the first semester. On behalf of plaintiffs and their counsel, I immediately applied to the Sixth Circuit for relief. We were joined by the United States in a memorandum prepared by Joel Selig and Drew Days. On January

16, the court of appeals enjoined the board "to cause [the] system-wide desegregation plan to remain in effect pending appeal or until further order."

Dave Greer then filed a motion asking the Sixth Circuit to require plaintiffs to post a penal bond in the amount of $358,000 as a condition precedent to the order maintaining the desegregation plan. We objected because the Sixth Circuit had entered its order on the express ground that it was "in the best interests of the parties and the public." The appeals court agreed and summarily denied Greer's motion. Systemwide desegregation would remain in effect until some appellate court finally determined that plaintiffs had failed to prove school segregation in Dayton, Ohio, unconstitutional. The Sixth Circuit would not abandon the plaintiffs to Justice Rehnquist or to Judge Rubin before it heard our case.

Nate Jones asked me to draft the initial brief for the Sixth Circuit in the Columbus case. I reviewed key portions of the record and Judge Duncan's opinions, the dangers of the Supreme Court's opinion in *Dayton* and Powell's view in *Austin,* and the thrust of Sam Porter's attack. I determined that our primary theme should be that the parties and the trial judge focused on the key issues of intent and causation from the beginning. Judge Duncan had not only fully heard but had directly and conscientiously addressed these two issues. Rather than independently argue the facts or law at length, our brief described how Judge Duncan decided the issues of intent and causation.

From this perspective, Porter's briefs might be viewed as a rhetorical bow to the views of Justices Powell and Rehnquist rather than a persuasive description of errors committed by Judge Duncan. For example, the trial court's discussion of specific instances of intentional segregation did not represent the sum total of the violation evidence and findings; as examples and subsidiary fact findings, they merely supported Judge Duncan's ultimate finding that segregative intent had infected school board conduct throughout much of the school district, from at least 1909 through the time of trial. Similarly, the "instances" of manipulation and deviation from so-called nonracial "neighborhood zoning" in racial fringe and pocket areas only provided evidence that segregation, not neighborhood, motivated board decisions. On the intent issue, then, the board's claim of consistent application of "neutral neighborhood" principles with only a few isolated exceptions had been pressed below and proven demonstrably false by the overwhelming weight of the evidence, as Judge Duncan had found.

On the causation issue, I argued that the board's wide-ranging discrimination in schools could not be neatly parsed from housing segregation and community discrimination. The racial identification of schools also identified neighborhoods by race which, in turn, maintained and exacerbated segregation in schools and housing. Karl Taeuber so testifed, and Robert Duncan so found. Whether or not the "incremental segregative effect" inquiry applied to a case with a continuing systemwide violation and history of dual schooling, Judge Duncan made the critical inquiry into causation and found, based on the evidence, that the school board's pervasive, intentionally segregative conduct did contribute to the current segregation of schools throughout the system.

The brief also contrasted Judge Duncan's trial with that of Judge Rubin. In Columbus, Duncan and the parties had focused on the issues of intent and causation from the beginning, while Rubin never allowed much proof on either. From the beginning Duncan applied the legal standards of the Denver, Arlington Heights zoning, District of Columbia employment, and *Swann* cases, while Rubin just read the Supreme Court's opinion in Dayton as creating a new body of law. Duncan wrote a reasoned opinion and made findings supported by substantial evidence, while Rubin concluded that school authorities, no matter how active their own discrimination, were constitutionally immune from challenge if residential segregation was complete because their actions could have no "incremental segregative effect." Rubin's view might well represent a fair interpretation of where Justice Rehnquist wanted to move the law, but it was not the only reading of the full Court's ruling in Dayton.

I was confident the Sixth Circuit would affirm Judge Duncan's judgment. I hoped that the appeals court would do so in a way that assisted reversal of Judge Rubin. But a bigger issue remained: would the Sixth Circuit's rulings then withstand further scrutiny by the Supreme Court and attack by Rehnquist and Powell? In Columbus, we had as sound and compelling a case of a dual system at the time of *Brown* and systemwide de jure conduct thereafter as we were going to find in an urban school district in the North. If the NAACP could not win in Columbus, it could not win anywhere.

In the appeal from Judge Rubin's dismissal in the Dayton case, Jones asked Caldwell to draft the brief for plaintiffs with my assistance. The brief discussed the controlling standards for appellate review in order to give the panel confidence that it could reverse clearly wrong findings and make supplementary findings when compelled by the evidence, as well as to overturn the erroneous use and application of legal standards. We used the Supreme Court's opinion to demonstrate the need for specific, direct, and complete rulings on all contested issues. After three previous appeals, we asked Sixth Circuit to review the entire case fully and to directly reverse Rubin for the first time.

The brief then attempted to demonstrate that Judge Rubin had misread Rehnquist's opinion and therefore failed to apply the correct legal standards for intent and causation, systemwide violation and systemwide impact, and actual desegregation as established by the Supreme Court's prior rulings. We argued that Rehnquist's opinion for the Court cited and confirmed rather than silently overruled *Swann* and the Denver decision. Three fundamental errors therefore marked Rubin's ruling. First, he "misapprehended the legal relevance of the Board's conduct prior to the time of *Brown I*. . . . [I]f the board was operating a dual system at the time of *Brown*, it thereafter 'automatically assume[d]' an affirmative duty to effectuate a transition to a racially non-discriminatory school system by eliminating all vestiges of state-imposed segregation.'' Second, the district court failed to utilize the "common sense . . . approach to discerning segregative intent" once plaintiffs demonstrated that a discriminatory purpose had affected a meaningful aspect of school board operations or a significant portion of the system, as with the overt faculty segregation, optional zones, and perpetuation of blacks-only schools following *Brown*. Third, on the causation issue, the trial court "failed—indeed refused—" to impose the burden of proof on the defendant wrong-doers to show that the current "segregation would have resulted even if they had not engaged in intentional discrimination." Once again, we challenged Greer to show how the systemwide desegregation plan was overly broad if we were right that the violation was extensive.

The brief analyzed how Rehnquist's opinion for the Court in Dayton need not be read by the panel as a command to give up the fight against urban school segregation in general or in Dayton in particular. It included a sixty-page appendix detailing the evidence of intentional segregation and the precise nature of the erroneous findings and conclusions drawn by Judge Rubin.

We could not be sure whether the brief would provide Judges Phillips, Edwards, and Peck with a way to reject the growing Rehnquist-Powell apology for urban school segregation in a fashion to persuade a majority of the Supreme Court, but at least the politics of this battle had evened somewhat. The Justice Department, in a brief written by Joel Selig and Drew Days, joined in the counterattack on Rubin's attempt to use housing segregation to excuse Dayton school authorities from meaningful responsibility for the color line in urban schooling. The United States pointed out that the evidence showed that the board's intentional discrimination and segregation was as great as any court was likely ever to see in a case where segregation was not mandated by state law. The Department of Justice's review of the record showed that "in 1954 the Dayton School Board operated two school systems, one primarily for white students, another primarily for blacks." Thereafter, the board did not dismantle this dual system. The government urged the Sixth Circuit to reverse the trial court and "rule on all contested issues and make detailed findings with respect to the facts and the law." In addition, President Carter gave no visible support to efforts to limit or to ban busing as a remedy for such unconstitutional segregation. Few southern school boards that had already desegregated their schools heard or responded to Rehnquist's call to retreat.

On the other hand, noted sociologist James Coleman, an early proponent of school desegregation, began to argue in a series of articles that desegregation limited to central city school districts merely increased the pace of white flight to all-white suburbs. The neoconservatives continued to argue that segregation resulted from choice, chance, ethnic clustering, economics, and anything else but racial discrimination. They added that "affirmative action" programs in employment, admission to postsecondary schools, and federal contracts amounted to "reverse discrimination" against innocent whites as much as "forced busing" that compulsorily transferred white children out of their chosen neighborhoods. Derrick Bell, a black law professor at Harvard and former LDF attorney, argued that school desegregation was a lost and enervating cause and urged civil rights lawyers to help all-black ghetto schools provide a better education. While public opinion polls showed increasing willingness to send children to integrated schools, the substantial majority continued to oppose busing as a tool to implement integration. Most politicians seemed willing to sit back and let the courts resolve the dispute. Although some senators and representatives responded to antibusing protests in some local communities faced with new desegregation decrees, the majority was unwilling to move beyond hamstringing HEW antisegregation enforcement to a confrontation with the courts.

In these conflicting crosscurrents, no one could predict how the courts of appeals would respond to Rehnquist's opinion in the Dayton case nor how the Supreme Court would in turn react to any appellate court that continued to find urban school segregation unconstitutional and to order actual desegregation. The Sixth Circuit would be the first and the most critical to face this issue.

The School Board's Response

Dave Greer's brief for the Dayton board warned the Sixth Circuit not to act as trier of fact. He argued that the Dayton board basically operated a "racially neutral policy of putting schools where the children are . . . in accordance with the directive" of Ohio law. With minor and historical exceptions of no continuing relevance at the time of the original trial, therefore, the board with its neighborhood schools was merely the innocent victim of residential segregation: "the worst thing that can be said in retrospect about the Dayton schools is that they reflect the racial imbalance of the geographical neighborhoods they serve."

Greer disputed plaintiffs' *Brown* theory:

Acceptance of this argument would insure that ultimately there would be racial balance in every school system in the country. . . . Simply looking at 1954 practices through 1978 glasses, no matter how innocent or well-meaning those practices may have been at the time, yield perceptions of segregatory activity. . . . Perhaps the predestined result of such litigation could be imposed on a nationwide basis by executive fiat at the suggestion and recommendation of the Department of Justice. . . . Where, as in Dayton, the School Board has done nothing to alter attendance boundaries in any significant manner or to otherwise channel black or white students to different schools for 24 years, the point of attenuation would clearly appear to have been reached even if there were anything 24 years ago to attenuate!

To support this thesis, Greer attached as an appendix the transcript of the questions that Justices Stewart, Powell, and Rehnquist asked Lucas in the oral arguments in the Dayton case the first time around. Greer concluded: "The questioning from the [Supreme] Court was unremitting on the point that the constitutional concern rests with what the facts were at the time of suit, not in 1952 or 1954 or any other prior year."

As to the causation issue, Greer argued that the "incremental segregative effect" command required plaintiffs to show not only the segregative intent of each board act in isolation but also its precise increment over the underlying housing segregation at the time of the original hearing. Greer concluded by posing residential segregation as the means to legitimize school segregation: "In this case the evidence has clearly established that the racial distribution of the Dayton school population simply mirrored the racial distribution of the Dayton residential population, and it follows that with or without any alleged constitutional violations by the board the racial mix of the school population would be the same." If the case could be turned around for view in this fashion, the NAACP challenge to school segregation would founder on the shoals of pervasive residential segregation in Dayton and everywhere else.

In our reply Bill Caldwell quoted former Supreme Court Justice Jackson: "present events have roots in the past, and it is quite proper to trace currently questioned conduct [back] to illuminate its connections and meanings." From this perspective, the Dayton board could be seen as a major actor in creating, maintaining, and expanding a basically dual system through the time of trial. As to any limits on the segregative impact of such systemwide violation, we argued that the burden of proof rested on the school board. Greer's failure to particularize which schools were not affected by the pervasive violation should be deemed a waiver: "The Court should expressly hold the defendants have had ample opportunity to question the scope of remedy, but instead they have elected to stick with their all or nothing position that there has been no system-wide violation."

This argument, however, had another side because Rubin had refused to allow plaintiffs to demonstrate any causal interaction between schools, housing, and the community color line of segregation: plaintiffs could not prove the current extent of the effects of the board's unconstitutional conduct either. Depending on the perspective from which the case was viewed, therefore, it could destroy either the Dayton board's claim of immunity or plaintiffs' claim to systemwide relief. We had been in similar positions before, in the first rounds of the Detroit and Dayton cases in the Supreme Court, and lost because the high court ignored our view of the case. We needed all the help we could get from the Sixth Circuit and the Justice Department if we were going to convince a majority of the Supreme Court justices.

The Columbus board in its response urged that the "incremental segregative" test "provides a new rule of general application in all northern school desegregation cases." Porter argued that Judge Duncan failed to make the inquiry. As a result "the District Court's judgments must be reversed . . . , or at least must be vacated and remanded with the direction that the District Court make the critical inquiry mandated by Dayton." He also urged that Justice Powell's separate opinion in the *Austin* case was now the law: school authorities were constitutionally liable only to the minor extent to which they exacerbated the underlying residential segregation in their pupil assignments. The limit of any wrong was deviation from neighborhood zoning, and the limit of any remedy was a return to neighborhood zoning.

Reading Porter's response, I had the sinking feeling that I had seen a similar argument before. Just like Bill Saxton in the Detroit case, Porter was not writing so much for the Sixth Circuit as for five votes on the Supreme Court. By parroting words from the Dayton and Austin opinions, Porter hoped to succeed without ever having to confront Judge Duncan's findings that the historic color line of racial ghettoization continued to divide the Columbus community.

Arguments

Judge Edwards chaired the panel with Judges Lively and Merritt that heard the appeals in the Columbus case. As Porter rose to begin his prepared remarks, Edwards advised him, "Mr. Porter, before you get started, you ought to know you have a big job here. You have to demolish the detailed, thorough and well-reasoned opinion of Judge Duncan." Indeed, Porter's task was too big this day, as his argument for the board could not convince the appellate panel. The judges repeatedly asked "how Judge Duncan was wrong" in his findings of segregative intent with respect to "optional zones," "construction," and "faculty assignment." Judge Edwards even asked whether Porter had been "consulted on the Innis-Cassidy alternative," an incident where the board broke its integration promises on bond issues and opened another school on a segregated basis in 1975. Judge Merritt also expressed his disbelief when Porter argued that optional zones, for example, were reasonable and innocent administrative techniques, not classic devices of segregation. "On this record, Mr. Porter, how can you claim that optional zones are not racial? Didn't the white kids really go all the way across the Town of Bexley to get to white schools?''

Judge Lively, however, expressed concern about the meaning of ''incremental segregative effect.'' In his oral argument Lucas attempted to translate the phrase in his usual commonsense fashion: ''Circumstantial evidence of segregative intent and effect builds slowly in Northern school cases. In this case, it built to a point where there was a pervasive picture of intentional segregation.'' It was not so much the *number* of segregative incidents, but the *kinds* and *extent* of unconstitutional conduct. ''A court can't count noses when talking about systemic discrimination. When dealing with a systemwide violation with manifestly wide-ranging consequences, courts have to deal with a qualitative not a quantitative measure.'' As Lucas had argued so many times, in public and private, there was no more a ''vernier caliper'' to measure the separate contribution of school authorities to current segregation than there was a ''magic door'' through which school authorities could escape the broader context of the local community color line.

In Dayton, Bill Caldwell opened the oral argument for plaintiffs. He claimed that Judge Rubin had committed fundamental errors of law and fact. He asked the Sixth Circuit, for the first and last time, to set the record straight, fairly, fully, and completely: Dayton school authorities first created and then augmented and perpetuated, rather than dismantled, a basically dual system of schooling right through the time of trial. The panel of Chief Judge Phillips and circuit judges Peck and Lively listened and interrupted with no questions of any substance.

Joel Selig followed on behalf of the United States. The ''Government's independent review of the record'' showed ''pervasive intentional discrimination with persistent, system-wide effects.'' The Dayton board created one set of schools primarily for whites, another for blacks; following *Brown,* the Dayton board failed to dismantle its dual system of schooling through the time of trial. Selig also urged the court to rule on all contested issues, point by point, in order to avoid further confusion. Only Judge Lively asked the tough questions about the meaning of ''incremental segregative effect.'' When Selig began to respond, Judge Lively interjected that it was ''only a question, a concern.'' Apparently, he was as perplexed by the meaning of the phrase as we were.

In response, Dave Greer referred to the trial court's findings that the Dayton board was not motivated by segregative intent and did not cause the school segregation at the time of trial. Greer painted the picture of a board that operated a racially neutral system to provide neighborhood schools close to where the children live. The racial composition of the schools had been determined by the racial composition of the neighborhoods, not by any intentionally segregative acts of the school board. Greer accused the plaintiffs of focusing on isolated trees rather than seeing the forest. Greer then took the three judges on a tour of the "forest" at the time of the creation of the so-called black schools on the West Side. At each interval, Greer argued, the racial composition of the schools merely reflected the underlying racial imbalance in housing. Indeed, "ever since the great flood of 1913," blacks concentrated on the West Side; surely, the Dayton board had no constitutional duty affirmatively to balance schools to overcome racially imbalanced neighborhoods. It was as if Dave Greer were still trying to confound Ella Taylor Lowrey by suggesting that when the Great Miami River crested in 1913, it washed Dayton of all responsibility for segregation.

Bill Caldwell rose to make his rebuttal. The panel had asked so few questions of Greer that it appeared the judges might also be confounded by Greer's persuasive imagery. Caldwell grinned slowly but responded directly: "My worthy adversary has made a capable argument for his client. But the Court should know that in his effort to paint the forest, he left out a considerable number of segregated trees; and the ones he did discuss, he forgot to tell you the order in which they grew." The stolid demeanor of the circuit judges was broken by a series of nods and a chuckle.

Decisions

While we waited to see whether the Sixth Circuit would continue to challenge urban segregation, the Supreme Court on June 28, 1978, issued its ruling on voluntary affirmative action in the admission of blacks to higher education in the *Bakke* case. By garnering only his own vote, Justice Powell controlled the judgment: because of the university's legitimate interest in achieving educational diversity, the race of an applicant may be considered as one relevant aspect of admission criteria; but totally separate admission tracks for whites and blacks are impermissible because all applicants must be judged as individuals and compete with all others. For Justice Powell, blacks were just another ethnic group, and justice just a matter of academic diversity. Stevens, Powell, Rehnquist, and Chief Justice Burger argued that, absent a showing that race must be considered in order to remedy the continuing effects of proven discrimination of the particular university, race could not be considered at all, even to achieve diversity, under the 1964 Civil Rights Act.

Brennan, White, Marshall, and Blackmun argued that a university may adopt a race-conscious admissions program that does not stigmatize blacks as inferior in order to overcome the current effects of past discrimination by the society at large and to integrate higher education. For these justices, all public institutions, not just the courts, are competent and should be encouraged to grapple sensitively and directly with the legacy of institutional racial bias in the country. The disparate opinions and lack of any clear majority in *Bakke* symbolized the lack of any coherent vision on the issues of race and responsibility.

On July 14, 1978, Judge Edwards wrote the opinion for a unanimous panel affirming Judge Duncan's finding of systemwide intentional segregation and order of systemwide desegregation. In the opinion, Edwards reviewed his understanding of the Constitutional history of the country and the concept of equality as it had developed. He recounted the Supreme Court's unanimous rejection of the separate-but-equal doctrine in *Brown*; the decision outlawed "public school separation by race imposed" by intentional state action as a violation of "the equal protection of the laws. . . . The date was May 17, 1954. This was 24 years ago." Reciting the progeny from *Green* to *Swann* to the decisions in the Denver and District of Columbia employment cases, Edwards noted that Justice Rehnquist's opinion in the first round in Dayton cited "with approval" each of these cases. "Indeed, in the long history of the United States Supreme Court desegregation law which has been written since 1954, no case has purported to overrule or cast in doubt any of the prior precedents which began with *Brown*."

For Judge Edwards and his brethren on the Sixth Circuit, there was *no* call to retreat in Rehnquist's "incremental segregative effect" conundrum. To Judge Edwards, school segregation in Columbus, and in many other cases he had reviewed, resulted from official racial discrimination. Urban apartheid in 1978 was the direct legacy of the "post-slavery system of segregation by race," the black codes, and slavery. The plaintiffs had proven that fact; Judge Duncan had found it; and Judge Edwards now bore witness to it, with all of the Barbee Durhams and Helen Jenkins Davises he had come to know, in the face of anything else some members of the Supreme Court might say otherwise.

To the school board's claim that the selection of segregative sites related only to a few isolated instances, Edwards cited the systematic pattern of opening racially identifiable schools and the "repeated instances . . . the Columbus Board chose the segregative sites" in the face of integrative alternatives. As to the claim that integration of teaching staff immediately prior to trial rendered prior faculty segregation proof moot, Edwards retorted: "Obviously it was no 'neutral' neighborhood school concept which occasioned generations of black teachers to be assigned almost exclusively to black schools until the Ohio Civil Rights Commission complaint was settled in July of 1974." With respect to the diverse deviations and manipulations in fringe and pocket areas, Edwards wrote: "These instances can properly be classified as isolated in the sense they do not form any systemwide pattern. They are significant, however, in indicating that the Columbus Board's 'neighborhood school' concept was not applied when application of the . . . concept would tend to promote integration rather than segregation." In sum, the evidence supported the trial judge's finding that "segregative intent" was a motivating factor throughout the Columbus board's operation of schools following 1954.

As to the causation and remedy inquiry into "incremental segregative effect" and possible "systemwide impact," Edwards noted that even the "most deliberate and willful violation of the Constitution in one of over a hundred schools would . . . call [only] for an order to take effective means to desegregate that school. . . . The isolated single violation obviously would not call for a systemwide desegregation order." Yet each such intentionally segregative "practice or episode inevitably adds its own 'increment' to the totality of the impact of segregation. . . . The question posed [by Justice Rehnquist] concerns the impact of the total amount of [such] segregation found after each separate practice or episode has added its 'increment' to the whole. It was not just the last wave which breached the dike and caused the flood."

Edwards read the Supreme Court's opinion in the first Dayton decision as involving limited violation findings concerning "three separate [and] relatively isolated incidences." In contrast, Edwards wrote, "school board policies of systemwide application necessarily have systemwide impact." Edwards identified five such pervasive violations in Columbus.

1. The pre-1954 policy of creating an enclave of five schools intentionally designed for black students [only] . . . clearly had a . . . systemwide impact.
2. The post-1954 failure of the Columbus Board to desegregate the school system in spite of many requests and demands to do so, of course, had a systemwide impact.
3. So, too, did the Columbus Board's segregative school construction and siting policy. . . .
4. So, too, did its student assignment policy which . . . produced the large majority of racially identifiable schools as of the school year 1975–76.
5. The practice of assigning black teachers and administrators only or in large majority to black schools likewise represented a systemwide policy of segregation. . . . It also served as a discriminatory, systemwide racial identification of schools.

As to each of these violations, Judge Edwards concluded, "we believe this record requires a finding that each policy or practice . . . had (and was intended to have) a systemwide application and impact. Each such policy or practice also added an increment to the sum total of the constitutional violation found. Beyond doubt the sum total of these violations made the Columbus school system a segregated school system in violation of the Fourteenth

Amendment and thoroughly justified the District Judge in ordering a system-wide remedy.''

The Sixth Circuit remanded Judge Duncan's liability finding against the state board for more detailed findings of segregative intent and impact with the "recognition that no practical delay in ending the unconstitutional practices which we have found above will result." In addition, the panel avoided full consideration of the proof and finding of community discrimination in housing as well as schools. Judge Duncan's considered conclusion that it was both factually impossible and legally unnecessary in a school segregation case to parse this unitary web of discrimination in all aspects of community life received no mention. The Sixth Circuit apparently was still afraid to embrace our view of ultimate responsibility of the state for all such discrimination under the Fourteenth Amendment.

On July 27, 1978, Chief Judge Phillips issued the ruling for the unanimous panel in the Dayton school case. Compared to Judge Edwards's work in the Columbus case, the *Dayton* opinion was short and the language unemotional. The result, however, was basically the same. After reviewing the "protracted" prior proceedings and the arguments of the parties on the pending appeal, Phillips concluded:

> the systemwide desegregation plan [previously] approved by this court should be reinstated. The record demonstrates conclusively that at the time of *Brown I,* defendants intentionally operated a dual school system and that subsequently, defendants never fulfilled their affirmative duty to eliminate the systemwide effects of their prior acts of segregation.

Detailing the evidence in sixty-three footnote citations to the testimony, exhibits, and party admissions, the chief judge calmly reversed the findings and conclusions of the trial judge. Phillips repeatedly held that Rubin's apologies for intentional segregation were "infected by legal error," were "clearly erroneous," "fail[ed] to apply the proper legal standards," "fail[ed] to shift the burden of proof to defendants," or "fail[ed] to attribute the proper legal significance to the evidence." Thirty-three times Phillips matter-of-factly reversed Rubin on grounds of law and/or unequivocal evidence.

There were going to be no more ambiguities concerning "cumulative violations" and "reserved issues" to cloud Phillips's view of the case. Based on a detailed analysis of the record, Phillips confirmed our original *Brown* argument:

- Prior to 1951, the Board forbade the assignment of black teachers to white or mixed classrooms pursuant to an explicit segregation policy. . . . [T]he Board ''effectively continued in practice the racial assignment of faculty through the 1970–71 school year.'' . . . At the time of *Brown I,* it was therefore possible to identify a ''black school'' in the Dayton system solely by reference to the racial composition of faculty. A blacks-only faculty meant a blacks-only school.

- The purposeful segregation of faculty by race was ''inextricably tied to racially motivated student assignment practices.'' In addition during the later 1940's and early 1950's, defendants operated one race classrooms in officially one race housing projects that ''were strictly segregated according to race.''
- ''Defendants' segregative practices at the time of *Brown I* infected the entire Dayton public school system. . . . Thus for 24 years defendants have been under a constitutional duty to desegregate the Dayton public schools. . . . The evidence of record demonstrates conclusively that defendants have failed to eliminate the continuing systemwide effects of their prior discrimination and have intentionally maintained a segregated school system down to the time the complaint was filed in the present case.''

Chief Judge Phillips concluded that systemwide desegregation was necessary to remedy ''(1) the failure of defendants to disestablish the pre-1954 segregated school system; and (2) post-1954 acts of systemwide impact which have contributed affirmatively to the construction of a segregated system.'' Dave Greer and the Dayton board failed to meet *their* burden, for this sytem ''with a history of segregation,'' of demonstrating that the current ''systemwide racial imbalance would have occurred even in the absence of their segregative acts.'' Greer had refused plaintiffs' repeated challenge to attempt to meet this burden of proof; the board was therefore bound to live with its all-or-nothing litigation strategy.

Nevertheless, Judge Phillips, like Judge Edwards in Columbus, felt constrained to say something about the ''incremental segregative effect'' language. Once again expressly rejecting Judge Rubin's view, Chief Judge Phillips held that the phrase ''was not intended to change the standards for fashioning remedies in school desegregation cases'':

The purpose of the remedy is to eliminate the lingering effects of intentional constitutional violations and to restore plaintiffs to substantially the position they would have occupied in the absence of these violations. The word ''incremental'' merely describes the manner in which segregative impact occurs in a northern school case where each act, even if minor in itself, adds incrementally to the ultimate condition of segregated schools.

The impact is "incremental" in that it occurs gradually over the years instead of all at once as in a case where segregation was mandated by state statute or a provision of a state constitution.

Although this understanding of the gradual process of intentional school segregation over time in the North marked many opinions, including Phillips's own opinions in the Detroit case, we had no idea whether Justice Rehnquist shared this view. More plausibly, Rehnquist did *not* have this concept in mind when he spoke of "incremental segregative effect" as the difference between school segregation as it now stands and the situation that would have existed in the absence of any constitutional violations.

Chief Judge Phillips, however, added two additional thoughts on the meaning of the phrase. First, he disapproved Rubin's isolated "act by act approach" as "no more valid than the school by school approach rejected" by the Supreme Court in the Denver case. Second, whatever the meaning of the phrase, Chief Judge Phillips held that Rubin "erred in allocating the burden of proof on the issue . . . to plaintiffs." Citing the Denver decision, Phillips held that "where plaintiffs prove, as here, a systemwide pattern of intentionally segregative actions by defendants, it is the defendants' burden to overcome the presumption that the current racial composition of the school population reflects the systemwide impact of those violations." If the Supreme Court was going to consider reversing the Sixth Circuit again, Phillips's opinion insured that the Denver precedent would have to be directly confronted rather than skirted once again.

Phillips's best answer to Rubin and Rehnquist, however, was his detailed analysis of the record evidence of intentional segregation that continued unabated from the 1920s. The careful evaluation of the record evidence, and explanation of the connections between various policies and practices of official racial discrimination, showed more clearly than could anything else the continuing de jure reality of segregation in Dayton schools. Phillips issued the opinion only days before he announced his retirement. His parting shot reversed Rubin's attempt to portray school segregation in Dayton as the de facto result of a school board operating blindly and neutrally in a series of isolated, unrelated, and nonracial events.

The July 27, 1978, ruling represented a fitting capstone to all of Judge Phillips's school opinions. It represented the maturing of his view of the reality of segregation in America. The opinions in *Deal* that Phillips joined in the 1960s adopted the narrow de facto doctrine of former chief judge Paul Weick and, in the process, almost announced the death knell for all challenges to school segregation. The opinions Phillips wrote in the Detroit case at the beginning of the 1970s launched the NAACP's de jure challenge to northern school segregation and attempted to broaden the inquiry to ultimate state responsibility and areawide desegregation. Phillips's final opinion in the Dayton case would stand or fall as the confirmation or the end of the legal challenge to the color line in urban schooling.

On July 31, 1978, the panel headed by circuit judge Edwards denied the Columbus board's motion to stay desegregation in Columbus for another year pending possible Supreme Court review. The Columbus community geared up for implementation of the plan. In an editorial, the *Columbus Citizen-Journal* assured that "school desegregation is working elsewhere. It will work here"; and the superintendent of the Columbus public schools publicly promised, "[W]e will be ready [for the opening of school] on September 7." In Dayton, school officials resigned themselves to desegregation for another year pending Supreme Court review.

One issue remained. Judges Phillips, Edwards, their brethren, the NAACP, Ella Taylor Lowrey, Phyllis Blackburn Greer, John Harewood, Wayne Carle, Helen Jenkins Davis, Barbee Durham, Nate Jones, Tom Atkins, Lou Lucas, Bill Caldwell, and many like them, black and white, young and old, still faced a disturbing question. Would a majority on the Supreme Court, and ultimately a majority of the American people, finally accept the understanding of the Sixth Circuit and Judge Duncan concerning the de jure reality of urban school segregation, if not the need for actual desegregation? Or would the high court adopt Judge Rubin's view that school authorities are not responsible for segregation in schools that just mirrors residential segregation, whatever its causes and consequences?

VI
Reprise and Preview: The Wilmington School Case, 1971–78

Chapter 13
Trial by Three Judges, 1971–75

The Sixth Circuit did not stand alone in rejecting the call to retreat sounded by Justice Rehnquist's opinion for the Supreme Court in the first round of the Dayton case. Four other federal courts of appeals—the Second, Third, Fifth, and Eighth Circuits—examined the issue of whether the "incremental segregative effect" conundrum legitimized all school segregation at the current level of segregation in housing. Each rejected such a view. These appellate courts determined that official discrimination by school authorities had contributed substantially to the de jure reality of school *and* housing segregation. Until explicitly told otherwise by the high court, each would insist that the remedy for such intentional segregation be actual school desegregation.

Perhaps the most important of these cases concerned Wilmington, Delaware, and its northern New Castle County suburbs. The case started before *Brown*; but a generation later it was still going strong. Along the way, it inherited the problems of the school district boundary barrier raised by the Supreme Court's decision in the Detroit case, as well as the incremental segregative effect defense offered by the Court's decision in the Dayton case. Thus, the Wilmington case was a microcosm of the entire legal challenge to segregation in America.

Visible Man

The conscience of one man spurred this thirty-year legal struggle in Delaware. Louis Lorenzo Redding was born at the beginning of the twentieth century and attended Delaware's state-mandated and state-financed colored schools in Wilmington with Negro children from all over New Castle County. His parents graduated from Howard University and had joined the NAACP, at its inception, to fight against racial caste. They remained active in Wilmington's local branch, where Redding's father served as executive secretary for twenty-five years.

Young Redding learned firsthand the "proscriptions and restrictions of segregation": Jim Crow laws and customs divided blacks from whites in every aspect of community life in Wilmington, except on the trolleys and in the library. In 1918 Louis Redding graduated from the blacks-only Howard High School with his black classmates from all parts of Delaware who, some fifty years after the First Reconstruction, were not yet free from Jim Crow segregation. He attended Brown University in the Ivy League and spoke at his class commencement in 1923.

Redding's father counseled him to become a physician, primarily because "lawyers, particularly Negro lawyers, starve for a long while, but doctors can serve humanity and earn a livelihood from the outset." While at Brown, however, Redding had been inspired by William H. Lewis, an assistant attorney general of the United States and a Negro, to become a lawyer. He was accepted at the Harvard Law School on a scholarship.

Redding, however, needed more money for living expenses to survive during his legal training. For a year, therefore, he became a vice-principal at the Fessenden Academy near Ocala, Florida, which was operated by the American Missionary Association. He spent another summer in Chicago as a night clerk in the post office and another year teaching English at Morehouse College in Atlanta in order to save enough money for his legal education. He matriculated at Harvard Law School in 1926.

While home for one Christmas vacation, Redding witnessed the Jim Crow system of justice in Delaware. He visited the county courthouse for the first time in his life and sat in the whites-only section. He was rudely greeted by three white bailiffs who told him, "You ain't supposed to sit here." It was the first shot in a prolonged battle between Louis Redding and Delaware "justice."

After graduating in 1929, Louis resolved to practice law in New York City with some friends, despite the entreaties of his father to break the color line of the Delaware bar. The elder Redding became insistent, however: if a son was going to reject a father's advice on careers, at least he could come home to practice law and to eat home cooking.

Redding wrote to Delaware lawyers, all of whom were white, to see if any would hire him for the six months of apprenticeship required by Delaware as a prerequisite to taking the bar examination. When none of the established lawyers expressed any interest, the elder Redding pressured the new United States senator from Delaware to serve as his son's mentor; political expediency, the black vote, and the senator's lack of contact with any active local practice of law combined to provide an apprenticeship.

Redding returned to Wilmington in the fall of 1929 to begin his legal career. When he arrived on the train from New York, the first touch of Delaware's Jim Crow soil prompted him to hop on the next trolley to Philadelphia. With a night's sleep he had the fortitude, and the foresight, to return: "Delaware's system of segregation presented quite a challenge." Redding became the first Negro admitted to the Delaware bar. An editorial in the local paper assuaged some of the fears of the local white community by announcing that he had passed the bar exam "with the highest mark ever." Redding took up residence in the family home and opened an office across the street from the police station and courthouse.

Redding immediately challenged the segregated seating in Delaware courts by filing protest letters with each chief judge. How could a judge or jury provide equal justice if black citizens had to rise to testify from a separate section of the courtroom? The chief judge of the municipal court instructed his bailiffs not to enforce segregated seating; but the chief justice of the state supreme court said it was a matter within the sole discretion of his bailiffs. At every opportunity, Redding tested this "discretion."

Redding served as a lawyer to any person in need of legal services, including political radicals incarcerated for exercising their First Amendment rights of free speech. Many Wilmington residents therefore viewed him as "communist" or "left-oriented." This was part of the price Redding paid for his belief in the American Constitution. For twenty years he practiced this creed in the office and at home in relative obscurity.

By 1949, other blacks began to join in the challenge to Jim Crow in Delaware. Thirty students from Delaware State College for Negroes applied for transfers to the whites-only University of Delaware but were rejected. They went to Redding, and he responded; he asked the university board of trustees to reconsider. When the board confirmed the decision, Redding challenged the "separate-but-equal" doctrine before the vice-chancellor of Delaware's chancery court, Collins Seitz, a graduate of the whites-only Wilmington High, University of Delaware, and Virginia Law School.

While Redding was preparing the case, Thurgood Marshall called to say that the Legal Defense Fund had a "young, white lawyer who needed to get his feet wet." Redding took Jack Greenberg, who later succeeded Marshall as head of the Legal Defense Fund, under his wing. They prepared the case together to prove that Delaware State College was not "equal," by any objective or subjective measure, to the University of Delaware. Based on the overwhelming record, Collins Seitz found the colored college "grossly inferior" to the white school and ordered the University of Delaware to admit the black plaintiffs at once.

Other racial barriers began to fall following this break in the color line. Downtown Wilmington theaters, the Delaware National Guard, and the Wilmington Hospital opened their ranks to Negro employees and patrons on something slightly better than a whites-only or strictly segregated basis. In 1951 two black families in Wilmington suburbs decided to challenge the inequalities of segregated schooling. One wanted to get her children into the nearby but whites-only Claymont High School, which had facilities superior to those of the more distant, black Howard High School. The other parent simply wanted the school bus for whites to stop by her house so that she would not have to drive her child to the distant, one-room colored school. They both petitioned the state board of education for redress. The state board, which supervised all Delaware elementary and secondary schooling, refused: "[T]he State Constitution requires separate educational facilities for colored and white children.'' That included whites-only high schools and whites-only buses: Delaware did not want either tainted by a single black child.

Both families then asked Redding to provide legal assistance. He agreed to handle their cases, but only if they wanted to challenge Jim Crow fully and directly. As later recounted by the woman dissatisfied with the school bus, ''He said he wouldn't help me get a Jim Crow bus to take my girl to any Jim Crow school, but if I was interested in sending her to an integrated school, . . . he'd help. Well, I thanked God right then and there'' (Kluger 1976, 435).

At that time, Delaware's public school system was a crazy-quilt organization. All colored schools were fully funded by the state; some operated as separate colored districts, some as separate schools run by the state board, some as separate schools run by otherwise white local districts. Whites-only schooling reflected a similar mix: local district boundaries were regularly breached by students living elsewhere, and the effective attendance areas for many schools covered an entire county, whatever the nominal school district boundaries. Only the state's color line and the supreme authority of the state board of education over all matters of educational policy and local school operations remained inviolate. Redding therefore made the state board the primary defendant in the twin lawsuits. Collins Seitz again heard the challenge to dual schooling, and Jack Greenberg again assisted.

The lawyers proved the material and intangible inequalities between Delaware's colored and white schools by direct evidence and expert evaluations. They demonstrated the stigma of the color line by eyewitness proof and expert opinions. Judge Seitz found that the state provided inferior facilities to the blacks-only schools manifestly unequal to those provided to the whites-only schools. Seitz added that the very system of ''state-imposed segregation in education'' adversely affected the ''educational opportunities'' of the black pupil. Although Seitz left to the Supreme Court the overruling of the *Plessy v. Ferguson* legal doctrine of ''separate but equal,'' he ordered the state board to admit the black child to white schools at once under *Plessy*: ''[Where] there is an existing violation of the 'separate but equal doctrine,' he is entitled to have made available to him the state facilities which have been shown to be superior. To do otherwise is to say to such a plaintiff, 'Yes, your constitutional rights are being invaded, but be patient, we will see whether in time they are still being violated.' ''

On the state's appeal, the Delaware case was joined with others from Kansas, Virginia, South Carolina, and Washington, D.C., in the United States Supreme Court. Redding shared the oral argument in the Delaware case with his younger associate, Greenberg. They argued that the admission of the black plaintiffs to white schools was insufficient: Delaware's law of dual schooling also had to fall. The Court first heard such oral arguments on the constitutionality of Jim Crow without regard to the appropriate remedy. In 1954, in *Brown I*, Chief Justice Warren ruled for a unanimous court: "[T]he policy of separating the races is usually interpreted as denoting the inferiority of the Negro group. . . . [I]n the field of public education the doctrine of 'separate but equal' has no place. Separate educational facilities are inherently unequal."

At the subsequent oral arguments on remedy in the consolidated cases, the lawyers for the plaintiffs pressed for immediate relief. The Court, however, permitted delay because of the public interest in an orderly dismantling of the entire system of dual schooling. The court ordered "transition to a racially nondiscriminatory system of schooling . . . with all deliberate speed." It authorized the lower courts to deal with the diverse local problems presented by each case, including, for example, through the "revision of school districts and attendance areas . . . local laws and regulations."

On the remand from the United States Supreme Court, the resistance to desegregation in Delaware was not as massive as in such states as Virginia, but it was nonetheless effective. The state board planned and approved a program of "gradual desegregation." In the Wilmington area, the Wilmington board, with the permission of the state board, continued the five de jure black schools as blacks-only schools through the racial assignment of black staff, gerrymandering of boundaries, and use of segregative "free transfers" and optional zones. These same techniques expanded this core of blacks-only schools in Wilmington with the opening of new black schools. For the next fifteen years, the historically all-white suburban elementary school districts around Wilmington also began to provide secondary schooling on a virtually all-white basis, thereby excluding most of the increasing number of black Wilmington pupils. As Louis Redding came to see this process, "there was basically a countywide system of schooling in the days of mandatory segregation; thereafter, the State shifted to separate and distinct districts as the center city schools became increasingly black." Downstate, the perpetuation of a segregated system of schooling was even more overt.

Black families again came to Redding. Once again he sued the state board of education, this time in federal court, to dismantle Delaware's system of dual schooling effectively, completely, and immediately. In 1957 the district court ordered the named plaintiffs admitted to white schools and ordered the state board to submit a plan for statewide desegregation. White mobs, spurred by the agitation of Byrant Bowles and his short-lived National Association for the Advancement of White People, greeted such decisions and Redding with outright racial hostility. Bowles sought money, pledges, and direct action to oppose any race mixing. For a time, he succeeded in effectively closing some downstate white schools to blacks, who could only transfer at their own considerable peril. As Bill Frank, the curmudgeon-at-large of the Wilmington press, remarked years later, Bowles was a classic example of "how an outside bigot can invade the State, euchre people out of money, promise them pie in the segregated sky and then shove off—leaving bruises that take too long to heal."

After four more years of litigation, the federal district court provisionally approved a desegregation plan that did not promise much relief. Although it spoke of the goal of a "wholly integrated system" for Delaware, it only ordered the immediate admission to white schools of those "Negro students desiring integration [by] transfer" and required the state board to develop a more thorough plan to be implemented in the years ahead. The court also mandated the formulation of a new school code in order to eliminate Delaware's "crazy quilt" of local school districts.

Although the opinion did affix primary responsibility for eliminating de jure segregation on the state board, Redding protested the failure to impose a timetable or any meaningful guidelines that would actually substitute one set of integrated schools for the two sets of segregated schools throughout the state. The purpose of his many challenges to dual schools had not been simply to allow a few brave blacks to transfer to otherwise white schools; he had sought to eliminate the systematic separation of basically black schools from white schools altogether. Subsequent proposals by the state board to the legislature to reorganize school districts to achieve desegregation fell on deaf ears. There was only one saving feature of the 1961 decree: the court accepted the state board's plan with the proviso that it would meet "the Board's constitutional duty only to the extent that it [proved] effective."

Redding moved on from the school cases to challenge segregation in public accommodations, most notably the whites-only restaurant in the Wilmington Parking Authority building, but he also challenged the Jim Crow practices of inns, hotels, and pubs. The Wilmington Parking Authority case reached the United States Supreme Court and tested the "state action" restriction grafted onto the Fourteenth Amendment by the *Civil Rights Cases* some eighty years earlier. He was assisted in these cases by a young black lawyer, Lenny Williams. Williams attended Wilmington's black schools, but Redding succeeded in opening the doors of the University of Delaware for him. After Williams graduated from Georgetown Law School, Redding agreed to serve as his preceptor in 1960 for the required apprenticeship. Thereafter Redding and Williams practiced law together for several years. As Redding fondly describes their first association, "Leonard carried my briefcase on the way to the oral argument before the Supreme Court in the Wilmington Parking Authority case."

In time, Lenny Williams, like Jack Greenberg before him, also learned how to argue a case for himself. Williams shared Redding's drive for racial justice. Williams, however, saw more potential in the political than the legal process. By 1966 Williams was named a judge on the Wilmington municipal court bench to hear criminal cases on a part-time basis and established his own private practice to handle civil matters.

During this period, the state board of education hired a new superintendent who began the task of dismantling the continuing system of dual schooling in the southern part of the state by closing or merging the small, separate black schools and districts into their nearby white counterparts. Although this initial process of desegregation was largely completed by 1967, the legislature refused any reorganization for the rest of the state, and the state board did nothing to confront the continuation and expansion of the historically black schools in Wilmington and of the white schools in suburban New Castle County. There were a few lone voices who suggested that the state confront the continuing dual system in northern Delaware. For example, a study team from New York University examined Wilmington schools and recommended either a consolidation into a countywide system or a pie-shaped redistricting of Wilmington and suburban districts in order to permit effective school desegregation.

Finally, the state board proposed an Education Advancement Act to permit the state board to consolidate school districts pursuant to several "educational criteria." The initial drafts did not mention Wilmington. The governor and state board appointed several blue-ribbon panels to hold hearings on the proposal and to generate public support. At these hearings, and elsewhere, several persons publicly and privately protested the failure of such a statewide reorganization to come to grips with the continuing problem of dual schooling between Wilmington and its neighboring northern New Castle County suburbs. At the time, Wilmington had an enrollment of 15,026 students, 66 percent of whom were black and isolated in an expanding core of black schools. The suburban schools, with the exception of those in the racially mixed DeLaWarr District, remained virtually all-white. The commissions duly reported citizen pleas concerning the need to redraw "existing boundaries to eliminate ghettoes" and the "provocative" proposals to remedy the school segregation between Wilmington and its suburbs.

With an ugly riot, National Guard reaction, and virtual martial law in Wilmington in 1968 freshly on their minds, the legislature responded by expressly excluding Wilmington from the discretion otherwise vested in the state board to reorganize public schooling throughout the state. The act, as passed, provided: "The [reorganized] school district for the City of Wilmington shall be the City of Wilmington with the territory within its limits . . . , the boundaries of which shall *at all times* be the same as the boundaries of the City of Wilmington." The state board then proceeded to reorganize all other Delaware school districts. It exercised its discretion to further the basic white character of suburban New Castle County schools: the board maintained the racially mixed DeLaWarr school population in a separate district despite educational, fiscal, and administrative recommendations to join it with adjacent white districts.

The Education Advancement Act effectively perpetuated Delaware's historic system of dual schooling in the northern third of Delaware—the urbanized Wilmington area—by establishing new but still racially separate districts. The state board never presented this statewide reorganization to the federal district court for approval. Redding watched this latest state approval of basically separate schooling with dismay. He had observed that the state custom of housing discrimination prevented blacks even from moving into the moderately priced suburban rental developments and single-family tracts. The Educational Advancement Act, therefore, would not only perpetuate the historic system of dual schooling but also would encourage the process of black ghettoization in Wilmington and whites-only development of the suburbs. As Redding approached his seventieth birthday, he did not know what to do. He did not believe that he had a roving commission to reopen the case and test the act against the 1961 judgment of the federal district court.

Thereafter, the Wilmington chapter of the American Civil Liberties Union (ACLU) received complaints from black and white families in Wilmington who protested the isolation of city schools in the state board's statewide reorganization of public schooling. Irving Morris and Joseph Rosenthal, partners in a prominent plaintiffs antitrust and securities firm and graduates from Yale and Harvard Law Schools, respectively, reviewed the complaints for the ACLU. The local press wrote that they had "developed a lucrative law practice out of helping the little guy, the long shot," in corporate disputes. That was no mean feat in Delaware, the legal haven for many corporations.

Morris came to Redding. Redding knew that "Irving was a broader-gauge fellow than most Wilmington lawyers. He came from a relatively racially liberated family and was aware of the continued racial stratification of community life in the Wilmington area." They discussed the possibility of reopening the case, and Redding agreed to interview the complaining members of the black community to determine whether they wanted to pursue interdistrict desegregation. Satisfied that the clients wanted to challenge the continuing school segregation in the Wilmington area, Redding consented to the drafting of an amended complaint in intervention to reopen the Delaware school case, largely dormant since 1961.

Redding, Morris, and Rosenthal filed the complaint in 1971. They alleged that the state board continued to operate a racially discriminatory dual public school system in New Castle County; that the Educational Advancement Act unconstitutionally confined most black students to black schools in Wilmington separate from most white students in white schools in the suburbs; and that the state of Delaware, through its laws, customs, and usages of racial segregation enforced, encouraged, supported, or acquiesced in public and private discrimination resulting in segregated schools.

Redding's signature was as visible on this pleading in 1971 as the man had been for the past forty years in the legal struggle for racial equality in Delaware. This would prove his ultimate challenge to the color line. Once again he named the state board of education as the primary defendant responsible for the continuing violation and the framing of an effective remedy. For Redding, the "objective of this lawsuit remains to rid Delaware's system of public schooling of all racial restrictions and proscriptions. The goal has never been to allow blacks to attend white schools but to substitute 'just schools' for the set of separate and identifiable 'white schools' and 'black schools.' Two-way integration, not one-way chasing by blacks of whites must be achieved."

Trial by Three Judges

Redding, Morris, and Rosenthal knew they needed assistance if they were going to marshall a substantial legal challenge to Delaware's continuing system of separate schooling in northern New Castle County. They needed legal resources and political allies. They looked to the Wilmington Board of Education to provide both. This biracial board began to show increasing interest in metropolitan approaches to racial desegregation so long as there was no retaliatory splintering of the Wilmington district or unfair treatment of black staff and pupils in any remedy. After considerable soul-searching, the Wilmington board determined to join plaintiffs to seek school desegregation for the greater Wilmington area. This represented a dramatic turn of events: the center city school board was admitting that black Wilmington students continued to be victims of intentional segregation but that the areawide extent of this violation required a metropolitan remedy, including the all-white suburban school districts whose constituency now dominated the state legislature. Despite the risks of political retaliation, the considerable resources of the Wilmington board were now available to the plaintiffs' cause.

The Wilmington lawyers also approached the Legal Defense Fund for assistance. Because of other pressing commitments, Jack Greenberg refused his mentor and dear friend, Louis Redding. Greenberg suggested that plaintiffs' counsel consult with Bill Taylor, director of a civil rights center in Washington, D.C., cocounsel with Lou Lucas in the LDF's challenge to metropolitan segregation in Richmond, and former staff director of the United States Civil Rights Commission. When the plaintiffs' attorneys consulted Taylor, he recommended Lucas as chief trial counsel. Lucas could not resist joining another areawide challenge to urban school desegregation.

The state board retained Bill Prickett, an experienced trial lawyer, to represent its interests. Prickett's method was to challenge every plaintiff assertion. During the first hour of the first deposition, Lucas and Prickett were at loggerheads and had to repair to a federal judge to resolve the first of their many disputes. During this pretrial skirmishing, the hostility between the adversary counsel did serve one useful purpose: it convinced a dissenting black member of the Wilmington board that separatism was a false road to equality in Delaware.

Because the lawsuit challenged the constitutionality of a state statute, a three-judge federal panel had to be convened. A major concern was how to get three federal judges to sit through a lengthy trial without becoming irritated with the imposition on their time. As Lucas noted, "It's hard enough just to get one judge's time and attention for a big school case, let alone three." Lucas therefore determined to focus on three basic points:

- Delaware's historic dual system had never been dismantled in Wilmington and northern New Castle County.
- The Educational Advancement Act had the purpose and effect of confining black students to a set of de jure black schools in Wilmington and protecting the historically white schools in suburban New Castle County.
- The state's custom of segregation and support of discrimination in housing operated in lockstep to herd black families into Wilmington schools and to steer whites to the suburbs.

As a backdrop for these arguments, Lucas argued the state board's primary responsibility for local schooling on a completely dual basis throughout the area as of the time of *Brown* and the board's continuing failure to dismantle the areawide system of segregation right through the statewide reorganization conducted under the Educational Advancement Act.

Prickett countered for the state board:

- Delaware had a tradition of public schooling by fragmented local districts.
- Separate colored schools and districts had been eliminated by 1967.
- The Educational Advancement Act merely continued the long-standing autonomy of the Wilmington school district in the consolidation of much smaller districts.

    Since the Fair Housing Act of 1968, housing segregation resulted from private choice, not official discrimination and, in all events, was not the responsibility of state or local school authorities.
- The Wilmington board should eliminate any vestiges of illegal segregation within its borders on its own.

Jack Sinclair, an urbane lawyer for the Delaware education establishment, joined to press these defenses on behalf of the Delaware School Boards Association that represented the interest of the white suburban school districts.

Two aging district judges, Wright and Layton, joined Third Circuit judge Gibbons to hear the case. Wright and Layton each had presided over one or another of the earlier stages of the Delaware school litigation in the late 1950s and early 1960s and were familiar with some aspects of Delaware's unique state system of dual schooling. Gibbons, one of the leading members of the Third Circuit's liberal bloc of judges, was familiar with some of the types of proof of official discrimination in housing from his previous decisions challenging segregation in public housing. All three were appalled at the lawyers' estimates that several weeks of trial time would be necessary. With varying degrees of patience, they sat through some fourteen trial days. Only lengthy stipulations of fact saved the judges and the counsel from a longer hearing.

As the trial progressed, Redding watched with considerable respect as Lucas presented their case to the three judges. As Redding remembers, "Louis Lucas was never an irritant in any association with his co-counsel, clients, witnesses, or the court. He has a certain presence and style that wins careful attention, even concurrence with what he's saying rather than hostility. His courtroom manner in this regard is most unusual and evokes a willingness by the trial judges to hear and to understand what he is saying." Lucas was not the only accomplished lawyer in the case. Redding still possessed a dignity and power in his studied gaze and his perfect diction. Irving Morris was the president of the Delaware Bar Association, Bill Prickett the president-elect, and Jack Sinclair no one's fool. In time, the state board would also retain Phil Kurland, the conservative constitutional law professor from the University of Chicago whose legal prowess matched that of Lou Lucas.

The liability hearing began on December 13, 1973. Lucas started cautiously with two suburban school superintendents. Both conceded that cross-district transfers and areawide schooling for educational reasons (e.g., special schools for the handicapped and vocational schools) still continued in northern New Castle County and that integrated schooling made sense as a matter of educational policy. The superintendent from the Mt. Pleasant district also testified that long-haul busing was no issue in the case because black Wilmington schools were only minutes away from suburban white schools. Suburban-urban commuting throughout most of the greater Wilmington area was a matter of five to ten minutes at most. As Lucas remarked privately, "Compared to Detroit or Richmond, this place is Lilliputland."

George Kirk, the superintendent of the Newark school district—with some fifteen thousand pupils, the only district of comparable size to Wilmington—summarized his experience in serving on one of the study committees preceding the passage of the Educational Advancement Act. He remembered references to proposals at that time to end the continuing and increasing racial isolation between black Wilmington and white suburban schools. Judge Gibbons interrupted to ask whether any of these committees referred to the district court's 1961 reorganization order. Kirk answered, "The presumption of our committee and, I believe, the presumption of most of the committees, was that integration in the State of Delaware as set forth by the [District] Court had already been accomplished." Gibbons retorted, "Now, that doesn't answer my question." Kirk then responded that no reference had been made to the decree.

Having set this stage, Lucas presented the proof of customary segregation and discrimination in Delaware through the testimony of a series of black realtists, a fair housing group that tested the covert racial discrimination in marketing in the month before the trial, local victims of discrimination, documentary admissions, and Karl Taeuber. The real estate agents described explicit and covert mechanisms of racial steering. For example, in the 1950s and 1960s, the state's real estate primer urged the agents to follow a version of the NAREB code of ethics that prohibited the introduction of any Negro in a white residential area. As another example, in the mid-1960s the Multiple Listing Service of the Greater Wilmington Board of Realtors designated only 7 percent of new listings in the suburbs as open to minority buyers but 51 percent of the listings in Wilmington as "open."

Such practices of discrimination continued through the time of trial in less overt forms: white brokers' refusal to cobroker with black agents in white areas; steering; different treatment of white and black home-seekers. When Judge Layton asked whether economics explained the suburban-urban racial separation, a black real estate agent answered, "Nope." He explained, "If you take a neighborhood separated by less than, well let's say five miles, one all-black and one all-white, and you have the same price house [in both]—let's think about that—they didn't get there because they wanted to be there. They got there because somebody put them there."

The black real estate agents also described the importance of segregated schooling throughout the area to segregated housing: "The first thing you teach yourself is know your school district because you sell houses in New Castle County based on [the racial identity of] school districts." Such direct testimony supplemented the documentary proof of FHA's early understanding that segregated schools are critical to maintaining a racially dual system of housing. It also confirmed the state Human Relations Commission's determination that the operation of virtually all-white suburban districts adjacent to Wilmington encouraged "escape" by whites from the expanding core of virtually all-black schools in Wilmington.

Karl Taeuber again recounted his research and applied it to the census data from the Wilmington area. After discounting choice, ethnicity, and economics as major explanations of the pervasive housing segregation, Taeuber concluded "racial discrimination in the housing market is a principle cause of these [segregated housing] patterns." Taeuber again detailed the diverse mechanisms of housing discrimination. Documentary exhibits from federal and local agencies confirmed both the general conclusions and the specifics.

Lucas inquired what role school racial identification played in housing choice. Prickett objected: "we are not trying a housing case. . . . Now, it seems to me, the order [of proof] is reversed. Here [Lucas] is asking what effect does schooling have on housing. . . ." Judge Gibbons cut Prickett off to overrule the objection: "I think [Lucas's] position is that [they are] interdependent." Taeuber proceeded to explain that schools play a major "part [in] the identification of neighborhoods [for the public]. . . . The racial characterization of the school district in which a given house is located is a very important consideration to a large number of in-migrants. . . . This has been a factor affecting the choice as to which part of the total metropolitan complex to move to." Taeuber concluded that the stark racial identification of school districts in the Wilmington area promoted racial choices in housing.

Taeuber then applied his segregation index to Wilmington area *schools.* On his scale from 0 (no segregation) to 100 (complete segregation), areawide school segregation increased from 72 in 1960 to 81 in 1973. If the Wilmington city schools were racially balanced within the district at the city-only racial ratio, the metropolitan school segregation index would dip only to 80.2. Judge Gibbons was astonished: "So what you are saying then is that hypothetically if the Wilmington School Board by its own action achieved a zero index [within the city], the county-wide index would nevertheless be 80.2?" Taeuber grinned as he saw the light of an idea glow in another judicial mind: "That is exactly correct." Judge Gibbons continued, "Would you put that down on a sheet of paper?" Judge Wright interjected, "Tell us just how you work that out. . . . Could you just work that out on a sheet of paper sometime when you don't have anything else to do and give it to us. . . . I would like to see." The truth hit home: "desegregation" within the city of Wilmington would do nothing to end the pervasive areawide segregation between black Wilmington schools and white suburban schools. When Taeuber prepared the requested "paper," it was marked "Court Exhibit 1."

On cross-examination Prickett succeeded in clearing up one ambiguity in Taeuber's published writings, that pervasive residential segregation persists regardless of local law concerning discrimination. Some, including Prickett, read this to mean that segregation laws and discriminatory customs did not "cause" and had little "effect" on the patterns of racial segregation. Taeuber responded, "That's not what I intended [to convey] by what I wrote." Instead, Taeuber explained that officially approved public and private racial discrimination in housing was so pervasive and its mechanisms so diverse that "regardless of the kinds of laws that happen to be around, the point is that there ha[s] been no concerted effort in the legal structure to get rid of this kind of [discriminatory] state action.''

Taeuber also dismissed Prickett's suggestion that segregation could be explained by a recent surge in black separatism. Noting that black separatism had a long history, Taeuber stated that it had never amounted to anything more than a minor movement in the twentieth century. Taeuber added, however, that the cultural ties of the many ethnic groups that had joined the mainstream had not been destroyed in the process; racial integration did not mean loss of ''black pride.''

Later, Jim Sills, former director of the People's Settlement Association and then professor of urban affairs at the University of Delaware and president of the Wilmington branch of the NAACP, added, ''There isn't a black separatist movement of any size in Wilmington. . . . The overwhelming majority of black citizens desire to move and be mobile in an integrated society. . . . The overwhelming majority . . . of black citizens in this city do not desire to have a segregated community of any kind.''

Redding closed plaintiffs' proof of Delaware's customary segregation by calling Judge Leonard Williams to the stand. The respected local black judge described how he moved back to Wilmington after law school in 1960 and looked for a home with his new bride. When they happened upon a house they wanted with a ''For Sale'' sign in the front yard, they contacted a real estate agent but were informed ''you can't see that house because [it] is not on the open occupancy list.'' Williams did not give up: ''I always felt that there is more than one way to skin a cat.'' The owner's name was O'Brien, undoubtedly a ''good Catholic'' like himself, so Williams contacted the parish priest who interceded on his behalf. When Mrs. O'Brien also determined that her son was a friend of Williams's from the University of Delaware, she agreed to sell the house. The Williams family stayed in this house near the Wilmington Medical Center for six years.

In 1966, after Williams became a judge and established a profitable law practice, he began to look for a larger house. He and his wife wanted a house in the relatively prestigious Rockford Park area which was not ''open'' to blacks. Nevertheless, they investigated about ten houses that were advertised for sale in the local papers: ''In every case when I would call the realtor's office to inquire about the property . . . once I identified myself . . . , I could not see the property. That was made clear to me. . . . I decided that this was ridiculous and that I should be able to [buy one of these houses].'' Williams then talked directly with the owners, some of whom were doctors and dentists, who said they ''couldn't break down to destroy [the] neighborhood and permit me to see the property.'' Of course, they claimed no ''personal prejudice.'' During his search, the medical center purchased and then began razing the houses around the Williams home. With winter approaching, Williams was getting ''kind of . . . desperate.''

Williams vowed somehow to see the next house that came up for sale in the area. Once again a straightforward inquiry led to a direct rejection. So he asked one of his white lawyer friends to investigate the house and to report back to Williams and his wife; the lawyer's description suggested that the house might make a good home for the Williams family. But Williams wanted to see the house for himself. At Williams's behest, the lawyer called the owner and asked if an electrician could check the wiring. One day at the lunch break from his court, Judge Williams doffed his robes and donned an old army khaki outfit to impersonate an electrician's helper. He "ruffled" his "head a little bit. I had a little more hair at that time and met the electrician in front of my house, and I got into the truck with him . . . to look at this house."

Having inspected the house with this ruse, Williams reported thoroughly and favorably to his wife. Judge Williams then obtained the sales contract on the house by paying the down payment to the white lawyer friend, who in turn negotiated for the sale and signed an agreement with the seller and then assigned the contract to Williams and his wife. On November 15, 1966, the Williams family completed the purchase and moved in before Christmas. At the time of the trial in 1973, Judge Williams remained the only black owner in the area. When Williams pointed out the location of the house to the three-judge Court, Judge Wright indicated that he was familiar with the area. Wright and Williams were neighbors.

Lucas called as witnesses three Wilmington legislators, one white, the other two black, to discuss the Educational Advancement Act. Each recounted how they had voted for the act even though they realized that race was a factor motivating the isolation of Wilmington in the reorganization plan. State senator Herman Holloway testified, for example, that he knew the act's effect would be "to scatter a few black public school students in the downstate areas and to contain and confine the larger portion of the black public school students within the city of Wilmington." All three explained how they suggested areawide desegregation alternatives in private sessions with legislators, but agreed to the final version of the act after it became clear that such solutions were unthinkable to the politically powerful suburban white lawmakers. In this legislative logrolling process tainted by bias, a representative did the best he could: financial benefits to Wilmington in the act, and the need to keep votes to pass a state fair housing act, led these Wilmington legislators to vote for a segregative education act.

Russell Dineen, a white Wilmington legislator, provided contemporaneous documentary evidence supporting this account. Dineen submitted his own copy of the first version of the act that excluded Wilmington from the reorganization plan, on which he had written "racial bias" during a markup session. Senator Holloway concluded these legislators' testimony: "[T]he Legislature was . . . establishing boundary lines . . . , establishing [Wilmington] as a [separate] school district, whereas prior to this time students from all over the State . . . were required to go to [Wilmington schools]. . . . Wilmington was being restricted to the boundaries of the City of Wilmington and hemming in most of the black students in the State."

Lucas also called Clarice Heckert, a white New Castle County representative and chairman of the House Education Committee, as a "hostile witness." This tactic permitted Lucas to cross-examine this defender of the act. Heckert argued that "much segregation is by choice." She conceded that, at the time of considering the act, she criticized proposals to desegregate Wilmington and the suburban schools because they called for "mammoth busing, [that] would take your [i.e., suburban] constituent children . . . into Wilmington schools and bus Negroes out." She also agreed that Wilmington city schools at one time served a much larger attendance area; as one pertinent example, her own children attended whites-only Wilmington city schools in 1954, even though she lived in the Alfred I. DuPont district in the suburbs. She boasted that the act had had enough financial and educational "goodies" that legislators "wouldn't dare vote against it."

Nonetheless, Heckert vigorously defended that act as "color blind," a nonracial attempt to consolidate small districts within Delaware's tradition of "community schools." In Heckert's view, desegregation in Delaware had been completed by the administrative action of the state superintendent long before the legislature and the state board tackled the reorganization issue. Judge Gibbons asked, "Did you ever give any thought to the consideration of the court's approval of [the Education Advancement Act] plan?" Clarice Heckert replied, "It was never mentioned. We never considered it at all. It was just assumed it had been complied with long since, and we were on the next job."

Lucas then proceeded to the school proof. Testimony of Gordon Foster and census maps and school boundary overlays by Bill Lamson showed that the original de jure black schools within Wilmington had never been desegregated. In 1953 the Wilmington board had added two new blacks-only elementary schools and converted a white junior high school to a colored school. They joined with the existing blacks-only elementary and blacks-only Howard High School to form a core of colored schools that served most black families in the northern half of Delaware. The state approved and fully financed all of these black schools. Thereafter, under the state board's supervision, the Wilmington board "desegregated" these black schools by gerrymandering of attendance boundaries, racial assignment of staff, "free transfers," and "racially dual optional zones" to allow all whites to avoid the still all-black schools. Such segregative practices, and the maintenance of the original blacks-only schools, continued through the time of trial.

State board attorney Prickett objected: "I don't think [the state] can be charged with [what] the Wilmington school district has done." Judge Gibbons responded: "Well, you are in the unfortunate position that the Wilmington school district, while it is a plaintiff in this lawsuit, is also a creature of the State of Delaware. . . . I don't think that you can separate the State from the school district."

Lucas then asked Foster about the alternatives reasonably available to the state to desegregate the historic black schools in Wilmington and the white schools in the suburbs rather than to restrict black pupils to the city of Wilmington. Once again Prickett objected, this time on the ground that such proof was relevant only to remedy, not to violation. Once again Judge Gibbons overruled the objection: "It goes to the question of what alternatives were available to the State of [Delaware] in complying with the Court's [1961] order."

Dr. Foster described one such alternative, based on the 1973 data, in which each virtually all-black Wilmington school could have been clustered with several nearby, all-white schools that would have resulted in each school having a 20–30 percent black student body. Judge Gibbons asked whether the 1973 figures were used "for illustrative purposes only. . . . The same techniques could have been utilized in 1968?" Foster answered "Yes" and explained that the technique had been used to desegregate Florida's countywide systems. He also added that other states' laws typically provided that local jurisdictions could use consolidation or interdistrict transfers to accomplish such areawide desegregation without disruption. In sum, such a cross-district desegregation alternative was educationally and administratively feasible and available to the state at the time of the Court's order in 1961 and the state's reorganization of schooling in 1968.

Lucas closed the school proof by calling the state superintendent of public instruction, Ken Madden. He detailed the pervasive state control of public schooling in Delaware:

- The state board authorized all new local school construction and financed 60 percent of the cost.
- The state board approved all transportation and paid for all busing costs.
- The state board reviewed and funded all operations of the designated colored schools.
- In 1968 the legislature and state board reorganized all school districts in the state.

A Lamson map graphically demonstrated that the vast majority of state school construction projects in New Castle County from 1950 through 1973 opened (and remained) as virtually all-black or all-white. Madden also conceded that at the time of passage of the Reorganization Act, he had written that some of the act's major provisions were added "to avoid consolidating any other district with Wilmington." At the end of Lucas's examination, the state superintendent vigorously denied that he or his staff had any contingency plan to desegregate Wilmington and suburban schools on an areawide basis should the court rule in plaintiffs' favor.

On cross-examination by his own counsel, Prickett, the state superintendent painted a different picture: by 1967, Delaware was in compliance with the 1964 Civil Rights Act, had eliminated the separate colored schools (outside Wilmington), and was preparing to consolidate small school districts. Once again Judge Gibbons interrupted to explain that the 1961 decree required more than the "elimination of colored schools." The decree was also "quite explicit" in requiring school district reorganization to dismantle the entire system of dual schooling and in retaining jurisdiction to measure the effectiveness of remedy.

Prickett opened his defense by calling John Parres, research director of the Wilmington schools and a former research director for the state board. Among other things, Parres testified that he had drafted a reorganization bill in 1961, one draft of which was duly submitted to the federal district court as well as the legislature. This draft did not mention Wilmington for consolidation, but neither did it exclude Wilmington from any statewide reorganization. Parres also testified that as a Wilmington staff member, he had actively opposed provisions of the Educational Advancement Act "locking Wilmington in." He had suggested to his state senator and the Wilmington superintendent and school board president that this section was "tinged with maybe some racial bias."

He advocated, in public and private, the countywide metropolitan approach recommended by the NYU study team. He sent the NYU report to all state board members in 1967. He testified that he made a slide presentation of the NYU recommendation to a white suburban audience including Clarice Heckert, but Mrs. Heckert expressed her firm opposition to consideration of any such proposal for areawide desegregation.

Prickett's next witness was Howard Row, the state board staffer who had written the first draft of the 1968 act. Row repeated the theme that the act's goal was primarily to consolidate small districts and that the express exclusion of the Wilmington school district and establishment of its boundaries at the city limits in the final drafts was intended only to track the historic law of Delaware. Row also testified that he had understood that the state board had already succeeded in eliminating the colored schools by the time he began drafting the act. On cross-examination by Lucas and Morris, however, Row conceded that the state board did not desegregate Wilmington's historically black schools in the preact phaseout or in the reorganization under the Educational Advancement Act. Row maintained, however, that he thought all

Wilmington schools were "in compliance." Circuit judge Gibbons was openly skeptical, and the two district judges seemed unconvinced by this suggestion.

Prickett called Earl Jackson, the first black superintendent in the history of the Wilmington schools. Jackson testified how he was hired in 1953, after receiving his Ph.D. from Harvard, as principal for the junior high school that had been converted to a black school that year. Jackson explained how the school after that never had a student body more than 4 percent white. Prickett challenged Jackson's failure to desegregate the school during his nineteen-year tenure as principal. Jackson, generally an impassive man, responded with emotion: he went "to everyone who had some influence to desegregate" the school and "complained over and over and over again." For example, Jackson testified, "the thing that disturbed me about the optional areas [for the school] is that they provided the opportunity for whites [in the area] to avoid and evad[e] going to the school." The white community hostility to the black schools that led to the creation of the "option" prevailed over Principal Jackson's pleas to the superintendent, however.

Having failed to pin responsibility for the state board's failure to desegregate Wilmington black schools on Earl Jackson, Prickett suggested that Redding was to blame for trying other civil rights cases rather than reopening the school case between 1961 and 1971. Judge Gibbons retorted: "His activities outside this case can hardly be the basis of an estoppel in favor of the State of Delaware which has [the] obligation under the fourteenth amendment."

Prickett completed his defense of the Educational Advancement Act by presenting an attorney who assisted Row in the drafting of the act, a civic leader who conducted community hearings, and a former state superintendent who had eliminated the separate colored school districts in the mid-1960s. Each supported the main lines of the state board defense. The civic leader conceded, however, that the Wilmington PTA had been excluded from the reorganization coalition and that he personally had rejected the Wilmington PTA's suggestion to seek desegregation of Wilmington's historic black schools in conjunction with the historic white suburban schools. Similarly, the former state superintendent conceded that he was aware of the continuation of the historic black schools in Wilmington but that the state board in its phaseout of the "colored districts" downstate did not inquire into the racially identifiable schools in the "remaining districts."

Prickett responded to plaintiffs' housing case by calling a prominent white realtor who testified that there had been no racial discrimination by "principals" in the "last several years and none by real estate agents since 1968." He further argued that most "native" Wilmington blacks "don't want" suburban housing. On cross-examination, he steadfastly maintained that his office never "steers" blacks but instead "shows them all listings" for which they have the requisite money. He did concede, however, that he regularly "guided" whites in order to "solve their shelter problems"; whites were steered to "similar sorts of folks. . . . Like seeing like." After all, he argued, whites would be "uncomfortable" in an "all black area." The witness then refused to acknowledge that one of his associates led a campaign to keep blacks out of a white area by distributing leaflets proclaiming the exclusivity of the area.

Judge Gibbons expressed curiosity over the realtor's admitted "lack of market penetration" within the city of Wilmington. After determining that such market share depended largely on the efforts and contacts of the employees of a real estate office, Judge Gibbons asked how many of the realtor's twenty-eight associates were black. The answer: "None." Having cornered the witness, Gibbons asked, of the 170 houses sold in a year by the witness, "how many are sold to blacks?" The answer: "I don't think it is a very high proportion, Sir." Gibbons asked, "Would it be as high as 5%?" The realtor answered, "There is a possibility of it," and retreated from the witness stand.

Lucas presented a brief rebuttal to Prickett's defenses. The reporter who covered the leafleting of the whites-only area of homes recounted the basis for his story and undercut any claim that Delaware's custom of segregation in housing had abated to any significant degree in recent years. The Wilmington PTA leader and the former education chairman of the state NAACP branch described how they publicly and privately protested the exclusion of Wilmington from consolidation in the Educational Advancement Act before study commissions, the state board, and the responsible civic coalitions that supported the act. They recounted how their pleas to desegregate the historic black schools and the all-white suburban schools fell on deaf ears.

Lucas closed his rebuttal evidence by recalling state superintendent Madden to the stand to discuss a February 24, 1972, report prepared by Madden's staff: it suggested several desegregation alternatives in the event the three-judge court ordered an areawide remedy. Although the superintendent had denied the existence of such a report in his previous testimony, the discovery of the document proved otherwise. On this note, the liability hearing ended on January 15, 1974.

The Three Judges' Decisions

The Supreme Court was still considering how to rule on Judge Roth's interdistrict desegregation decision in the Detroit school case. In view of this uncertainty, counsel for both plaintiffs and defendants in the Wilmington case urged the court to resolve all legal and factual issues rather than limit any ruling to the largely "remedy" theory of interdistrict relief adopted by the Sixth Circuit. Lucas, like Lenny Williams, had learned that "there is more than one way to skin a cat.'' From the beginning, Lucas framed and proved the case so that it could be distinguished from the lower court findings and theories in the Detroit and Richmond cases, if necessary to keep the cross-district issue alive in the Wilmington case and in the nation.

In their July 12, 1974, opinion, district judges Layton and Wright ignored the advice of counsel. They reserved ruling on the constitutionality of the Educational Advancement Act and the plaintiffs' claim that Delaware's custom of discrimination contributed to segregated schools throughout New Castle County. They first wanted submission of Wilmington-only and metropolitan plans to ''remedy the continuing school segregation in Wilmington'' and labeled any decision on the interdistrict liability issue as ''premature.'' The majority ruled only that the state board had the primary duty to desegregate Delaware public schools and that this affirmative duty had not been met effectively with respect to Wilmington and its five ''pre-*Brown* colored schools that continued to be operated as virtually all-black schools.''

Circuit judge Gibbons filed a separate opinion chastising his brethren for deferring a decision on the metropolitan issues squarely presented by the parties and the evidence. Although Gibbons agreed that vestiges of the state's dual system remained in Wilmington, he argued that similar vestiges persisted on a reciprocal basis in the suburbs: ''in suburban Wilmington the formerly all-white schools remain identifiably white by any relevant measure.'' He distinguished the situation in Wilmington from that of Detroit or Richmond by noting that Delaware's dual system of schooling at the time of *Brown* pervaded the entire area pursuant to express state control over local schooling. In this context, Gibbons found that the Educational Advancement Act had the effect of preventing the state board from carrying out its mandate in *Brown II* to disestablish the still basically dual system of schooling in northern New Castle County. In Gibbons's view, ''the State Board should be ordered to submit a plan for the desegregation of city and suburban schools disregarding those provisions'' of the act that effectively isolated black Wilmington schools from their white suburban counterparts.

The antibusing Neighborhood Schools Association and its coordinator, John Trager, greeted the district court's decision with a call for massive resistance to any desegregation. The local newspapers responded by counseling restraint:

Mr. Trager is a man with considerable support and uninhibited by any feeling of civic responsibility. His leadership thrives on fear. . . . [H]e presumes to have the power to allow or not to allow a court order to be implemented. It is demaguery of a very dangerous kind. . . . Whatever is the final decision [of the court], it [should] receive the obedience of all segments of the community.

United States senator William Roth countered that, ''it would be tragic if [the decision] meant massive busing in New Castle County.'' Senator Roth pledged his support for antibusing legislation to avoid any such specter.

Lucas was disappointed that the two district judges had not gone further, but he was confident that Judge Wright would eventually join circuit judge Gibbons at the remedy stage by finding Wilmington-only relief inadequate. Lucas's confidence was shaken two weeks later when the Supreme Court issued its opinion reversing the metropolitan relief and rejecting an areawide remedy for what the Burger majority perceived as Detroit-only segregation. Lucas was concerned that Judge Wright might react by inferring that the ''whole metropolitan ball game was over.''

Lucas called on me to review the record in the Delaware school case and to draft a brief showing how the Detroit decision authorized rather than prohibited cross-district relief in northern New Castle County. Lucas told the Wilmington press that the Detroit ''decision neither helps nor hurts. Wilmington is an entirely different animal.'' Bill Prickett had a different view: ''The place where [Layton and Wright] found the violations was in [the city of] Wilmington, and that's where the [only] remedy should be.'' The *Evening Journal* commented that the issues cited as ''premature'' by Wright and Layton ''seem to have matured now.''

The three-judge court responded to the Detroit decision by inviting all of the suburban school districts to intervene as defendant parties and to present any new evidence they wished. Surprisingly, after these districts intervened, they determined to stand on the existing record. Nine chose to be represented by Jack Sinclair and simply joined with Prickett and the state board to argue that any violation was confined within Wilmington and so too must any remedy.

In reviewing the pleadings, record evidence, and the detailed findings of fact prepared by plaintiffs' trial lawyers, I determined that we should focus on Delaware's particular form of state-imposed school segregation prior to *Brown*. At that time Delaware had a unique ''state-controlled and state-mandated, racially dual system of public schooling'' throughout New Castle County area schools. Far from ''separate and autonomous local districts,'' Delaware operated a state system of public school segregation with most blacks-only schools located in the city but serving the entire county. As a result, the case involved an ''areawide'' (not just an ''interdistrict'') violation from the beginning. From this perspective interdistrict relief was authorized, because state defendants following *Brown* acted—in the face of marked residential segregation, itself caused by racial discrimination—to perpetuate one-race schooling by creating and maintaining white schools in the suburbs and black schools in the city. As a result, the state both failed to dismantle the historic black schools in the city and white schools in the suburbs and actively opened 86 percent of its school construction projects in New Castle County on a virtual one-race basis.

Given this history of continuing interdistrict de jure segregation, the Educational Advancement Act was ineffective as a plan to desegregate either the historic areawide system of dual schooling or the continuing interdistrict system of segregation: the act and ensuing state board reorganization of schooling throughout the state simply reinforced the system of blacks-only schooling within the city of Wilmington and white schooling in suburban New Castle County. I also argued that the act could properly be measured by a remedial or effect test rather than a violation or intent standard, given the continuing interdistrict violation.

In sum, the Detroit decision did not proscribe cross-district relief. Instead, it authorized interdistrict desegregation in the particular circumstances of the Wilmington case. Where there were proven interdistrict violations, the chief justice's opinion in Detroit counseled, there was "a duty to prescribe appropriate remedies."

On March 27, 1975, Judge Wright, joined by Judge Gibbons, found a continuing areawide violation with significant interdistrict effects. Reviewing the history of dual schooling in Delaware before *Brown*, they found a "substantial interdependence of the Wilmington and suburban systems." Unlike the situations in Richmond and Detroit, "*de jure* segregation in New Castle County was a cooperative venture involving both city and suburbs. . . . At that time, in other words, Wilmington and suburban districts were not meaningfully 'separate and autonomous.' "

Thereafter, the districts began gradually to separate as Delaware's state-approved custom of community discrimination herded black families into neighborhoods in the expanding core of center city black schools and directed white families into the burgeoning neighborhoods served by white schools in the suburbs. Gerrymandering of attendance boundaries, free transfers, and optional zones contributed to the perpetuation of the blacks-only Wilmington schools. "Since *Brown* governmental authorities have contributed to the racial isolation of city from suburbs . . . and are responsible to a significant degree for the increasing disparity in residential and school populations between Wilmington and its suburbs in the past two decades."

In *this* context, the majority also held that the Educational Advancement Act, even if not racially motivated in a subjective sense, amounted to an unconstitutional racial limitation on the state board's power to reorganize districts. The act "played a significant part in maintaining the racial identifiability of Wilmington and the suburban New Castle County school districts."

Although Wright's analysis of the act reflected much of the uncertainty over the meaning and application of diverse "effect" and "intent" standards prevalent among judges and commentators at the time, the opinion in other respects provided a sensitive resolution of the issues presented by the parties. Wright, joined by Gibbons, concluded:

> We have found (*a*) an historic arrangement for interdistrict segregation within New Castle County, (*b*) significant governmental involvement in interdistrict discrimination, and (*c*) unconstitutional exclusion of Wilmington from consideration for consolidation by the State Board pursuant to reorganization powers now lapsed.

The district court declared unconstitutional those provisions of the act that excluded Wilmington from eligibility for consolidation and ordered the parties to submit alternative city-only and metropolitan plans of desegregation.

Judge Layton dissented on all points. He took a different view of the "root causes" of segregation in New Castle County based on the Fourth Circuit's restrictive view in the Richmond case:

> What the majority does not face up to is that there seems to be no definite explanation for the huge tide of black immigration into the nation's cities, and the white flight therefrom, in the past two decades. One theory based upon persuasive logic is that the cause is economic; that thousands of blacks have left the South and other predominantly rural areas in the past twenty years out of a natural desire to seek the better job opportunities and higher wages available in the cities. There they have settled and, as is true of most ethnic groups, have tended to band together. . . . I cannot agree that the disparity in residential and school populations between Wilmington and its suburbs is the result of discriminatory state action.

As to the reorganization, Layton found that the act only maintained the existing boundaries for Wilmington and "had no interdistrict effect. . . . I would direct that our recent [Wilmington-only violation] opinion be supplemented by a plan for the elimination of the dual system of education [within] Wilmington."

Reactions

Louis Redding felt that the evidence *compelled* the majority's finding of pervasive interdistrict violation: Delaware's state system of public school segregation had yet to be dismantled in northern New Castle County. In 1961 he had warned the district court that the state would not do the job of desegregation without explicit instructions. In 1975, fourteen years later, Judge

Wright finally recognized that Redding had been right all along. Redding's continued presence in court had served as a reminder to conscience.

For Lucas, the Delaware decision was a gratifying trial court triumph; but he had come to know that it did not mean victory on the inevitable appeals to the Supreme Court. In fact, Judge Wright's ruling would provide a clear test of whether the Supreme Court's opinion in the Detroit case actually left room for metropolitan school desegregation in any circumstances.

The state PTA responded to the ruling by passing a resolution opposing busing. The state senate attempted to add an amendment to Delaware's constitution requiring a referendum before changing the boundaries of any school district. The *Evening Journal* retorted that this suggestion was another "false hope," because a state lacked the power under the Constitution of the United States to interpose obstacles to federal court decrees; the state senate's action merely represented another example of legislative default. James Venema split from John Trager and the Neighborhood Schools Association to form a larger and better organized antibusing group, the "Positive Action Committee." The state board and suburban defendants responded by filing a direct appeal with the Supreme Court.

On November 17, 1975, the Supreme Court in a five-to-three decision summarily affirmed the interdistrict violation ruling of the district court. Justice Marshall did not sit, and the majority issued no opinion, as is common in summary dispositions of direct appeals from three-judge court decisions. Justice Rehnquist, joined by Chief Justice Burger and Justice Powell, dissented on the procedural ground that the 1968 act had had *no* effect after the onetime state board reorganization was completed in 1969; therefore the case was not properly one for decision by a three-judge court and direct review by the Supreme Court. Because of these "difficult jurisdictional questions," Rehnquist added, "the Court's summary affirmance, in my opinion, . . . leaves totally beclouded and uncertain what is decided."

Lucas breathed a sigh of relief. The summary affirmance appeared to vindicate his public claim, and private hope, that the Detroit case called for areawide desegregation where there were interdistrict violations. The *Washington Post* commented:

[In the Detroit case, the Supreme Court] ruled that there had not been a sufficient finding of officially created interdistrict segregation in the Detroit metropolitan area to justify an interdistrict busing program. A lot of people took this to be a final closing of the door on area-wide desegregation orders. That interpretation of the Detroit decision rested on a reading that ignored the implications of what was said—namely, that if such a finding of interdistrict discriminatory practice *were* made, a cross-district busing solution might be in order. That, for all its tentativeness and frailty, is what the Wilmington affirmation suggests.

Although Lucas was not satisfied with the particular road map suggested by the majority in the Detroit case, he was driving a bus in the Wilmington case through the cross-district loophole.

Chapter 14
The Interdistrict Remedy, 1976–78

Provisional Remedy

The road to cross-district desegregation in the Wilmington area would prove long and rough. The three-judge court received city-only plans and interdistrict proposals ranging from "free transfers" and "magnet schools" between existing districts to countywide consolidation. The Wilmington board proposed actual desegregation by clustering schools as originally suggested by Gordon Foster; but it proposed that the existing districts be retained to operate these desegregated schools, at least for an interim period while the Delaware General Assembly developed an alternative governance structure. The Wilmington board's plan also included a comprehensive program for ancillary relief to prevent discrimination against minority students and staff during the desegregation process.

The close-in suburban districts in this compact metropolitan area proposed plans that included their somewhat more distant neighbors who argued, in turn, for limiting any plan to the close-in districts. Other proposals sought to exempt elementary grades or to rely solely on one-way assignment of Wilmington blacks to suburban schools. The state board proposed a redistricting plan to divide Wilmington into five parts and to attach each part to one or more of the existing suburban districts.

Bill Prickett suggested to Lou Lucas that the case be settled on the basis of voluntary transfers between existing districts. Lucas presented the state board's offer to the Wilmington board and to the private plaintiffs. The proposal was not what Louis Redding and his clients had been fighting for; and the state board's threat to dismantle the Wilmington school district and administration only confirmed the commitment of the new president of the Wilmington board, Wendell Howell, to fight for a fair, two-way plan that would also protect Wilmington's black students, staff, and community from state retaliation.

During the extensive remedy hearings before the three-judge court, Lucas stressed that a conservative approach to any judicial reorganization of school districts should be followed. The state, as in reapportionment cases, should be given the first crack at changing school district boundaries. In the interim, actual two-way desegregation should proceed between the existing districts, with any disputes resolved by a court-appointed monitoring commission. Lucas also stressed that the scope of remedy should be no greater than necessary to remedy the areawide violation.

The suburbs proceeded to battle with one another over which should be included and which should be excluded in any desegregation plan. In addition, the defendants argued that any compulsory interdistrict desegregation premised on retaining existing school district boundaries was impractical and would inevitably involve the district court in resolving disputes concerning the administration of the schools. Any areawide desegregation remedy, argued the suburbs, should be limited to voluntary transfers and magnet schools.

At the remedy hearing, the presence of Wilmington's superintendent, Thomas Minter, had its first impact on the case. Minter, who had served as a regional school superintendent in New York City and Philadelphia, took over as Wilmington superintendent in the midst of the school case. His job was to lead the district to a fair and effective metropolitan desegregation solution. He testified that magnet schools and voluntary plans, as a primary remedy, were ineffective and expensive and catered to racial choices. Dr. Minter asserted, "If we are going to . . . desegregate, it's [got to be] a two-way process." If children of both races attend desegregated schools located in black as well as white areas, he noted, "then both groups are accepting, both groups are looking out one for the other."

When the defense lawyers sought to argue that one-way desegregation plans reflected "freedom of choice in a democracy," Minter replied:

I don't believe any of us, if I may be philosophical, has complete freedom of choice. . . . In terms of schools, even when children go to schools within their own districts, they are *assigned* to schools. . . . I don't know of anyone who has absolute freedom of choice in the matter of going to public schools.

Other suggestions for blacks-only desegregation and even a complete black school closing program were made. Gordon Foster, who had assisted hundreds of school districts to desegregate throughout the South, responded: "[That] would buy several years of politically oriented, racial difficulties with the school operations. . . . In terms of desegregation plans, it is just bad news." Magnet proposals also fell before Foster's experience: "The sudden popularity of 'magnet' programs . . . when desegregation is threatened [is] essentially a racist idea. [Their premise is] that if you make schools [in the black community] supergood, then whites will come in." Foster described how some school authorities even went so far as to close down, paint, and fumigate *new* black schools in order to assuage white fears prior to desegregation. Foster added that magnet schools, like "free choice" transfer programs, had proven ineffective as primary tools to desegregate dual systems of schooling.

On May 19, 1976, Judge Wright, joined by Judge Gibbons, issued the opinion for the three-judge court. Noting that the area primarily affected by the violation included only 251 square miles and 80,678 students, 19.4 percent of whom were black, the court first reiterated the areawide extent of violation in order to define the proper scope of remedy. The continuing interdistrict violations previously found "had a substantial . . . effect on the enrollment patterns of the separate districts." The unconstitutional actions of the state legislature and the state board of education "[are] a substantial and proximate cause of the existing disparity in racial enrollments in the districts of Northern New Castle County." As a result, city schools contained almost 85 percent black pupils, while white suburban schools housed less than 5 percent black pupils. Any plan limited to the city schools would not restore the black "victims of the violation" to the "position which they would have occupied had [the continuing areawide] violation not occurred." Instead a city-only plan would just "result in the maintenance of the racial identity previously established by State action."

The court also rejected so-called voluntary and magnet school plans because none promised to accomplish much desegregation. Further, the court rejected all of the desegregation proposals that reorganized the entire area either by redistricting or by maintaining existing boundaries and assigning students across district lines. The court found that redistricting was better left to the state legislature, while desegregation across existing school district lines might require too much ongoing judicial supervision of school operations.

The court therefore ordered a provisional consolidation of districts with a plan of actual desegregation to be prepared by an interim board appointed by the state board from the elected board members of the existing local districts. This consolidation would go into effect and continue only for as long as the legislature failed to adopt an effective alternative. The court delayed implementation of any desegregation plan for secondary schools to September 1977 and to September 1978 for any elementary school plan. The court authorized the interim board to prepare plans for pupil reassignment and for administration of the consolidated district. The promulgation, implementation, and operation of a constitutional system of schooling was placed squarely on the shoulders of the responsible state and local school authorities.*

Lucas was disappointed that desegregation would be delayed at least another year, but he lauded the court's restrained exercise of discretion and sensitive approach to solving the practical problems of interdistrict remedy.

---

*Judge Layton agreed that Wilmington-only and magnet plans were inadequate to remedy the interdistrict violation but dissented on the ground that the extent of any violation was narrower than found by the majority so any remedy should be more limited.

The legislature and the antibusing groups were outraged. Apart from authorizing "free choice" transfers between existing districts, the legislature determined to do nothing except to cheer appeals of the ruling by the state board and the suburban districts. James Venema, the leader of the Positive Action Committee, stumped for an antibusing constitutional amendment. Senator Joe Biden, a Democrat, joined Senator Roth, his Republican counterpart, in bipartisan opposition to "forced busing." The state board and suburban districts again appealed the judgment of the three-judge court directly to the Supreme Court.

First Appeal

The Supreme Court, however, determined that the remedy ruling could have been entered by a single judge and therefore should be reviewed in the first instance by the Third Circuit. Of the nine Third Circuit judges, Judge Gibbons could not sit because he had participated in the trial and joined in district judge Wright's rulings; and Collins Seitz, now the chief judge of the circuit, recused himself because his son worked in the state attorney general's office. That stripped the Third Circuit of two of its members who would have been sympathetic to the goal of the trial court. When the Third Circuit agreed to hear the case *en banc* with the seven remaining judges, the probability of a closely divided decision loomed. Given the uncertainty over the meaning of the Supreme Court's summary affirmance of the original interdistrict violation ruling, the parties could not be sure even of the scope of appellate review.

By this time I had joined Lucas, Taylor, Redding, Morris, and Rosenthal as co-counsel for plaintiffs. We argued that the Supreme Court had already affirmed the existence of a significant and continuing interdistrict violation, and that the only issue for the Third Circuit was whether Judge Wright abused his discretion in remedying the constitutional wrong. Given the substantial nature of this violation, we argued, the district court had a duty under the Detroit decision to prescribe an interdistrict remedy. The areawide interim remedy not only fit the violation, it represented a model of judicial restraint and deference to the legitimate interests of the state and local school authorities in shaping and in implementing relief. The defendants countered that the trial court had failed to tailor the remedy to fit the segregation actually caused by any violation.

While we waited for the Third Circuit's ruling, the district court twice heard pleas by the state board and suburban defendants for another year's delay in provisional consolidation and actual desegregation. Although the interim board had long since established diverse committees to develop plans for pupil reassignment, administration, finance, and curriculum for the new provisional consolidation, the defendants claimed that desegregation should be delayed until all appeals had been completed in view of the large "super-district" that would otherwise result.

By this time the three-judge court had disbanded to allow a single judge to hear any remaining aspects of the case. Judges Gibbons, Wright, and Layton left the case in the hands of district judge Murray Schwartz. Judge Schwartz, a recent Nixon appointee, had been a corporate lawyer before his appointment. In his brief term on the bench, he had become known as a thorough, hardworking judge who was not afraid to stand up to established state tradition if necessary to right constitutional wrongs. Schwartz rejected defendants' stalling tactics and denied the applications for stays: "the delay of [another] year or more in implementation of a desegregation remedy would cause the [irreparable] loss to each of the members of the Plaintiffs' class of another year of the [constitutional] education to which he or she is entitled under current decisions of this Court."

On May 18, 1977, while the appeal in the first round of the Dayton case was still pending in the Supreme Court, the Third Circuit narrowly affirmed the three-judge court's remedy ruling by a four-to-three vote. The majority and dissenting opinions, however, gave little guidance to the lower court. Judge Aldisert, writing for the majority, held that Judge Wright's previous liability ruling constituted "the law of the case" in view of the Supreme Court's summary affirmance and that the three-judge court's remedy concept represented a sound exercise of equitable discretion. Paraphrasing the legal standard applied by Judge Wright in his remedy ruling, Judge Aldisert added, "The school system and its students are to be returned, as nearly as possible, to the position they would have been in but for the constitutional violations that have been found." The majority only reiterated that the district court opinion did not require "racial balance": any desegregation should only overcome the segregation caused by the constitutional violations.

The Third Circuit also directed the district court to reissue the three-judge court's remedy order with a minor clarification: If the state failed to file a report within sixty days demonstrating a successful effort by the Delaware legislature to promulgate an effective remedy, the circuit court directed the lower court to appoint a planning board of local school officials to promulgate a provisional remedy. This "clarification" apparently ignored the existence and work of the interim board over the past year.

The three dissenters, in an opinion by Judge Garth, agreed that the Supreme Court's summary disposition on liability was a binding decision on the merits but argued that the Third Circuit somehow had to decide which specific violation findings had been affirmed. Garth defined eight separate practices that might be violations but ignored altogether the continuing violation rooted in Delaware's interdistrict dual system in New Castle County at the time of *Brown*. Garth argued that the case should have been remanded to the district court to determine which specific practices were "intentional" and then to calibrate the interdistrict segregative effects of each isolated violation. To Garth, the duty of the federal courts was to separate the segregation caused by constitutional violations from that "attributable to economic and social forces, to private actions, and to nondiscriminatory governmental actions." Under Garth's prescription, the federal courts had no power to remedy the latter.

The opinions of the Third Circuit did not signal the immediate end of litigation nor the beginning of desegregation in northern Delaware. In both the trial and the appellate courts, the state had only fallen one judge short of avoiding interdistrict desegregation. Defendants asked the Supreme Court to review the case and prepared for more hearings before Judge Schwartz. Both would give the state several more opportunities to win the one vote it needed.

Confusion and the New Judge

On the remand to implement the Third Circuit's mandate, district judge Schwartz faced ambiguity in the law, default by the state legislature, and public confusion. On June 27, 1977, the Supreme Court added "the incremental segregative effect" test when it ruled in the Dayton case. This ruling fueled public consternation in Delaware, fired the hopes of the antibusers, and provided new grist for the defendants' old arguments in Delaware. It also steeled the General Assembly to do nothing about reorganization and desegregation except to urge the state board and suburban districts to press their petitions for review of the entire case in the Supreme Court and to prepare for more litigation in the lower courts.

With the time for the report on the state legislative action drawing near, the state board adopted a one-way plan of blacks-only desegregation proposed by state senator Arnold and his special joint legislative committee on the school case. The plan "assigned" all black Wilmington students to white schools but provided that each might "opt out" at any time by returning to Wilmington schools. The board appropriately dubbed the plan "reverse volunteerism." The state board then included this plan in its report as an alternative to the legislature's refusal to act.

The report amounted to a lawyers' brief that questioned the Third Circuit decision. In the Dayton ruling defendants found renewed hope to reexamine virtually the entire case, either in the Supreme Court or before Judge Schwartz. Although arguing that Judge Schwartz should conduct a hearing on the "incremental segregative effect" of any constitutional violations, the report conceded that "it is not feasible to determine what today's situation would be . . . but for the alleged constitutional violations."

With the default by the legislature, the patently discriminatory plan of reverse volunteerism, and the forbidding specter of the Dayton decision, plaintiffs faced a practical and legal bind. First, there was no fair and effective pupil assignment plan ready to be implemented for secondary schools. The interim board, whose existence had been ignored by the Third Circuit, was apparently going out of business. Its proposed desegregation plan utilized a grade-center approach to close all early elementary and senior high schooling in Wilmington proper and to assign suburban children to city schools for two years at middle schools.* This "ten-two" plan smacked of the same type of racial inequity as "reverse volunteerism."

Second, there was no sure way to avoid the psychological if not the potential legal hazards of the Dayton decision. Neither the Dayton decision nor the Third Circuit opinion, however, compelled us to retry the entire case. As Lucas remarked, "Let's hoist the State with its own petard: they have conceded that it's not possible to make the 'incremental segregative effect' inquiry."

Third, we had to worry about the nature as well as the scope of any plan. Louis Redding had not fought for thirty years to settle for a plan premised on discrimination or designed to cater to white fears of two-way desegregation at the expense of black children.

Judge Schwartz convened a hearing on the state board's report and the defendants' request for a stay of any desegregation pending review in the Supreme Court. Schwartz proceeded to ask tough questions to get straight answers. He started with the defendants' lawyers: Did the Third Circuit mandate permit court-ordered implementation of any interdistrict plan not approved by the legislature? If not, what authority did the district court have even to consider "reverse volunteerism"? Wasn't the only alternative to order the state board to appoint the new planning board? How did "reverse volunteerism" relate to any equitable principle? Had any court ever considered such a proposal? With respect to the extent of violation and scope of remedy, how did defendants expect the court to make the "incremental segregative effect" inquiry that they represented was not "feasible"? Wasn't the scope of remedy already established except insofar as the Supreme Court might review the case? What proof did defendants plan to offer to show how the impact of the violation was limited? If defendants offered no new evidence, would the extent of violation and scope of remedy remain as found by the three-judge court?

Judge Schwartz then turned to plaintiffs' counsel. Judge Schwartz asked

---

*Under a "grade-center approach," *all* students in the desegregation area attend former white schools for certain grades and former black schools for other grades. Under the interim board's plan, for example, all students might be assigned to suburban schools in grades one to six and nine to twelve but to Wilmington schools in grades seven and eight; all Wilmington schools would then be reorganized to serve only as middle school "grade centers."

whether he could depart from the Third Circuit's mandate. If not, he could not hear any pupil assignment plans now but must appoint a new planning board to develop a plan of pupil desegregation.

Judge Schwartz then moved to the state's argument concerning the extent of any violations that might support the areawide scope of remedy ordered by the three-judge court. In an attempt to address the problem of the "but-for" and "incremental segregative effect" tests of Detroit, Dayton, and the Third Circuit, he asked me first to describe how each of the eight violations identified in Judge Garth's dissenting opinion was motivated by segregative intent and then to evaluate the precise extent to which each intentional violation contributed to the current school segregation. The very framing of this question suggested that Judge Schwartz might believe the inquiry into segregative impact required by the Dayton decision had yet to be made. I responded generally by arguing that Judge Wright's ruling had already established the interdistrict extent of violation and areawide scope of remedy. The issues raised by the state board had already been tried by the parties and decided by the three-judge court in its violation and remedy rulings.

Judge Schwartz was not satisfied; he wanted an answer to his questions. So I responded. Judge Garth's list of eight violations omitted the most critical violation, the foundation on which the three-judge court ruled: complete long-standing interdistrict school segregation in Delaware in 1954. The dominant motive of this state-compelled de jure segregation was racial discrimination. The local districts were not separate and autonomous at the time but were engaged in a cooperative venture to implement the state system of segregation throughout the area.

The three-judge court had found that this interdistrict dual system had never been dismantled. The state had only splintered this single system of interdistrict segregation into separate districts, channeling whites to virtually all-white suburban school districts and containing blacks in the expanding core of Wilmington's black schools.

Although some of the specific practices in question were intentionally discriminatory, the appropriate test was whether these actions effectively dismantled the single system of complete, interdistrict, de jure segregation of 1954. The types of practices cited by Judge Garth clearly had perpetuated and even exacerbated the original unconstitutional system of areawide dual schooling.

I continued: "The way the Third Circuit dissent says there are eight violations is the wrong reading of the three-judge court's opinion. . . . [A] fairer way to read the opinion [is to] look at what is a detailed description of the history and the context and the development of this whole area and the school system . . . rather than parse it into separate violations." From this perspective, Judge Wright had made a thorough and informed analysis of the facts: the opinion carefully traced the continuation of the original interdistrict dual system through the time of trial. At the remedy stage, defendants again had failed to show that the violation was limited, or that it was anything but a substantial, proximate cause of the racial disparity in pupil enrollments between Wilmington and its suburbs. Thus, Judge Wright, not Judge Garth, had conducted a "sensitive inquiry" and made the "reasoned statement of legal principles" required by the Supreme Court decisions in Arlington Heights and Dayton.

Judge Schwartz asked whether the three-judge court had made all the findings required by Dayton. I answered yes, but added that he could supplement these findings. After two hours of this question-and-answer argument, I sat down. Lucas whispered to me, "You just re-won the case with the new judge."

Each of the defense lawyers tried to challenge my statement of the basic facts and findings of the three-judge court. They called my description a "fantasyland." I responded, "I can understand the concern of the defendants' counsel with the facts as I've described them because they lead inexorably to [the] result [of areawide desegregation]. . . . [Defendants'] burden, however, is those are the facts that the three-judge court found."

At the evidentiary hearing which followed on the state board's "reverse volunteerism" proposal, Tom Minter again testifed. By then Minter had become deputy commissioner of elementary and secondary education at HEW. Minter first dealt with the events leading to the state board's proposal. He described the interim board's prior "ten-two" grade-center concept as "patently discriminatory" on its face: only black and Hispanic children would have to be bused early in their elementary careers; only black high schools would be closed; only Wilmington children were assigned out of their area for ten years. Lucas asked whether there was any reason for this discrimination. Minter responded: "I don't know if you call it a reason. [Suburban administrators said,] 'The point is Wilmington brought the case, so Wilmington has to suffer, that's too bad, but that's kind of the way it is.' "

"Reverse volunteerism" was even worse, in Minter's view. "The only people who move are blacks. . . . I think it's insulting to the [black] parents and children [who] are again the victims. . . . [T]he majority society is again putting the burden [on the minority]. It's almost saying 'Go out and heal yourself.' "

Bill Prickett in his defense of the plan countered that "reverse volunteerism" was appropriate to avoid "unfairness to these [black] people. [T]hey should not be marched around by the Federal Court if they don't want to be. . . . We don't think the Federal Court ought to impose its will if [black] people, given a choice, can stay where they belong [in black Wilmington schools]." Minter responded: "To me it is insulting to say, '. . . close down the schools in Wilmington and let everybody move out to the suburbs' [, except] as Mr. Prickett said . . . [for black] people being where they *belong*. . . . I am not sure that anybody in the society is where he *belongs*. There is no place for *belonging* other than in the mainstream. So I react very emotionally and very strongly against the plan, both as an educator and as a black—it just seems that it is patently unfair.''

Sam Russell, the lawyer for the prestigious Alexis I. duPont district to which many Wilmington blacks had voluntarily transferred in the past year, still didn't understand the white racism inherent in one-way, blacks-only desegregation, let alone in the state board's plan of ''reverse volunteerism.'' He asked, ''Isn't it rather demeaning to the black population in Wilmington to suggest that they don't know what is good for them, that they should be told where they go and not have an option to make the choice themselves?'' Minter answered somberly, ''That is a very difficult statement to respond to because the statement itself is really the basis of my objection—the way you phrase the statement is in itself [racially insulting], if I may say so.'' Russell interjected ''Well, I am not trying to be.'' The dramatic exchange continued:

Minter.   I know you aren't. That is why it is difficult to respond to. . . . Desegregation or mandatory assignment is not just telling people where they should go to maintain—to acquire a constitutional right. We tell people as school children all over this state and other states where they should go to school. We tell everybody where they should go to their school, the boundaries, you know, the whole thing.

My point is that we have a population, a segment of the population, a minority segment, that has been discriminated against. So let's go back over the history of it. We are not coming from a Tabula Rasa; we are coming with a history. The history is overt, legal and other, discrimination. Now, . . . the minority people didn't do it to themselves. . . . So when they petition for relief, they don't expect to be told, ''Well, you may have your relief at your own expense, if you will endure all of what I will call indignities, inconveniences, and so forth, and come on to our turf, fine, we will accept you.'' That is what is degrading. I don't want you to accept—well, I don't want to be personal—black people don't want you to accept them. That is the issue.

Russell tried to recover: ''So it is the disparity in the burden—''

Minter.   That is right.

Russell.   —coming back and forth, which you primarily object to in the State plan?

Minter.   Yes; it is basically one group that has been discriminated against being forced to bear the total burden of the remedy, and at the same time it is reinforcing the either overt or covert beliefs that there must be something wrong with that group because the other group is not affected at all. We either accept you or we don't.

Russell.   But to remedy that we have to impose the same burden on another group?

Minter.   We share the burden. We are not imposing a burden. We are sharing the burden.

To the credit of the staff of the state board, they merely explained the mechanics of "reverse volunteerism" but agreed on cross-examination that the proposal was not educationally sound, had been drafted by the lawyers rather than the school officials, and gave no promise of accomplishing substantial desegregation.

No Compromise

At the close of the hearing on "reverse volunteerism" and defendants' application for stay of desegregation, Judge Schwartz convened a "settlement conference" among counsel for all parties in his chambers. He suggested consideration of voluntary transfers for all black children in Wilmington coupled with a variety of magnet schools and programs in Wilmington to attract suburban white children. He outlined his perception of the remaining litigation risks for both sides. For the defendants, he described a possible Supreme Court affirmance and a complete two-way plan with the certain consolidation of existing school districts into a single district pursuant to the Third Circuit's mandate. He turned to Louis Redding and described plaintiffs' risk—a Supreme Court reversal that could end "Mr. Redding's thirty-year struggle to allow blacks to go to white schools."

Schwartz had failed to grasp the object of Redding's struggle, namely to eliminate the caste system of segregation with all its racial restrictions and proscriptions. As Redding later recalled this incident, "I did not then and do not now give a damn about allowing black kids 'to go to white schools.' But I did care about how to win Judge Schwartz in this case." After considerable discussion, plaintiffs' counsel all agreed that the appropriate response was to write a letter to Judge Schwartz, which included a statement of how we felt:

Mr. Redding, other plaintiffs' counsel and their clients do not seek, nor have they ever sought, for black children the right in the Court's words

". . . to go to a white school." Furthermore, the elimination of official segregation and its effect is not a process of improving the "quality" of education in particular Wilmington schools to attract suburban children. Plaintiffs seek only an equitable transition to racially nondiscriminatory schooling—not "black schools" or "white schools" but just schools. Thus, the suggested parameters for settlement would require a basic compromise of constitutional rights. Indeed, these parameters have already been rejected by the three-judge court.

Two weeks later, on August 5, 1977, Judge Schwartz issued his ruling on "reverse volunteerism" and the state's motion for delay. As a matter of procedure, he held that the Third Circuit's mandate did not contemplate the district court ordering a state board proposal if the legislature failed to enact a reorganization plan. Upon the legislature's continued default, the Third Circuit instead required the "appointment of the New Board [by the state board] and implementation of the one-district plan." On the merits, Judge Schwartz rejected the proposal for "reverse volunteerism," noting that "[t]he most obvious and significant flaw is that the proposal places the entire burden on those whose rights have been violated. . . . One would find it difficult to create a more graphic paradigm of an inequitable remedy than one which assigns to those who have been wronged the [sole] responsibility of correcting those wrongs."

Judge Schwartz also expressed "no difficulty in concluding that the three-judge court was correct in its rulings." As to the extent of violation, he agreed that "the trier of fact found that the vestiges of an interdistrict *de jure* segregated school system had not been completely dismantled." Although agreeing that Judge Wright's remedy ruling was also supported by application of the standards subsequently promulgated by the Supreme Court in Dayton, Judge Schwartz recognized that the law was perhaps in a state of flux in the Supreme Court. This "complicating factor" suggested that defendants' petitions seeking Supreme Court review of the Third Circuit's judgment (and the entire case) were not frivolous. Judge Schwartz noted that the education of all area children would suffer "irreparable injury" if a single district was created in September and then subsequently dismantled by the Supreme Court. The judge therefore stayed the pupil desegregation and provisional consolidation that already had been scheduled for eighteen months to begin in September.

Judge Schwartz ordered the state board to appoint a new planning board from the elected members of the existing local districts "to begin immediate development of a [single district] plan to desegregate grades 1 through 11 in the public schools of the 11 affected districts in September, 1978, and grades 1 through 12 in all subsequent years." He directed the new board to hire whatever experts and staff were necessary to complete the planning job. He ordered the state board and the existing districts to provide complete cooperation, including their own staff and funds, to the new board. Unless the Supreme Court granted certiorari to review the Third Circuit's judgment, Judge Schwartz would order consolidation and desegregation to begin in September, 1978. He scheduled hearings to begin on October 18, 1977, on the pupil reassignment and administrative plans to be developed by the new board in order to avoid any further delays. In all, the opinion revealed a district judge trying to work his way out of the confusion by proceeding fairly, if perhaps cautiously, while giving the Supreme Court another chance to signal its intentions before he implemented the mandate of the narrow majority on the Third Circuit and the three-judge court.

On October 4, the Supreme Court denied the defendants' petitions to review the case by a four-to-three vote with Justices Marshall and Stevens not participating. The Chief Justice and Justices Powell and Rehnquist filed a one-line dissent: they "would grant the petitions [to review the case], vacate the judgment and remand . . . to the . . . Third Circuit for reconsideration in light of Dayton." Although some antibusing elements in Delaware still claimed that the case was open to reversal on appeal from any final order by Judge Schwartz approving a plan of desegregation, other Delaware citizens believed that a plan would eventually go into effect and that the only issue was the form it would take.

Wringing Out Discrimination

The new board took up where the interim board left off. It adopted a "ten-two" grade-center approach that assigned city students to suburban schools for ten years and all suburban students to city schools for two years. This approach represented a compromise among all of the suburban school board members appointed to the new board. Instead of attempting to determine which if any areas might be excluded from the plan, it was easier to include all suburban schools; and, given the relatively short bus rides involved, the suburban members decided to share the burden of desegregation but otherwise to disrupt suburban schools as little as possible. The plan therefore promised complete desegregation and touted the fact that all suburban children would be treated the same—ten grades in their "home" schools and two grades "away" in city schools. The new board's plan, like that of the interim board, also eliminated all early elementary and high school education in the city schools. It also failed to utilize the full capacity in Wilmington schools: a plan that assigned three grades to the city schools would have reduced the extra burden of reassignment borne by black children compared to white from eight years (ten-two) to six (nine-three).*

---

*Under such a grade-center plan, Wilmington schools had sufficient capacity, that is, classrooms or pupil spaces, to house all students in the desegregation area for three grades in the city. Under this alternative, all students would then attend suburban schools for nine grades.

Wendell Howell, the Wilmington board president and minority representative on the new board, denounced "ten-two" and directed Superintendent Joe Johnson to prepare an alternative. Johnson and Parres devised "Plan W," touted as a "regional concept" which attempted to achieve as much desegregation as possible around high schools situated between neighboring black and white pupil populations. It involved redrawing boundaries between nearby black and white high schools where possible, then pairing and clustering more distant white suburban schools with city black schools. A primary goal of this approach was to assure that *some* high school education would continue in the city after desegregation.

As the hearing approached, Lucas asked me to take over primary responsibility in Wilmington because of his trial on remand in Dayton before Judge Rubin. As I reviewed the two plans, I became convinced that it would be a mistake to view either proposal as a complete and final plan for pupil reassignment. Both contained many technical errors and practical problems that needed attention. Instead, the two proposals presented competing methods of reassignment and concepts of fairness. Judge Schwartz could only resolve the basic conflicts and then order the new board to develop a complete and detailed plan for actual reassignments.

Bill Prickett suggested a four-district alternative to the single school district consolidation, but Judge Schwartz informed him that under the Third Circuit's mandate any such redistricting was a matter for the legislature, not the court. Prickett then joined suburban lawyers in supporting the legislature's program of voluntary transfers between existing districts as an adequate remedy. The defendants indicated, however, that they liked the ten-two plan better than Plan W.

Reporters needed a score card just to keep track of players. The defendants were represented by thirteen different attorneys. The new board was represented by Henry Herndon, a corporate trial lawyer who prepared his cases thoroughly and tried them professionally. Wendell Howell, the minority board member, retained Lenny Williams to represent his interests. Louis Redding, approaching eighty years of age, joined me and Joe Rosenthal at plantiffs' counsel table. Tom Lodge, attorney for the 52 percent black DeLaWarr school district, sat with the press in the jury box to separate himself and his clients from the white suburbs and the black plaintiffs. In the spectators' section, Earl Jackson, the retired Wilmington superintendent, watched every day from one side of the aisle. He was usually joined by Joe Johnson, Al Plant (Wilmington's fiery black representative in the state house), other concerned black citizens, and John Parres. On the other side of the aisle sat John Zebley, a retired grandparent who had been permitted to make an argument in the Third Circuit and who continued to file letter briefs and plans in the district courts. He was joined by school officials from the state board and suburban districts and several mothers who supported neighborhood schools and opposed busing.

The new board, through its first witness, Dr. Phyllis Magat, argued that the eight-year disparity borne by black Wilmington students in reassignments under the ten-two plan did not discriminate against Wilmington's black pupils. The witness argued that the racial composition of the total pupil population should determine the number of grades and the number of years in which that student would be reassigned under a grade-center plan. But in a system that was closer to 25 percent black, all students would be assigned to the former black schools for three grades and to the former white schools for nine grades, rather than two and ten as proposed by the new board.

The working assumption underlying the new board's concept was also faulty. The limiting factor on assignments was school capacity, not racial composition. By refusing to use available capacity at the city schools, the new board's ten-two approach maximized, rather than minimized, the disparity in years of reassignments borne by the black children compared to white. Because city schools had enough space to serve area students for three grades, a nine-three plan was feasible.*

Judge Schwartz understood the harsh facts concerning the disparate burden of reassignment to be borne by black students: "because of the [existing school capacity in Wilmington], it is inevitable that blacks have to be bused more than whites. . . . [T]here will be . . . disproportion. The issue is whether it is going to be maximized or minimized." The first remedy issue had been drawn: on the average, would each black student ride the reassignment bus eight (ten-two) or six (nine-three) more years than his white counterparts?

Dr. George Kirk, the superintendent of the Newark school district, then testified on behalf of the new board in defense of the ten-two plan. Kirk vigorously defended the approach as a complete school desegregation plan that treated all suburban children "equitably" in that each would be assigned to Wilmington schools for two years. On cross-examination, however, he conceded the possibility of instituting a nine-three plan, in reducing the disparity in the number of years black compared to white students were assigned, and in maintaining some early elementary grades and high school education in city as well as suburban schools.

Judge Schwartz then interjected: "Excuse me, Mr. Dimond. If that were done, would plaintiffs be satisfied?" I responded by suggesting that if the new board majority and the state board agreed to the fair implementation of a nine-three plan throughout the entire grade span in both city and suburban schools,

---

*Former black schools could house about twenty thousand pupils in a system with close to seventy thousand students; less than four full grades could therefore be served in these schools.

I would take the proposal back to the plaintiffs and the Wilmington board to see if our remaining dispute between the administrators over how to organize the high school plan could be set aside. Judge Schwartz was dissatisfied with this answer: "So, in answer to my question, then, plaintiffs are not interested in settlement?" When I responded that I had yet to hear from the other side, Judge Schwartz suggested that I meet with opposing counsel and then asked me pointedly, "Have you . . . ever settled . . . a school case?"

I had the distinct impression that Judge Schwartz's critical tone reflected his personal frustration at the stern rebuke we had sent him following his last settlement conference. I admitted that I had never seen a school case settled on equal and effective terms because nondiscrimination in the pupil assignment method was usually not acceptable to the white majority. After canvassing the views of opposing counsel and hearing their opposition to any nine-three plan, Judge Schwartz responded hotly: "What a settlement would promote would be stability so that we could get on with the business of education instead of litigation. . . . If the parties don't want to settle, I could care less."

At this point Lenny Williams took over: "Let me just get down to the basic fundamental issue and why it is so difficult to talk about settlement. . . . Number one, we're not talking about settling a [fender bender] injury case. We're talking about determining the rights of people, particularly people who have been carrying the burden for an exceedingly long time." Williams then attacked the ten-two plan: "It's as if black kids are going to be told that you are going to carry 100 pounds and you carry that load wherever you got to carry it on that bus. And white kids are going to be told you carry [only] 20 pounds. . . . [L]et's relieve an *extra* ten pounds [from the black children] if you can." Williams continued:

> There are people in this courtroom, and I'm one of them, who [had to wait] around for 25 years and [have] seen this [segregation] thing continue forever and ever. . . . There is room to settle. . . . [But] how [can] you compromise the rights of people who have been suffering for a long time? And that's the key issue here. We're not trying to retain a Wilmington school system per se. We're talking about lessening the burden on the people who are the victims, the people who have [supposedly already] won [this lawsuit], who the Court had said [their Constitutional rights] have been offended, who have suffered, not making them continue to pay in a disproportionate fashion. . . . That's the key here.

Williams concluded by noting any settlement therefore required "some sensitivity" to this basic issue, "and that's what I don't know is present among [the white majority in the suburbs] who have to deal with that."

I then suggested to the court a procedure for resolving the assignment issue: plaintiffs would agree to Superintendent Johnson and a designated suburban superintendent working together full-time, as "officers of the court," to iron out their differences and present an alternative plan to the court. The judge asked Johnson to meet with Carroll Biggs, the most politically influential of the suburban superintendents, to determine whether they could work together to develop a single plan. Biggs would not budge much from ten-two, and Johnson could not agree to anything below nine-three. If this second abortive settlement effort served any useful purpose, it proved that racial realities stood in the way of any equitable settlement.

At this point, Prickett suggested to Judge Schwartz that the portion of the three-judge court's order exempting students entering the twelfth grade from reassignment in the first year of desegregation made no sense under the new board's ten-two plan. The exemption had originally been included to permit seniors to graduate from the same high schools that they had already attended for the past two years. Under the new board's ten-two plan, however, the two Wilmington senior high schools were turned into two-grade centers for middle school students. It did not make much sense to have a lone twelfth grade class with two junior high grades.

Schwartz asked me whether plaintiffs agreed with the state board's suggestion to drop this exemption. I responded in a fashion that would test the racial bias of the state and suburban defendants: plaintiffs would agree to include Wilmington seniors in the ten-two plan *if* the defendants would also agree to include all of their high school seniors in *any* desegregation plan, including a plan which assigned suburban high school students to Wilmington high schools.

Judge Schwartz responded: "If [the state board and the suburbs] want it one way, they have to take it the other." There was a flurry among the defense lawyers. Prickett expressed concern about assigning suburban seniors to Wilmington high schools. Once this opposition was revealed, Schwartz wanted to know how including seniors in the reassignment plan could be good for black students reassigned to former white schools but bad for white students reassigned to former black schools: "Mr. Prickett, what else does [your concern] have to do with except white or black?"

After these interruptions, I returned to questioning George Kirk. I asked him to assume that he had been ordered by the district judge to consider a center plan alternative to ten-two that would "minimize racial inequities [between black city students and white suburban students] in terms of the number of years in and out." With Kirk's cautious but honest answers, we developed the outline of a nine-three plan that in the first nine grades assigned all students to former black schools in three grades and to former white schools for six grades. I then asked Kirk "to put a cover over your ability to tell" the current racial and school district identity of the high schools. Operating from this assumption that racial identity was irrelevant, Kirk agreed that both Wilmington high schools were good educational facilities and centrally located for ease of access for both white and black students. Judge Schwartz watched the development of this racially nondiscriminatory plan intently.

Kirk expressed concern over whether there was sufficient capacity in the city schools to implement a plan once the details of actual assignments were considered; Kirk speculated that a nine-three grade-center plan was not feasible because the Wilmington staff never presented such a plan. I responded by suggesting that Joe Johnson and Wendell Howell instead had proposed the "regional concept" as an alternative to any grade-center approach. By the end of the day, Judge Schwartz wanted to know whether any effort had been made by the new board or its staff "to ascertain whether the three-grade [center plan] structure is possible or not." Neither the interim nor new boards had ever considered the feasibility of using such three-grade centers.

Judge Schwartz began to ask questions about testing the feasibility of a nine-three plan that included high schools, as well as early elementary centers (grades one to three) in Wilmington. After ascertaining that it would take the new board's pupil assignment committee a couple of weeks to develop and test such a nine-three plan, Judge Schwartz moved to resolve the issue: "Dr. Kirk, I will now ask you to get all information that can be obtained from your pupil assignment team on the feasibility of [a] 9 and 3 [plan] within 20 days." After considerable badgering from me, Judge Schwartz also asked Kirk to develop an alternative grade-center plan without using the "basic precept of the majority plan" of treating all suburban children alike; instead "[follow] the basic precept that you treat all black and white children as similarly as possible" given the nonracial constraint of school capacity.

Kirk's honesty led to one final surprise. The mandate of the Third Circuit required the state board to share in the planning expenses of the new board. Kirk had submitted an itemized bill for the new board to the state superintendent. Instead of sending a check, however, the state superintendent sent a letter saying that the legislature had not yet funded the new board. In the same words argued by Michigan in the second round of the Detroit school case, here was the beginning of Delaware's claim to immunity from paying to remedy the state's long-standing constitutional violation.

Prickett expressed surprise over the state superintendent's letter and, within a matter of days, assured the court that the new board's bill would be paid promptly pursuant to the mandate of the Third Circuit. Prickett refused to concede, however, that the state's claim of immunity fell under the Supreme Court's second decision in the Detroit case. On my motion, Judge Schwartz therefore added the state treasurer as a defendant to cut off the possibility of further default by the state on paying its fair share of the costs of planning and implementing a remedy.

Lenny Williams put Wendell Howell, Wilmington board president and minority member of the new board, on the stand to explain his opposition to ten-two and his support for Plan W. Howell explained that the basic purpose of his plan was to "lessen the burden [of] transportation, particularly as it affects minorities. . . . We're viewing children as children, not treating them separately as a group. [The ten-two premise] seems to me to be somewhat of a sophisticated form of separate but equal." Howell also described his inability to make the majority on the new board "explore, you know, with some real sense of commitment" any alternatives to ten-two. The lawyers for the state board and the suburban districts could not wait to cross-examine this fast-talking, cocky, brash black leader. For two days they challenged his assertions, but he would not budge. The details of Plan W came under heavier attack, but Howell deferred to his own superintendent for discussion of its mechanics.

On the Outside Looking In

Joe Johnson then had the task of explaining Plan W, including the several weak points in the hurried version filed with the court. Johnson explained the basic concepts: to avoid racially discriminatory assumptions, to lessen the disparity in years of reassignment between blacks and whites, to include early elementary and high school education in the former black as well as white schools, and to use a "regional concept" where practical. Judge Schwartz was curious about the meaning of the regional concept. Johnson explained that wherever concentrations of blacks and whites lived in close proximity, they should be assigned to nearby schools in order to minimize busing and to maximize the incentives for desegregated housing. Johnson used a rough two-mile limit for "walk-in" attendance at high schools under Plan W—W for walk-in. The regional concept would work best at Wilmington and P. S. DuPont High Schools, located at the western and northern boundaries of the city. In northern New Castle County there was such pervasive residential segregation that few other high schools were strategically positioned to permit the implementation of such a regional concept.

Johnson had grown up under the thumb of Wilmington's oppressive color line. His father was an electrician for the Pullman Company and his mother a domestic. They lived across the street from a white school and a white community center. Both had been closed to Johnson in his youth. The state compelled him to attend the blacks-only schools, including Howard, where he met Lenny Williams, his lifelong friend. To this day, Johnson vividly remembers the many times he stood as a small boy outside the fence of the community center and looked in on a hot summer day as white children ran around the base paths and cooled off in the big swimming pool. The white and black children played stickball in the street together, but when the gates of the whites-only community center opened a race wall rose to separate them. As a boy, Johnson thought that the playing field "looked like the biggest softball diamond in the world and the pool like an olympic oasis." The sting of this racial insult has not much lessened in thirty years even though, as Johnson has come to see, "the pool is [now] about the size of a postage stamp for waders, the ball diamond doesn't even have an outfield, and now only blacks use the center."

In 1966 Williams called Johnson: the Wilmington superintendent was looking for vice-principals for several secondary schools, and the jobs were open to blacks. Johnson applied and accepted an appointment at a former whites-only junior high located in an area from which he had been shooed by the police as a too energetic, and too black, twelve-year-old bicyclist. 1966 was a time when the white Wilmington power structure wanted some blacks in visible positions of responsibility, but not as neighbors. The white realtor informed Johnson that only certain housing was "open." The front doors of white housing were closed to blacks. It had been no coincidence that Williams had made it in the front door of such a house only as an electrician's helper with Johnson's father to inspect the house Williams wanted to buy.

With Tom Minter's departure to the Carter administration, Johnson took over as the superintendent of the Wilmington school district in order to run the schools and lead the fight for a transition to a fair and effective system of integrated schooling throughout northern Delaware. With the string of discriminatory desegregation proposals emanating from the legislature, the state board, and the new board, Johnson feared that Delaware's historic color line still controlled the process of developing a remedy for de jure segregation. Johnson was still not sanguine about the prospects for genuine integration on equal terms in schools, housing, or community life in his native home.

As the direct testimony and cross-examination of Johnson progressed, the problems with Plan W emerged. The first was whether the plan would foster unpopular school closings. By Johnson's calculations, the decline in school age children throughout the suburbs meant that some twenty-seven white schools should already have been closed and could be closed under Plan W. Would any judge be bold enough to utilize all Wilmington schools under nine-three or Plan W, *and* face the white community's hostility to the prospect of seeing many schools closed in the suburbs at the same time? Johnson suggested an alternative: closing schools, while perhaps economically justified, was not warranted now because of its "extra burden to desegregation." Closing of schools was an issue to be decided by the school authorities and their constituents later, after Judge Schwartz approved a pupil assignment proposal.

On cross-examination, one of the suburban lawyers expressed his disbelief at the possibility of closing twenty-seven suburban schools but "no Wilmington schools. . . . Is that your idea of parity or equity?" Johnson responded:

> [M]y ideal parity or equity doesn't deal with schools, it deals with people, and the only way that we can develop parity among youngsters and reduce the disparity between youngsters is to have a place in Wilmington for them to attend school, and if it means leaving every school open in Wilmington so they don't have to get on the bus for ten years, then that's my definition of parity.

Subsequently, we showed that nine-three only reduced the average utilization of suburban schools from their current 70 percent to 67 percent of their state-rated pupil capacity. The argument that an equitable plan would be the cause for wholesale closing of white schools was false. If suburban schools were to be closed, it would be due to declining birth rates over the past decade, not to school desegregation.

The attendance zones that had been drawn for illustrative purposes on the Plan W map equidistant between Wilmington high schools and their nearest suburban counterparts presented more major problems. Although calculation of the school population within these boundaries would have revealed only a few hundred white students, defense lawyers failed to pin Johnson down on these specifics until cross-examination by the ninth defense lawyer.

Johnson countered by unveiling a new map that he had developed overnight. He used a ninth-to-twelfth rather than tenth-to-twelfth grade structure in Wilmington, P. S. DuPont, and several suburban high schools, including Mt. Pleasant, and extended the boundaries around P. S. DuPont and Wilmington High further into the suburbs. These new boundaries were still within one-and-one-half miles of these "regional schools" and at least one-half mile from any other suburban high school. Johnson explained that Wilmington and P. S. DuPont would serve sizable integrated student populations, and Mt. Pleasant High could be added as a third "walk-in" school by extending its boundaries back into Wilmington.

Such modification, however, demonstrated that Plan W, like the ten-two and nine-three proposals, still remained only a concept in the making, far from a workable finished product. As the new board's pupil assignment committee was working on fleshing out only the nine-three concept, the prospects for Plan W seemed dim. Yet the basic concept of more equitable sharing of the burdens of desegregation might still prevail.

Jim McKinstry, the lawyer for the Claymont district, called a personable high school counselor to the witness stand to attack Plan W's disparate impact on suburban children. The witness objected that Plan W reassigned Claymont kids to Wilmington schools for more years than it did their suburban neighbors. The witness described the spirit of his largely blue-collar clients and the Claymont community's suspicion of any plan that might appear to favor some of the wealthier suburban neighbors. On cross-examination, Williams pounced: How would the Claymont community feel if they were bused for ten school years to desegregated schools in a hypothetical "white acres" district, while the "white acres" children came to Claymont for only two years? After some verbal sparring, the counselor finally answered Williams's question: "The Claymont people would object very strenuously to having their children bused for ten years, yes."

Williams then asked the clinching question: "In your capacity as a leader [in] . . . the school system, if under the 10-2 plan a black Wilmington youngster comes to you from Wilmington, who is now transported into your District [and] says . . . 'tell me why I've got to travel up here ten years while the [Claymont] kids up here only go down [to Wilmington for] two years?' How would you handle that?" The counselor stammered, paused, objected, and finally responded: "At the moment it is a difficult question to answer . . . I've got to admit that. . . . [Y]ou really got me shook, Mr. Williams." Williams replied, "I'm shook too. I've got to answer that question one of these days [in the black community]." Judge Schwartz finally cut off the painful questioning.

On November 22, 1977, the new board's pupil assignment committee filed its "Special Report." It included five illustrations of how a nine-three plan could be feasibly implemented. The hearings which followed provided no evidence indicating otherwise.

While the hearings on the nine-three plans proceeded in court, the state board finally convinced the governor to act to provide an alternative reorganization plan. Governor P. S. duPont responded by delivering a letter on November 28, 1977, to Judge Schwartz's home. The letter informed Schwartz that the governor intended to call a special session of the legislature within the next two weeks to reorganize school districts in northern New Castle County in order to "reestablish" the state's "constitutional authority over the boundaries and governance of its public schools . . . [rather than] vest almost all control in the United States District Court." Claiming his purpose was neither to delay nor impede the elimination of "racially identifiable schools," duPont requested a "communication" from Schwartz indicating if such a course of legislative action were appropriate. The governor recognized that the judge might have an "obligation" to enter the letter "as part of the record."

On November 29, Schwartz responded and distributed both letters to all counsel in open court. Judge Schwartz wrote:

I am sure you realize that federal courts cannot give advisory opinions regarding legal principles and a judge should not comment on the merits of a matter pending before him. It necessarily follows any response must be limited to that which has been adduced on the record in [this case].

Judge Schwartz proceeded to detail the state's two-and-one-half-year default in failing to respond to the courts' invitations to act. Noting the "unprecedented lengths to minimize federal court intrusion," Judge Schwartz informed Governor duPont that the federal district court would proceed to a decision on the pupil assignment plan and measure any legislation passed against "constitutional standards . . . [and] the time frame and context of the present litigation."*

The governor did convene a special session of the legislature, and the state board proposed a four-district plan that dismembered only the Wilmington school district. But James Venema and his antibusing Positive Action Committee lobbied successfully against the legislative proposal on the grounds that it was a "busing bill" and that the case was still "wide open" on appeal from any orders Judge Schwartz might eventually enter. Opposition to the governor's reorganization bill also came from another corner. Wendell Howell and the black Wilmington legislators, who supported fair and effective desegregation, had also opposed the splintering of the Wilmington constituency into four suburban districts and the further delay inherent in redistricting at this late date.

The Decision

Hearings on the nine-three plans concluded on December 6. On January 8, 1978, Judge Schwartz issued his decision. The opinion detailed his reasoning in resolving the relatively narrow but important remedial issues that remained. Twenty years of litigation should have settled the extent of the interdistrict violation and the scope and contours of the areawide remedy. The opinion recounted the repeated refusal of the state to come forward with a plan alternative to the provisional consolidation ordered almost two years before by the three-judge court. It then cited the state board's default in submitting an ineffective and inequitable plan of "reverse volunteerism": "defendant state

---

*During the discussion of these extraordinary events the next day, I submitted a copy of a resolution passed by the Delaware House requesting President Carter to remove Judge Schwartz from office. Judge Schwartz interrupted me to ask whether any member of the Delaware legislature had voted against the resolution. A federal judge may be appointed for life in order to insulate against such majority opposition of the moment, but the reality of standing alone is another matter.

board fairly can be characterized as channeling its energies toward preservation of its legal position, rather than attempting to redress the constitutional violation.'' Given this context, the district court's duty, under the mandate of *Brown* and the Third Circuit, ''is to insure the elimination of the inter-district racially discriminatory dual school system that has persisted in New Castle County . . . [by] ordering into effect a [plan] for desegregation that meets [this] goal in a practical and equitable manner.''

Judge Schwartz also rejected the ten-two plan submitted by the new board. The assumption underlying the ten-two plan, namely that a ''complete mix'' of pupils should be determined by the percentage of black students in the area, led to the conclusion that three-grade rather than two-grade centers for white reassignments into the former black schools were warranted. The new board ''arbitrarily chose'' two grade centers without any nonracial reason. Equally revealing, the board's ten-two plan converted all of the black high schools to two-grade, middle-school centers, although Wilmington High, for example, was an excellent facility and was sixty feet from an existing white district. Similarly, the new board had responded to white concerns about sending younger elementary students on the bus by reassigning only black children in grades one to four. ''At the very least,'' Judge Schwartz advised, ''fundamental fairness demands that decisions that have the effect of maximizing the [reassignment] burden on black students be supported by justifications of a non-racial nature.'' Schwartz held that the new board failed to provide *any* nonracial explanation. He also withheld approval from Plan W, based on his doubts concerning its workability at its current stage of development.

The opinion then turned to the feasibility of the nine-three plan. This concept only modified the board majority's chosen assignment method by utilizing educationally sound three-grade rather than two-grade centers. Judge Schwartz first agreed with Superintendent Johnson to approve a pupil assignment concept and to leave the subsequent decisions on school closings to school officials. He then found that ''9-3 is a concept that promises to meet the constitutional goal of effectuating a unitary racially nondiscriminatory school system in an effective and equitable manner.'' He approved the new board's development and implementation for September, 1978, of a desegregation plan using three-grade centers as long as it encompassed a full grade span and included at least one high school in Wilmington. Plan W died aborning, but it had fostered consideration and approval of a fair alternative.

To the white community, Judge Schwartz explained the need to avoid discrimination between racial groups. To the black community, he described the reality that black and white schools could not be desegregated without black children being reassigned for more school years than white children. Judge Schwartz did not plead for sympathy and understanding: he gave both.

Judge Schwartz also approved additional relief that he found "necessary and essential to accomplish the transition to unitary, racially non-discriminatory schooling and to overcome the vestige effects of *de jure* segregation in Northern New Castle County." He included general directions to the new board concerning in-service training, reading and communication skills, a review of curriculum and texts, counseling and guidance, school site selection and closing, human relations programs, discipline, and faculty desegregation. Judge Schwartz ordered the state defendants to share in the costs of this ancillary relief.

Given the state's default in addressing the reorganization issue, Judge Schwartz applied the existing state law model for school district consolidation with some important modifications. Thus, for example, he required a ward system of school board elections to insure fair representation for minorities on the board. He also set a ceiling on the authority of the newly consolidated school board to levy property taxes. The legislature would have power to alter the property tax ceiling, but otherwise the court left to the new board the decision on the tax rate it would establish, as well as the decision on whether to "level up," "level down," or maintain separate salary schedules for the staff and teachers of the eleven component districts.

Finally, Judge Schwartz addressed the defendants' arguments concerning the Supreme Court's decision in Dayton, that the approved pupil assignment concepts "were formulated without exacting consideration of whether they returned the Northern New Castle County schools to the precise position they would have assumed 'but for' the constitutional violations found." To Judge Schwartz, defendants were simply trying to relitigate an issue they had already lost before the three-judge court and in their unsuccessful appeals to the Supreme Court and the Third Circuit. Equally dispositive, the defendants had offered no evidence to suggest that the grade-center or regional concepts exceeded the effect of the violation of interdistrict dual schooling. Judge Schwartz concluded:

[T]he firmly established constitutional violations in the case are the perpetuation of a dual system and the vestige effects of pervasive *de jure* interdistrict segregation. . . . Eradication of the constitutional violation to the scope and extent enumerated by the three-judge court is all that any of the plans and concepts submitted [by the new board] purport to accomplish, and that is all the concept endorsed by [this] Court does accomplish.

Judge Schwartz, like Judge Duncan in Columbus, had refused to read Justice Rehnquist's opinion in Dayton as a call to retreat. Although initially more cautious in reaching this judgment, Judge Schwartz was ultimately just as firm in requiring complete, effective, and equitable relief from the continuing color line in schooling.

Louis Redding paid tribute to the decision. ''Judge Schwartz issued a reasoned statement of the law established by the prior litigation. He found the facts compelled by the evidence. He evenhandedly applied equitable principles. That is what a federal judge is appointed to do.''

The reaction of the white community to the opinion was not as positive. The state board and suburban defendants immediately appealed to the Third Circuit. James Venema, founder of Delaware's Positive Action Committee and now head of the National Association of Neighborhood Schools, campaigned for Joe Biden's Senate seat on an antibusing campaign. In response, Biden continued his opposition to school desegregation in northern New Castle County and sponsored legislation to limit busing. The governor again convened the legislature to pass a reorganization bill that would inevitably delay actual desegregation for another year. In response, the legislature gave the state board authority to implement new school district boundary lines. The state board's proposed ''four district plan,'' however, failed to provide for an orderly transition to opening schools on a desegregated basis in the fall.

The new board members and staff now had three masters: the existing eleven districts, the new four districts, and the single district. Chaos was rapidly coming to grip public schooling in Delaware. On behalf of the new board, Henry Herndon asked Judge Schwartz to enjoin the four-district plan pending a full hearing on its constitutionality. Judge Schwartz enjoined the state board plan and ordered the new board to follow the single district pending a full hearing. The state board did not appeal this judgment and never asked for a hearing on its four-district plan. Meanwhile, the state legislature passed a bill to lower the tax cap authorized by the court. For the first and only time, Judge Schwartz overreacted to the state's prior default and obstruction: despite his previous invitation to the legislature to act on the tax issue, he struck down the tax bill.

In the spring of 1978 Judge Schwartz had to intervene several times to keep the desegregation plans alive. When, for example, the state board refused to pay for the buses in the absence of a specific enforcement order, Judge Schwartz issued such an order. The new board, under the guidance of counsel Henry Herndon, continued its own preparations for desegregation within a new, single district, despite the lack of legislative support and the vocal opposition of many politicians and antibusing groups.

Seven More Judges

In their appeals to the Third Circuit, the various defendants did not seriously challenge the district court's approval of three-grade in contrast to two-grade centers nor the district judge's meticulous implementation of the Third Circuit's mandate in the face of the state legislature's default. Instead the briefs focused on the claim that the three-judge court and the district court had never applied nor followed the Supreme Court's decision in Dayton. Defendants argued that the case required the lower courts to identify with particularity the constitutional violations, and to remedy only the "incremental segregative effect" that the identified violations had on increasing segregation in the schools above the underlying residential segregation. Defendants argued that this "mandatory inquiry" had never been undertaken and that areawide desegregation far exceeded the segregative effect of any violation.

Bill Taylor drafted the response for plaintiffs. The brief was short and direct: "defendants in this appeal persist in regarding no issue in this case as having been settled even to the point of urging that the case be dismissed without any remedy at all." The brief summarized the prior proceedings and findings, and concluded that the district court's approval of the new board's grade-center plan was correct: the Dayton opinion expressly authorized thoroughgoing desegregation to remedy a continuing constitutional violation with "system-wide impact," such as was found in Wilmington.

On May 10, 1978, Phil Kurland and Lou Lucas again faced each other and the seven judges on the Third Circuit. Once again Chief Judge Seitz and Judge Gibbons did not sit to review the case. Once again, the arguments for each side were punctuated by pointed questions from the judges. The presence of one new judge, Leon Higginbotham, former civil rights advocate and continuing legal historian on the matter of color in America with thirteen years experience in hearing civil rights cases in the district court, added depth to the court's probing.

Some members of the court were troubled by the apparent failure of the trial courts to parse and then to calibrate the amount of segregation caused by nonracial factors. Lucas responded by detailing how the three-judge court made its sensitive inquiry into this causation issue in both its violation and remedy rulings. Substantial governmental involvement in interdistrict discrimination in schools and housing perpetuated the complete system of interdistrict de jure school segregation at the time of *Brown* right through the time of trial. The three-judge court carefully inquired into the causes of this segregation. Although other interlocking factors also played a part, the three-judge court found that the continuing interdistrict violation substantially and proximately contributed to the racial disparity in enrollments between the school districts in the area. Judge Garth challenged Lucas to point out where the three-judge court had made such findings. In rapid fire, Lucas quoted each specific finding concerning the nature and extent of the continuing interdistrict violation and its areawide impact.

Lucas then explained how defendants never offered any evidence suggesting how specific schools were not affected by this systemwide violation. Judge Aldisert interrupted to articulate his understanding of the issue on appeal: "[I]n light of the fact that neither plaintiffs nor defendants put on evidence before Judge Schwartz on the issue, should the case be decided by who bears the burden of proving the extent, or the limits, of the impact of the segregation violation?" Lucas responded in two ways. First, the burden of proof rested squarely on the wrongdoer, not the victim; on the defendant school authorities, not the plaintiff schoolchildren. Aldisert seemed skeptical in light of the Dayton decision, but Lucas quoted that portion of *Swann* that placed the burden of proof for limiting systemwide remedy in a historic dual system on the school authorities. Second, Lucas argued that the Dayton decision did not create new law or reverse *Swann, Green,* or the Denver case.

Noting Chief Justice Burger's numerous statements of concern about crowded dockets in the federal courts, Lucas concluded in his best Southern accent that Dayton "surely does not require federal judges to pull out their vernier calipers to attempt precise measurements concerning deeply rooted constitutional violations. If the violations were isolated, such a mathematical inquiry might be possible. But in cases like this, with a longstanding and wide-ranging systemic violation, a much more sensible, and sensitive, inquiry has to be made: and that is just what the three-judge court and District Judge Schwartz have done." The judges chuckled at the reference to Burger's widely publicized "docket control" remarks, but Aldisert did not appear entirely convinced by the response.

Judge Arlin Adams expressed concern about the ancillary relief ordered by Judge Schwartz. Adams did not understand the authority for such relief. When Lucas explained the standard established in the second Detroit decision, Adams remained skeptical; he feared that it gave federal courts an open-ended invitation to take over public schooling and raid the state treasury to pay for a "wish list" supplied by local administrators. Lucas responded by suggesting that Judge Schwartz strictly applied the test laid out by the Supreme Court in the second Detroit decision to order only that supplemental relief that was "necessary and essential" to root out discrimination and to insure an effective transition to integrated schooling. Lucas invited the Third Circuit to scrutinize the evidence and the district court's findings and exercise of discretion closely. There was no danger of a blank check for the federal courts on the public fisc.

This prompted a question concerning the legislature's act lowering the tax cap. That issue, however, was not yet part of the pending appeal. Lucas apologized for "not knowing much about that decision. I was not involved in the hearing on that matter." Lucas added pointedly, however, and in complete consistency with his argument on ancillary relief, "About all that I do know is that plaintiffs did not bring that motion and did not oppose the State tax cap in the district court."

Governor duPont, Senator Biden, and other Delaware politicians attended the oral arguments. They could not gain much comfort from the proceeding. But neither could we be sure that we had avoided the Dayton roadblock in the Third Circuit. Defendants' latest appeals did not challenge the actions of Judge Schwartz so much as the rulings of his predecessor, Judge Wright, for the three-judge court.

While we all waited for the decision, the state board and suburban defendants petitioned Judge Schwartz for another stay of desegregation and the provisional consolidation for another school year pending appellate review. On June 14, 1978, Judge Schwartz denied the petition. On July 1, Governor P. S. duPont announced the cancellation of $2.5 million previously authorized for the expansion of P. S. duPont High School. With that, the governor and the new board completed the downgrading of Delaware's most illustrious public school: P. S. duPont High School was converted into a seventh-to-ninth grade center. The state also challenged the tax injunction directly in the Third Circuit.

On July 24, Judge Aldisert wrote for a unanimous court of appeals and affirmed Judge Schwartz. The opinion was as sharp as the questioning at oral argument. We had finally succeeded in convincing the appeals court of the nature and extent of the violation: "[T]he three-judge court found interdistrict *de jure* segregation throughout Northern New Castle County . . . [that] 'had a substantial, not a de minimis, effect on the enrollment patterns of the separate districts. . . . Racially discriminatory acts of the State and its subdivisions were a substantial and proximate cause of existing disparity in racial enrollments in the districts of Northern New Castle County.'" The three dissenters from the Third Circuit's previous ruling agreed that this view was "now the law of the case." Reiterating that the appeals court had previously approved the scope and basic concept of the remedy ordered by the three-judge court, Aldisert turned to the specific issues at hand.

The Third Circuit agreed that "reverse volunteerism" failed to comply with the previous mandate. Among other things, "reverse volunteerism" would "improperly shift the 'entire burden of remedy' onto 'those whose rights had been violated.' . . . [T]he plan's most basic defect [is that it] 'assigns to those who have been wronged the responsibility for correcting those wrongs.'" In this context, the Third Circuit's affirmance of the district court's rejection of "ten-two" in favor of three-grade centers was a foregone conclusion.

The Third Circuit also determined that the evidence and findings concerning ancillary relief and governance supported the decree ordered below. Judge Schwartz had been meticulous in his evaluation of the evidence, factual findings, and application of the proper legal standards to these issues. On the issue of local taxation, however, the Third Circuit held that the act of the legislature setting a lower cap on local property taxes should have been accorded a "presumption of regularity" and not viewed as an eleventh-hour scheme to frustrate desegregation. The appeals court vacated the injunction against the tax bill and remanded to Judge Schwartz, who subsequently found the act constitutional.

With respect to the key issue concerning the Dayton decision, the seven judges of the Third Circuit unequivocally joined their brethren on the other courts of appeals in rejecting the notion that the Dayton decision foreclosed actual desegregation. Judge Aldisert first noted that the Supreme Court mandated use of the "incremental segregative effect" standard for cases where mandatory segregation by law had long since ceased. In contrast, the findings of the three-judge court and Judge Schwartz were "that the mandatory segregation of the races did not cease long ago. . . . [B]ecause the dual school system was never dismantled, the consequences of the mandatory segregation of the races in New Castle County have continued up till the present day." Judge Aldisert disputed any suggestion that individual violations could be viewed in isolation: "[I]t is the *combined* effect of all the separate violations that must cured by the remedy."

Judge Aldisert recognized that under *Dayton* there was a broad range between isolated violations and complete intentional segregation: At some point in this range the remedial burden of proof on the extent of impact shifted from plaintiffs to defendants. In this case—with the historic interdistrict, de jure segregation; with the proposal of a "racially reasonable plan" to remedy the continuing areawide effects; where the defendant was in the "best position . . . [but] admits that it is not feasible to separate out the incremental segregative effects of the constitutional violations from the segregative effects of demographic changes"; and "where the defendant [state board] has dragged its heels and obstructed progress toward desegregation for 26 years" —the burden did shift to the defendant. Aldisert chided the state board for its apparent claim that because this burden was impossible to meet, there should be no relief: "Desegregation remedies [are] drawn from the heart of equity. [N]o court could be so callous as to accept the contention that although vestiges of *de jure* discrimination pervade to this day, it is helpless to fashion a remedy to root them out."

Judge Aldisert then reminded the state board that the state of Delaware had been directed for twenty-six years by judicial decrees to fashion a remedy to eliminate the vestiges of statutorily mandated, de jure segregation. Judge Aldisert concluded by denouncing "the persistent attempts by [the state board] to have the federal courts re-examine the findings of constitutional violations in New Castle County. . . . [T]he latest effort [is] to argue, albeit indirectly, that the decision in Dayton commands a different result. . . . [W]e disagree that Dayton alters the law in this case." If that was the goal of a new majority on the Supreme Court, it would have to do its own dirty work. For the seven judges on the Third Circuit, only equitable and effective desegregation on an areawide basis could remedy the continuing interdistrict system of basically dual schooling in northern New Castle County.

Many Delaware politicians and antibusers decried the decision, but most responsible officials prepared for actual desegregation in the fall within a single district and exhorted their constituents to comply with the decree in an orderly, peaceful, and cooperative fashion. Even while continuing to work in the Congress to ban busing, Senator Biden assisted the new board in securing federal school desegregation assistance to pay for most of the ancillary relief. Governor duPont actively encouraged and supported the efforts of civic, business, school, and law enforcement leaders to plan and to work together to assure a peaceful transition.

Joe Johnson held an "open house" to acquaint white suburban families with the Wilmington schools they had long since forsaken. Eleven thousand showed up, walked the corridors, examined the classrooms and libraries and gyms, skipped along the playgrounds, and met the teachers and administrators, black and white. Many of the visitors expressed amazement at the attractiveness of the well-kept school facilities situated next to large parks. For these white families, it was a chance to overcome their fears of the unknown. Joe Johnson, sometimes joined by suburban school staff members, also attended many meetings in the black community to discuss the desegregation plan and to respond to concerns about education and fears of mistreatment in suburban schools. Many people in New Castle County, Delaware, like their counterparts in Columbus, Ohio, were ready to tackle the challenge of school desegregation in the fall of 1978.

The conscience of Louis Redding brought New Castle County to this turning point. His thirty-year legal struggle in the Wilmington school case seemed close to final vindication. His story was both a challenge to urban school segregation and a preview of what might be achieved in the years to come. Only one more hurdle remained—the Supreme Court.

VII
The Supreme Court and the School Segregation Cases, 1978–80

Chapter 15
The Briefs and Arguments in the
Supreme Court

Preemptive Strike

While schools in Columbus and the Wilmington area were finally poised to begin actual desegregation in September, 1978, the Dayton, Columbus, and Wilmington cases were coming up for final review by the Supreme Court. On August 1, 1978, the Columbus Board of Education had filed an application for delay of school desegregation with Potter Stewart, the justice responsible for overseeing the activities of the Sixth Circuit. With rare exception, circuit justices, whatever their personal misgivings or view of the merits, routinely denied such requests for delay. One day after receiving the Columbus board's request, Potter Stewart denied the application for stay without opinion.

Sam Porter was not daunted. As the *Columbus Citizen-Journal* reported, he just "shop[ped the] Supreme Court for a justice to delay busing." William Rehnquist, the associate justice to whom the board's attorney next delivered the stay application, directed plaintiffs to respond in writing by August 10. Such renewed requests for stay "are not favored" under the Supreme Court rules and are granted even more rarely by any second justice. Yet the call for a response meant that Rehnquist was actively considering just such extraordinary action.

Lucas drafted a reply to set the record straight both on what the lower courts ruled and on how a stay at this late date would cause extensive disruption. The Columbus board and community were fully prepared for desegregation, not a precipitous return to segregation. The board had already purchased and received the buses, hired and trained drivers, reassigned pupils and notified parents, reassigned teachers, closed certain schools, reorganized curriculum, and undertaken an extensive community relations program. On the afternoon of August 10, Lucas filed a response arguing that "the most costly and disruptive action which could now be taken would be to undo the work of thousands of people, community leaders, school administrators, teachers, parents and pupils, all of whom are geared for the commencement of desegregation."

On the morning of August 11, Justice Rehnquist issued a printed order and opinion granting a stay pending the board's petition for Supreme Court review. Rehnquist accepted the board's representations concerning the projected fiscal burden of desegregation and pointed to "the personal dislocations that accompany the actual reassignment of 42,000 students, 37,000 of whom will be transported by bus.'' Rehnquist could not see that a community preparing for desegregation for the last eighteen months might be considerably set back by the notion that all this effort was a false start.

Rehnquist was even more abrupt in discussing the lower court's declaration of black plaintiffs' right to a system of desegregated schooling. He conducted a preemptive first strike to interpret the meaning of the Supreme Court's opinion in the first Dayton case that would curtail sharply, if not ban, all busing. Rehnquist wrote that the ''incremental segregative effect'' test ''mandated . . . specific findings on the impact discrete segregative acts had on the composition of individual schools within the system.'' This may have been the meaning intended by Justice Rehnquist when he wrote the first Dayton opinion. But it represented the restrictive principle articulated in his *dissent* in the Denver case and the separate *minority* opinion in the Austin case, not the *full* Court's opinions rejecting any such school-by-school, violation-by-violation approaches in the Denver and *Swann* cases. With his stay opinion, Rehnquist staked out a reading of the first Dayton opinion that the full court had not been willing to embrace: Rehnquist's opinion for the Court in Dayton had expressly relied on, rather than reversed, the full Court's opinions in Denver and *Swann*.

Displaying his frustrations with the refusal of the appeals court to heed his call to retreat, Rehnquist stated, ''the Sixth Circuit has misinterpreted the mandate of this Court's Dayton opinion.'' Quoting only one phrase, out of context, to support his reading of the Sixth Circuit's rulings, Justice Rehnquist asserted:

> The Court of Appeals employed legal presumptions of intent to extrapolate systemwide violations from what was described in the Columbus case as ''isolated'' instances. The Sixth Circuit is apparently of the opinion that presumptions, in combination with such isolated violations, can be used to justify a systemwide remedy where such a remedy would not be warranted by the incremental segregative effect of the identified violations.

Justice Rehnquist distorted Judge Edwards's use of the phrase ''isolated'' in the Sixth Circuit's opinion. First, Judge Edwards had used the phrase to describe the Columbus board's manipulation of ''neighborhood'' zoning principles through discontiguous attendance areas, optional zones, and gerrymandering in relatively discrete racial fringe and pocket areas. Second, Edwards noted that such deviations demonstrated the board's consistent intent to segregate schools throughout the district, particularly in those areas where ''neighborhood'' zoning normally would have resulted in substantially integrated schools. Finally, Edwards identified several *systemwide* violations, including the board's intentional perpetuation of its historic system of dual schooling, its racial assignment of faculty, and its segregative school construction policy. Rehnquist ignored these facts.

Justice Rehnquist appeared to want to limit relief in the Columbus school case to two "discontiguous attendance areas that resulted in white children being transported past predominantly black schools. . . ." Acting as a single justice, Rehnquist was attempting to "sink the ship of integration," pursuant to the very legal strategy developed by the Nixon Justice Department but twice squarely rejected by the United States Supreme Court.

Rehnquist chastised plaintiffs for their response to the stay application: "Plaintiffs . . . take an 'all or nothing approach' and do not offer any suggestions as to how the . . . judgment of the Court of Appeals can be stayed only in part consistent with the [Columbus board's] legal contentions." Having blamed plaintiffs for not conceding error, Rehnquist added, "I therefore have no recourse but to grant or to deny the stay . . . in its entirety." Not surprisingly, Rehnquist granted the stay "in its entirety."

The *Columbus Citizen-Journal* commented wryly that Rehnquist's stay was "one more milestone in the long legal route of the case. There will be more." The newspaper noted that two things were clear: First, all participants were getting their day in court; second, the people of Columbus were somewhat confused. At the same time, the *Columbus Dispatch* reported on the substantial task facing school officials to reorganize for a school opening on a segregated rather than desegregated basis. Antibusing forces were now more amenable to abrupt educational changes and offered to help the school system get ready for opening of school on a segregated basis; they would stuff envelopes, move furniture, or do anything else school officials wanted done. Nevertheless, the Metropolitan Columbus Schools Committee announced that it "was going ahead in its programs to help citizens deal with desegregation" if and when it came.

Lucas was furious with Rehnquist's ruling. Nate Jones was incredulous. Rehnquist's goal was now clear: his action as a single justice revealed that he was intent on ending all meaningful challenge to urban school segregation and the color line of ghettoization. The ultimate danger was not so much that actual desegregation would be delayed for another year in Columbus, but that the sustained NAACP effort to show the de jure reality of urban segregation now faced a complete and final defeat.

Jones felt that some response was necessary. The immediate problem was that the Court was on vacation, and the justices were scattered about the country. It was unlikely that the full Court would convene for a special term to reconsider Rehnquist's action. On the other hand, a motion seeking a special term of the Court could serve to emphasize from the outset the actual meaning of the lower court opinions and to highlight the attempt by Rehnquist to rewrite the Supreme Court's opinion in Dayton to reverse the Denver decision. As full review of the Sixth Circuit's rulings was now virtually certain, an emergency motion to the full court to reconsider Rehnquist's grant of a stay in Columbus would notify all of the justices—friend, foe, and swing vote—that the plaintiffs did intend to fight to the end for "all or nothing," as Rehnquist phrased it. In addition, such a motion would warn all of the justices to expect other school districts to seek immediate stays from their circuit justice and then to go shopping with Justice Rehnquist with a renewed application.

Jones filed his extraordinary motion on behalf of the plaintiffs on August 14. He asked Justice Stewart to refer the motion to the entire court for consideration. The motion attacked Justice Rehnquist's reading the Supreme Court's opinion in Dayton, the lower court opinions in Columbus, and the facts concerning the injury of a stay relative to that of actual desegregation. "No one has ever found that a desegregated education harms children." The motion also noted that Rehnquist's opinion amounted to an "invitation" for other stay applications "and if unsuccessful with one Justice, further shopping expeditions to secure another . . . result." The stay here "is the reinstatement of segregation at the hand of a Single Justice." When Potter Stewart refused to circulate the motion, Jones worked with Bill Taylor and presented a motion to the chief justice on August 21 to convene the full Court for a special term.

Jones and Taylor also asked Solicitor General Wade McCree to join in the motion to vacate the stay. Within days, McCree filed a "Memorandum for the United States as Amicus Curiae" advising the full Court that "the stay entered by Mr. Justice Rehnquist on August 11, 1978, should be vacated." McCree cited the lower court findings concerning a history of overt dual schooling, the interaction between school and housing segregation, and the continuing systemwide school segregation directly caused by the board's intentionally segregative actions. McCree argued that Judge Duncan's "finding of liability was not limited to discrete acts having specific, identifiable effects within the system. Rather the court found a pattern of conduct on the part of the Board that led to the creation and persistence of racially identifiable elementary, junior and senior high schools [throughout] Columbus."

The solicitor general also analyzed Judge Edwards's use of the phrase "isolated" in describing the board's departure from the "neighborhood school concept" in fringe and pocket areas: the board chose not to apply the "neighborhood" criteria whenever its application "would tend to promote integration rather than segregation." Given the wide-ranging nature of the long-standing and continuing violation, the United States approved the application of the burden-shifting principle on remedy announced by the Third

Circuit in the Wilmington school case. In sum, "a stay . . . is improper in Columbus because of the Board's total failure in the courts below" to demonstrate that "a more limited remedy is appropriate." McCree concluded, "To our knowledge, this Court has never before granted a stay of the implementation of a school desegregation plan found by both a district court and a court of appeals to be appropriate to undo far-reaching constitutional violations in the operation of a school system. . . . [T]his case does not present an appropriate occasion for a departure from that practice."

On August 25, after distributing the motion to the full Court, the chief justice ruled: "[A] majority of the Justices having responded and no affirmative votes having been received to convene a special term of the Court, the motion is denied."

There was no time for the shock to set in. On August 23, the Dayton board filed an application for stay with Circuit Justice Stewart seeking leave to resegregate Dayton schools based on Rehnquist's stay opinion in Columbus. After the full Court refused even to hear the motion to vacate the Columbus stay, Lucas pocketed his pen for the rest of the summer. He refused to write any more responses: "The Justices are going to do just what they want to do regardless of what we say."

On August 28, Stewart denied the application in an opinion distinguishing the Columbus stay:

> Columbus had never been the subject of a school desegregation remedy; the Dayton system, by contrast, will enter its third year under the current [desegregation] plan on September 7. In Columbus, the status quo was preserved by granting a stay; here it can be preserved only by denying one. To avoid disrupting the school system during our consideration of the case, the stay should be denied. This disposition, of course, does not reflect any view on the merits of the issues presented.

The same day, Dave Greer renewed the application for stay with Justice Rehnquist. Two days later Justice Rehnquist denied the stay: "I am in complete agreement with Mr. Justice Stewart that there is a difference between the status quo in the Dayton school system and that in the Columbus school system."

Relying on Rehnquist's stay opinion in Columbus for a restrictive reading of the Court's Dayton decision, the Delaware Board of Education and nine of the eleven suburban school districts had also filed an application on August 21 for stay of the areawide desegregation in Wilmington with the justice for the Third Circuit, William Brennan. On September 1, Justice Brennan denied the stay in a full opinion. Brennan first distinguished the facts. The Court's first Dayton opinion involved findings concerning three isolated violations; in the

Wilmington area, there was a completely dual system at the time of *Brown* that "had been perpetuated through constitutional violations of an interdistrict nature. . . . The District Court's finding of these interdistrict violations was summarily affirmed by this Court, and it thus constitutes the law of the case. . . . [T]he record before the Court of Appeals in [this] case was replete with findings justifying, if not requiring, the extensive interdistrict remedy ordered by the District Court."

Next, Brennan staked out his position on the meaning of the full court's decision in the first round of the Dayton case: "[T]he remedy of the District Court [in the Wilmington area] was fashioned to implement the familiar rule . . . that equitable relief should be tailored to fit the violation." Finally, Brennan weighed the relative administrative harm to defendants if a stay were denied against the injury to plaintiff schoolchildren if a stay were granted:

> This case has been in continuous litigation for the past 21 years. . . . "The rights of children to equal educational opportunities are not to be denied, even for a brief time, simply because a school board situates itself so as to make desegregation difficult." In such circumstances, I cannot conclude that the balance of equities lies in favor of [those seeking a stay].

Four days later, Jim McKinstry filed a renewed application with Justice Rehnquist on behalf of seven of the suburban districts. With schools scheduled to open on an integrated basis in less than a week, the state board and three suburban districts refused to join in McKinstry's plea for disruption. Nevertheless, the clerk of the Supreme Court called me that afternoon: Justice Rehnquist wanted a response from plaintiffs in *two* days, by September 7. I was aghast. Our summer's nightmare seemed to have no end.

My response on behalf of the plaintiffs, the Wilmington board, and Louis Redding's thirty-year struggle minced no words. As to the generally disfavored renewal of stay applications, I added that it would be unseemly for a single justice, who had already dissented twice in this much litigated case, to suggest that he could speak for four votes, let alone a majority in the Supreme Court. "Judicial integrity" should counsel Justice Rehnquist to deny the renewed stay application, "leaving any remaining disagreement on the merits of the case with [Justice Brennan] to consideration by the full court."

Having appealed to Rehnquist's sense of propriety, I then turned to the hard realities. With four days remaining until the scheduled opening of Wilmington area schools on a desegregated basis, "no alternative is available at this time. Put bluntly, the only plan of pupil, teacher and staff assignments which can feasibly be implemented, . . . is already in place. Unlike the situation in Columbus, there is no alternative to the desegregation plan currently available; and all implementation activity for the desegregation plan has already taken place." Citing the affidavits of board member Jim Sills and Superintendent Biggs, I noted the substantial cost of segregation at this time: a several-week delay in school opening, payment to the idled teachers in the interim, and $5 million in additional contracted costs that federal desegregation funding would no longer defray. "In these circumstances, the interest in good order and stability counsels denial of the stay in order to permit the plan already in place to continue in operation . . . rather than to attempt the physical, administrative and community upheaval and substantial delay and disruption entailed in reassigning all teachers, staff and pupils to their formerly segregated schools."

I also described the restrained effort of the lower courts "to order a remedy which will place the victims of the violation in substantially the position they would have occupied had the violation not occurred" and to permit the state every opportunity to shape a remedy before imposing a provisional plan to forestall further state default. "[T]he Wilmington case does not involve 'isolated instances' of constitutional violations in a state where racial discrimination in public schooling has long been illegal. To the contrary . . . , New Castle County [has] a pervasive, interdistrict system of virtually complete segregation which had its roots in state-compelled racial dualism and was nurtured to its current pervasive form by persistent governmental involvement in interdistrict discrimination. As found by the courts below, this continuing areawide constitutional violation is a 'proximate cause of the existing disparity in racial enrollments in the districts of Northern New Castle County.'"

Although I felt we had no hope of persuading Justice Rehnquist on the law and the de jure reality of urban segregation, I added an extensive and combative footnote to let him know that we were ready for the battle. "[T]here is, in our view, no warrant for the patent misreading of a lower court's opinion concerning 'isolated instances' as in [Rehnquist's Columbus stay opinion] as a pretext to allow a single Justice to question in an off-hand fashion and without citation the evidentiary presumptions so painstakingly and recently articulated for the Court [in Denver for] school cases. It hardly bespeaks judicial candor for a single justice to espouse his dissenting views in [the Denver case] in the guise of interpreting [the Court's Dayton decision] to do what the entire Court most assuredly did not do: reverse [Denver], *Swann,* and *Green* and every other case giving practical meaning to *Brown.*" After challenging Rehnquist's "school-by-school" approach on both legal and practical grounds, the footnote concluded:

[I]f an inference from the [Columbus stay opinion] is that the remedy must be limited only to the "increment" that unconstitutional school practices "increase" school segregation over supposedly underlying residential segregation, the inference not only requires express reversal of [Denver] and *Swann*; it also contradicts the facts of record proven and specifically found in numerous school cases including this one: intentionally segregative school practices *do* racially identify residential neighborhoods, thereby causing residential segregation by families who choose their houses based on the racial identification of schools which in turn causes further school segregation and so on. This is precisely the "environment for segregation" which is at the core of the dismantling requirements of *Brown II, Green, Swann* and [Denver]. To refuse as a matter of law to permit proof of this factual circumstance would be, in truth, finally to render *Brown* itself void without even a candid admission that such constitutionally revolutionary and regressive action is being undertaken at all, let alone in complete contradiction of the facts.

I asked the Supreme Court clerk to transmit a copy of our response to Brennan in the event that it might become necessary to seek the circuit justice's assistance in reversing any stay and thereby precipitating emergency consideration by the full Court.

Justice Rehnquist refused to issue a stay opinion in Wilmington. He did confirm, however, that he was ready to lead the fight to legitimize segregation. "For all the reasons expressed in [his] dissent" to the summary affirmance of the interdistrict violation, he could not "agree" that areawide liability represented the "law of the case." By this comment Rehnquist invited the defendants to seek relitigation of all violation issues. On the Dayton issue of the "incremental" extent to which any violation caused current school segregation, Rehnquist noted that he had serious reservations and that the issue, in his view, was also open. But "in good conscience," he added that he could not "suggest that four justices of this Court would vote to review the case to consider [either the violation or causation issues] at this time." Justice Rehnquist apparently understood the appearance of impropriety and for the time being backed off on the issues on which he had previously dissented in the case.

On the consolidation of the school districts and reassignment of pupils pursuant to a grade-center approach, however, Rehnquist argued vigorously: "I believe that before a remedy of this drastic nature is finally imposed, not merely on one Board but on 11 previously independent school boards, four Justices of this Court would wish to review the case and consider that question on its merits. . . . If the Court meant what it said in Dayton that 'local autonomy of school districts is a vital national tradition,' I think it would give plenary consideration to a case where the District Court has treated a series of independent school districts which were found to have committed constitutional violations much as if they were a railroad in reorganization.''

It did not matter to Justice Rehnquist that the decision in the first round of the Detroit case expressly recognized the *duty* of district courts to afford interdistrict relief on finding interdistrict violation; that the defendant school authorities in Wilmington argued against retaining existing districts in affording such areawide relief; that the lower courts deferred to the Delaware legislature for three years to come forward with an effective plan and ordered consolidation only as a provisional or interim remedy pending the state's substitution of any workable alternative; and that the local school authorities argued for the grade-center approach to accomplish actual desegregation. To Justice Rehnquist such facts of record did not matter in his attempt to posit ''local control'' as the final protection for white suburban segregation of black schoolchildren in center city schools.

Nevertheless, Justice Rehnquist denied the stay: ''The consolidated school system has been subject to the desegregation order, without interruption, since January 1978. It would simply be too disruptive to upset established expectations now.'' As I had argued, there was no alternative. Rehnquist concluded by noting that ''this disposition, of course, does not reflect any view on the merits of the issues presented.''

Areawide desegregation therefore began as scheduled in northern New Castle County within a consolidated district. School opened peacefully; there were only two picketers at one school. Although the first year would be marred by a five-week teacher strike and the ''white flight'' of 5 percent of the students to private academies and to public schools across the nearby state line, all of the schools operated with integrated staffs and stable pupil racial compositions between 15 and 35 percent black. Education also continued. In fact, the rate of overall student progress on achievement tests in the district would become the highest in years. Whether the school desegregation plan would also serve, in time, as a catalyst to breaching the color line in all aspects of community life in Delaware remained in doubt. There would be little incentive for the civic, business, and political leadership to place a high priority on such multiracial development in housing, jobs, and social networks until the Supreme Court finally acted either to deny review or to affirm the judgments of district judge Murray Schwartz and the seven judges of the Third Circuit.

With the possible exception of the Wilmington case and its lengthy prior history of adjudication in the Supreme Court before a reduced court of seven justices, however, plenary review of all the school cases now seemed inevitable to me. In conversation with Jones and our other co-counsel, I described the coming term of the Supreme Court as ''the Armageddon for school cases.'' Bill Caldwell argued, however, that we still might convince the Court not to review the cases if ''we make strong factual demonstrations that these are dual school systems in the practical sense, and that this conclusion is inevitable under any legitimate approach to fact finding.'' The key was to limit votes for review of the case to the ''Austin three (Burger, Powell, and Rehnquist).'' Bill thought we might do so if we could make ''our attacks on Rehnquist['s stay opinion] appear . . . lawyer like.'' Having nothing to lose by the effort, Caldwell and I vigorously argued the law, the facts, and the lower court rulings in our oppositions to the school board petitions to review the school cases.

It came as no real surprise that the full Court decided, on January 8, 1979, to review both Dayton and Columbus on the merits. It seemed as if the Court just would not allow plaintiffs to win any more school desegregation decrees through the traditional expedient of refusing to review lower court judgments. Even in Wilmington, the Court sat on the defendants' petitions to review the case. Just as foreboding, Lucas received a number of calls from Supreme Court watchers in the media who claimed to have ''inside information'' that the Court had taken the Dayton and Columbus cases to set an absolute bar on the relevance of proof of intentional segregation prior to the time of *Brown*. Such a limitation on proof of the roots of segregation could be another step in a strategy to absolve almost all northern school segregation and to invite southern districts to return to the segregation prevailing prior to *Swann* and *Green*.

Preparation

The major problem facing Jones and his co-counsel now was how to win single-district school cases in the Supreme Court. The dream of challenging metropolitan segregation was fading into the nightmare that a majority on the Court would use the color line in housing to legitimize school segregation even within school districts. The danger was no longer painful punches from a single justice, but a knockout from the full Court in the Dayton and Columbus cases. The common wisdom was that the Court generally reviewed lower court decisions that it wanted to reverse rather than affirm. Counting votes, it seemed obvious that Rehnquist, Powell, and Burger wanted to reverse the Sixth Circuit again and legitimize most school segregation. We hoped that Justices Brennan, White, and Marshall would just as staunchly stand by the efforts of the courts of appeals to tackle the de jure reality of urban school segregation. Justice Marshall, who did not sit in the first round of the Dayton case, might recuse himself again. We had to win two of the three votes from Justices Stewart, Stevens, and Blackmun.

Jones convened a conference of all of his lawyers to plan for the battle ahead. It was not a happy time. Tom Atkins, Lou Lucas, Norm Chachkin, and Bob Murphy of the Lawyers' Committee, Richard Austin, Bill Caldwell, Bill Taylor, even Nick Flannery, and I discussed the dangers we faced and the vast amount of work that needed to be done if we were going to have any chance of prevailing. The mood was grim but not despairing. We determined to set to work immediately rather than wait for the school board briefs. We already knew the issues and obstacles we faced; there was no need to wait for Dave Greer and Sam Porter to repeat them to us. We tentatively agreed that Chachkin and Atkins would draft the brief in Columbus and Atkins would make the oral argument; and that Caldwell and I would draft the brief in Dayton and Caldwell would make the oral argument. Jones was under active consideration by the Carter administration to take the vacancy on the Sixth Circuit resulting from Judge Peck's retirement; we all hoped that he would be a federal circuit judge by the time of the oral arguments.

Jones asked Caldwell and me to coordinate our research effort and to circulate a memorandum describing the nature and extent of our burden. By January 15, we drafted and transmitted a seven-page "division of labor" that described nine related activities and work groups, named leaders for each task, and prayed for "additional research resources." Chachkin, with assistance from Atkins and me, would review the Columbus record, work with defendants' counsel to designate those parts of the evidence and lower court proceedings that should be printed in an appendix for distribution to each justice, and draft a statement of facts for our brief. Caldwell and I would perform the same function in Dayton, as well as draft a memorandum on a "violation argument" to explore the possible reach of the Reconstruction legislative history, develop an Arlington Heights–type catalog of intent evidence from school cases, support reasonable burden-shifting principles, and undercut the neighborhood school defense. Richard Larson and Bert Neuborne of the ACLU offered assistance on the burden-shifting argument and research on the 1866 Civil Rights Act. Nick Flannery (who later dropped out due to the press of other commitments) and I would research the legal support for "stigma or racial identification" as a way to persuade the Court of the far-reaching and enduring nature of the intentional segregation injury.

Bill Taylor would collect the best thinking on the causation issue and the interaction between school and housing segregation. Critical to this effort was the need to determine whether and how to inform, explain, distinguish, or undercut the "incremental segregative effect" standard, as well as how to mount a defense to Powell's charge that actual school desegregation was not in the public interest of the country nor the private interest of affected families. In some way, our arguments had to convince the key swing votes that court-ordered busing was worth the trouble. Lucas was to describe the practical understanding of the evidence of segregation from the point of view of a trier of fact.

Lucas and Jones would draft a short "Armageddon" statement, outlining the increasing show by Rehnquist and Powell that they were attempting to get the Court out of school segregation entirely and to undermine *Brown* and hence any meaningful remedies in a broad range of cases. This statement could then be distributed selectively to awaken any potential allies to join us. Jones, with Taylor and Murphy, would take responsibility for coordinating friend-of-the-court briefs to support our position from the United States, social scientists, labor, the National Education Association, the Legal Defense Fund, the ACLU, and others. In time, Taylor would also coordinate the development of a "statement" by leading social scientists on the interaction between school and housing segregation, the discriminatory causes of segregation, and research on desegregation and white flight that could be attached as an appendix to the Columbus brief.

In addition, Chachkin agreed to review federal equity cases, including the antitrust precedents, in order to understand and to resolve the apparent "tension between limiting relief to the precise impact and contours of the violation and broad, flexible equity powers." Finally, Richard Kohn of the Lawyers' Committee agreed to research two procedural issues: (1) the weight the Supreme Court traditionally accorded findings affirmed by both lower courts (as in Columbus) as compared with appellate court reversal and supplementation of the trial court findings (as in Dayton); and (2) the extent to which we could argue claims in Dayton arising out of constitutional and statutory provisions other than the equal protection clause.

On January 18, Jones again convened his lawyers by conference call. We all agreed to the division of labor and set about the work. On February 5, Caldwell and I established a tight deadline for transmission of initial work products and a conference in Washington to discuss the defendants' briefs, our research, and the best strategies for our own briefing. Everyone contributed. It was as if we each felt a collective responsibility for what we had been about during the entire decade. We reread the briefs, the oral arguments, and the social science statement in *Brown*.

We also read Richard Kluger's *Simple Justice,* the moving narrative of Thurgood Marshall's efforts to prepare his forces for the frontal attack on segregation in *Brown*. We were looking for inspiration. Instead, we were awed by the thoroughness and depth of Marshall's preparation; we could try to do no less. All of us were willing to contribute our experience, our time, and our insight to explore every conceivable way to make a majority on the Court see and deal with the de jure reality of segregation. The draft statements and memoranda began to circulate on each assigned topic. Letters and phone calls followed with comments, suggestions, and revisions.

It became clear that of the possible approaches, some could not be stressed. For example, arguments based on the Thirteenth Amendment or the legislative history of the 1866 or 1871 Civil Rights Acts could still be made; but, because the lower courts had not considered these standards and sources, it would be better to reserve such novel legal issues for any remand proceedings rather than ask the Supreme Court to consider them without a lower court record. Other approaches were useful in supporting our primary arguments. For example, the concepts of stigma and racial identification as used in prior judicial opinions could lend credence to the substantial, wide-ranging, and continuing impact of intentional school segregation and its interconnection with housing segregation over time; of particular note, this concept permeated Justice Blackmun's decisions in school cases when he sat on the Eighth Circuit. Frontal use of the concept, however, might suggest that the evidentiary presumptions established in the Denver case were subject to reconsideration. It was also unlikely that the concept, no matter how powerful, could alter the world view of a Stewart or a Powell; they were not prepared to accept that any color line in urban schooling subjected the black minority to a second-class status as effectively and as insidiously as Jim Crow, the Black Codes, or slavery.

Similarly, we could not argue as a primary thesis that the mere incorporation of residential segregation and housing discrimination by school authorities violated the Fourteenth Amendment. Such an approach invited a wooden ruling by a Rehnquist majority that school authorities did not control and were not responsible for residential segregation. Moreover, Karl Taeuber's concept of "unity," the interlocking web of discrimination in schools, housing, and community life, was the vision portrayed by the record evidence. Our job, without distorting or stretching the evidence, was to highlight the school authorities' integral part in this systemic discrimination and then to show its extensive consequences over time on current school segregation. If we could not win on the record evidence, prior precedent, and our de jure vision of the case, we could not prevail, no matter how inventive or powerful any new argument might be.

Chachkin's draft of the statement of facts in Columbus turned out to be a stroke of genius. As in our prior briefs in the case, he traced the history of the development of the core of five blacks-only schools through 1954. Our previous briefs and the lower court opinions had dropped this historical narrative at this point in time and analyzed the board's conduct after 1954 in terms of separate techniques of segregation, such as faculty and staff assignment, school construction, optional zones, discontiguous areas, and gerrymandering. Instead, Chachkin merely summarized the nature of each of these administrative devices and how they could be used for segregative or integrative ends. He then proceeded to continue the historical analysis from 1954 to date, year by year, with a focus on the interlocking nature and wide-ranging consequences of the seemingly endless incidents of segregation.

By the time any reader completed this narrative, he would be convinced that the board's intent to segregate hit every geographic area in the system and pervaded all operations of the district. The sheer volume and repetition of the blatantly segregative incidents, year after year, in the core and in all corners of the district was numbing. The detail might be overwhelming, but so was the brutally objective picture of the board's unrelenting intent to segregate the entire system. The draft statement of facts made a mockery of Rehnquist's claim that there were only "isolated instances" of constitutional violations by Columbus school authorities. It supported Judge Duncan's summation that the intentional segregation violation covered the entire system—rather than resting "on three specific violations, or eleven, or any other specific number."

Chachkin's draft also provided a means to tie the factual statements and legal arguments of our separate Columbus and Dayton briefs together. The Dayton statement could stress the pre-*Brown* proof to show the existence of a virtually complete and openly dual system at the time of *Brown*; the legal argument could then emphasize the board's failure thereafter to dismantle this dual system. In contrast, the Columbus brief could emphasize the board's systematic intent to segregate schools following *Brown* right through the time of trial and stress our de jure argument under the Denver and Arlington Heights decisions. Yet the different emphases would not undercut either case; as both cases had fairly extensive pre-*Brown* violations, the separate *Brown* and de jure arguments would support each case. Even with this strategy, we could only realistically hope for an affirmance in Columbus and a remand in Dayton for yet another round of hearings on the continuing impact of the violation and scope of remedy. We feared, however, that a majority on the Court would vote to reverse in both cases by offering current residential segregation as an excuse for continuing school segregation.

The Briefs

Sam Porter's brief for the Columbus board outlined the substantial growth in the geographic size and enrollment of the Columbus schools following 1954 and the pervasive residential segregation, and portrayed a school board committed to providing nonracial neighborhood schools as close to the children as possible. Once again Porter assumed that the *only* violations involved the specific examples identified in Judge Duncan's rulings. The brief sought to give nonracial explanations for these isolated instances and to demonstrate their limited impact on segregation. With respect to faculty, Porter emphasized that teaching staffs had been integrated prior to trial. Porter concluded by downplaying the pre-*Brown* proof as "hearsay," with "no attempt to demonstrate a current impact on the racial composition of schools in the Columbus system."

With this factual predicate in place, Porter argued that the lower courts refused "to make the required factual determination concerning the current incremental segregative effect of the remote and isolated constitutional violations described in their opinions." Porter proceeded to attack the lower courts for using a "fruit of the poisonous tree analysis" based on erroneous legal presumptions of intent and effect. "By equating intent with disproportionate impact," the lower courts sought to "attribute to school officials the responsibility for imbalanced residential patterns. . . . [T]he conclusion reached below can be defended only through the application of legal fictions to broad factual generalizations which are not supported by record evidence."

The brief ran the risk of destruction at the hands of a full exploration of the evidence of pervasive school board discrimination. It did, however, neatly argue Rehnquist's view of the facts, the law, and the Sixth Circuit: The facts showed only isolated violations and residential imbalance beyond the board's control. The law required a careful calibration of the extent to which such isolated instances aggravated segregation in schools beyond the underlying residential segregation at the current time. The Sixth Circuit was bent on using legal fictions to accomplish racial balance.

Dave Greer's brief for the Dayton board offered more of the same, but he dressed it in more colorful language. "On the issue of intent, the [Sixth Circuit] began by looking at the past instead of the present. It reasoned [from this 'false premise'] that the existence of segregatory acts or practices in 1954 placed the Board under an affirmative duty to diffuse black and white students throughout the school system. . . . When the distorting lenses of the presumptions created by the Sixth Circuit are withdrawn . . . , the conclusion is inexorable that for at least the past twenty years none of the actions of the Dayton school board has been tainted with segregative intent." Greer was just as caustic about the Sixth Circuit's failure to apply the "incremental segregative effect" test "from the remedial perspective as the difference between the distribution of a school population as it is and as it would have been in the absence of constitutional violations." Once again he portrayed residential segregation in Dayton as a natural phenomenon that started with the "great Dayton flood of 1913."

Greer concluded his imagery by arguing that the "natural expansion of the black residential community is simply reflected in the changing composition of the Dayton schools. . . . The changing racial compositions of the schools in the Dayton system over the past twenty years have, without any manipulation by the Board, simply reflected ['residential housing'] patterns. In the absence of any incremental segregative effect from Board action, the proper remedy was a dismissal of the plaintiffs' complaint." Once again, Greer had written an entertaining brief to invite the Court to minimize board discrimination and to use "natural" residential "imbalance" as the apology for the color line in schooling. The Ohio and Delaware boards of education also filed *amicus* briefs adopting this whitewash. They were joined by the Pacific Legal Foundation, the "public interest" law center of California conservatives like Edward Meese.

The brief for plaintiffs in Columbus detailed the massive evidence of the board's long-standing, pervasive, and continuing intentional segregation. Chachkin's detailed statement of the facts found by the lower court refuted Porter's claim that the violations were isolated. As we had learned from the Detroit case, however, whether five justices would review Duncan's subsidiary and ultimate findings fairly in light of the record was not certain. Nevertheless, the factual statement and legal argument presented a persuasive case to reaffirm the Denver decision by interpreting or limiting the "incremental segregative effect" test of the first Dayton decision to cases with only a few isolated violations. Citing the Court's respect for meaningful relief in all variety of equity cases, the brief concluded by attacking the school board's "mechanistic" reading of "incremental segregative effect": The school board's restrictive approach would "prune only the most prominent branches [of intentional segregation], leaving the roots intact and permitting discrimination to flourish again. Little can be imagined that would be more destructive of the nation's long struggle, supported by the [Supreme] Court, to eliminate official racism from our society than to strip the equal protection clause of the Fourteenth Amendment of *practical* meaning."

Appended to the brief was a "Social Science Statement" on school and housing segregation written by forty of the nation's leading scholars. Robert Crain of RAND, Edgar Epps and John Hope Franklin of the University of Chicago, Tom Pettigrew of Harvard, Karl Taeuber of Wisconsin, and Robert Weaver of Hunter College were among the most prominent. Kenneth Clark—the primary draftsman of the social science statement concerning the nature of segregation in *Brown,* and the author of the origins and deprivation of urban segregation in the *Dark Ghetto*—provided the most historic support. The very principles of *Brown* were at stake; and Clark was once again placing his vision of reality on the line. The statement summarized the findings of current research:

- "The ethnic enclave for whites was temporary and, to a large extent optional, while for blacks . . . segregation has been enduring and can, for the most part, be considered involuntary. Every major study of the housing of blacks and whites in urban America has identified racial discrimination as a major explanation of the observed segregation." Economic factors and nonracial personal choice explain little of the current segregation.

- "Racial discrimination was institutionalized throughout American society. . . . Discriminatory practices and racial segregation in each aspect of life [e.g., in housing, schooling, employment, social affairs, and political activity] contributes to the maintenance and reinforcement of similar practices and segregatory outcome in other aspects."
- "There is an interdependent relationship between school segregation and neighborhood segregation. Each reinforces the other. Policies that encourage development and continuation of overwhelmingly racially identifiable schools foster residential segregation. This residential segregation in turn fosters increased school segregation. . . . Discriminatory acts by school authorities that contribute to the racial identifiability of schools promote racially identifiable neighborhoods."
- "Th[e] process of 'racial succession' or 'ghettoization' has been perceived [by some] as a relentless 'natural force,' yet it is in fact governed by institutional policies and practices and is not at all inevitable."
- "The actions of school officials are part of a set of discriminatory actions by government agencies and other institutions. This web of institutional discrimination is the basic cause of school and residential segregation."

By giving concrete examples and references to published studies to illustrate the basis for these conclusions, the statement rebutted the claims of Justice Stewart that the causes of "Negro concentration" are "unknown or unknowable," of Powell that voluntary preference and economics are the "primary determinants" of segregation, and of Dave Greer that segregation and expansion of the black "ghetto" are "natural" ethnic phenomena.

The statement then focused on Rehnquist's interpretation of the phrase "incremental segregative effect":

Some social scientists have been asked to refine these general conclusions and provide precise answers about specific causal relationships in particular places and times. . . . What is the incremental effect on current school attendance patterns that results from direct and indirect effects of individual discriminatory actions taken in the past by school officials? Social scientists cannot answer such questions with precision. The questions can be rephrased to call for stating what the present would be like if the past had been different in certain specified respects. . . . [But] history can not be unreeled and reeled back differently. The present state of empirical knowledge and models of social change do not permit precise specification of the effects of removing particular historical actions.

The statement concluded, "historical reconstruction simply cannot meaningfully quantify what the racial distribution of pupils or residents would have been if particular school officials had acted differently. Delimiting the wrong that flowed from specific acts and righting the wrong are matters of jurisprudence, not social science." In short, Rehnquist's violation-by-violation, school-by-school incremental comparison between current reality and what would have been was a fiction to which considered justice, not pseudoscience, must provide the answer.

Our brief for plaintiffs in Dayton detailed the development of the explicitly dual system at the time of *Brown* and its perpetuation and expansion thereafter. With this predicate, the brief explained the direct analogy between the facts in Dayton, Ohio, and Charlotte-Mecklenburg, North Carolina: "[W]ho is responsible for the flourishing of the basically dual system in the years following *Brown*? And who bears the burden of explaining the continuation of a system of basically one-race schools following *Brown* through the time of trial?" The answer in Dayton in 1979, we argued, had to be the same as in Charlotte in 1971 because "there is no constitutionally principled way to distinguish [the two] on the undeniable facts of record." In short, unless *Swann* and *Green* were to be reversed, the Dayton board's continuation of a historic dual system through the time of trial also required actual desegregation to provide any meaningful remedy.

Once again we challenged Greer's refusal to show by any offer of evidence how the existing systemwide plan exceeded the systemwide violation. We also refuted his portrayal of a one-way relationship between housing and school segregation. When the Dayton board converted, opened, and maintained four schools designated for blacks only on the West Side while operating whites-only and blatantly discriminatory "mixed" schools in the rest of the district, it sent a message to black and white families alike: The West Side was the place for blacks, and other areas were favored for whites.

Only by ignoring the fact that "[p]eople gravitate toward school facilities, just as schools are located in response to the needs of people" [as *Swann* noted], can it even be suggested that such pervasive school discrimination does not promote segregated residential patterns which, when combined with neighborhood zoning, "further lock the system into the mold of separation of the races."

By the time of *Brown,* "four decades of such overt discrimination" had plainly locked the Dayton system into the mold of segregation of the races. The brief continued,

> This observation is . . . buttressed by two additional facts. First, the official racial discrimination by school authorities built upon, incorporated and encouraged the corresponding and continuing local custom of racial discrimination, exclusion, and duality of housing. . . . Second, the intentional school discrimination continued after 1954 through the time of trial. . . . Intentionally segregative Board practices with respect, for example, to optional zones, the similarly "haphazard" school construction program resulting consistently (and only) in a widespread pattern of one-race schools and additions, and the coordinate assignment (through at least 1971) of racially identifiable staffs to "black," "changing," and "white" schools, all served as signals to the community of the racial designation of residential areas.

The brief concluded by challenging the school board's plea for immunity: the upshot of the board's interpretation of the first Dayton opinion was that the desegregation remedy in school cases should stop at the current level of residential segregation to which the board's actions contributed and which remained almost complete. In short, the "remedy" would be "continued one race schooling." On *Brown's* twenty-fifth anniversary, the Dayton board offered "Dayton's black school children almost complete resegregation in separate one-race schools, now and hereafter. Such a racially stigmatizing lesson would only 'affect their hearts and minds in a way unlikely ever to be undone,' [quoting *Brown I*]. . . . Instead, this Court should inform both the Dayton school children and the Dayton school authorities that the systemwide plan of desegregation now in effect remains the proper remedy for the basically dual system of schooling existing through the time of trial."

We were joined by many friend-of-the-court briefs filed, for example, by the United States, by the Legal Defense Fund and the UAW, by the ACLU and the Union of Electrical, Radio, and Machine Workers, and by the NEA. The government supported our reading of the evidence of wide-ranging school board discrimination and the law of violation and remedy in school cases. Its brief argued that "the causes of current racial separation in the Columbus and Dayton schools must be evaluated in light of the historical creation and maintenance of dual systems." The burden of proving the propriety of limiting relief in such cases of systemwide violation rests with the wrongdoing school authorities, not the victimized black schoolchildren and their parents. Because the boards here did not establish that a less extensive remedy would cure the effects of their systemwide violation, systemwide remedies were appropriate. Drew Days, speaking for the government, concluded:

> [The school boards here] seek to impose on the plaintiffs in school desegregation cases the burden of proving, with mathematical certainty, school by school throughout a district, the precise degree to which a school board's widespread racially discriminatory conduct affected the racial composition of the student body. A similar approach was rejected in [the Denver case]. . . . Much of the [school boards'] argument constitutes an attack on the remedial principles of [Denver] and *Swann*. . . . [They] have suggested *no* justifications for overruling these decisions. . . . Overruling or limiting *Swann* and [Denver] would call into question the validity of every one of [the desegregation] plans [currently working in some 400 school districts throughout the country]. The potential for disrupting settled expectations is enormous.

This stance of the chief civil rights enforcement official of the Carter administration represented a far cry from his predecessors in the Ford and Nixon administrations who had pleaded for restrictions on violation and remedy in school cases, argued against the *Swann* and Denver rulings, sought repeal of *Green,* and supported school segregation under the guise of "free choice," "neighborhood schools," and "local control." The view of the elected administration had obviously changed; but so had the view of the Court. The two seemed to be moving in opposite directions; it was not at all clear that the affirmative entreaty of Drew Days and the United States could persuade the swing votes on the Court in 1979 any more than the negative views of the prior administration had done in 1973 or 1971.

The Legal Defense Fund presented much the same argument as the United States had, but with the perspective and prestige of fifty years of experience in proving official racial discrimination. In particular, James Nabrit III added his insights into the proof and process of intentional segregation to lend support to our reading of the evidence, the law, and the lower court opinions.

> The Columbus and Dayton school boards ask the Court to make a fundamental turn away from the course it charted from *Brown* to [the Denver decision]. Indeed, they seek to reverse [the Denver decision] by . . . turn[ing] the "incremental segregative effect" language of Dayton I into a rule that would measure the rights of minorities with a "micrometer." . . . Such a retreat from [the Denver decision] would cut off any hope of integrating the schools of many of our nation's communities and

represent a tragic turning away from *Brown*. . . . Segregated schools [have been] an integral part of the ghettoization of blacks. Who can know to what extent the ghettos of Dayton and Columbus would be different, if the schools had been operated on a nondiscriminatory basis, and had taught a lesson of nondiscrimination and equality instead of a lesson of white supremacy. The specter of endless segregation of the races in the public schools of the North haunts these cases [if the Court adopts the school board's] position . . . Those who have devoted their lives to laboring in the vineyards for an integrated society believe they have earned the right to speak plainly: If this Court were to accept the [school board's] position, segregated schools (and as a consequence a more segregated society) will be the legacy of this Court, just as surely as a segregated society was the legacy of the Court that decided the *Civil Rights Cases* and *Plessy v. Ferguson.*

Sam Porter filed a short reply brief. He argued that Chachkin's detailed statement of the board's proven discrimination should be ignored because the citation of specific incidents in the lower court opinions represented the sum total, not examples, of the violation. Such a claim could only appeal to a Court predisposed to reverse by holding, precisely as Justice Rehnquist had done in his stay opinion in Columbus, that "isolated" violations do not support systemwide remedies. Porter also challenged the weight, truth and relevance of the "Social Science Statement." We had used the statement, however, only to undercut the credibility of the neoconservative views espoused by Powell, Rehnquist, and Stewart. Porter's reply therefore only *added* to the problems of *any* justice who wanted to argue that residential segregation resulting from economics or choice and not discrimination caused almost all urban school segregation.

Oral Arguments

On April 24, 1979, Chief Justice Burger called on Sam Porter to proceed. Unlike the oral argument in the first round of the Dayton school case, Justice Marshall did not walk out. He was not about to recuse himself again when the soul of *Brown* was at issue. Porter opened by challenging the lower court's application of presumptions of intent in order to extrapolate a judgment of systemwide liability from isolated findings of violations. Justice Rehnquist quickly took the offensive by urging Porter to agree that the "incremental segregative effect inquiry" must be made even if there is a finding of system-wide violation. Porter responded, however, that Judge Duncan had identified only a few isolated violations: "They are not examples, and his opinion is clear that they are not examples." Justice Stewart then added, "They were the sum total [of the violation]. . . . And racial segregation has been illegal under the law of Ohio since, what, the 1880's?''

With such questions, it seemed like Porter was not so much engaged in oral argument before the Supreme Court as a moot court with his co-counsel. Porter concluded: "Five or six or eight or ten [violations], in a system of 170 square miles does not constitute a dual system." Porter's reception in the Supreme Court was considerably more friendly than the one he suffered at the hands of the Sixth Circuit. As I listened at counsel table with Atkins, Caldwell, Chachkin, Days, and Jones, I had a sense of déjà vu, the sinking feeling that the decision, as in the Detroit case five years earlier, had already been made.

Atkins stepped forward quickly and resolutely. He would go down fighting with his chin up and his wit intact. Before Atkins could finish his opening summary of the case, Rehnquist pounced. The junior justice, bent on sinking the ship of integration, juxtaposed Duncan's ruling with the "incremental segregative effect test." Duncan said it was not now possible to parse school from housing segregation and that such a fruitless attempt was not required; in contrast, "our language in Dayton mandated a comparison between the current situation and what it would have been in the absence of violations." Rehnquist asked Atkins, "Don't you see some inconsistency there?"

In our preparations with Atkins and Caldwell prior to oral arguments, we predicted that this would be Rehnquist's opening gambit. After some debate, we had resolved that the answer should be no, followed by a lengthy explanation of Judge Duncan's care in evaluating all the evidence, including the two-way interaction between schools and housing to plumb the cause of school segregation, and culminating with Duncan's finding of "systemwide intentional segregation." Given the stakes, Atkins had decided that he was not brave enough to argue forthrightly that Rehnquist's "incremental segregative effect" test was a fool's game; we could survive that standard if it were interpreted, consistently with the Court's opinions in *Swann* and the Denver case, as applying only to cases with a few isolated instances of school board discrimination.

While Atkins proceeded to give the short no and the lengthy response, Justice Rehnquist became visibly frustrated. Rehnquist then asked what Atkins meant by "systemwide segregation." With that opening, Atkins launched into a more complete explanation of the basic facts: a dual system in 1954; the racial assignment of faculty thereafter; the construction of schools intended for one race, "warehouses being built for black students"; and the reciprocal effect of such intentional policies in creating and maintaining "white schools." Rehnquist interrupted to ask if just one intentionally segregative site selection would justify a finding of systemwide segregation in a school system the size of Columbus because of some "ripple effect." Atkins responded directly, "No. We think that is not common sense." Rehnquist asked what, then, was the "intermediate step" between a single segregated act and the imposition of a systemwide remedy. Atkins again returned to Judge Duncan's careful evaluation of the overall intent of the school policymakers in Columbus, their wide-ranging segregative actions, the lockstep interaction with housing, and the patent dual system in Columbus in 1954.

At that point, Stewart interrupted abruptly to ask what the situation was at the time of filing the complaint; he was not any more impressed in 1979 by the "ancient history" at the time of *Brown* than he had been in the first round of the Dayton case in 1977. Atkins responded hotly by pointing to some seventy-seven specific violations directly segregating 149 schools, over and above the 1954 dual system and the continuing systemwide policy of faculty segregation: "This was not a case of 'isolated instances.'"

Atkins concluded by summarizing the violations and the lower court opinions that brought the "systemwide remedy flush with the systemwide violation. We ask this Court to affirm that remedy and to permit the students in Columbus to receive, for the first time in a century, fully adequate and fully constitutional education in the public school system. . . . If you don't permit that to happen, the [Columbus school authorities] will certainly not make it happen. We have no place to go from here. . . . [W]e *are* approaching the 25th anniversary of the *Brown* decision. In Columbus it hasn't meant a thing—we ask this Court to send *Brown* to Columbus." Atkins was determined to hold the Court to a "moral decision," to force the Court to confront the meaning of the calls of Rehnquist and Powell for a complete retreat and the call of Stewart for a "statute of limitations on original sin."

Drew Days followed with a low-keyed recitation on behalf of the United States. He noted the basically dual nature of schooling in Columbus and the board's failure to meet its affirmative duty to dismantle such a system of intentional segregation. Days argued that the "incremental segregative effect" test created no new standard but merely "reiterated the settled precept that a remedy must be tailored to cure the condition that offends the Constitution by eradicating the effect of the violation":

> When there have been only isolated and sporadic acts of school board discrimination affecting a limited number of schools or students, a similarly limited remedy is appropriate. That is what we understand to be the teaching of Dayton. On the other hand, where there has been a general policy of discrimination in the operation of the school system as a whole . . . , a systemwide remedy will generally be required.

Days then addressed the burden of proof at the remedial stage: "[B]ased upon the teachings of *Swann* and [the Denver case], the burden of showing to what extent the system-wide remedy is inappropriate falls upon the school board.'' Again, Rehnquist expressed his dissatisfaction by inquiring what question a court should ask itself in determining whether there is a system-wide or only isolated violation: ''At what point does the burden shift?'' At first Days responded with his own tautology, when there is a systemwide violation; but he then proceeded to discuss the record evidence of pervasive discrimination in Columbus as an example of when the burden should shift.

Days concluded that any ''risk of uncertainty'' about the scope of remedy for a systemwide violation ''should not be borne by the victims of the illegal action.'' In such circumstances, a systemwide remedy would remove ''the racial identifiability of the dual system. . . . [It] would also visibly rectify the stigma of inferiority which is the product of pervasive violations. If a school board wishes to contend that a less inclusive decree would purge all taints of its proven system-wide racial discrimination, it has the burden of showing exactly what the limitation entails.'' Days had stood Rehnquist's ''incremental segregative effect'' test and assumptions of ''isolated violation'' on their head in the Columbus case.

As Drew Days moved from the lectern to sit down, Justice Stevens asked whether there was any significance in the different findings of Judge Duncan in Columbus and Judge Rubin in Dayton. Days answered no; his personal review of the record evidence demonstrated that the Supreme Court should uphold the court of appeals findings of systemwide violation in Dayton, not the clearly erroneous, contrary findings of Judge Rubin. That single statement undercut Dave Greer's facile opening remark to the Court: ''I at least was pleased by having the [plaintiffs] in the Columbus case open by asking that this Court affirm the findings of the trier of facts, the trial court, and I would hope that they would open their argument in this case with the same request.'' Greer proceeded to respond to Days's legal argument by suggesting that the Dayton test of ''incremental segregative effect'' was the ''culmination'' of the Court's rulings in the *Swann,* Denver, and Detroit cases: ''to restore the victims of discriminatory conduct to the position they would have occupied absent such conduct.'' This rationalization of the cases, however, was a two-edged sword: if there was a systemwide violation, the propriety of a system-wide remedy was virtually conceded. Greer seemed to fall further into this trap by arguing that, ''as the trial court found, there was no systemwide violation.''

Greer then tried to extricate himself by arguing that the ''incremental segregative effect test'' also applied to findings of systemwide violation: ''[T]he remedial purpose is restorative [not punitive]. It is not to compare what is to what ought to be in some ideal world in which none of us can ever live. It is an effort to compare what is to what would have been in the absence of the violations. . . . In justifying a system-wide remedy in this case, the Sixth Circuit completely abandoned that comparative test and it redefined the whole concept of incremental segregative effect in terms of a snowballing process of cumulative violations.''

Stewart interrupted with a slightly different tack to reach the same end. ''The District Court on remand in this case, Judge Rubin, found that there wasn't a systemwide violation, didn't he? . . . And he dismissed the case didn't he?'' When Greer answered affirmatively, Stewart then sought to impale plaintiffs on the findings of the trial court: ''Did he find any specific isolated constitutional violations?'' Greer responded with alacrity, and unmistakable pleasure, at this turn in the questioning by describing the ''pre-1951'' policy ''of assigning black faculty to teach in black schools'' and the creation in 1933 of the black Dunbar school ''that went out of existence in 1962.''

Thurgood Marshall could stand no more. He interrupted Greer by asking in an exasperated voice what happened to Dunbar and what the school was named now. Greer explained that the old Dunbar had been turned into McFarlane Elementary and a new Dunbar had been opened. Marshall would have none of it:

Q. They are still predominantly Negro, I assume, because Dunbar was a Negro.

A. Well, the fact that Paul Lawrence Dunbar was a great Negro poet has no relationship to the fact that Dunbar High School, new Dunbar or the old McFarlane, are attended primarily by black students today. The fact is established by the residential complexion of the neighborhoods they serve.

Q. There are 24 new schools constructed between '50 and '72, and 22 of them were Negro or white.

A. Correct.

Q. It was accidentally or deliberately, either one, it ends up that way.

A. Building the schools was deliberate, sure.

Q. In 1971, 75 percent of the Negroes were assigned to Negro schools?

A. By virtue of their neighborhood proximity.

Q. Answer my question and then add to it. Yes?

A. Yes is the answer, Your Honor.

A. . . . I think the complete answer to that is that while that is all entirely true, it overlooks the fact that there was no feasible alternative for the board other than the location of these schools as they were. As the plaintiffs' own witnesses have testified, the only alternative to the program that you have just described was, one, build a single campus in the City of Dayton and bring all students bused to that, or, two, to adopt some systemwide busing plan to—

Q. Mr. Greer, that is as old as 1955.

A. Well, whether it is new or— . . . all right, if it is not new, it is a fact in this case, that because of the residential patterns in Dayton, those were the only available alternatives.

As Marshall badgered, Greer remained unflappable. The board attorney returned to complete the answer to Stewart's question: the third, and final finding, related to physical isolation between and within a few schools in the 1920s, 1930s, and 1940s. Stewart asked, "This lawsuit was brought when?" Greer responded, "1972, April" and proceeded to provide Stewart with the argument he wanted to hear: the trial court "specifically found that there was no continuing effect of these prior practices in the three areas which I have described."

Greer then attacked the Sixth Circuit's legal standard for finding constitutional violations: it substituted "a bed of procrustean presumptions for the judicial analysis that is contemplated by Arlington Heights, [the District of Columbia employment case,] and Dayton I decisions of this Court. . . . The way that the [Sixth Circuit's] analysis seems to work is that whenever there is a condition of current racial imbalance in the schools, which there certainly was in Dayton at the time suit was filed, then it is fair game to go back in the past as far as may be necessary to find some constitutional violation and then to juxtapose the current condition of racial imbalance with a historical situation of a constitutional violation by the welding material or glue of a concept of an affirmative duty to diffuse the races throughout the system. . . . It is not a real presumption, it is an outcome determinative approach to finding violations."

Finally, one of the swing votes, Justice Stevens, interrupted with a question that showed concern.

Q.   Mr. Greer, I don't think you are really stating the theory of the Court of Appeals though, are you? They didn't start from the fact there is presently imbalance and then infer violation from that. Didn't they start from the notion that there was proof of intentional violation as of 1954, and a failure [thereafter] affirmatively to correct the situation? They relied entirely on the duty to take affirmative action in effect.

A.   They are talking about 1954—

Q.   Right.

A.   It is our contention that there was no dual system in 1954 or in 1972 or any of the years in between.

Q.   Right.

A.   But what they are doing is instead of focusing on the existence of a violation at the time suit was filed, it is using a double focus. One is a condition of racial imbalance at the time of suit, and the other is a finding of an unconstitutional act at some time in the past. They picked the year 1954 which I would submit has the logic only of being the date of the *Brown v. Board of Education* decision.

Q.   Well, they say as of that date there was a clear duty on the part of the board to change a situation they found to exist. Now, I know you don't accept the finding [of a dual system] as of that time and [that] a failure to have corrected in the interval amounts to a present violation today.

A.   And that is where you get what I call the glue or the weld, and that is this affirmative duty—and the words of the Sixth Circuit are an affirmative duty to diffuse black and white students throughout the system.

Q.   Well, there would be such a duty, would there not, if they are right about the dual system in 1954?

Justice Stevens, at least for purposes of questioning Greer, was pinning the Dayton board with plaintiffs' original *Brown* argument. When Greer responded that there was *no* affirmative duty on dual systems following *Brown,* Stevens pressed harder:

Q.   Let me just test that, because this goes really to the heart of the case.

A. It does, indeed.

Q. Supposing you had a *de jure* situation with all black and all white schools, totally the same, and then all they did was change rules and say anybody can go to any school within three-quarters of a mile of his home or whatever the boundary was, but there was no change in boundaries. You would have to change the boundaries to correct the situation, and you say there is no duty to change boundaries?

A. That's correct.

Q. Let's take a school system in that region of the country which up until 1954 had legislation on the books requiring the segregation of school children based upon the color of their skin, and in 1954, in *Brown v. Board of Education,* that legislation was held to be unconstitutional. Certainly it then became incumbent upon the school boards of some school districts in that part of the country in a state which had had such legislation to do something about it, didn't it?

A. It absolutely did and—

Q. To desegregate, wasn't it, an affirmative duty?

A. But the duty is to provide a system in which no one is denied access to a school because of race or color. That I would submit to you is different from an affirmative duty to create some balance of races throughout the school system.

Marshall bristled at this response and almost shouted: "What has happened to that good old phrase 'root and branch' [in dismantling dual systems]?"

With this new hope, Bill Caldwell rose as Greer retreated. Caldwell spoke to solidify our position with Justice Stevens and to win the crucial fifth vote, either from Justice Blackmun who had said nothing or from Justice Stewart who remained so vocal in opposition to plaintiffs' claims. Caldwell opened:

My case, as apparent, is quite different from the case that has been presented by the [Dayton defendants]. Their case is that racial discrimination has been the rare exception in the operation of the Dayton public schools. My case is that it has been the rule.

Their case in effect contends that deliberate segregation has affected the schools on only a few occasions at random and with very limited and precisely definable impact. But our case and the undeniable facts show that school segregation in Dayton not only was predictable, it was predicted by purposeful design and operation for a period of at least sixty years. From 1912 to 1972, the board operated a systematic program of racial segregation that was circumscribed by neither geography nor administrative function. Throughout this time, the board operated a covert dual school system.

Stewart quickly interrupted: "What were the District Court's findings on the 1972 situation again? What did the District Court find about the condition in 1972?" After skirting Rubin's opinion, Caldwell responded to Stewart by stating the *facts* of unremitting intentional segregation beginning in 1912. As to the core of blacks-only schools at the time of *Brown*, Caldwell concluded "these were full-blown state-imposed segregated schools." Stewart wouldn't accept that as a legal possibility because the Ohio legislature had long since outlawed dual schooling. Caldwell responded that the de jure schools in Dayton were nevertheless imposed by the state of Ohio acting through its local school board. Stewart responded: "Well, all of these things that you have told us happened in spades in that region of the country where the legislatures required them to happen. Does that mean that school districts in those areas of the country are always going to be tainted by their historic illegal unconstitutional action?" Caldwell would not let the Court break faith with *Brown*:

Your Honor, [they] will be until they have done something to undo this horrendous wrong that they have committed. And what I am trying to convince you is that by the time of *Brown*, the Dayton school authorities had essentially accomplished the same results that North Carolina accomplished in Charlotte-Mecklenburg and that thereafter they should have been under the same constitutional duty.

With that shot, Stewart got up from his chair and disappeared through the curtain in back of the justices.

In his absence, several members of the Court gained the floor to ask how the Sixth Circuit could make its own findings of fact rather than send the case back with some instructions to the trier of fact, Judge Rubin. Caldwell responded that the courts of appeal have to review the evidence to determine whether findings are "clearly erroneous." Citing the leading Supreme Court case on the subject, he argued that such determination often amounts to making a new finding. Rehnquist interjected that, even assuming that the violation finding was correct, "the school board is entitled to shoulder the burden of proof that the violation did not cause an incremental segregative effect so as to be system-wide, is that correct?'' Caldwell agreed the school boards then ''have the option of carrying that burden,'' but countered that in this case the board had effectively conceded that if the violation were system-wide, the existing systemwide remedy was as right as any.

Caldwell then returned to argue the facts showing a systemwide violation. In 1954, ''except for the absence of the written state law permitting this result, the Dayton system was basically . . . the same as the systems that were before the Court in *Brown,* and it was basically the same system that existed in Charlotte. The minor slight factual distinction is that there was a minimal level of tolerance of racial mixing.''

At this point, Stewart returned to his seat and immediately interjected: ''Wasn't that true of almost every big city in the United States—New York or Chicago or. . . . That there is a great deal of de facto concentration of one race or another in various schools?'' Caldwell responded: ''In my case, I am talking about de jure concentration. I am not talking about de facto concentration. It may well be that the pattern exists.'' Stewart again interrupted:

Q. In New York City, every time they build a new school in Harlem, I suppose it could be reasonably anticipated that that would be populat[ed] 100 percent by Negro children, couldn't it?

A. It is certainly possible. The question is how did it get that way, and I don't know that there has been litigation on that issue.

Q. No, I don't either. . . . It has just occurred to me that what you were telling us was probably characteristic of every sizable city in the United States.

A. Well, if it is, Your Honor, it is a sad state of affairs because these people [the school authorities in Dayton] did the same thing that the Charlotte-Mecklenburg Board of Education did.

Stewart responded, ''Perhaps so,'' but added, ''the issue in this case is whether or not there was a constitutional violation at the time the lawsuit was brought and, if so, what the appropriate remedy should be.''

Justice Stewart had ''gotten off the school bus'' at the school district line in the Richmond and Detroit cases: within districts, he was ready to reject any school busing predicated on the ''affirmative duty'' of *Brown* to dismantle dual school systems as required in *Green, Swann,* and the Denver case. This represented a substantial retreat, even for a justice who had long since substituted a de facto perception for his original view of the de jure reality of urban segregation.

When Caldwell argued that the segregation policies and practices of the Dayton school authorities "funneled black people to part of the system and preserved the rest of the system for whites," Stewart again displayed his antipathy: "Well, where is that finding? Judge Rubin obviously did not so find." Caldwell referred to the opinion of the court of appeals and gave an "example of such a finding":

[T]he Dunbar High School, which was operated from 1933 to 1962, the Court of Appeals found that through discriminatory practices in other parts of the system that the board by counseling, by discriminating against black students that went to predominantly white schools, in effect forced blacks to go to this system-wide blacks-only high school. Any person who would observe that situation would make a residential choice on the basis of the board's segregation policy. A white family seeking a residence in Dayton certainly would not move to the Dunbar High School area where their children couldn't even be [admitted] because they couldn't have any contact with black teachers; at the same time black families were not inclined to move into the white parts of town where they would have been subjected to humiliating discrimination and never had contact with black adults.

Phyllis Greer had borne witness to this point. Caldwell would not let the Court ignore this harsh reality of Dayton's color line.

Caldwell concluded by completing the analogy between Charlotte and Dayton. From 1954 through the final decision in *Swann,* "the court recognized that the school officials persisted in discriminatory conduct, had played a substantial role in this pattern of [segregated] development. . . . Those findings are fully applicable to Dayton, and [*Swann*] should be fully applicable. The judgment [of the Sixth Circuit] should be affirmed."

Drew Days argued again for the government. After skirmishes over the meaning and application of various presumptions and legal standards, the assistant attorney general concluded:

The principles that have been articulated by this Court in its opinions are grounded on considerations of fairness and policy and are designed to provide practical and effective means of eliminating longstanding and pervasive segregation of the public schools in violation of the Fourteenth Amendment. . . .

We think that [the] records [in these two cases] make unavoidable the conclusion that the principles enunciated in *Brown, Green, Swann* and [Denver] are as applicable to Columbus and Dayton today as they were to Topeka, Kansas in 1954, New Kent County, Virginia in 1968, Charlotte, North Carolina in 1971, and Denver, Colorado in 1973.

Dave Greer chose to make the rebuttal in the Dayton case that his counterpart Sam Porter in *Columbus* waived. To protect his flanks, Greer argued that he did contest remedy, contrary to Caldwell's assertions. Justice Brennan expressed his doubt whether the board even raised the question in its petition for Supreme Court review. Rather than suggest that the remedy was too extensive, however, Greer proceeded to argue the absence of *any* violation: he treated the Supreme Court to a forest of racially neutral school board action growing innocently upon a floor of racial separation in housing. The root case was a "natural" racial concentration: "[T]he incremental segregative effect [of school board actions] here is zero, and the appropriate remedy is dismissal of the complaint." Greer asked the Court to reject John Harewood's testimony against racial segregation by sacrificing public school desegregation on the altar of supposed natural "residential imbalance."

At 1:15 P.M. on April 24, 1979, the Dayton and Columbus cases, and the fate of all future challenges to urban school segregation, rested with the consciences of nine justices. Although counting votes following oral argument is always chancy at best, the outcome seemed to rest on one justice. Rehnquist, Powell, Burger, and Stewart seemed disposed either to reverse, to sharply undercut, or to explain away *Swann* and Denver; Marshall, Brennan, White, and Stevens seemed just as committed to confirming the affirmative reading and practical meaning of *Brown*. Perhaps a Stevens, a Stewart, or even a Burger might be persuaded one way or the other after a careful review of the evidence and lower court rulings in Dayton or Columbus. For the most part, however, the swing vote seemed to rest squarely with Harry Blackmun, who had said not one word in the oral arguments and previously had joined with the majorities in *Swann, Denver,* Detroit, and Dayton I without expressing any independent view. The fate of the color line of ghettoization and the hope for a racially unified alternative hung in the balance.

In the NAACP camp there was no sense of impending victory, only a nagging concern that the Second Reconstruction was now under siege. Nate Jones wrote to me: "Just a word to say thanks for the role you played in the *Columbus/Dayton* Supreme Court project. You have helped to protect something that is most precious. Because of your contribution, I feel confident that *Brown* will be saved." Given Nate's personal compassion, I wondered whether his remarks were meant to absolve his co-counsel from responsibility and guilt if the Supreme Court finally gutted *Brown* after our ten-year legal challenge.

Chapter 16
The Decisions from the Supreme Court, 1979–80

Waiting and Hoping

There was nothing to do but wait. The members of the Court usually cast their votes on a case at the first conference following argument, but the results of such conferences rarely leaked out. We had no idea how the justices had voted, who had been assigned to write the majority decision, or what other cases and legal challenges might be affected. The only certainty was that the final decisions in the Dayton and Columbus school cases would once again be the last announced by the Court in the term. That meant the wait would be long and agonizing.

One bright moment broke the spring's discontent. On the twenty-fifth anniversary of *Brown* at a reception for six hundred civil rights leaders in the East Room of the White House, President Carter announced the appointment of Nate Jones to fill the Ohio vacancy on the Sixth Circuit Court of Appeals left by the retirement of Judge Peck. The nomination of the NAACP general counsel signaled the president's official support for the principles of *Brown* at the end of one critical decade and the beginning of another. Jones had earned this just reward from the president; the Supreme Court would determine whether his legal challenge would survive his tenure at the NAACP.

Other days that spring were not so bright. For example, Nina Totenberg, the informed Supreme Court expert of National Public Radio, invited Bill Taylor to appear on a panel show to commemorate *Brown*'s quarter century. Taylor spoke of the promise of *Brown* and his hope that the proof of discrimination in Dayton and Columbus would compel the Court to reaffirm the principles of *Swann* and the Denver decision; but Totenberg predicted that the Court would just halt desegregation in order to get out of the busing thicket. On another occasion, Taylor, Ken Clark, and I were invited to participate with about fifteen others in a silver anniversary of *Brown* for the National Academy of Education sponsored by HEW's assistant secretary for education. The session turned into a divisive debate about the meaning and relevance of *Brown*. Neoconservatives touted ethnicity, separatists and pragmatists argued for the need to make the best of segregation, some academics ignored their own findings of discrimination as the cause of urban segregation, and integrationists argued for a unified, multiracial, multicultural society. The moderator of this group even threatened to resign his commission to end the squabbling at one point, and his final summary of the groups' diverse views could only reflect the wide divisions.

As the first weeks of June passed without a decision, the wait became intolerable. On each day that the Court was scheduled to hand down opinions, Chachkin dutifully attended so that he could broadcast the news to Jones and his co-counsel scattered across the country. Chachkin was joined in the Supreme Court vigil by Sam Porter, the Columbus board's attorney, who flew in from the midwest. Some counsel avoided the phone and the radio out of fear of bad tidings; others stayed by the phone and the all-news radio stations to get the verdict as soon as possible.

As June drew to a close without a decision, an informed court-watcher from the media passed the rumor to Bill Taylor that Rehnquist was writing the opinions for the Court in both school cases to restrict desegregation by giving school authorities immunity from any acts of intentional discrimination other than the most recent. If true, the news meant defeat, and the only remaining issue would be the depth of the setback. Chachkin tested the gossip against the only available facts. He analyzed the opinions already issued by the Court from the two weeks of oral argument during which the Court heard the two school cases; he found that only Justice White had written none of the majority opinions, while Justice Rehnquist had already written two—probably his full share. Chachkin surmised that White was writing the opinions for the Court and renewed our hope.

June ended on a disheartening note for the NAACP: a majority of the House of Representatives signed a "discharge petition" requiring the Judiciary Committee to stop bottling up Representative Mottl's antibusing amendment and to permit a vote in the full House on the explosive proposal. Although a two-thirds vote was needed to send the amendment on to the Senate, Don Edwards, chairman of the Judiciary Subcommittee on Constitutional Amendments, feared "as long as Democrats are joining Republicans in this, any petition will have hopes of success. It's a sad day in the House." Judiciary Committee chairman Rodino headed the opposition to the amendment: "in areas of the country that have had this problem, it's been emotion-packed at first, but afterwards it's been demonstrated that busing does work in everybody's best interest." Clarence Mitchell, the NAACP's longtime lobbyist, fondly known as the 101st senator, walked across the hall to the House to lend his perspective and prestige to halt the latest attempt to gut *Brown*. Nevertheless, the success of the discharge petition at this very moment highlighted the strength of the opposition and the continuing threat to the Supreme Court's "independence" if it did not knuckle under by continuing to restrict school desegregation or by stopping it altogether.

Decision

The Court announced that Monday, July 2, would mark the last day of the 1979–80 terms. Either the decisions in Dayton and Columbus would be announced that day or the cases would be held over for reargument in the fall.

Chachkin and Taylor watched as the Justices emerged from behind the curtains at precisely 10:00 A.M. to render their judgment. The Court announced the result in several cases before the chief justice intoned that Justice White would announce two decisions. Without expression, White stated that "for the reasons set forth in the opinions filed with the clerk, the judgments of the Court of Appeals for the Sixth Circuit are affirmed" in Columbus and Dayton. Justices Brennan, Marshall, Blackmun, and Stevens joined Justice White. Justice Stewart, joined by Chief Justice Burger, concurred separately in Columbus and dissented in Dayton. Justices Rehnquist and Powell dissented in both. White's short announcement seemed almost anticlimactic after years of pitched battle.

Chachkin, Taylor, and members of the Justice Department team listened with restrained joy and unrestrained relief. Sam Porter shook Chachkin's hand; they expected desegregation would now go forward in Columbus in the fall without a hitch. Chachkin and Taylor dashed to the clerk's office to get copies of the opinions to learn the extent of the NAACP victory. Their immediate sense of triumph and vindication was marred only somewhat by the Court's failure to rule on the petitions to review the Wilmington case, even while denying review in the pending single-district cases requiring systemwide desegregation in Austin and Minneapolis. Confirmation that the first Detroit decision left open the possibility of metropolitan relief would just have to wait.

As Chachkin and Taylor drove back to their offices, they read White's opinion, the dissents of Rehnquist and Powell, and the concurring and dissenting opinions of Stewart and Burger. That afternoon, before another National Public Radio interview, Nina Totenberg had the temerity to suggest to Bill Taylor, "I guess we had it all wrong on our earlier show." Taylor was gracious: he just remarked that the Columbus and Dayton decisions were a "ringing reaffirmation" of Denver, *Swann,* and *Brown.*

In Columbus, White wrote, "the Board's conduct at the time of trial and before not only was animated by an unconstitutional segregative purpose, but also had current, segregative impact that was sufficiently systemwide to warrant the remedy ordered by the District Court." Speaking for the Court, White agreed with lower court judges Duncan and Edwards that as of 1954 the Columbus board had created a basically dual system, including five blacks-only schools identified as such

> through all-white to all-black faculty transfers that occurred each time the Board came to consider a particular school as a black school. . . . [T]here is no magical difference between segregated schools mandated by statute and those that result from local segregative acts and policies. . . . [W]e fail to see why there should be a lesser constitutional duty to eliminate that [dual] system than there would have been had the system

been ordained by law. . . . Each instance of a failure or refusal to fulfill
[the] affirmative duty [to dismantle such a dual system] continues the
violation of the Fourteenth Amendment.

The Court then adopted our *Brown* argument: "Whatever the Board's current
purpose with respect to racially separate education might be, it knowingly
continued its failure to eliminate the consequences of its past intentionally
segregative policies." Decades after they suffered and years after they testified, Helen Jenkins Davis and Barbee Durham had been vindicated.

As to our de jure argument following *Brown,* the Court agreed that the
board had undertaken a series of intentionally segregative actions through the
time of trial, including racial assignment of faculty, segregative construction
of schools, and the various, invidious deviations from the board's "avowedly
strong preference for neighborhood schools" in fringe and pocket areas
"when neighborhood schools would have tended to desegregate the involved
schools." The Court rejected Porter's claim that the examples cited by Judge
Duncan included *all* violations found; the district court's opinion "made it
quite clear that its broad findings were not limited to these [specific] instances." The Court also held that Duncan had properly used the anticipated
and foreseeable segregative consequences of board action as only one relevant
aspect of the evidence of the board's continuing intent to segregate schools
and properly "found purposefully segregative practices with current, systemwide impact."

To Porter's claim that residential segregation would have caused the
extensive school segregation regardless of any unlawful conduct by the board,
the Court responded that the board failed to counter plaintiffs' contrary proof
at trial. Justice White added that the phenomenon of the continuation and
expansion of residential areas as black following the creation and maintenance
of blacks-only schools "seems only to confirm, not disprove, the evidence
accepted by the district court that school segregation is a contributing cause of
housing segregation."

Karl Taeuber's view of the unity of an interlocking web of discrimination
may have influenced White's thinking. The opinion, however, never mentioned the concept, Judge Duncan's thoughtful exploration of the issue, or the
invidious nature of the color line of ghettoization in both urban schools and
housing. The opinion only rejected the defense that pervasive housing segregation somehow immunizes even the most intentional school segregation
from constitutional attack under the Fourteenth Amendment: school officials
could not hide behind such a "magic door" in communities riven by racial
discrimination. But just as the Court had refused in its earlier rulings in *Swann*
and the Detroit case to evaluate the proof of (and state responsibility for) a
system of racial ghettoization in schools and housing, so too White's opinion

focused on a similarly restrictive conception of school officials' violations in Columbus.

In Dayton II, Justice White followed a similar course. He distinguished the Supreme Court's prior ruling in the case as relating to limited trial court findings, which originally had not been disturbed by the Sixth Circuit, of a few isolated violations that did not justify a systemwide remedy. In contrast, the final time around "the court of appeals performed its unavoidable duty in this case and [properly] concluded that the district court" made clearly erroneous fact findings and applied the wrong legal standards. At the time of *Brown*, defendants were intentionally operating a dual school system. The district court had simply "ignored" the legal significance of the intentional maintenance of a substantial number of blacks-only schools in the system at the time of *Brown*. In addition, "the purposeful segregation of faculty by race was inextricably tied to racially motivated student assignment practices." The court of appeals had correctly concluded that an unconstitutional dual system existed in Dayton in 1954. Justice White continued, "[T]he court of appeals was quite right in holding that the Board was thereafter under a continuing duty to eradicate the effects of that system."

This the board failed to do. Instead, the board compounded the original constitutional breach after 1954 through a series of intentionally segregative actions (for example, racial assignment of faculty and segregative optional zones and school construction) which "actually exacerbated the racial separation existing at the time of *Brown I*." The Court agreed with Phyllis Greer's claim that "dynamic gradualism" in faculty assignment was only a subterfuge for unremitting, purposeful discrimination. Moreover, the Court held that the "measure of the post-*Brown* conduct of a school board under an unsatisfied duty to liquidate a dual system is the effectiveness, not the purpose, of the actions in decreasing or increasing the segregation caused by the dual system." In sum, the Court agreed with John Harewood's view that a school board has an affirmative duty to confront and to remedy the continuing legacy of historic discrimination rather than use it as an excuse for segregating "children where they are."

Finally, Justice White, speaking for the Court, directly rejected the school-by-school, violation-by-violation reading of the "incremental segregative effect" standard:

> [School authorities] contend that [Judge Rubin] correctly interpreted our earlier decision in this litigation as requiring [plaintiffs] to prove with respect to each individual act of discrimination precisely what effect it had on current patterns of segregation. This argument results from a misunderstanding of [our prior opinion], where the violation that had then been established included at most a few high schools.

White distinguished such limited findings of violation from Harry Phillips's final ruling for the Sixth Circuit that found a dual system in 1954, a total failure thereafter to dismantle this system, and a continuing program of intentional segregation that "clearly was systemwide in that actions perpetuated and increased public school segregation in Dayton." Reiterating the holdings in both the Denver and Columbus cases, White's opinion for the Court concluded: "[P]urposeful discrimination in a substantial part of a school system furnishes a sufficient basis for an inferential finding of a systemwide discriminatory intent unless otherwise rebutted. . . . [G]iven the purpose to operate a dual school system, one could infer a connection between such a purpose and racial separation in other parts of the school system."

Put bluntly, although the causal interaction between schools and housing had not been examined by the courts below in Dayton, Dave Greer was hoist with the petard of his considered refusal to address this inquiry once plaintiffs proved substantial and continuing discrimination by school authorities. Greer had lost his "all-or-nothing" defense because the Court would not accept the incredible post hoc rationalization that the great Dayton flood of 1913 parted the races. In the end Dave Greer did not confound Ella Taylor Lowrey or the Supreme Court.

In both cases, Justice White noted the repeated refusal of the school boards in Dayton and Columbus to respond to notice of the effects of their actions or omissions. At times the boards themselves had expressed recognition of their responsibility, but ultimately they did "nothing." The detailed proof of segregative practices and available desegregative alternatives provided by Gordon Foster and Bill Lamson combined with the notice provided by the likes of Barbee Durham, Wayne Carle, and John Harewood to convince the Supreme Court that urban school segregation resulted in substantial part from intentional school board discrimination, not happenstance, voluntary choice, or economics.

This conclusion, however, was not readily accepted by Burger and Stewart and was totally rejected by Powell and Rehnquist. Burger joined Stewart in "defer[ring] to the trier of fact." Somehow, both Carl Rubin and Robert Duncan were right. For Burger and Stewart, it was the facts, not the trial court opinions, that differed. This anomalous result was abetted because both the chief justice and Potter Stewart refused to embrace our *Brown* argument that proof of a dual system at any time after 1954 imposed an affirmative duty on school authorities to desegregate. Burger also shared "many of the concerns expressed by Mr. Justice Powell with regard to use of massive transportation as a remedy. It is becoming increasingly doubtful that massive transportation really accomplishes the desirable objectives sought. Nonetheless our prior decisions have sanctioned its use when a constitutional violation of sufficient magnitude has been found. We cannot retry these sensitive and difficult issues in this Court."

Stewart also found himself bound to abide by prior precedent to this extent. Although arguing that "it is unrealistic to assume that the hand of 1954 plays any major part in shaping the current school systems in either Columbus or Dayton," he agreed with Judge Duncan that the extensive violations continuing right through the trial created under the Denver decision a probable case of systemwide liability, which the board failed to rebut. In addition, Judge Duncan had given Porter every opportunity to show that specific white schools "were so far removed from the center of Negro population that the unconstitutional actions of the board may not have affected them at all. But the defendants did not carry the burden necessary to exclude these schools." In Stewart's eyes the school board had to pay for Porter's refusal to present evidence at the remedy hearing on this issue in the face of Judge Duncan's express invitation.

As to Dayton, Stewart reached the opposite result by concluding that the court of appeals "seems simply to have differed with the trial court's factual assessment, without offering a reasoned explanation of how the trial court's finding fell short." I doubted that Potter Stewart could make such an assertion to Harry Phillips face-to-face. For Stewart, the rule in school cases appeared to be to let the trial judges decide whatever they wish on the issues of intent and causation, without meaningful review by the courts of appeals and by the Supreme Court.

For Justice Powell, White's opinions in Columbus and Dayton were "profoundly disturbing." They "seem remarkably insensitive to the now widely accepted view that a quarter of a century after [*Brown*], the federal judiciary should be limiting rather than expanding the extent to which courts are operating the public school systems of our country." Such rhetoric extended to his characterization of White's opinion: "[T]he Court indulges the courts below in their stringing together of a chain of 'presumptions,' not one of which is close enough to reality to be reasonable." Elsewhere, Powell characterized the Court's legal standards as fictions and its legal reasoning as unprincipled. He called all current segregation de facto, based on the assertion that the "type of state-enforced segregation that *Brown* properly condemned no longer exists in this country." Powell reached this conclusion by labelling de facto the continuing segregation considered by the Court in *Swann*. In short, Powell sought to legitimize urban segregation, North and South, on the claim that it resulted from "familiar segregated housing patterns . . . for which no school board is responsible," nor apparently *any* other government agency—local, state, or federal. Justice Powell chose to ignore the contrary proof, findings, and perspective of Judge Duncan.

Powell proceeded to add one other defense for continued segregation. Court-ordered busing, not the continuing process for ghettoization, in his opinion, was responsible for "resegregation" in the nation's cities. The majority's "wholesale substitution of judicial legislation for the judgments of elected officials and professional educators derogates the entire process of public education.'' The former Richmond school board president concluded his opinion by conceding that courts "should confront discrimination wherever it is found to exist" but advising in the next breath that "the responsibility for public education, including the bringing about and maintaining of desired diversity, must be left with school officials and public authorities.'' In the end, Lewis Powell viewed racial segregation in America as a matter of "voluntary choice," just as he viewed integration as a matter of "voluntary diversity.'' Powell apparently wished both were beyond the purview, and the jurisdiction, of the federal courts.

Justice Rehnquist was even more direct in his dissent. Although he joined in expressing his distaste for federal court displacement of local authority, he called the majority opinions "a lick and a promise.'' He sought to interpret *Brown*'s progeny as requiring school boards "to do no more than simply permit black students to attend white schools and vice versa.'' He suggested that the majority's rulings in Columbus and Dayton II "dramatically depart from [the Denver decision] by relieving school desegregation plaintiffs from any showing of a causal nexus between intentional segregative action and the conditions they seek to remedy.'' Rehnquist then rewrote the facts to argue that school authorities in Columbus and Dayton engaged in at most "isolated" segregative acts with incremental effects of limited scope and duration. He criticized the majority's "preoccupation with 'an affirmative duty' exhumed from the conduct of past generations to be imposed without regard to the forces that actually shaped the racial imbalance.''

For Rehnquist, segregation remained the natural and nondiscriminatory norm:

> Virtually every urban area in this country has racially and ethnically identifiable neighborhoods, doubtless resulting from a melange of past happenings prompted by economic considerations, private discrimination, discriminatory school assignments, or a desire to reside near people of one's own race or ethnic background.

Rehnquist discounted the evidence and Duncan's findings concerning the origins of the urban color line and the causal interrelationship between school and housing segregation on the twin assumptions that residential segregation exists wholly apart from discrimination and that the precise impact of housing and school segregation can be parsed.

Given Judge Duncan's focused inquiry, and the marshalling of proof by all parties to address the issues of intent and causation, Rehnquist's final conclusion was a fantasy: "[I]t is clear in this case that critical questions regarding causality and purpose were not asked at all.'' The real problem for

William Rehnquist was that both questions were addressed and answered by Robert Duncan, but the answers went contrary to Rehnquist's personal view of reality.

The Reaction

After several years of increasingly bitter internal strife on the Court over the issue of urban segregation, the *Washington Post* commented, the "sharp language of the dissenters—in particular, that of William Rehnquist—will most likely rekindle the drive for a constitutional amendment on school busing." The *Post* added:

> It provides the picture of a court divided within itself, inconsistent, and prepared to see its members exchanging cheap shots on almost any occasion. Perhaps it was fitting that the last day of the term had its own peculiarity. In an unprecedented action, the chief justice announced the court was adjourning for the summer but its "term" would be extended until October 1. No one, except the justices, knows what that means. It sounds as if they need a vacation.

The antibusing forces, however, were not ready to take a break. In Columbus, they threatened a school boycott, began to prepare kits for "home instruction," and swore their allegiance to Representative Mottl's antibusing amendment. By a vote of seven to two, the Columbus Board of Education endorsed such a constitutional amendment. In Dayton, school superintendent John Maxwell added, desegregation is "killing us. Nobody wants it. . . . Looks like we're dead unless we get a constitutional amendment." At the same time, both boards authorized the filing of petitions in the Supreme Court to rehear the cases. Expressing indignation at the Court's action, Dave Greer wrote:

> The net effect of the majority opinion in this case, we respectfully submit, is the achievement of racial balance among students in public school classrooms at the expense of Constitutional, equitable and jurisdictional doctrines carefully developed in prior cases. Those doctrines should not be lightly altered to achieve a result, no matter how socially desirable such a result may seem to be. Nor is the desirability of the result unequivocal. In a free and open society, neither a court by fiat or a school board by discriminatory action should select its own society and shut the door.

But such visceral reaction was not shared by others. Columbus mayor Tom Moody declared that the community "can live with [the Court's] decision and build upon it.'' Tom Atkins was even more matter of fact: ''My principal reaction is the decision will mean that the desegregation plan that was to go into effect last September will go into effect this September.''

John Harewood continued in his retirement to work with community groups for peaceful integration, racial understanding, and educational excellence; but he feared that the S.O.S. board, as symbolized by Superintendent Maxwell's remarks, was not working to implement this goal. As Harewood looked back over the ten-year court struggle, he was disheartened that

> all this time has been spent on something so open and shut. Objectively, Dayton has been an intentionally segregated community in schools and housing. It's too bad the case had to drag on this way so long. But, in the end, I *never* doubted that right would eventually prevail. Now we can get about the unfinished business of genuinely integrating the Dayton Public Schools and breaking down the white suburban barriers to racial equality. That may require a change in local leadership and the invocation of metropolitan solutions. But the greater Dayton community *will* eventually see that all our schools and facilities must be put to good use to educate all our children. We'll learn that no one, black or white, is entitled to a racial sanctuary or a one-race preserve; and that we must learn to live, work, and educate together if the Country is to move forward rather than split asunder.

Phyllis Greer felt much the same way. She had been disheartened by the utter futility of the delays imposed by Judge Rubin, the murder of Charles Glatt, and the S.O.S. board's failure to address educational needs with its preoccupation with fighting segregation. But she had not given up, and the new decision renewed her hope that people and commitment could make a difference and allow a new beginning for the Dayton community.

Helen Jenkins Davis also felt vindicated by the Court's decision. The majority on the high court had not yet become immune to pleas for racial justice. Now it was time for the children to go to school together to learn about one another firsthand ''in a little United Nations'' rather than through the ''hate propaganda of segregation.'' For Barbee Durham, the Court's decision represented a culmination of his life struggle against ''separatism.'' Others, such as Maynard Dickerson, did not live to witness the decision. Barbee Durham and his wife took Mrs. Dickerson to dinner on the night of the Court's ruling to break bread together and to share the moment and all of their memories. Barbee Durham also viewed the impending desegregation of Columbus schools as only a start: the students deserved a good integrated education, and the white suburban havens would eventually have to be opened in order to eliminate the color line of white protection and to reverse the engine of caste, racial ghettoization.

The vote in the House of Representatives on Mottl's antibusing amendment was scheduled for July 24. The *Washington Post* urged the House to reject the proposal: Busing "can be useful and sometimes is the only tool available to break up historic patterns of open discrimination. By voting to bar its use in any situation, the House would be declaring that the constitutional rights of some students to equal treatment can *never* be enforced. The House should reject this effort to cripple the ability of courts and school boards to correct racial injustices." The *New York Times* asked whether desegregation opponents wished to trivialize the Constitution by adding a "right to walk." The *Times* continued: the proposed amendment "flies in the face of evidence, validated by the Supreme Court, that deliberate school segregation persists and that busing is the only suitable remedy. . . . To forbid all mandatory busing would leave *no* remedy of such indisputable wrongs. It would overturn an important meaning of the Fourteenth Amendment and virtually rescind the 1954 *Brown* decision." The House Republican Policy Committee and the House Republican Conference refused to endorse the Mottl amendment. Democratic House leaders, the Black Caucus, and Clarence Mitchell's coalition of labor, civil rights, religious, and minority groups led the opposition. The antibusing forces lobbied just as intensively in the halls and anterooms of Congress.

During an emotional four-hour debate, Republican representative John Anderson received a standing ovation when he said, "We are seeking to elevate above equal protection of the law the neighborhood school. You are going to divide this country. . . . If you have no remedy to enforce [the] right [to be free from intentional segregation], what a hollow, meaningless thing it becomes. . . . This is the wrong time, the wrong place, the wrong way in which to tamper with the Constitution of the United States." Mottl retorted: "[F]orced busing is the creation of a judiciary run amok. . . . [It's] judicial terrorism." Democratic representative Mendel Davis, a conservative from South Carolina, answered: "We should be more concerned for the welfare of the children rather than the emotions of the parents. . . . [A ban on busing] would turn the clock back on the cause of human rights." Arkansas representative Bill Alexander added, "The question of busing has been resolved. I can see no value in resurrecting this issue." William Gray, a black Democrat from Philadelphia, concluded: "It's not the yellow bus, it's the black and brown and red and yellow us."

The final vote told the story. The proposal failed to gain a simple majority, much less the necessary two-thirds majority. The vote was 216 to 209 *against* Mottl, with 176 Democrats and 40 Republicans joining together to stop the antibusing amendment in its tracks. Louis Stokes, Mottl's counterpart from the black core in Cleveland, expressed his hope that the vote would "end once and for all the simmering dispute and send a clear signal to the Country that Congress will not stand in the way of court-ordered reassignment of school children'' to end segregation. Although Pat Buchanan had advised President Nixon at the beginning of the decade that the "ship of integration is sinking," it was still afloat at the end.

To Nate Jones that represented a more important triumph than his appointment to the Sixth Circuit. In the Court's decisions in Dayton II and Columbus and the defeat of the Mottl amendment, the retiring NAACP general counsel "hoped for finality in the law on the reality of *de jure* segregation. That could lead Congress, the Executive and its agencies, the states and local school and housing officials, and private business to take responsible, affirmative action to formulate policies and implement programs to eliminate segregation in our great metropolitan communities. I think we have reversed the drive to preserve and promote segregation that Nixon spawned." At the very least, the events of the summer of 1979 reminded black leaders that segregation is an integral part of the overall problem of institutional racial bias in this country.

The Supreme Court, however, had not been direct in reminding America that the Second Reconstruction has yet to be completed. White's ruling took the narrowest tack in affirming the Sixth Circuit. There was no more analysis of the interlocking web of discrimination found by Judge Duncan in the Columbus community than there had been of Judge Roth's similar findings in the Detroit school case. There was no discussion of broader state responsibility to afford protection from such a caste system of racial ghettoization; the focus was still on the acts of the local school board viewed in isolation from the greater wrong.

The results in Dayton II and Columbus were different from the results in Dayton I and Detroit; but the Court was still talking in terms of narrow legalisms rather than a broader appeal to the nation as a whole to confront any legacy of racism that may still divide the country into two societies. Justice White never explained to the people his summary rejection of the Rehnquist/Powell thesis that racial separation in the country is an innocent matter of personal choice and voluntary ethnic clustering. There certainly was no assurance in White's opinion that a majority of the Supreme Court would support the lower courts in the Wilmington case.

Epilogue

There were additional hitches in implementing systemwide desegregation in Columbus. Under the Court's rules, Sam Porter's petition for rehearing automatically stayed the Supreme Court's mandate because of the Court's curious continuation of the 1978–79 term until the justices returned from their summer vacations in the fall. As this mandate was the "further order" that would ordinarily have lifted Justice Rehnquist's stay, plaintiffs faced the prospect of yet another year's delay due to an unintended procedural mix-up. While the Columbus board, Sam Porter, and Judge Duncan dutifully planned for fall implementation unaware of the problem, Chachkin filed a motion asking the Court either to issue the mandate forthwith or to vacate Rehnquist's stay so that relief would be delayed no longer. Seizing on his last hope, Porter opposed Chachkin's motion and asked the court to stay the issuance of the mandate until it acted on the rehearing petitions.

On July 28, 1979, the full Court cut through the procedural foul-up: "It is ordered that the stay entered by Justice Rehnquist on August 11, 1978, is vacated. It is further ordered that the judgment of this Court shall issue forthwith. Mr. Justice Rehnquist took no part in the consideration or decision of these orders." With that statement, systemwide desegregation could finally begin in Columbus at the start of the 1979–80 school year, more than six years after the case had been filed. On October 1, 1979, the Court perfunctorily denied the rehearing petitions of the Columbus and Dayton boards.

In the days before the opening of school in September, the *Columbus Citizen-Journal* called desegregation "the law of the land. . . . [A]ll citizens should obey it. . . . More important, all citizens should cooperate in the peaceful implementation of that law—for the sake of all Columbus children and the future of our community." The Metropolitan Columbus Schools Committee, which worked so hard to make desegregation work, took out a full page ad with a more upbeat message: "New faces, new places. But school is *still* school. And we wish every Columbus parent and student an enjoyable and successful school year." School opened to a full house. There was no boycott, no violence, only the beginning of the business of children learning together rather than apart. Only a plot to bomb the school attended by Judge Duncan's children marred the calm; but local officials and federal authorities intervened before any damage could be done. The difficult problems of within-school discrimination, "white flight," the racial barriers of some all-white suburban sanctuaries, and the continuing job of teaching all the children still had to be faced. Columbus had the resources, and the incentive, to face these new challenges.

There was also a new beginning in court before Judge Duncan. On the remand from the Sixth Circuit to determine the liability of the state board of education for the intentional school segregation in Columbus, Atkins and Caldwell discovered that the state regularly made reports until 1955 on the "Number of Separate Schools for Colored Children" in at least eighteen different school districts. In the face of the state defendants' claim of ignorance throughout a decade of litigation with the NAACP, these reports dramatically demonstrated the state's knowledge, and continued support and funding, of separate schools. All along, the state had known what the plaintiffs in Dayton and Columbus had taken years painstakingly to prove: School authorities throughout Ohio created and maintained two separate sets of schools, one for whites and another for blacks. Moreover, this dual system was not a local aberration; segregated education was the state's covert but nonetheless intended policy and effective custom at the time of *Brown*. In 1955 the state board stopped reporting on "separate schools" but continued to fund the state's system of dual schooling.

As a result, Caldwell and Atkins amended the plaintiffs' complaint in order to seek statewide relief against the state board of education to dismantle Ohio's system of school segregation. Although Judge Duncan limited his ruling to finding the state school authorities liable for school segregation in Columbus, the decision could mark another critical turning point in the NAACP struggle against urban segregation throughout Ohio. The Sixth Circuit eventually affirmed this judgment against state officials, and the Supreme Court declined the state's petition to review the decision. The stage was thus set in Ohio for a broad statewide legal challenge to segregation, in schools and housing, throughout each major metropolitan area.

In Delaware, the second year of areawide desegregation in northern New Castle County opened and continued as peacefully as the first. Chief Justice Burger's description in the Detroit case of the supposedly insurmountable practical problems with interdistrict desegregation had been disproven by the careful work and leadership of district judge Murray Schwartz and the majority of parents, students, and teachers in the black and white communities in the Wilmington area. That cross-district remedies are administratively, financially, and governmentally feasible should have come as no surprise to a nation which had witnessed the successful consolidation or reorganization of literally thousands of school districts during the past thirty years. In truth, the mechanics of interdistrict relief present no real barrier to metropolitan school integration.

There were, however, many challenges in the desegregation of New Castle County schools. The legislature and state board initially provided no active support for the new board and the single district and finally split the consolidated district into four smaller, albeit still desegregated districts. At the same time, there was growing concern in the black community that the mostly white suburban staff, particularly at some junior and senior high schools, was meting out discipline more harshly to blacks than whites and steering minority youngsters into "slow classes" and "dead-end tracks" with little prospect of learning, college, or employment. Some parents, and many representatives in the legislature, called for a no-nonsense crackdown on alleged disorderly conduct in the schools. "White flight" caused another 5 percent drop in enrollment, but 10 percent of the whites who had fled New Castle County public schools in the prior year returned. Many blacks and whites shared a commitment to break down all aspects of the color line in school life so that black and white children could learn, achieve, and live together in the years ahead. For almost two full school years the continuing pendency in the Supreme Court of the state board's petition to review the entire case, however, prevented many more from giving their full support.

At times, Joe Johnson was frustrated by the lack of commitment by state and local officials: "[U]ntil every member of the community, black and white, knows that a full and equitable program of integrated schooling is the rule and the practice of top leadership, there will be continuing racial division and distrust in Delaware." He also feared a national retrenchment on the issue of race and segregation.

Despite the many symbols of racial equality minted by the Carter administration, the president's first three years in office were also marked by:

- an HEW that Congress stripped of all enforcement power to halt school segregation except through the tedious process of referral to the Justice Department for suit;
- a Justice Department that initiated only a handful of suits against school segregation, refused to prosecute all but one of the school cases referred by HEW, and had no effective plan to challenge continuing racial ghettoization in schools, housing, and the location and development of industry and community facilities; and
- a HUD that was only beginning to consider the practical alternatives to continued subsidization of segregation.

In its fourth year, however, the Carter administration had begun to move. Under Drew Days's guidance the Civil Rights Division initiated metropolitan school and housing cases in several communities and successfully challenged exclusionary white suburbs elsewhere to open their doors to blacks who wanted to move closer to expanding job opportunities. HUD began to develop areawide housing assistance programs based on the *Gautreaux* principle to provide black families with a wider range of housing choice, while stimulating capital investment and jobs in the central cities.

In addition, the Supreme Court, in a opinion by Chief Justice Burger, affirmed and encouraged Congress's power to act creatively and effectively to remedy the persisting effects of caste discrimination in all walks of American life. In a separate concurring opinion, Justice Powell added: "Congress properly may—indeed must—address directly the problems of discrimination in our society. . . . [There is] a compelling governmental interest in redressing racial discrimination." Justice Marshall, joined by Justices Brennan and Blackmun, concluded, "If we are ever to become a fully integrated society . . . , we must take steps to open . . . doors [that] . . . for far too [long] have been shut to Negroes."

Johnson, however, feared that the majority in the country was unsympathetic to any further action against racial inequality, and he worried that many in the black community were either losing hope or coming grimly to accept segregation as the hard reality of black life in white America. He feared that the election of Ronald Reagan would mark a turn for the worse on the public mood and national commitment to racial justice. With the ''built-in time bomb of impoverished single-parent black families in urban ghettoes'' and ''black unemployment doubling'' and tripling during another numbing recession, Joe Johnson feared that a new wave of riots was in the offing: ''[B]lack people can't take the continued pressure of caste inequality forever. Too many are still forced to look at whites-only opportunities from the outside, fenced out just as I was as a boy from the white community center across the street from my home.'' To a large degree the opening and then racial transition of that community center only marked a shift in the whites-only fences, not the end of racial segregation.

Yet Joe Johnson was still acting to break down the barriers between white and black in the Wilmington area; appointed as the superintendent for one of the four new districts in the Wilmington area, he still worked to make schooling and integration work. He just wasn't ''sure there is enough time or commitment to get the job done.'' He concluded, ''Our best hope for the time being rests with the courts and the black community hanging tough on the segregation issue; that may yet force public consideration and constructive action.''

District judge Murray Schwartz appeared to share Johnson's frustration. The state's continued appeals to overturn his decisions, the state's initial refusal to support the plan and quality education for all Delaware schoolchildren, and the local administrators' failure to use desegregation as an opportunity to come to grips with the educational crisis in American public schooling, all seemed to rankle Schwartz as a concerned citizen. Like so many other federal judges who determined to follow the law, however, he could not interfere; having set out the constitutional ground rules, the courts had to rely on the responsible federal, state, and local officials, the administrators and teachers, and the parents and children not only to implement the decision but to make the schools work to achieve excellence and a genuinely integrated society without racial caste, hostility, or suspicion.

Perhaps one incident at the height of concern over initial implementation of the desegregation plan symbolized the limited role of the trial judge. Judge Schwartz requested that federal marshalls provide protection to his family at home. Murray Schwartz recounted the response: ''They told me there was no need for concern at home but advised me to wear a bullet-proof vest while sitting on the bench in a heavily guarded federal courthouse.'' The independence of the federal judiciary can be very lonely at times. In the end, a federal judge could only point a direction; others must then step forward to lead the way to insure a safe, and ultimately redeeming, journey. When Delaware sought to divide the single school district into four separate districts, Judge Schwartz delayed approval only for so long as it took the legislature, the state board, and the new districts to establish a framework of coordination and oversight that offered some promise of insuring the workability of desegregated schooling throughout the area.

Louis Redding, whose conscience had stirred Delaware for the past fifty years, did not view the battle as over. When asked whether the metropolitan plan would work in northern Delaware, he replied:

> I don't know. It will depend on a whole spectrum of opportunity in housing and jobs. School integration is critical, but it is only one factor in eliminating the color line. It's taken 25 years to get this far in Delaware to dismantle dual schooling; and we still have a ways to go. Ultimately, I hope my work will contribute to making this community, and this nation, a decent, democratic place to live for all people. Without such efforts over the past decades and the years ahead, that full and free life will remain beyond the reach of most Negroes in America.

Louis Redding then lowered his voice and raised his sad eyes and proud head: "It hasn't been an easy life for me in Delaware compared to many of my white classmates at Harvard Law School. But I have reaped some reward. I believe that efforts like mine have made life a little better for blacks and, I believe, will bear even sweeter fruit in the future."

Redding's eyes then brightened considerably as he described his twenty-six-year-old daughter's medical research in Tanzania. Her graduation from Cornell Medical School and further training at the University of North Carolina Medical School made her father proud. Her plan to specialize in tropical diseases, however, concerned Louis Redding. He remarked ruefully:

> I've fought all my life so that America would give her the opportunity to live a decent, full and humane life. After all this, she may be planning to practice medicine for a good portion of her career in Africa. I can only hope that any such decision will be based on purely philanthropic reasons not because America found no way to accept the Negro citizen on free and equal terms at home. At that point, I will count my blessings but miss my daughter's close company.

The *Wilmington News Journal* summed up: "In northern New Castle County, we have made a beginning, but no more than that. . . . [T]here is promise in the beginnings, not of a perfectly integrated society in our time, but of increasingly better opportunities for all our children."

In Detroit, however, there was only more waiting for a new beginning.

Hearing on the amended complaint for interdistrict relief was still mired in procedural wrangling as proceedings on all aspects of "desegregation" within the Detroit school district finally wound down before a special panel of three federal district judges. Judge Edwards had displayed his frustration at the oral argument on the latest appeal: "The black schools in the inner core were the primary target of the intentionally segregative conduct found by Judge Roth in his 1971 ruling. As a result of the violations found, they were virtually all black in 1971. They are still the all-black product of the violation ten years later."

On April 14, 1980, senior judge Phillips had so held for a unanimous panel:

> [T]he [state and local] defendants' discriminatory policies helped to drive whites from the Detroit school district and to contain blacks in an ever-expanding core area of the city. . . . [T]he unconstitutional actions of the defendants, both local and state, contributed to the segregated residential patterns and the one race [blacks-only] schools that now exist in Detroit. . . . [T]he record demonstrates that [the] population changes themselves are in part vestiges of past discrimination.

The tragedy was that the Sixth Circuit's understanding of this broader wrong and the interdependence of school and housing segregation had not been articulated in its initial rulings in the Detroit case; then, perhaps, a majority on the Court could not have avoided the issue. Phillips concluded by reminding the district court of its *"obligation* to proceed with the *interdistrict* litigation, if pursued by plaintiffs." Whatever the final outcome, the late Judge Roth's concern still haunted the protracted proceedings: "I wonder how many minority children have, during the pendency of this case, forever lost their right to attend a nonsegregated school."

On April 28, 1980, the Supreme Court finally refused to hear Delaware's claim that areawide desegregation of New Castle County schools exceeded any conceivable interdistrict segregation violation. Justice Rehnquist, joined by Justices Stewart and Powell, dissented from this final denial of Supreme Court review by calling the "county-wide remedy more Draconian than any ever approved by this Court." Once again substituting rhetoric and his personal vision of reality for the evidence, facts found, and remedy ordered by the courts below, Rehnquist likened the cautiously tailored pupil reassignments and provisional consolidation to a "railroad in reorganization."

Once again, Justice Stevens took no part in consideration of the case; but this time, Thurgood Marshall joined Justices Brennan, White, and Blackmun to deny any further state attempt to overturn the case. Marshall's move offset Stewart's defection to the Rehnquist line. In the face of a divided court of only eight justices sitting, Chief Justice Burger also chose to vote to decline review of the case, even while agreeing that the issues raised "merit review here but only when a *full* Court is available to consider the important issues present-ed." With a similarly uninformative summary disposition of the Atlanta case, in which a trial court rejected interdistrict school desegregation relief, the high court by a five-to-three vote (Justice Marshall not sitting) obscured its ultimate view of proof of areawide, intentional segregation and the propriety of any areawide remedy.

Justice Powell still refused to accept the majority's final decision that discrimination is a fundamental cause of racial segregation of schools in urban areas. When the chief justice joined Justices White, Brennan, Marshall, Blackmun, and Stevens to dismiss review of a case of systemwide violation in the Dallas school district, Justice Powell was joined by Justices Stewart and Rehnquist in another bitter dissent making yet another call to constitutionalize segregation:

> [T]his case presents a long-needed opportunity to re-examine the consid-erations relevant to framing a remedy in a desegregation suit. . . . [U]se of the busing remedy to achieve racial balance . . . [has] had the primary affect of stimulating resegregation. . . . In large cities, the principle cause of segregation in the schools is residential, which results from demographic and economic conditions over which school authorities have no control. . . . By acting against one-race schools, courts may produce one-race systems [as white] parents with school-age children [exit] to the suburbs.

Powell's "white flight" defense for continued central city school segregation, of course, was premised on white America's perpetuation of a virtually all-black core for minorities and exclusive suburban sanctuaries for whites. Jus-tice Powell urged the federal judiciary to leave any solution to the problems of segregation entirely to legislators and executive officials, rather than exercise its constitutional mandate to decide the cases and controversies brought by minority petitioners on their actual merits.

Like many others, Justice Powell sought once again to avoid responsibil-ity for the continuing engine of racial caste—black ghettoization and white protection—in metropolitan America. While other members of the Court at least left this issue open, the Lewis Powells of the land still preached the default of the Nixon segregation legacy. After a decade of struggle to keep the Second Reconstruction alive in the courts and throughout the nation, they inconsistently preached that racial discrimination had been largely conquered, had little to do with continuing segregation, presented an intractable problem, or was someone else's responsibility.

At times, President Reagan seemed bent on this same abdication of responsibility. He decried "forced busing" and "judicial activism," opposed affirmative action to overcome any continuing effects of past discrimination, supported tax exemptions for racially discriminatory private schools, virtually ignored the ghetto and racial exclusion in whites-only enclaves altogether, and promised the appointment of justices who would leave decision (and default) on such policy issues to popularly elected officials. On other occasions, however, the president proclaimed his opposition to racial discrimination against historically disadvantaged minorities, personally extended his sympathy to black homeowners terrorized by Klan intimidation in an otherwise white suburban area only minutes from the nation's Capitol, and extolled the right of every American to move and to live anywhere in the land. Viewed together, Reagan's diverse statements revealed little understanding of the basic race issue, while his administration acted consistently to reverse the belated initiatives by his predecessor to begin to challenge racial segregation in metropolitan America.

In opposing busing without providing any alternatives and obscuring the discriminatory underpinnings of segregation in America, the Justice Powells of the Court and the country seek to allow the American people to avoid the fundamental dilemma posed by pervasive racial segregation in metropolitan America. Until that condition is directly faced, the hard lessons of the segregation cases of the 1970s will have yet to be learned. Over time, desegregation of compulsory systems of public schooling may, or may not, prove a part of an overall remedy. The efficacy of such "forced busing," however, has never been the important issue. The challenge is not how to invent another excuse for refusing to act to end segregation but how to proceed in the years ahead to eliminate any continuing color line from the American landscape. The critical question remains whether this one nation will ever act together to overcome a caste system of racial ghettoization that has divided the people of our nation into two societies. The segregation cases of the 1970s did not resolve this issue, but they did succeed in keeping it alive.

Conclusion

The preceding chapters have attempted to tell a story of the school and housing segregation cases of the 1970s from the inside as they happened. In this sense, the book may offer a limited perspective because it portrays the apparent certitude of one side in the midst of a complex, adversary struggle. Yet the narrative avoids the false certainty that many pundits seem to find with the benefit of hindsight and the dubious objectivity of others who claim to be neutral observers rather than participants in the continuing debate over the nature, causes, and consequences of the extensive racial separation that still pervades our schools, housing, and community life. My contemporaneous understanding of the cases, therefore, may offer some insights that merit reflection.

Consider the constraints imposed by traditional legal thinking on the Supreme Court's review of the segregation cases of the 1970s. This view of the judicial process is premised on a bipolar controversy in which a court decides a dispute between two parties and then provides a complete remedy to the plaintiff victim to overcome the precise effects of any particular wrong committed by the defendant. This approach does not begin to comprehend what a case challenging pervasive discrimination is all about. In *Brown,* the Warren Court recognized as much when it declared Jim Crow segregation unconstitutional because it was hurtful to human beings, even though the Court could not define the nature of the wrong with any clarity and deferred consideration of the scope of any meaningful remedy for years.

In the segregation cases of the 1970s, Justices Rehnquist and Powell nevertheless argued that the judicial inquiry must be narrowly focused on wrongdoing by particular local officials, viewed in isolation from the historic context of any larger wrong and from any constitutional duty of each state as a whole to afford protection from community customs of caste. Any remedies would then be carefully tailored to do no more than overcome the incremental effects of a particular defendant's specific wrong on current conditions. From this perspective it was easy for these justices, who did not have to confront the conflicting evidence in person at trial, to rationalize racial segregation as the product of ethnic pluralism and voluntary choice rather than racial discrimination. Their concern over the apparent hostility to mandatory school desegregation remedies prompted use of such techniques to avoid consideration of the two basic violation issues: Is the almost complete separation of blacks from whites across metropolitan America a legacy and continuing engine of caste? If so, should we as a people, through our state and federal governments, be held responsible for refusing to confront any such wrong? Instead, these justices sought to absolve white America from responsibility for the ghetto.

Yet other members of the Supreme Court, who seemed more sympathetic to minority claims of discrimination, also sought shelter in narrow legalisms: like their brethren on the Burger Court, they used the shibboleth that the nature of the violation determines the scope of the remedy, but to desegregate schools within local school districts rather than to rationalize racial segregation. For example, Justices White and Brennan focused their majority opinions for the Court in the Dayton, Columbus, and Denver cases on intentionally segregative acts of particular local officials and ignored the people's broader responsibility for pervasive racial separation in schools and housing.

District judges like Roth, Duncan, Wright, and Schwartz grappled with the evidence and their own conscience for months. They found an interlocking web of racial discrimination that contributed to racial segregation in all aspects of community life. Yet in every one of these cases the majority on the Burger Court sought to avoid the broader issue, whether the ruling legitimized or condemned particular aspects of racial separation. It was as if all of the justices were trapped by their fears that the only role for the Court in the shifting political tides concerning race in America was to justify (or to avoid) particular remedies by narrowing the focus of the judicial inquiry of right and wrong to clearly identifiable, racist acts by specific officials.

In the process, the advocates who tried their cases in trial courts to prove a broader understanding of caste discrimination in America generally had to narrow their cases in the appellate courts in order to have a better chance of ultimately prevailing. When they could not, as in the first round of the Detroit case in the Supreme Court, a majority of the justices simply refused to plumb the deepest meaning of *Brown* for the issue of racial containment in a metropolitan context. Instead, Chief Justice Burger hypothesized extreme difficulties for cross-district busing, rhapsodized about local autonomy, blamed Judge Roth for looking beyond the boundaries of the center-city school district, criticized plaintiffs for not raising any broader issue at the outset of the case, and refused to review the proof and findings of an areawide system of racial containment. In contrast, in Columbus, where Judge Duncan also found such a pervasive system of racial ghettoization in all aspects of community life, the plaintiffs prevailed in the Supreme Court only on the narrowest theory of school officials' intentionally segregative conduct that would justify systemwide school desegregation.

This book's narrative story of the segregation cases of the 1970s, of course, reveals other trial judges who were at least confused by the high court's narrow vision. Yet, for those trial judges who were willing to put up with extensive hearings, the evidence and argument did move them as human beings responsible for making independent judgments. While Judge Roth may provide the most dramatic example of such a conversion, even Judge Rubin was moved a little by the limited evidence he was willing to hear, at least until he chose to follow Justice Rehnquist's apparent call to immunize school authorities from any responsibility for incorporating pervasive residential segregation in neighborhood schools. Yet Rubin still rejected the rationalization adopted by Powell and Rehnquist that residential segregation is a matter of voluntary choice and ethnic pluralism unrelated to public and private customs of caste discrimination.

Liberal or conservative, black or white, Republican or Democrat, most of these trial judges did not completely close their minds nor their rulings to the existence of some wrong if they were willing to hear evidence concerning the nature of the pervasive racial separation in metropolitan America. Indeed, the broader their purview, the more likely that findings of systemic wrong would emerge. In addition, the hearings on violation in the trial courts focused on the nature and extent of the wrong rather than on the scope of any remedy. Only after some appreciation of the depth of the wrong had been grasped and violation rulings made did trial judges consider similarly sweeping relief at subsequent hearings on remedy.

In contrast, the Supreme Court proceedings were limited to a written brief and a thirty-minute oral argument. Several justices were more concerned with the limited authority of courts to intervene to impose remedies than with the duty of courts independently to declare rights and wrongs based on considered review of the evidence and constitutional values. In this context, it is not surprising that the Chicago public housing case was the only time the full Court in the 1970s unequivocally and unanimously embraced an areawide view of the wrong of racial ghettoization: any remedy would involve only the opening of federal housing subsidies to a few hundred black families each year who might choose to escape the officially designated blacks-only projects in the center-city ghetto by renting apartments in garden townhouses in otherwise whites-only suburbs.

Even in that case, however, the Court avoided any real consideration of the potential wrong of pervasive segregation in a major metropolis. Justice Stewart, who wrote the opinion, made no reference to his 1968 ruling in *Jones v. Mayer* wherein he had declared that when racial discrimination herds blacks into ghettos and excludes minorities from whites-only communities, that, too, is as much a relic of slavery as Jim Crow and antimiscegenation laws. After all, how could Justice Stewart writing in the Chicago housing case in 1976 make any such ringing declaration of the wrong after he had written in the Detroit school case in 1974 that the causes of racial isolation of blacks from whites in urban America are unknown and unknowable?

As the desegregation cases moved from South to North in the 1970s, public opposition to desegregation also expanded. When the cases challenged segregation in their own backyards, northern whites could no longer safely blame bigoted white southerners for a regional race problem. In his pre–

World War II survey of *An American Dilemma,* Gunnar Myrdal had predicted that a system of social segregation would endure much longer than blatant Jim Crow laws: the spatial separation of blacks from whites in schools, housing, and community affairs would allow white America to live comfortably with a separate and unequal society because whites would not have to face blacks in daily life. This would allow whites to avoid feeling any personal responsibility for unequal conditions and any collective guilt for the continued racial segregation. The barrage of race cases in the 1970s rattled this smug complacency.

The ensuing controversy, however, did not narrow the perspectives of all of the justices on the Court. For example, although Justice Blackmun wrote relatively little in the major race cases in the 1970s, he moved to a broader appreciation of the wrong at issue at the same time as Stewart pulled back. While Stewart was moving to join Rehnquist and Powell in opinions denouncing school desegregation and proclaiming the innocence of most racial separation in America, Blackmun was moving to join Brennan, Marshall, and White in condemning school segregation in Dayton and Columbus and in refusing to overturn the experiment in metropolitan school desegregation for areawide caste discrimination in the Wilmington school case. In another case he added, "We cannot—we dare not—let Equal Protection perpetuate racial supremacy" under the guise of "colorblindness." Even in the face of the narrowing process of Supreme Court review in the Burger Court, the full range of segregation cases in the 1970s did not move every justice in the same direction.

I am often asked whether the benefits of the busing remedy to achieve school desegregation are worth the costs. Does desegregation lead to better education for black children? Will it assist in breaking down any caste barriers that may still separate blacks from whites in housing, jobs, and community life in metropolitan America? Has it worked well in any areas? Doesn't it fragment black political power? Doesn't it just promote white hostility to black deprivation and needs? Isn't it opposed on grounds of pragmatism and principle by large segments of black and white leadership who view it as counterproductive or just plain wrongheaded? Doesn't it inevitably impose greater burdens on black than white children and lead only to guaranteeing the subjugation of black minorities in majority white schools? Won't it lead to whites opting out of mixed public schools by transferring to private schools or moving to the next ring of whites-only suburbs?

I do not have any sure answers to these instrumental questions, and the narrative in this book offers none. The case histories only show that the fears about programs to expand minority housing opportunity and to implement systemic school desegregation remedy have not materialized in fact in these communities. Elsewhere, I have written about a range of policy options—including school, housing, job, and community development initiatives now being tried in a few communities, as well as innovative, comprehensive market approaches on the horizon—that can work together to begin to overcome segregation in all aspects of community life and to expand opportunities for all Americans in the decades ahead. I have also elaborated a constitutional standard—the anticaste principle—that could aid the Court and the country in facing the problem and considering such a broad range of remedial reforms in the years ahead. But such proposals are only suggestive, and many others may emerge if we have the will to look. The courts alone cannot implement any remedy, but can only stimulate thought by the people and action by the other institutions in our society. Thus, the purpose of the school and housing segregation cases of the 1970s, and this book, has been to pose a question for the courts and for the people: Is racial separation in America a legacy and an engine of caste discrimination, or is it a matter of voluntary choice and ethnic diversity? On that question, I have no doubt.

Perhaps, Judge Roth said it best:

> Residential segregation within the city and throughout the larger metropolitan area is substantial, pervasive and of long-standing. Black citizens are located in separate and distinct areas within the city and are not generally to be found in the suburbs. While the racially unrestricted choice of black persons and economic factors may have played some part in the development of this pattern of residential segregation, it is, in the main, the result of past and present practices and customs of racial discrimination, both public and private, which have and do restrict the housing opportunities of black people. . . . [T]he black population in the city grew and largely was contained therein by force of public and private racial discrimination at all levels. . . . On the record there can be no other finding. Governmental actions and inactions at all levels, federal, state, and local, have combined, with those of private organizations, such as loaning institutions and real estate associations and brokerage firms, to establish and to maintain the pattern of residential segregation throughout the . . . metropolitan area. . . . While it would be unfair to charge the [state and local school authorities] with what other governmental officers or agencies have done, it can be said that the actions or the failure to act by the responsible school authorities, city and state, were linked to that of these other governmental units. When we speak of governmental action, we should not view the different agencies as a collection of unrelated units. Perhaps, the most that can be said is that all of them, including school authorities, are, in part, responsible for the segregated condition which exists. We recognize that causation . . . is both several and com-

parative. The principal causes undeniably have been population movement and housing patterns, but state and local governmental actions, including school board actions, have played a substantial role in promoting segregation. . . . We need not minimize the effect of the actions of federal, state, and local governmental officers and agencies, and the actions of loaning institutions and real estate firms, in the establishment and maintenance of segregated residential patterns . . . to observe that . . . the ghetto is at once both a place of confinement and a refuge. There is enough blame for everyone to share.

Yet, it is easy for both white and black Americans to avoid consideration of the issue altogether because the very fact of separation means that we do not regularly confront the issue that much on a personal basis. There is no longer a Jim Crow law that openly proclaims white supremacy myths in conflict with our deepest ideals of liberty and equality. It is therefore easier to focus on short-term cost-benefit concerns about the scope of remedy than to confront the issue of the nature and extent of any wrong inhering in the racial separation that still pervades where we live, go to school, break bread, work, and go to church and with whom we socialize, communicate, make money, and network in our daily lives. It is easier to rationalize this separation as a matter of liberty and voluntary ethnic clustering than to recognize it as discrimination. It is easier to feign ignorance and claim innocence than to confront the issue and accept responsibility.

The Supreme Court is a uniquely independent judiciary. It could play a vital role in making us confront the basic issue by bringing it to the forefront of our national conscience. We are not well served by a Court that whitewashes claims of violation, argues that the judiciary ought not hear claims of general social injustice unless specific judicially manageable remedies running against particular wrongdoers are apparent, is so concerned about the extent of effective remedies that rationalizations of wrongs as innocent conditions overwhelm, or orders sweeping remedies on the narrowest judicial prescription that particular wrongs require specific remedies.

This narrow mind-set has trapped the vision of much of the Court and of the country. It is time for all of us to think again about the wrong of segregation in America and the right to be free from racial caste. If we confront that issue as lawyers and judges and elected officials and citizens, we may begin to see both our individual obligation and our institutional duty to accept responsibility for current segregation.

Compare the judicial decisions at the turn of the century following the end of the First Reconstruction with the Court's ruling in *Brown* signalling the beginning of the Second. In 1883 the Supreme Court held the 1875 Civil

Rights Act unconstitutional on the ground that Congress had no authority to protect blacks from private discrimination even in the face of a massive state default. The Court thereby effectively immunized community customs of caste from federal redress and authorized the states simply to look away from racial restrictions on the use of inns, theaters, restaurants, other public accommodations, and transportation and to turn a deaf ear to Klan subjugation, lynchings, and other forms of night-rider intimidation. In 1896 the Supreme Court ruled that a Jim Crow law requiring separate seating for blacks and whites on a public conveyance was constitutional on the specious grounds that it was not intended to impose any badge of inferiority on blacks and that it guaranteed formal equality under the law. In the wake of this decision, Jim Crow segregation became the American way of life. In 1903 the Supreme Court refused to find a violation of the Fifteenth Amendment when Alabama barred all blacks, even the tens of thousands who had voted for decades after the Civil War, from further voting on the dubious ground that the Court was powerless to provide any meaningful remedy in the face of the supposed massive white opposition to black suffrage. In the wake of this decision, the political voice of millions of blacks was effectively silenced for generations to come.

In 1954 the Warren Court also faced substantial opposition, had no idea of the appropriate remedy, and possessed less power to implement any meaningful relief. Nevertheless, the Warren Court pointed a new direction by declaring Jim Crow segregation unconstitutional. *Brown* marked the beginning of the Second Reconstruction, which gathered momentum through the civil rights movement and the national political response symbolized by the 1964 Civil Rights Act, the 1965 Voting Rights Act, and the 1968 Fair Housing Act.

We are still reaping the benefits of this watershed that finally eliminated official Jim Crow racism. Perhaps the most tangible has been the growth in the political power of racial minorities that has accompanied increased registration of black voters under the Voting Rights Act and the inspiration of the likes of Martin Luther King and Jesse Jackson. Thus far, this black political leadership (and the increasing number of elected black officials) still strives to open the doors of white economic, political, and community power to black folk, even while seeking to secure the wherewithal to allow poor black families to survive day by day, often hand to mouth, in inhospitable urban ghettos and rural poverty.

Yet the terms for securing wider support for survival and uplift are set in large measure by the caste segregation that still divides us. In Michigan, for example, Mayor Coleman Young, state representatives Sanders and Vaughan, and school board president Golightly have been informed by the white majority in the state, successive national administrations, and a one-vote majority on the

Supreme Court that they may seek solutions to the problems of racial ghettoization only from within the resulting area of black containment. Some increased state and federal aid will sometimes be forthcoming to ease the most immediate burdens of being confined within a center city that has lost and continues to lose much employment, business, tax base, and private capital to neighboring white suburbs; but any political logrolling by black interests will be limited to whites finally ceding local control of blacks-only ghettos to blacks. This limitation on the terms of the political debate harks back to the years immediately preceding *Brown* when many whites offered to put resources, and sometimes even black control, into woefully underfunded blacks-only schools as the price to maintain Jim Crow. Working together to solve the myriad problems of metropolitan America by breaching the basic color line has thus far proved beyond the ken of white America. For the most part, state legislatures, the national political process, and often the Burger Court have refused to look at the causes and consequences of the racial segregation that still pervades much of the country.

Perhaps we are all captives of the political pressures and legal formalisms of our time. As Justice Marshall wrote in his dissent from the Supreme Court's decision in the Detroit school case, "Today's holding, I fear, is more a reflection of a perceived public mood that we have gone far enough in enforcing the Constitution's guarantee of equal justice than it is the product of neutral principles of law. In the short run, it may seem to be the easier course to allow our great metropolitan areas to be divided up each into two cities—one white, the other black—but it is a course, I predict, our people will ultimately regret."

I persist in hoping, however, that some day again the Court will confront the wrong inhering in such pervasive racial segregation. If the Court would ever face *this* issue, we could still be inspired to do more than regret our contemporary, albeit substantially sanitized, form of apartheid. The Court's frank declaration of the basic wrong would provide a start. That might allow black political leaders like Jesse Jackson to point as boldly today to the gap between declared wrongs and current conditions as Martin Luther King did from 1957 through 1968. It would encourage local black community leaders like Joe Johnson and Lenny Williams to take up where Louis Redding left off in Delaware. It would offer hope to those who follow Nate Jones, Phyllis Greer, John Harewood, and Barbee Durham in communities throughout the country to continue to rebel against segregation. It might help precipitate understanding of the crises that we face today, just as John Kennedy was finally forced to confront the defenders of Jim Crow on a moral ground as a matter of political necessity. It would encourage all of us to think about whether we are willing to work together to complete the job of the Second Reconstruction or whether we are satisfied to end it on a compromise note as dissonant as the chord that closed the First Reconstruction.

Sources

The primary sources for this book are my personal observations as the events described unfolded, on-site investigations of fifteen urban areas from 1979 through 1981 to study the extent and impact of desegregation efforts, and my review of trial records, briefs on appeal, and judicial decisions. In addition, newspaper accounts, other secondary sources, and interviews with witnesses, lawyers, public officials, and concerned citizens that were conducted from July, 1979, to February, 1980, are utilized as follows.

Part 1:   Gerber, *Black Ohio and the Color Line*; and interviews with Phyllis Greer and John Harewood.

Part 2:   Bill Grant's numerous articles in the *Detroit Free Press*; Grant, ''The Detroit School Case''; E. Hain, ''School Desegregation in Detroit''; and interviews with Nate Jones, Bill Grant, and Lou Lucas.*

Part 3:   Interviews with Phyllis Greer, John Harewood, Nate Jones, and Lou Lucas.

Part 4:   Interviews with Alex Polikoff, Kale Williams, and David Tatel. Farley et al., ''Barriers to the Racial Integration of Neighborhoods''; Garland, ''Cabrini-Green to Willow Creek'' and ''Willow Creek Revisited''; ''The Gautreaux Decision and Its Effect on Subsidized Housing,'' Hawley and Rock, eds., *Segregation in Residential Areas*; Hermalin and Farley, ''The Potential for Residential Integration in Cities and Suburbs''; HUD, ''The Gautreaux Housing Demonstration'' and ''Preliminary Findings of the 1977 Housing Market Practice Survey''; Orfield, *Must We Bus*; Polikoff, *Housing the Poor*; Roof, ed., Symposium on ''Race and Residence in American

---

*Professor Wolfe, in her book *Trial and Error* (1981), challenges Judge Roth's understanding of the basic facts, and criticizes the evidentiary restrictions and tactical limitations on the types of inquiry undertaken in the case based on her reading of the written transcript. Although she concedes that the evidence of racial discrimination in housing was abundant (p. 80), she challenges the causal link between the current racial separation and that history of discrimination. She also challenges the proof that the school authorities acted intentionally to segregate any schools; and, even if they had, she questions whether their actions had any long-term impact in view of the pervasive racial separation that she sees as an innocent matter of voluntary clustering common to all ethnic groups and of socioeconomic life-style choices, neither of which school boards control. Her review of the transcript, however, misses all of the nuances and dynamics (e.g., visual exhibits, credibility of witnesses, electric revelations in demeanor) that might test her conception. In contrast, Judge Roth, who shared Wolfe's basic worldview before the trial in the case, was moved by the presentations in his courtroom to see a larger responsibility of the state as a whole for an interlocking web of public and private activities fueling a discriminatory system of racial ghettoization, in which school authorities play an important, but only contributing, part.

Cities''; Sorensen et al., ''Indexes of Racial Residential Segregation''; Taeuber, ''Demographic Perspectives in Housing and School Segregation'' and *Negroes in Cities*; Van Valey et al., ''Trends in Residential Segregation, 1960–1970.'' I also reviewed various presidential papers, congressional hearings, and HUD evaluations of federal housing programs.

Part 5:   Interviews with Helen Davis, Barbee Durham, Tom Atkins, Lou Lucas, and Nate Jones. I also reviewed articles on the Columbus school case from the *Columbus Citizen-Journal* and *Columbus Dispatch*.

Part 6:   Interviews with Louis Redding, Joseph Johnson, John Parres, Lou Lucas, and Bill Taylor. I also reviewed articles on the Wilmington school case from the *Wilmington Evening Journal, Wilmington Morning News,* and *Washington Post.*

Part 7:   Interviews with Nate Jones, Lou Lucas, Bill Caldwell, Bill Taylor, Norman Chackhin, Louis Redding, and Tom Atkins. I also reviewed articles on the Dayton, Columbus, and Wilmington cases in the *New York Times, Washington Post, Wilmington News Journal,* and *Columbus Citizen-Journal*

Selected Bibliography

Abrams, C. *Forbidden Neighbors.* New York: Kennikat Press, 1971.

Bardolph, R., ed. *The Civil Rights Record: Black Americans and the Law, 1849–1970.* New York: Crowell, 1970.

Bell, D. *Race, Racism and American Law.* Boston: Little, Brown and Co., 1980.

Bickel, A. "The Original Understanding and the Segregation Decision." 69 *Harvard Law Review* 1 (1955).

Black, C. "The Lawfulness of the Segregation Decisions." 69 *Yale Law Journal* 421 (1960).

Brauer, C. M. *John F. Kennedy and the Second Reconstruction.* New York: Columbia University Press, 1977.

Cahn, E. "Jurisprudence." 30 *New York University Law Review* 150 (1950).

Cataldo, E. F.; Giles, M. W.; and Gatlin, D. S. *School Desegregation Policy.* Lexington, Mass.: Lexington Books, 1978.

Chesler, M. "Institutional Changes to Support School Desegregation." *Law and Contemporary Problems* 174 (1978).

Courant, P. "Racial Prejudice in a Search Model of the Urban Housing Market." 5 *Journal of Urban Economics* 329 (1978).

Dardin, J. T. "Migration and Segregation." 13 *East Lakes Geographer* 20 (1978).

Deskins, D. *Residential Mobility of Negroes in Detroit, 1837–1965.* Ann Arbor: Department of Geography, University of Michigan, 1972.

Dimond, P., "The Anti-Caste Principle." 30 *Wayne Law Review* 1 (1983).

———. *Discrimination in the Provision of Public Services.* Lexington, Mass.: D. C. Heath, 1979.

———. "Strict Construction and Judicial Review of Race Discrimination under the Equal Protection Clause." 80 *Michigan Law Review* 462 (1982).

———. "Toward Ending Segregation in the 1980's." 13 *Urban Review* 73 (1981).

Downs, A. *Opening Up the Suburbs: An Urban Strategy For America.* New Haven: Yale University Press, 1973.

DuBois, W. E. B. *The Souls of Black Folk.* Reprint. New York, 1961.

Duncan, H. G. *Changing Race Relations in the Northern Border States.* Philadelphia: University of Pennsylvania, 1922.

Ely, J. H. *Democracy and Distrust.* Cambridge: Harvard University Press, 1980.

Epps, E. G. "City and Suburbs: Perspectives on Interdistrict Desegregation Efforts." 10 *Urban Review* 82 (1978).

Fairman, C. "Foreword: The Attack on the Segregation Cases." 70 *Harvard Law Review* 83 (1956).

Farley, R. "The Changing Distribution of Negroes Within Metropolitan Areas: The Emergence of Black Suburbs." 75 *American Journal of Sociology* 512 (1970).

———. "Trends in Racial Inequalities: Have the Gains of the 1960's Disappeared in the 1970's?" 42 *American Sociological Review* 189 (1977).

Farley, R.; Bianchi, S.; and Colasanto, D. "Barriers to the Racial Integration of Neighborhoods: The Detroit Case." 441 *Annals of the American Academy of Political and Social Science* 97 (1979).

Franklin, H. *In-Zoning.* Washington, D.C.: Potomac Institute, 1974.

————. *Equal Housing Opportunity.* Washington, D.C.: Potomac Institute, 1976.

Franklin, J. H. *Racial Equality in America.* Chicago: University of Chicago Press, 1976.

Garland, B. "Cabrini-Green to Willow Creek." *Chicago Magazine,* June, 1977.

————. "Willow Creek Revisited." *The BPI Magazine,* February, 1979.

"The Gautreaux Decision and Its Effect on Subsidized Housing." September 22, 1978, Hearing of Subcommittee of Government Operations Committee. Washington, D.C.: Government Printing Office, 1979.

Gerber, D. A. *Black Ohio and the Color Line, 1860–1915.* Urbana: University of Illinois Press, 1976.

Grant, W. "The Detroit School Case." 21 *Wayne Law Review* 851 (1975).

Hain, E. "School Desegregation in Detroit: Domestic Tranquility and Judicial Futility." 23 *Wayne Law Review* 65 (1976).

Hawley, A. H., and Rock, V. P., eds. *Segregation in Residential Areas.* Papers on Racial and Socioeconomic Factors in Choice of Housing. Washington, D.C.: National Academy of Sciences, 1973.

Hermalin, A., and Farley, R. "The Potential for Residential Integration in Cities and Suburbs: Implications for the Busing Controversy." 38 *American Sociological Review* 595 (1973).

Jencks, C., et al. *Inequality.* New York: Basic Books, 1972.

Kain, J. F. *Essays on Urban Spatial Structure.* Cambridge, Mass.: Ballinger Publishing Co., 1975.

Kluger, R. *Simple Justice.* New York: Alfred A. Knopf, 1976.

Myrdahl, G. *An American Dilemma.* New York: Harper and Brothers, 1944.

Ogbu, J. *Minority Education and Caste: The American System in Cross-Cultural Perspective.* New York: Academic Press, 1978.

Orfield, G. "If Wishes Were Houses Then Busing Could Stop: Demographic Trends and Desegregation Policy." 10 *Urban Review* 108 (1978).

————. *Must We Bus.* Washington, D.C.: Brookings Institute, 1978.

Panetta, L. E., and Gall, P. *Bring Us Together: The Nixon Team and the Civil Rights Retreat.* New York: J. B. Lippincott Co., 1971.

Polikoff, A. *Housing the Poor: The Case for Heroism.* Cambridge, Mass.: Ballinger Publishing Co., 1978.

Pollack, L. "Racial Discrimination and Judicial Integrity: A Reply to Professor Wechsler." 108 *University of Pennsylvania Law Review* 1 (1959).

Report of the National Advisory Committee on Civil Disorders, March 1, 1968. New York: Bantam Publishing Co., March, 1968.

Raffel, S. *The Politics of School Desegregation.* Philadelphia: Temple University Press, 1984.

Rist, R. C. *The Invisible Children: School Integration in American Society.* Cambridge: Harvard University Press, 1978.

Roof, C. V., ed. Symposium on "Race and Residence in American Cities." 441 *Annals* 1 (1979).

Sorensen, A.; Taeuber, K. E.; and Hollingsworth, L. J., Jr. "Indexes of Racial Residential Segregation for 109 Cities in the United States, 1949 to 1970." 8 *Sociological Focus* 125 (1975).

St. John, N. H. *School Desegregation Outcomes for Children.* New York: John Wiley and Sons, 1975.

Taeuber, K. "Demographic Perspectives in Housing and School Segregation." 21 *Wayne Law Review* 833 (1975).

————. "Housing, Schools, and Incremental Segregative Effects." 441 *Annals* 157 (1979).

Taeuber, K. E., and Taeuber, A. F. *Negroes in Cities: Residential Segregation and the Neighborhood Change.* Chicago: Aldine Publishing Co., 1965.

U.S., Department of Health, Education and Welfare. Prejudice and Pride: The *Brown* Decision After Twenty-Five Years, May 17, 1954–May 17, 1979. Report from the National Academy of Education, Washington, D.C., 1979.

"The Gautreaux Housing Demonstration: An Evaluation of Its Impact on Participating Households." October 18, 1979. Mimeograph.

"Preliminary Findings of the 1977 Housing Market Practices Survey." Mimeograph.

Van Valey, T. L., "Trends in Residential Segregation: 1960–1970." 82 *American Journal of Sociology* 826 (1977).

Vose, C. E. *Caucasians Only: The Supreme Court, the NAACP and The Restrictive Cases.* Berkeley: University of California Press, 1959.

Weinburg, L. *A Chance to Learn: A History of Race and Education in the United States.* Boston: Cambridge University Press, 1977.

Weston, R., ed. *Blacks in Ohio History.* Ohio Historical Society, Columbus, 1976.

Wilkins, R. "The Sound of One Hand Clapping." *New York Times Magazine,* May 12, 1974, 43.

Wilkinson, J. H. *From Brown to Bakke: The Supreme Court and School Integration: 1954–1978.* New York: Oxford University Press, 1979.

Wolfe, E. *Trial and Error.* Detroit: Wayne State University Press, 1981.

Woodward, B., and Armstrong, S. *The Brethren.* New York: Simon and Schuster, 1979.

Table of Principal Cases

Alexander v. Holmes County Board of
Education, 396 U.S. 19 (1969): 31,
86, 96

Austin Independent School District v.
United States, 429 U.S. 990 (1976):
165–68, 178–79, 203, 249, 251,
265, 271, 283, 344, 377

Barrick Realty, Inc. v. City of Gary,
491 F.2d 161 (7th Cir. 1974): 203

Belton v. Gebhart, 87 A.2d 862
(Del Ch. 1952), 347 U.S. 483
(1954): 285–87

Bradley v. Milliken, 433 F.2d 897 (6th
Cir. 1970), 438 F.2d 945 (6th Cir.
1971), *on remand,* 338 F. Supp. 582
(E.D. Mich. 1971), 345 F. Supp.
914 (E.D. Mich. 1972), *aff'd,* 484
F.2d 215 (6th Cir. 1973), *aff'd in
part and rev'd in part,* 418 U.S. 717
(1974), *on remand,* 540 F.2d 229
(6th Cir. 1976), *aff'd,* 433 U.S. 267
(1977); 620 F.2d 1143 (6th Cir.
1980) (Detroit school case): v, 34,
38, 68–72, 77–86, 90, 93–95, 110–
18, 154, 167, 174–76, 212–13,
278–79, 302–3, 386, 392, 396

Bradley v. School Board of Richmond,
462 F.2d 1058 (4th Cir. 1972), *aff'd
by an equally divided Court,* 412
U.S. 92 (1973): 40, 77, 90–91, 92,
97, 100, 113–14, 122, 302–3, 305–
6, 372

Brinkman v. Dayton Board of Education, 503 F.2d 684 (6th Cir. 1974),
518 F.2d 383 (6th Cir. 1975), 539
F.2d 1084 (6th Cir. 1976), *rev'd,*
433 U.S. 406 (1977), *on remand,*
583 F.2d 243 (6th Cir. 1978), *aff'd,*

443 U.S. 526 (1979) (Dayton school
case): 137–39, 147–80, 262–66,
276–79, 347–94, 396–97

Brown v. Board of Education, 347
U.S. 483 (1954) (Brown I): v, 21,
40, 84, 95, 110, 111, 116–17, 129,
141, 147, 169, 172, 256, 274, 286–
87, 350, 354, 361, 369–75, 385,
395, 401–2

Brown v. Board of Education, 349
U.S. 294 (1955) (Brown II): v, 21,
64, 79–80, 111, 129, 141, 151, 154,
158, 169, 256, 268, 287, 303, 332,
350, 369–75

Burton v. Wilmington Parking Authority, 365 U.S. 718 (1961): 288

Civil Rights Cases, 109 U.S. 3 (1883):
401

Clark v. Universal Builders, Inc., 501
F.2d 324 (7th Cir. 1974): 202

Columbus Board of Education v. Penick, 443 U.S. 449 (1979) (Columbus
school case): 343–88, 396–97

David v. School District of Pontiac,
309 F. Supp. 734 (E.D. Mich.),
aff'd, 443 F.2d 573 (6th Cir. 1970):
26, 58–59

Dayton Board of Education v.
Brinkman, 433 U.S. 406 (1977)
(Dayton I): 176–80, 225, 253–79,
283, 314–17, 320, 333, 335–39,
344, 357–59, 361–65, 379–80

Dayton Board of Education v.
Brinkman, 433 U.S. 526 (1976)
(Dayton II): 347–94, 396–98

Deal v. Cincinnati Board of Education,
369 F.2d 55 (6th Cir. 1966), 419

Deal v. Cincinnati Board of Eduation
(*continued*)
F.2d 1387 (6th Cir. 1969): 26, 29,
33, 43, 58–59, 63, 87, 90, 93–94,
121, 131–32. 149, 249, 278
Delaware Board of Education v. Evans,
446 U.S. 923 (1980): 347–51, 392–
93
Dred Scott v. Sanford, 60 U.S. 393
(1857): 117

Ellis v. Board of Public Instruction,
423 F.2d 203 (5th Cir. 1970): 170
Estes v. Metropolitan Branches of
Dallas NAACP, 444 U.S. 437
(1980): 393
Evans v. Buchanan, 393 F. Supp. 1218
(D. Del. 1974), *aff'd,* 423 U.S. 962
(1975), 416 F. Supp. 328 (D. Del.
1976), *aff'd,* 555 F.2d 373 (3d Cir.
1977), 435 F. Supp. 832 (D. Del
1977), 447 F. Supp. 982 (D. Del.
1978), *aff'd,* 582 F.2d 75 (3d Cir.
1978), *cert. denied,* 446 U.S. 923
(1980) (Wilmington school case):
287–88, 303–8, 311–17, 320–22,
331–39, 346–51, 386, 388, 392–93,
396

Fullilove v. Klutznick, 448 U.S. 448
(1980): 389

Gautreaux v. Romney, 448 F.2d 731
(7th Cir. 1971), 332 F. Supp. 366
(N.D. Ill. 1971), *rev'd,* 457 F.2d
124 (7th Cir. 1972), 363 F. Supp.
690 (N.D. Ill. 1973), *rev'd,* 503
F.2d 930, 939 (7th Cir. 1974), *aff'd,*
425 U.S. 284 (1976) (Chicago public
housing case): 209–25
Gautreaux v. CHA, 265 F. Supp. 582
(N.D. Ill. 1967), 296 F. Supp. 907
(N.D. Ill. 1969), 304 F. Supp. 736
(N.D. Ill. 1969), 436 F.2d 306 (7th
Cir. 1970), 342 F. Supp. 827 (N.D.
Ill. 1972), *aff'd,* 480 F.2d 210 (7th

Cir. 1973), *aff'd,* 425 U.S. 284
(1976) (Chicago public housing
case): 207–12
Giles v. Harris, 189 U.S. 475 (1903):
401
Gladstone Realtors v. Village of Bellwood, 441 U.S. 91 (1979): 201–2
Green v. County School Board, 391
U.S. 430 (1968): 28–29, 56, 79, 98–
99, 129, 174, 274, 336, 349, 350,
352, 360, 370, 372

Higgins v. Board of Education, 508
F.2d 779 (6th Cir. 1974): 123, 154
Hills v. Gautreaux, 425 U.S. 284
(1976) (Chicago public housing
case): 218–25, 389, 397

Jones v. Alfred H. Mayer Co., 392
U.S. 409 (1968): 113, 397

Kemp v. Beasley, 423 F.2d 851 (8th
Cir. 1970): 355
Keyes v. Denver School District No. 1,
303 F. Supp. 279. (D. Colo. 1969),
rev'd in part, 445 F.2d 990 (10th
Cir. 1971), *rev'd* 413 U.S. 189
(1973) (Denver school case): 97–99,
111, 151–52, 155, 157, 159, 161,
165–66, 168–69, 179, 203, 249,
256, 267, 274, 278, 336, 344, 349–
50, 355–56, 358, 362, 364–65,
372–73, 380–82, 396

Milliken v. Bradley, 418 U.S. 717
(1974) (Detroit school case, Milliken
I): v, 110–18, 154, 171–72, 175,
213–20, 225, 283, 304–8, 316, 333,
351, 378, 386, 388, 392, 396–97,
402
Milliken v. Bradley, 433 U.S. 267
(1977) (Milliken II): 174–76, 180,
326, 336

Oliver v. Kalamazoo Board of Education, 346 F. Supp 766 (W.D. Mich

1971), *aff'd*, 418 F.2d 635 (6th Cir.
1971), 368 F. Supp, 143 (W.D.
Mich. 1973), *aff'd*, 408 F.2d 178
(6th Cir. 1974): 122–23

Parker v. University of Delaware, 75
A.2d 225 (Del. 1950): 285
Pasadena City Board of Education v.
Spangler, 427 U.S. 424 (1976): 161–
63
Penick v. Columbus Board of Education, 429 F. Supp. 229 (S.D. Ohio
1977), *aff'd*, 583 F.2d 787 (6th Cir.
1978), *aff'd*, 443 U.S. 449 (1979):
249–57, 274–76, 343–94, 396
Plessy v. Ferguson, 163 U.S. 537 (1896):
95, 101, 116–17, 286, 363, 401

Regents of the University of California
v. Bakke, 438 U.S. 57 (1978): 273–
74, 398

School District of Omaha v. United
States, 433 U.S. 667 (1977): 179, 283
Shannon v. HUD, 436 F.2d 809 (3rd
Cir. 1970): 210

Sipes v. McGhee, 334 U.S. 1 (1948):
42–43, 46
Swann v. Charlotte-Mecklenburg Board
of Education, 300 F. Supp. 1358
(W.D.N.C. 1969), 306 F. Supp.
1299 (W.D.N.C. 1969), *aff'd*, 402
U.S. 1 (1971): 56–58, 79, 98–99,
105, 114, 129, 145, 149, 155, 159,
161, 252–56, 261, 267, 274, 336,
344, 349–50, 352, 360, 362, 364–
66, 372–73, 378, 381

Village of Arlington Heights v. Metropolitan Housing Development Corporation, 429 U.S. 252 (1977), *on
remand*, 558 F.2d 1283 (7th Cir.
1977): 197–200, 267, 317, 353, 356,
368

Warth v. Seldin, 422 U.S. 490 (1975):
188–90
Washington v. Davis, 426 U.S. 229
(1976) (D.C. employment case):
162–63, 267, 274, 368
Wright v. Council of the City of Em-
poria, 407 U.S. 451 (1972): 92